The Tallyman's Campaign Handbook

THE TALLYMAN'S CAMPAIGN HANDBOOK

Election 2016

Noel Whelan

with Kathryn Marsh

The Liffey Press

Published by
The Liffey Press Ltd
Raheny Shopping Centre, Second Floor
Raheny, Dublin 5, Ireland
www.theliffeypress.com

A catalogue record of this book is
available from the British Library.

ISBN 978-1-908308-85-6

Printed in Ireland by SprintPrint

Contents

Constituency by Constituency:

The Tallyman Team

Noel Whelan is the author or co-author of a number of previous books on politics, elections and electoral law in Ireland. These have included the series of Tallyman's Guides to Irish elections. He writes a weekly political column for *The Irish Times* and is a regular commentator on politics and current affairs for the broadcast media. He worked previously as a political organiser at Fianna Fáil headquarters and then as a special adviser. He works currently as a barrister specialising in Criminal and Constitutional Law. He was one of the Leaders of the Democracy Matters campaign which sucessfully opposed the 2013 Seanad Abolition Referendum. He was Strategic Adviser to the Yes Equality Campaign for the 2015 Marriage Equality Referendum.

Kathryn Marsh is an experienced editor and researcher who has worked on several books on politics and elections including *The Sunday Tribune Guide to Irish Politics* (2002) and *Showtime or Substance* (2007). This is the fourth Tallyman's pre-election guide that she has collaborated on. She has also been a member of various public bodies concerned with environmental and agricultural issues and had a monthly local radio slot dealing with horticultural matters. Wearing her hat as an environmental activist, she was formerly the Director of Sonairte, the National Ecology Centre.

Contributors

Richard Colwell is CEO of RED C Research, the company he founded in 2003, having spent five years at Lansdowne Market Research, and eight years at ICM Research and Research International in London. He has worked extensively developing and analysing political polling both in the UK and Ireland. Richard writes a regular column analysing political polls in *The Sunday Business Post*, and is a frequent commentator on polling and consumer trends in Ireland and worldwide. He is Vice President of WIN Gallup International group, a collaboration of 75 independent polling agencies worldwide, and Chairman of AIMRO, the body that represents polling and research in Ireland.

Larry Donnelly is a Boston-born and educated attorney, and a Lecturer and Director of Clinical Legal Education in the School of Law at NUI Galway. He writes monthly columns about American and Irish politics for TheJournal.ie and IrishCentral.com and is a regular contributor to Irish and US broadcast media outlets on politics, current affairs and law. Twitter: @LarryPDonnelly

Niamh Gallagher is Co–Founder and Board member at Women for Election. She has spent more than ten years working in politics and policy in Ireland, the UK and Brussels. She is a regular columnist with the *Irish Independent* and winner, with Michelle O'Donnell Keating, of the Social Entrepreneurs Ireland IMPACT award and the IMAGE 2015 Social Entrepreneur of the Year Award. Niamh is a graduate of Trinity College Dublin, the London School of Economics and the UCD Michael Smurfit School of Business, where she recently completed her MBA.

Jim Nolan analysis elections at national and constituency level for Paddy Power.

Professor Michael Marsh is Emeritus Professor of Political Science in Trinity College Dublin and was formerly Professor of Comparative Political Behaviour. He has published a number of books and over 100 professional articles on parties and elections, including the report on the first ever Irish Election Study, *The Irish Voter* (Manchester University Press, 2008). He coedited the last four books in the How Ireland Voted series, published by Palgrave and he has also contributed extensively to print and broadcast media.

Dr Brian Murphy lectures in Communications, Applied Writing and Cultural Tourism at the Dublin Institute of Technology. He hold a PhD in Modern Irish History from the School of History and Archives, University College Dublin. Brian's monograph on Douglas Hyde and the genesis of the Irish Presidency will be published later this year by the Collins Press. He previously co-edited *Brian Lenihan: In Calm and Crisis,* the bestselling book on the public career of the former Minister for Finance. Brian is a former speechwriter to two Taoisigh.

Michelle O'Donnell Keating is Chair and Co-Founder of Women for Election. With 20 years' experience in the private, political and not-for-profit sectors, Michelle is currently in the School of Law and Government in DCU where she lecturers on International Relations and Political Economy. Michelle has an MA in International Relations from DCU and is completing her PhD at DCU exploring the impact of IMF programmes upon women.

Dr. Liam Weeks is a college lecturer in the Department of Government, University College Cork, and author of *Independents in Irish Party Democracy* (forthcoming with Manchester University Press)

Author's Note

This is the fourth edition of *The Tallyman's Campaign Handbook* to be published in advance of a Dáil election. The preparation of this guide has again been challenging with a range of new political parties and entities and a record number of independent candidates.

The parties selected their candidates earlier than usual on this occasion. Sinn Féin, for example, had some of their candidates selected a year ago. Speculation about the prospect of an election in November 2015 also brought selection meetings forward as well as flushing out many independents who were delaying making up their minds or announcing. It is never possible in a publication like this to include details of all the candidates because nominations do not close until a week or so after the Dáil is formally dissolved, but we have made a particular effort again in this edition to include even more details about all the candidates who are known at the time of going to print.

One of the questions we ask candidates when we email, text or phone them at strange hours of the day or night is, 'what was it that motivated you to go into politics?' Very often the answer is that they grew up stuffing flyers into envelopes. We both come from that sort of family and it is one of the reasons we enjoy working together on the research, writing and analysis in this book. The political party press offices, the posters of online resources and the hundreds of candidates or potential candidates and their staff and families we have talked to have all helped us get a clear picture of who was standing where, what their past performance suggests about their prospects in these elections, and what factors would shape the terrain in which they will compete in each constituency. We are, as always, grateful not only for their time and assistance but overwhelmed by the passion for public service that drives most candidates.

Given the time pressures involved, and since almost every sentence in this book contains several election-related facts, some errors will inevitably have slipped through. For those, we alone accept responsibility and we would be happy to be notified of them.

The quality of the publication on this occasion has been enhanced further by the involvement of The Liffey Press. We are grateful to David Givens and his staff not only for their editing and design skills, but also for their patience and courage in taking on a publication framed by the time constraints of the at times volatile electoral cycle. Once again this book has been made possible by the involvement of Paddy Power and their support for this project. Jonathan Williams again showed confidence in the potential of this publication and was, as ever, a reassuring support.

Pulling together the material that ultimately became the Tallyman's pre-election guides began as a personal pastime before the 2002 election. That it has now becomes a standing feature of the lead-in to Irish general election campaigns owes much to the faith and assistance of many. It is also possible because of the extensive public data generated largely through voluntary effort by a number of experts and enthusiasts about the Irish electoral process. Their work is reflected in a whole range of useful and fascinating internet sites and online resources containing candidate and constituency detail about Irish politics and elections. We have drawn on many of them in shaping our analysis and sourcing and checking data for this work. We are particularly indebted to Dr Adrian Kavanagh and his very comprehensive postings on election-related issues at http://adriankavanaghelections.org. We are grateful also to www.guthanphobail.net for its collations of polling and election data. For the purposes of this project we are grateful, and more generally all interested in Irish elections are grateful, to Christopher Took and Seán Donnelly for their work on www.electionsireland.org, which remains the definitive searchable archive of Irish election data. On this occasion we also wish to thank and acknowledge the work of Jason Kelleher at http://irishpoliticalmaps.blogspot.ie for his contribution to analysis on elections and permission to draw on his work. Notwithstanding this explosion of online election-related resources, we are still happy to know that there is enduring demand and support for a handheld guide to the election, containing all the details between one set of covers.

Our gratitude also goes to Kathryn Byrne and her team at Limelight Communications.

We are also delighted that we have managed to supplement the guide to the constituencies on this occasion with useful insights and analysis from some of Ireland shrewdest election observers. We thank Richard Colwell, Larry Donnelly, Niamh Gallagher, James Nolan, Brian Murphy, Michele O'Donnell Keating and Liam Weeks for taking the time to put down their thoughts on specific aspects of the forthcoming election.

At both a national and constituency level the 2016 elections is going to be packed with drama, intrigue and colour. It has all the elements to be the most dramatic election for our party system in almost a century. In addition to including as much detail as possible and as is consistent with making this guide accessible we have at points embarked on projections and predictions. At this stage, given the volatility in the context of the election, the shift still to come in the patterns of public support and the fact that candidate lineups have yet to be finalised in some instances, these projections can only be tentative. We do hope, however, that whether you access this book for work, pleasure or curiosity you will find everything you need here to shape your own assessment of what might happen in election 2016.

We also wish to thank the Franchise Section of the Department of Environment, Communities and Local Government who were typically helpful in providing information.

We wish also to thank Michael Marsh and Aidan Marsh not only for their contributions, patience and forbearance when asked to live on takeaways, but for trying hard not to sigh when Kathryn asks them if they have any spare minutes to check a few figures.

Finally, we wish to thank Noel's son Seamus for tolerating Daddy's distractions and his wife Sinead McSweeney for her support and for her knowing smile when he again promises that this will be his last book.

Noel Whelan and Kathryn Marsh
14 January 2016

Introduction: An Earthquake Election?

Noel Welan

Election 2011: A hard act to follow

Seismic is the adjective I settled on three weeks before the 2011 general election to describe the likely impact of its results on our political system. The election results certainly lived up to that dramatic billing.

While the people of some other long established democracies were, or were on the verge of, rioting in the streets this time five year ago, the Irish rioted at the ballot boxes. In the polling booths on 25 February 2011 our electorate delivered one hell of a kicking to the outgoing government. Not only did the election give rise to a change of government – the first such real change in 14 years – but the new government was given the largest mandate ever, with an unprecedented majority.

The 2011 election also gave rise to the most dramatic shift in personnel in Dáil Éireann in the country's history. Almost two-thirds of those who sat in the chamber when the house first met after the 2011 election had not been TDs four weeks earlier when the Dáil was dissolved.

In party terms the 2011 election also had a dramatic impact. Fine Gael went to the top of the political league table and achieved both the largest share and the largest number of Dáil seats in its history even though it fell short of the votes won under Garret FitzGerald in the early 1980s. Labour became Ireland's second largest party in Dáil Éireann. The Greens were eliminated from the Dáil, at least for the time being. Sinn Féin achieved critical parliamentary mass in the south. Most dramatically of all, Fianna Fáil collapsed. The near dominance that Fianna Fáil had asserted upon the Irish political system for decades is worth reflecting on to contextualise the scale of the reverse they suffered in the last general election. Founded in 1926 Fianna Fáil had been in government for all but nineteen of the intervening years. Since 1932 it had never got less than 39 per cent of the vote in Dáil elections. Until 1991 the party had won every presidential election. Until 2004 it had always been the largest Irish party in the European Parliament.

Yet in the general election of February 2011 Fianna Fáil suffered a political meltdown. It lost two thirds of its Dáil seats. Not only did it lose power, but it also came in third behind Fine Gael and Labour and only just ahead of Sinn Féin. It was an extraordinary political disaster. The 2011 election, as Fine Gael's Brian Hayes put it, inelegantly but accurately, was about the other parties fighting over the carcass of Fianna Fáil. In that fight Fine Gael proved the better carnivores.

It should be difficult to see how the 2016 election could possibly match 2011 for drama and impact, but it is showing all the signs that it might.

A Post-Traumatic Election

While the economic and social circumstances in which the 2011 elections were held were traumatic, those in which the 2016 election take place are post-traumatic and therefore potentially even more turbulent.

One of the most complex assessments of the 2011 Irish election was published shortly afterwards by the Sligo-born political scientist Peter Mair, one of the leading European experts on parties and elections. In a lengthy piece examining the 2011 election in its wider context, which was published in Michael Gallagher and Michael Marsh's edited study *How Ireland Voted 2011*, Mair, while noting that 2011 had been a change election, suggested that it was 'perhaps paradoxically, a change that might eventually be reversed and that might not have done very much to disturb the fundamentals.' We cannot do justice to Mair if we summarise his work here, but he cautioned against seeing the 2011 outcome as being seismic of itself, or on its own. While Fianna Fail's vote collapsed to a historically low level, the long established pattern of switch-

so, it is worth noting, they forgot the advice that a British political scientist, Tim Bale had given them when they invited him to the Árd Fhéis in 2012. Bale spoke to the Fianna Fáil faithful about the lessons to be learnt from the British Conservative Party's recovery after they lost so badly to Tony Blair's New Labour party. He set out ten rules for a party seeking to recover from a collapse on this scale. One of his strongest warnings was rule number 9: 'Don't be fooled by "success" in second-order elections.' The Tories under William Hague and Iain Duncan Smith had convinced themselves they were on the way back when they did well in local, European and by-elections, only to suffer defeat again when the general election came around. The stock line of Fianna Fáil politicians, even now as the Dáil election approaches, is to point to how well they did in the 2014 local elections and suggest that they should not be underestimated.

The outcomes of the May 2013 mid-term elections fade into the background now as all attention turns towards the 2016 election. Since the Dáil resumed its sittings on 13 January after the Christmas break the parties, their candidates, and the media have effectively been in full campaign mode. Before considering what the approaches of the parties might be to the campaign it is worth observing two particular factors, which will add to the enduring volatility in our party system and in public support patterns and shape the political environment for this campaign.

The layout of the playing pitch

The first is that the layout of the playing pitch has changed quite radically. Whereas in 2011 we had 43 constituencies, this time we have forty. Whereas the last Dáil had 166 seats, the next one will have 158. In advance of this election we have had the most dramatic redraw of constituencies ever. In some areas, particularly in Dublin and in the midlands and mid west, the constituencies have been redrawn beyond recognition, and beyond comparison with previous elections. The particulars of the boundary adjustments and their potential implications are detailed in the constituency sections of this book. Adrian Kavanagh, Maynooth University political geographer, has observed that cumulatively the boundary adjustments are most likely to benefit Fianna Fáil. Whatever their impact on parties or candidates, the constituency changes will certainly contribute to the sense of political disorientation which will be felt anyway by many voters in this election for other reasons.

Recalibrating for gender balance

Although the most recent redraw of constituencies has been more challenging for the parties than previously, party managers at least have experience of recalibrating their constituency organisation and candidate strategies to reflect boundary changes. They have no experience of having to adjust for gender considerations. For this election such adjustment have been imposed upon them. As Niamh Gallagher and Michelle O'Donnell-Keating detail in their piece in this book, the provisions of the Electoral (Amendment) (Political Funding) Act 2012 require that in order to qualify for (substantial) state funding after the election the parties must ensure that at least 30 per cent of their candidates in the election are of each gender. The incentive has worked; record numbers of candidates have been selected. The look of the ballot paper will be transformed by the fact that about a third of all the photographs thereon will be of females. The figures and profiles prepared for this book suggest that the financial incentive to political parties has also had a collateral effect in inspiring more women to stand as independents and prompting smaller parties unlikely to benefit from state funding to increase the gender equality of their candidate lists. An unfortunate feature of the coverage of the impact of the incentivising of greater gender diversity is that internal party rows in a handful of constituencies over the selection of candidates have created a distorted narrative of the 'gender quota' factor. When looked at more closely, as is done to some degree in this book, these constituency rows said to be over female candidates owe more to the, at times haphazard, efforts of party headquarters to manage candidate strategy generally rather than merely on a gender basis. This will be the most female election ever. Whether it means we will have the most female Dáil ever remains to be seen. International precedent suggests that it should but we don't know yet whether or what particularly Irish factors may come into play.

The nature of the campaign

While all of these factors shape the context of the election it is the parties and candidates themselves who will shape the nature of the campaign. The manner in which they will compete is already apparent.

Fine Gael will emphasise what it will characterise as its economic achievement over the last five years in restoring confidence and bringing about a recovery. If one follows the teachings of Karl Marx and James Carville on the relationship between economic and political developments then Fine Gael should be set for certain victory in this election. The pace of recovery is rapid and the rise in employment is particularly dramatic. There is no doubt but that this is accruing to Fine Gael's benefit to some extent. However, it is also facing the problem that many voters are not feeling the recovery, or their sense of it is muted by the enduring traumas of austerity. Moreover, elections are never about the past, they are almost always about the future. Fine Gael has reflected that in its campaign slogan, which emphasises the need to 'Keep the Recovery Going' and by suggesting, quite brutally one suspects in the last weeks before polling, that this recovery is somehow dependent on it being in government, and/or that a stable alternative government can not and will not be formed without it. There are two things, however, which threaten to undermine its chances of re-election. The first has been its inability to tackle some serious social problems, like housing, homelessness and hospital A&Es and to implement large-scale projects, like Irish Water. The other is hubris. As an incumbent government, with an economy growing at least half a per cent per month, it wants above all else in this campaign to present an image of competence and cohesion.

In the phoney war before the actual election campaign Fine Gael has made some ground with this contention, in part because Fianna Fáil, to the extent that it has been clear about its post election position, has said it will not participate in government with either Fine Gael or Sinn Féin after the election. On any rational examination of the possible outcomes of this election that suggests that, if the party sticks to its promise after the election, Fianna Fáil is extremely unlikely to be in government at all. Determined and at times tetchy attempts by Fianna Fáil to insist that talking about election outcomes is premature and that the focus should be on policies will continue to be undermined while the risk of irrelevance after the election remains stark for it.

Fianna Fáil's policy offerings on key taxation and economic questions are unlikely to differ much from those of Fine Gael, although there are areas of divergence, for example in capping the wage levels at which it will reduce the universal social charge. Its principle line of attack will, it seems, be on highlighting government failures in public services, especially health. Fianna Fáil can draw some comfort from the fact that its vote share in the local elections was higher than polls had suggested in advance – and indeed higher than the exit poll suggested on polling day itself. Even allowing for this adjustment, however, Fianna Fáil is likely to do no more consolidate its position in number and seat terms and have a small improvement in this election. It should, however, be sufficient for it to portray this as the first block in a building towards political recovery.

Labour is on a containment mission in this election. It could hold about a third of its seats but there is a risk it will do even worse than that. It is seeking to limit its losses by claiming a need for it to be in the next government to balance the more right wing excesses of Fine Gael policy. Labour's hopes rest on more voters giving it some credit for the recovery and on a hope that the notion of Fine Gael in government unrestrained, perhaps even as a single party government, is something voters will come to fear so much in the last weeks of this campaign that they will want Labour there in sufficient numbers to restrain it. It is a risky, even desperate strategy, but it may save some of its seats.

Sinn Féin is on the up. It may double its percentage vote and almost double its seats. It argues that its capacity to turn votes into seats is hampered by organisational limitations in some parts of the country. However, as its European election performance shows, the quality of its candidates could more than compensate for that. A close examination of its local election performance and its candidate strategy for this election illustrates that, as ever, Sinn Féin is playing a long game. It is slowly building candidate profiles in all of the Dáil constituencies. In policy terms it is offering voters the starkest contrast to what the government parties are. It is the major party arguing most strongly for greater public expenditure on services before tax reductions. It will play well to its growing audience.

Separately Sinn Féin and its prospects is likely to be one of the central issues in this campaign. There is a large cohort of the middle ground for whom Sinn Féin is anathema because of its history and its present day defence of it. The risk of Sinn Féin being in government, however unrealistic, will determine which of the other parties many of these voters will vote for.

Meanwhile the performance of each of the two newest parties in Dáil Eireann will be shaped by its personalities rather than its policies or organisation. The number of TDs, if any, which Renua Ireland has in the next Dáil will be determined by whether its current TDs can hold their seats outside Fine Gael. The analysis of the constituencies in this book suggests that each of them faces real difficulties in doing so. By comparison, the Social Democrats are led by three politicians, each of whom is likely to hold his or her seat comfortably. Otherwise, however, it seems the Social Democrats have not had the time, money, people or opportunity to leverage the standing of Rosin Shortall, Catherine Murphy and Stephen Donnelly to shore up their new candidates to the extent necessary to win additional seats.

The efforts of the far left politicians to group themselves under the Anti-Austerity Alliance – People Before Profit banner may also have minimal impact on their individual campaigns. Again, however, most of them seem likely to hold their seats and there is at least one constituency where, even if he were still under the Socialist party banner, their candidate would have been well placed to gain a further seat.

The final grouping worth watching, of course, is that of the independents. There is, as Liam Weeks suggests in this book, something uniquely Irish about the extent to which our voters support independents. Whether that support is at anything approaching the level that independents have attracted in polls over the lifetime of the outgoing Dáil or that they achieved in the local elections is one of the central questions in this campaign. If independents become crucial to government formation this March then the personalities who win will be as important as how many independents win. We have identified in this book several independents who could be new deputies after this election. Many of them could bring their own dynamic to the independent benches for the next Dáil.

At the starting line

At this point, in the middle of January 2016, standing at the starting line we can only guess how this race might end.

The only significant shift in party support patterns in the last twelve months, year on year, is some strengthening of the Fine Gael position. This is attributable to the economic recovery and the sense that this recovery is holding and spreading. It has the potential to drive further growth in Fine Gael's support in the next month

The next government is more likely to be a coalition of Fine Gael and Fianna Fáil than any other configuration. This is what the last twelve months of published polls, and indeed betting patterns suggests. Despite protestations from both parties that they will not go in to government with each other, they will if they have to. If the outcome of the next election is that those two parties combined (or with the help of a handful of others) make up the only workable majority, they will go to go into government together. The electorate will not thank them if they don't

The improvement in Fine Gael's position does makes the prospect of a 'Fine Gael–Labour and Others' government after the election more likely than it was a year ago. However, the Fine Gael –Fianna Fáil option remains the most likely outcome.

The 2011 election disrupted the Irish party system and the economic and social crisis has transformed the political landscape. We are, for a period anyway, going to see a Balkanisation of our political system. It will take at least the current election and probably another one after that for our politics to settle down into whatever its new pattern will be. It will be fascinating to watch it unfold.

Shouting the Political Odds

Jim Nolan, Paddy Power election analyst

The 2011 General Election broke many records since proportional representation based elections started in Ireland in 1921.The biggest loss of seats by any party (Fianna Fáil), the biggest bonus of seats won relative to party share of the vote (Fine Gael), the biggest defeat for any outgoing government since the electoral system of PR commenced, were all features of that election. Fine Gael, with 76 seats, and Labour, with 37 seats, also won more seats in the Dáil than in any previous election. With such a level of electoral turmoil how did the punters fare?

There are a number of answers to that question! At the time the election was called it was blindingly clear who the successful parties (and non-parties) would be, and Paddy Power's odds reflected that probability. One astute Midlands punter did back Enda Kenny at odds of 3/1 in late September 2010 (with a bet of 500 Euro) to be the Taoiseach after the next election. On the day of the election in February 2011 the odds on Enda winning were 1/300! On the same day the odds on a Fine Gael/Labour Government were 1/100. Clearly, with odds available for Taoiseach, Tanaiste, and next Government more akin to current day ECB interest rates, punters were always likely to focus far more on the 43 individual constituencies.

Because of the sudden nature of that election's arrival Paddy Power's odds on individual candidates were being produced literally as the candidates declared their intentions and some pricing mistakes did happen. However, punters quickly moved in to educate us as to what the correct odds should have been. Early on we had priced Independent candidate Stephen Donnelly at 10/1 in Wicklow, and later extended the odds to 20/1. At that price punters became interested and by election day the odds had tumbled to 15/8. Definitely 1–0 to the punters!

Due to the media being under financial pressures there were fewer individual constituency polls sponsored by the media than in 2007, and the reduced level of hard information provided difficulties for both odds compilers and punters alike. But punters rose to the challenge and when the complete list of 165 elected TD's were announced Paddy Power's final odds had 137 of the successful TD's as favourites. Of the 28 candidates who were not among the favourites, most were still at relatively short prices. The biggest price of any successful candidate at the death was Fianna Fáil's Robert Troy in Longford–Westmeath, where his odds of 6/1 took into account that he had to overcome two more fancied party colleagues in order to claim the sole Fianna Fáil seat. The shortest priced losers (based on final odds) were Fine Gael's Deirdre Clune at 1/6 in Cork South Central, Fine Gael's Tom Sheahan at odds of 2/11 in Kerry South, Fine Gael's Fidelma Healy-Eames at odds of 2/11 in Galway West, and Sinn Féin's Eoin Ó Broin at odds of 1/3 in Dublin Mid-West.

Allowing for the relative shortage of verifiable constituency opinion polls sponsored by the electronic or print media, the final comparison of odds versus results showed a keen appreciation of the realities in most constituencies by those who were willing to put their money down. On occasions there has been concern expressed that bets placed could cause a punter to change their vote in the privacy of the polling station. Conversations with political punters suggest that this was not the case and that people who had strident political views often backed political opponents as a form of insurance.

Overall, the 2011 General Election betting results produced a small percentage loss for Paddy Power and good luck to any who beat the odds on that occasion. The 2016 Election will, very likely, be different from that of five years ago, but the same challenges remain for bookmaker and bettor alike.

Whilst there is a perception that massive amounts are won and lost on elections this perception is definitely over the top. Most of the thousands of bets placed are small (less than 20 Euro on average) and total bets laid on an Irish election would be far smaller than the amounts bet on an Aintree Grand National or an All Ireland football final between Dublin and Kerry!

The Tallyman's Guide will give everyone interested in the 2016 Election a deeper appreciation of the leaders, candidates, parties, groups, constituencies, and election related facts which active citizens will relish. Paddy Power are pleased to contribute as sponsor to this publication by a long-term journalist and broadcaster on Irish politics.

Polls Paint the Landscape for 2016

Richard Colwell, Managing Director, Red C

A plethora of polls have been conducted since the last General Election in February 2011. They have charted the contrasting fortunes of the parties during what were tough economic times for most.

The back drop to this upcoming election is of course what went before. Voters turned on Fianna Fáil at the last election as anger mounted over the country being forced to give up its economic sovereignty, and the severity of the recession that was upon us became clear. The backlash was so great that some questioned if the party that had once dominated Irish politics for years would ever recover. Voters turned instead in great numbers to the coalition of Fine Gael and the Labour party, with such a significant majority that many predicted an easy second term in five years time.

The intervening years, however, have been tougher than anyone could have imagined. Despite a campaign that was characterised by the 'burn the bondholders' slogans, the reality of the country's economic fortunes changed all that. The new coalition, shocked at the real state of the country's finances, was forced to follow the plan put in place by its predecessors, leaving many voters feeling betrayed.

The introduction of new taxes, in particular the unpopular water charges, as well as the perceived capitulation to the Troika, meant the overriding feeling among many voters was that they had been let down by those that they voted for.

This has led to a political landscape not seen before in Irish politics. As we might expect, support for government parties has declined mid-term. However, while this is a familiar trend seen for government parties across the world, the big difference in Ireland has been where this support has moved to. Rather than see it move back to the traditional heartland of Fianna Fáil, voters who perhaps had not yet forgiven the party moved on to new homes. The rise of support for independent candidates and other anti-establishment parties is the main feature, along with very strong gains for Sinn Féin.

The longer term rise of support for Independents is driven by people from very different backgrounds, which is perhaps unsurprising given that the candidates themselves represent a very wide ranging set of beliefs and doctrines. If we look at those voters who now claim to support Independent candidates, they have switched from all parties, but having said that, almost half supported the current government at the last election.

Figure 1. Percentage of seats and votes won by independent candidates at Dáil elections, 1922–2011

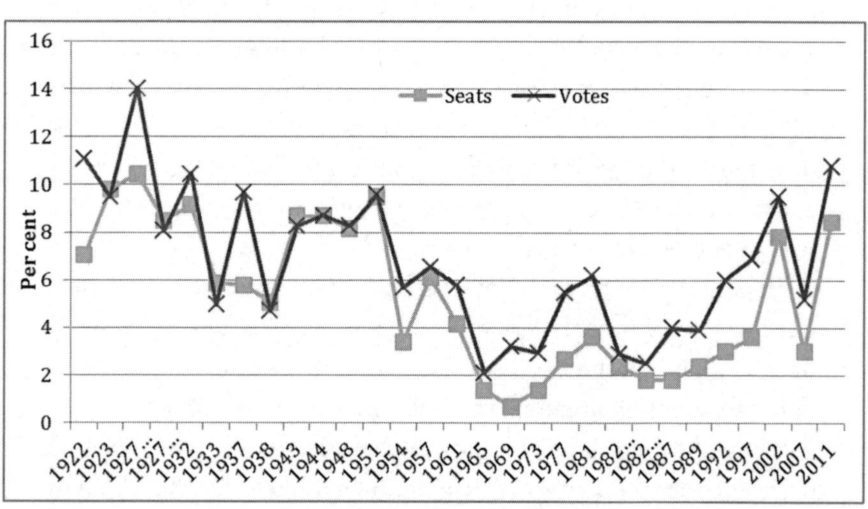

Without any clear identity, a big question in the run up to the next election is how strong really is the claimed support for independent candidates. Or rather, whether claiming you will vote independent to pollsters at mid-term is a different way of expressing your anger at the established parties, one that may be reversed as the realities of who you will vote for at the ballot box draws near. In the last two years independent candidates have tried to cash in on this apparent rise in support by starting new parties and alliances. Renua Ireland and the Social Democrats are two such new parties launched on the back of this voter discontent. However, according to the polls at the time of publication, both are struggling to break through, with the Social Democrats doing somewhat better by securing 3%, and Renua Ireland just 1% of the first preference vote. The Independent Alliance, another grouping formed in order to try and retain claimed independent votes, is not a party as such but a collection of independent candidates that have agreed to work together, and this grouping is currently securing 2–3% of the vote.

Sinn Féin has also made significant gains during the last five years, building support to highs of 22% at the peak of public anger against Water Charges, having only secured 10% at the last election. However, quite regularly Sinn Féin has done well in between elections in the polls, but fallen away as the election approached, and not matched this poll success with real votes cast in polling booths on Election Day.

In the past, support for the party has perhaps been too heavily biased toward those in society who are simply less likely to vote, while a vote for Sinn Féin has to some extent also been seen as something of a protest vote, but without the ability to actually work in government. There are signs, however, that this forthcoming General Election may be different.

Firstly, there are many who have simply lost trust in the established parties. They are those who originally voted for Fianna Fáil, but now will not forgive that party for its role in the collapse in the economy and the austerity that followed as a result; then moved on to the Labour Party in the belief that it would stand up for fairness and equality, but have now also given up on Labour, having felt let down, and are turning towards Sinn Féin to fight for their cause. It will be a tough fight for either Labour or Fianna Fáil to win these voters back at the next Election.

Secondly, there is evidence of increased acceptance of voting Sinn Féin among a wider proportion of the population generally. Not that long ago the party had those who would give it a first preference vote, but not many supporters outside of that group. Now, when we analyse second preference vote behaviour, there is a further 13% of voters who would not give Sinn Féin a first preference at this stage, but would be prepared to give it their second preference vote. The possibility of gaining a more normal rate of transfers is something the party has not had in the past and could mean it does well even if first preference support falls away on Election Day.

Finally, there is the fact that those claiming they plan to vote for Sinn Féin no longer appear to be quite as flaky as they used to. The demographic breakdown of supporters for the party is far more closely aligned to the population than it used to be, with less dependence on the more fickle younger voters who were less likely to turn out to vote, and far more voters from different backgrounds and persuasions. At the time of publication support for Sinn Féin has dropped slightly from the highs seen at one stage, but still remains significantly higher, at around 18%, than they achieved at the last election. Garnering anything even close to this will be a major success for the party, and result in a significantly increased presence in the next Dáil. The key will be seeing how well it retains support in the final weeks and whether it can motivate supporters to vote.

So both Sinn Féin and independent candidates appear set to perform better than ever at the next election judging by the polls at this point in the campaign. But what is expected now of the more established parties? Despite the decline seen for the government parties up to the end of 2014, there has been a clear shift back to the establishment for voters as the general election moves closer and the economic condition of the country as a whole improves. Whether this is due to voters linking the party to the current economic success, or more likely seeking stability as the economy improves, is unknown. However, it is clear that certainly Fine Gael and to some degree Labour have seen fortunes improve.

For some time RED C has championed the theory that a significant proportion of those currently claiming they will vote for Independent candidates may simply be using this option to hold fire on where their final loyalties might lie. They are torn between anger at the austerity and broken promises they believe this government is responsible for, and the reality that the parties they voted for at the last election are still probably the safest bet for not rocking the boat over the next five years.

Our prediction was that as voters moved closer to the realities of an actual General Election, they may well start to shift back to the government parties, and away from their claimed support for independent candidates. That shift certainly appears to be materialising to some extent for Fine Gael. The downward trend in support for independent candidates and other parties seen over the past four months, is very closely matched by the upward trend in support for Fine Gael. In fact when you add up small increases over the past four months, a consistent upward movement has delivered overall gains in support of +6. That leaves Fine Gael securing 31% of the first preference vote at Christmas, just a few weeks before the General Election. The key for the government parties is persuading those who voted for them in 2011 to do so again in 2016. This appears to be precisely what Fine Gael is managing to do better over the recent past, while Labour is still struggling to woo back lost voters. The past four months has seen Fine Gael improve its voter loyalty by 10%. In July the party was only retaining 60% of those who voted for them in 2011, but by November this had improved to 70% retention of past voters.

Labour on the other hand are only managing to secure 30% of those that voted for the party in 2011, with a mass exodus of past voters to other parties. It is around Labour's vote that much of the speculation lies in the run up to the General Election. Consistently recording around 6–7% support in polls during 2015 has left the party very nervous. This is because the difference between relative success and failure is based on very small margins. If the party secures a 10% share or more they are likely to get a much better seat return than if they secure 6–7%.

Finally what of Fianna Fáil? In the past the party has secured close to 40% of the first preference share, but those days appear now to be a long way away. Having secured 17% at the last General Election, there were initially promising signs in the first half of the government's term, when it clawed back support to obtain around 26–27% of the first preference vote. However, this support fell away again in 2013 and early 2014, and since then it has remained static at between 18–20%. There is a possibility that some 'Shy Fianna Fáil' voters still exist, and historically they have performed slightly better on Election Day than the polls have suggested they would. But there are few signs that this will mean a significant rise in support, having been so static over the past two years.

So what do the polls suggest might be the make-up of the next government? Clearly at the present time Fine Gael are likely be the largest party by some distance, putting it in pole position to lead the next coalition, with Enda Kenny as Taoiseach. However, this will all depend on the fortunes of other parties that are prepared to go into coalition with it, as it also appears somewhat unlikely that it would increase support sufficiently to secure a majority. It has already declared its preference for a return of the current coalition, but that may not be possible unless the Labour vote share improves. Even a small improvement would mean that the current government could be returned, with support from some independent candidates.

If Labour does very poorly, however, this leaves the door open to other coalitions. The potential alternatives would be ground-breaking in Irish politics. A coalition of Fine Gael with Fianna Fáil, Fine Gael with Sinn Féin, or even Fianna Fáil with Sinn Féin in government, are all options that may be very difficult to agree between all parties and the potentially instability of which the current coalition partners will be quick to promote in the weeks ahead.

Does It Matter Who Runs for the Party?

Dr. Michael Marsh,
Emeritus Professor of Politics, TCD

This book tells you an awful lot about the candidates running for office in 2016: where they come from, what they do, whether other members of their family are, or have been in politics, as well as what they believe in and what they want to achieve. In some countries this would be a case of 'too much information'! All I want to know, says a typical voter, is what party are they running for, and what that party has done or says it will do, and who is its leader. Here in Ireland it is widely believed that the candidate really matters: hence the detail provided in the Tallyman's Guide.

This contribution will explore this belief and the evidence that might support it a little further, using the information provided by academic surveys carried out just after the elections of 2002, 2007 and 2011 as part of the Irish National Election Studies as well as some analysis of voting patterns over a longer period.

Let us start with election results. It is impossible to dismiss the importance of party. From 1981 up to 2011 Fianna Fáil on average took 41% of the vote, Fine Gael 31% and Labour 11%, with independents and a wide range of other parties taking the rest. Fianna Fáil candidates consistently won more votes than those of Fine Gael. Excepting 2011, Fianna Fáil's vote varied between 39% and 47%, a narrow range. Fine Gael's support has been more volatile, ranging between 22% and 39%, and Labour's has been between 6% and 20% but typically it has been close to 10% while Fine Gael's has been close to 30%. This all suggests that party is very important.

The respective importance of party and candidate can also be explored by looking at vote transfers. Where party is most important to voters, we expect them to prioritise the candidates of one party over supporting any other candidates. Where candidate is primary we would expect preferences to go haphazardly across parties. In recent years 60–70% of those voting for Fianna Fáil and Fine Gael transfer within the party. This is down from 80% in the 1980s and earlier but even so this points to the pre-eminence of party over candidate, at least in the big parties. It is lower among Labour voters but still over 50%.

Yet when we look at support for parties at constituency level we see that where a party runs more than one candidate, the votes each candidate pulls in are certainly not equal. Some do a lot better than others. Parties do their best to manage things, by restricting candidates' campaigns to certain areas and advising party supporters which candidate should get their No 1 vote so as to maximise the chances of winning two or more seats. While their success in doing this testifies to the importance of party, their need to do it in the first place highlights candidate differences: some are simply more popular than others, even within the same party.

Various survey questions have been designed to try to find out the respective importance of party and candidate to the voter. Since the 1970s people have been asked which of several factors were most important in their choice from a list including the party leader, the set of potential ministers, the party's policies and a candidate who will promote local needs. The last of these consistently won out, with between 40% and 50% of voters indicating that the candidate was more important than the party for a larger minority of voters. While this would not be inconsistent with the information about transfer patterns if the candidate-centred voters were followers of independents and minor parties, in fact many of them vote for Fine Gael and Fianna Fáil. Voters might say that the candidate is critical, but still appear to vote for a party.

The Election Studies mentioned earlier asked survey respondents two questions to explore this further. The first was simply whether the candidate or the party was the most important factor in their vote. The second question was whether the respondent would have supported the same candidate had they sported a different party label. Putting these two questions together we found that for about a third of voters, candidate was said to be key: respondents said they valued candidate over party and would follow their candidate across party lines. About a quarter of voters plumped for party: they said party was most important and said they would not have voted for the same candidate had their candidate run for a different party. The remainder are a mixed bunch. Some said 'candidate' was most important, but would not have ignored labels, while for others it would depend on which other party the candidate moved to. A few said 'party' was most important, but would still have followed a candidate who moved party. We did find that there were fewer clear 'candidate' voters in 2011, perhaps because the economic crisis focussed attention on the needs of the country over and above the constituency.

The Irish Election Studies (see www.tcd.ie/ines) also asked people to rate the various parties and their local candidates on 11 point scales, where the ends of the scales indicated strong likes or dislikes. Not surprisingly, for most voters the candidate they liked best ran for the party they liked best. In that case the obvious choice was the one followed in more than 8 out of 10 cases. When the best candidate did not represent the best party, voters were about four times as likely to go with the best candidate rather than the best party. Again though, party seemed to matter a little more in 2011.

While it is not surprising, the coincidence of judgements of best party and best candidate is remarkable. Parties and candidates each probably contribute to that. 'Good' candidates may look for a party that will help them, and parties want candidates who can add something to their ticket. This raises the question of what makes a good candidate. An important feature is name recognition; another is a record of achievement on behalf of the constituency. This can sometimes be inherited: parties like to pick candidates closely related to former TDs, and of course those from such families are more likely to think about a political career. For the voter a good candidate should probably come from their part of the constituency, particularly when the constituency crosses county boundaries. Almost all analyses of candidate success and failure over the past decades have highlighted the importance of incumbency and previous general election experience but have also underlined the importance of party labels. The most striking thing about the candidates detailed in this book is that so many more this time are women. There has been some controversy over whether female candidates are outperformed by male candidates. The best evidence is that they are, but generally because men tend to have more electoral experience and are more likely to be incumbents. The financial incentives for parties to nominate more women this time has promoted the nomination of many women with relatively little electoral experience and it will be interesting to see what impact this has on their success. The continued flux in our party system suggested by the polls may point to a significant turnover in personnel this time with many elected who have not come into politics in the usual way as they stand for new parties and sometimes new ways of thinking about politics; and sometimes, because they have established a formidable reputation outside traditional party politics. Look for yourself!

Independents: The Party Crashers?

Dr. Liam Weeks, School of Government, University College Cork

If in 2016 independents can maintain the levels of support they received at opinion polls across 2014 and 2015, then record numbers of them will be elected to the 32nd Dáil. This would continue an upward trajectory for independents, as they had a relatively successful 2011 Dáil election, winning fifteen seats, the most since 1927. Furthermore, support for them continued to grow during the lifetime of the 31st Dáil. In particular, independents' popularity surged in 2014, when they won an unprecedented 23% of the vote at the local elections held in May, before becoming the largest political grouping in opinion polls a few months later, a position they maintained almost continuously up until the spring of 2015. Even as support for independents inevitably began to wane in the run-up to the 2016 election they have remained the second most popular choice of voters.

Such a presence is without parallel in any other democracy, where few independents run for political office at the national level, let alone win seats in parliament. In part, this is because many European countries tend to use list electoral systems, under which voters opt for political parties, not candidates. In addition, in many other countries political competition and culture is centred on parties, with the consequence that many voters are ignorant of their local candidates. In contrast, Ireland uses what political scientists agree is the most candidate-centred electoral system – proportional representation by the single transferable vote (PR–STV). Combined with a political culture where voters' number one priority at elections in Ireland has been to choose a candidate to look after the needs of the local constituency, this creates conditions conducive to the emergence and election of independents.

To put the performance of independents in Ireland into international context, 2011 was the first national parliamentary election since 1950 in any mainstream democracy where independents won an aggregate vote of more than 10%. In addition, while there were fifteen independent TDs after that Dáil election, in total there were only seventeen elected independents sitting in the national parliaments of all other western democracies. So, almost 50% of the world's independent national parliamentarians are in Ireland, a remarkable statistic, which could well rise even further in 2016.

This significant presence of independents has not been a constant feature of Dáil elections. Although elected to every Dáil since 1921, independents have experienced mixed electoral fortunes. Up to the 1950s they were a considerable electoral force, winning an average twelve seats per election, to a Dáil smaller than the current version. However, they entered a period of decline in the 1960s and 1970s, as just two new independent TDs were elected between 1961 and 1981. Independents were thrust back into the limelight in the 1980s, first as several of them contributed to the defeat of the Fine Gael–Labour coalition's budget of January 1982, followed secondly by the infamous Gregory Deal, the basis on which independent Tony Gregory voted for Charlie Haughey as Taoiseach. Since then, other independent TDs such as Tom Foxe in Roscommon, Jackie Healy-Rae in Kerry, Mildred Fox in Wicklow, and Tom Gildea and Harry Blaney in Donegal, have all negotiated arrangements with different Taoisigh in return for their Dáil vote. This leverage has contributed to independents remaining an important political actor in Ireland, when they have long since disappeared from the national political landscape in most democracies.

The Rise of Independents

Figure 1 indicates the historical fluctuation in support for independents. In recent decades, apart from a hiccup in 2007, support for independents has been steadily on the rise, with more independents elected at almost every Dáil election since the 1980s. For example, at the ten Dáil elections between 1961 and 1997, just eight new independent TDs were elected. At the four elections between 1997 and 2011, however, twenty-three new independent TDs were elected, including five in 1997, nine in 2002, and nine in 2011. This resurgence of independents may be part of a wider European phenomenon of the rise of populism, which in other countries has taken the form of parties, such as Podemos in Spain or the Five Star Movement in Italy. Many independents in Ireland preach an anti-establishment message and are able to profit from the general malaise amongst voters towards the political system, a malaise that was especially prevalent at the height of the financial crisis.

Perhaps testament to this populist streak has been a change in the independent vote. Where once it was tied solely to the local independent candidate, there now appears to have developed a genuine independent brand, where voters are willing to support whatever candidate wears this label, almost akin to party voters. Hence, in the polls in the run-up to the 2016 election, one in four voters expressed their preference for an independent before such candidates had even declared their interest in running. In tandem with this, there is now also a different type of nationally-oriented independent, who came to prominence with the election of the likes of Mick Wallace and Shane Ross in 2011.

With the increased support for independents in opinion polls in 2014 and 2015, many of these more national independents sought to mobilise this vote in advance of the 2016 election. Lucinda Creighton, one of the most high-profile independents following her resignation from Fine Gael in 2013, set the ball rolling with the establishment of the Reform Alliance, a loose parliamentary grouping of former Fine Gael TDs. This morphed into a new political party, Renua Ireland, in March 2015, which attracted some independent councillors to its ranks. An informal independents' network of TDs, councillors and MEPs was launched in January 2014 to provide support to independent candidates in the run-up to that year's elections. In 2015 a separate independent alliance, headed by TDs Shane Ross and Michael Fitzmaurice, and chaired by Senator Fergal Quinn, emerged, which outlined ten key principles, but was keen to emphasise it was not a party. It did not have a binding manifesto, nor did it plan to operate a whip, but, if supporting a government, it promised to do so on votes of confidence. This alliance clearly envisaged a role for itself in government, while at the same time retaining the independent brand. Concurrently, three independent TDs came together to launch a new political party, the Social Democrats, in July 2015. It remains to be seen which strategy will prove the most successful for independents – whether to compete on their own, or to pool their resources against the established parties.

The 2016 Election

The burning issue for independents is whether their popularity at opinion polls can be replicated at the ballot box. An important point of note is that the category of 'independents' reported from polls includes 'others', which refers to anyone outside of the four main parties, including Renua Ireland, the Social Democrats and the alliance between People Before Profit and the Anti-Austerity Alliance. As a consequence, although support for 'independents and others' has not been below 20% in the polls since early 2014, the actual support for independents outside of these groups and parties is likely to be lower, perhaps between 10% and 15%, not too far from the 11% they attracted in 2011.

While determining the true level of support for independents is difficult, converting a national vote into constituency seat returns is an even trickier matter. Winning 15% of votes does not necessarily equate to 15% of seats under the Irish voting system, and independents' percentage of seats won tends to be less than their equivalent proportion of votes. In 2011, they won 8.4% of seats with 10.8% of votes, in 2007 3% of seats with 5.8% of votes, and in 2002 7.8% of seats with 9.5% of votes. Likewise, although 'independents and others' won more votes than any party at the 2014 local elections, they won less seats than both Fianna Fáil and Fine Gael.

One reason why it is difficult to convert the independent vote into seats is because of the very low rates of transfer solidarity between independent candidates. When an independent is elected or eliminated, on average only one in four of these votes go to a fellow independent. While this level of transfers may improve in 2016 simply because of the greater number of independent candidates likely to run, the transfer rate will still be far below the equivalent within the main parties, which averages around 60%. In other words, when one of the candidates of the parties is elected or eliminated, 60% of their votes go to their running mates. Independents' failure to attract higher levels of transfers from other independent candidates means that the independent vote will gradually be reduced as the counts progress. Many votes for independents will transfer to party candidates or be non-transferable. This is one of the factors motivating the form of independent alliances, to ensure that independent votes remain with independent candidates. The problem of transfers and too many candidates diluting an independent vote was highlighted in Laois–Offaly in 2011. Ten independent candidates between them won 1.2 quotas, but no seats, while Sinn Féin won one seat with 0.65 quotas and Fianna Fáil two seats with 1.6 quotas. A record number of 173 independent candidates contested the 2011 election, a figure that may be exceeded in 2016, and which will only dilute the independent vote further, resulting in more scenarios similar to Laois–Offaly.

Where are independents likely to do well? Table 1 indicates the average vote for independents per constituency across three periods, all the way back to 1923. In the table several constituencies had to be merged because of a change in electoral boundaries over time. One obvious pattern is the prominence of independents in the border constituencies in the early decades of the state, as is their decline in the time since. Donegal has proved somewhat of an exception, as independent support has been pretty consistent in the county across all three electoral phases. Indeed, an independent has been elected in Donegal at 23 of the 28 general elections between 1923 and 2011. Their diversity, ranging from independent unionists to independent republicans to independent farmers, suggests there is something of an independent vote in this region that is itself independent of the nature of the candidacy.

In terms of constituencies not conducive to independents, Carlow–Kilkenny, Cork East and Cork North-West have not been hotbeds of support for them in recent years, despite the rising national vote for independents. Not only was no independent elected in these three constituencies at any Dáil election since 1981, their electoral performance has been pretty negligible. No independent candidate ran at seven of the Dáil elections in Cork North-West (no independent has run there since 1997) in this period, and on only one occasion when one did run was support greater than 1%. In Carlow–Kilkenny half of the general elections between 1981 and 2011 did not feature an independent, and in the five that did the average independent vote was just over 2%. It was even lower in Cork East, at 1.3%, where independents have not contested four of the last ten Dáil elections.

A health warning about analysing historical levels of support for independents is that it is quite volatile and primarily depends on the availabiltiy of a suitable candidate. Tipperary, for example, traditionally had a very weak vote for independents, until first Michael Lowry ran in 1997, followed by Seamus Healy in 2000 and Mattie McGrath in 2011. This means that no constituency should be seen as a no-go area for such candidates, even the likes of Cork East or Carlow–Kilkenny. Where a prominent and capable independent decides to run, he or she can potentially receive a sizeable vote, particularly if a national swing to independents materialises, a possibility that has never been greater than in 2016.

Table 1. Average % vote for independents per constituency at Dáil elections, 1923–2011

	1923–61	1965–77	1981–2011
Cavan–Monaghan	26.3	4.01	6.7
Dublin North (C, N, NE, MC, NW)	22.0	4.07	7.1
Donegal	13.0	11.34	15.8
Cork City	10.3	4.53	5.3
Dublin County (S+SW+W+MW)	9.6	3.63	4.4
Wicklow	8.7	2.12	9.3
Cork South-West	8.7	0.00	3.4
Sligo–N. Leitrim	8.7	3.22	7.9
Longford/Westmeath/Roscommon	8.4	9.35	7.2
Laois–Offaly	7.7	2.79	3.3
Cork Mid	7.3	0.00	0.6
Cork East	7.3	2.65	0.8
Dublin South (SC+SE+DL)	6.7	2.48	3.8
Clare	5.9	1.67	7.4
Waterford	5.5	1.10	4.8
Kerry	5.3	49.5	8.0
Louth	4.4	2.09	8.2
Limerick	3.6	3.96	5.5
Carlow–Kilkenny	3.3	0.36	1.3
Tipperary	3.0	0.51	13.3
Galway	2.2	2.47	5.6
Mayo	1.9	0.47	5.8
Meath	1.5	2.39	4.6
Wexford	1.4	1.14	4.5
Kildare	1.0	1.35	3.2

How many seats can independents expect to win? If we take the sitting independent TDs first, of the fifteen elected in 2011 all bar one is running again (Luke 'Ming' Flanagan resigned his seat following his election to the European Parliament in 2014, with independent Michael Fitzmaurice winning the by-election to replace him), with two running for parties – Stephen Donnelly and

Catherine Murphy for the Social Democrats. Two independents are running as the sole Dáil representatives of registered parties – Mick Wallace for the Independents 4 Change and Seamus Healy for the Workers and Unemployed Action Group. Two other independent TDs elected under a party banner in 2011, Joan Collins and Clare Daly, have an ambiguous affiliation with the United Left party, which they helped establish in 2013, but will run as independent s, describing themselves as independent socialists. These fifteen independents will be joined at the election by four other TDs who fell out with their respective parties in the lifetime of the 31st Dáil – Eamon Maloney and Tommy Broughan with Labour and Peter Matthews and Denis Naughten with Fine Gael. Historically, the average re-election rate of independent TDs standing again is 80%, so if this is repeated in 2016, we can expect 15 of the 19 to retain their seats. In terms of new additions to this cohort, on average five new independent TDs emerged at each of the five Dáil elections over the past twenty-five years. Taking these two historical patterns into account, we can expect to see twenty independents in the next Dáil. Indeed, this is the exact number predicted by The Irish Times in its series of constituency profiles published in November 2015. The new independents it tips as likely to emerge include Kieran McCarthy in Cork East, Michael Collins in Cork South-West, former Green TD Paul Gogarty in Dublin Mid-West, Sean Canney in Galway East and Catherine Connolly in Galway West. Someone with a greater financial interest in the outcome than The Irish Times, the bookmakers Paddy Power, had in late 2015 independents and others to win 33 seats. Assuming that the minor parties will win at least ten of these seats, this also puts independents close to the figure of twenty. Of course, this is all speculation that very much depends on the support independents can attract. All things being equal, the more votes they get, the more seats they can expect, and if the election turns out to be 'Independents' Day', many more than those mentioned here will come into the reckoning when the votes are counted. If this happens, independents will be a serious political force in the 32nd Dáil.

Righting a Historic Imbalance: Selecting Female Candidates

Niamh Gallagher amd Michelle O'Donnell-Keating, Women for Election

Friday the 25th of February 2011, the date of the last general election in Ireland and an historic day. As the results rolled in it became clear that this Dáil, the 31st, would have a higher number of women than ever before. Cause for celebration? Perhaps, or perhaps not. This making of history saw a record 25 women walk through the gates of Leinster House as newly elected TDs, 25 women of 166: 15%.

In 2011, that this figure was progress is deeply disheartening. In a country where women run multinationals, play leading roles in the legal system and continue to grow in number and in influence across the professions, that politics lags so far behind society is not only embarrassing, but troubling. Our Dáil is where the important decisions about our society and economy are made; yet women's voices are absent. How are women influencing the decisions that affect them? And how can we, Irish people, be certain that decisions are made in all of our best interests: men, women, girls and boys.

Background to the Gender Quota Legislation

A Joint Oireachtas Committee Report on Women's Participation in Politics published in 2009 highlighted five barriers women face to entering politics, which mirror those experienced internationally, but with an Irish flavour, particularly in relation to candidate selection.

Those barriers are summarised as the '5 Cs', and are by now well rehearsed. They are culture: Irish political culture is dominated by men and built to accommodate men, particularly within political parties; candidate selection procedures: they favour men and are difficult to navigate for those from outside the system; confidence: women are less likely to go forward for selection than men; child-care: women are more likely to have this primary responsibility, which limits their ability to be available in the manner required for Irish politics; and cash: women in Ireland traditionally have access to less cash resources than men do.

The Report concluded that given the variety of barriers the single most effective reform to increase the number of women in Irish politics is the introduction of mandatory positive action measures through legislation, which would require political parties to adopt gender targets or quotas in their selection processes. In its election manifesto the Labour Party committed to introducing quotas, and, by the conclusion of coalition negotiations between Fine Gael and Labour the Programme for Government included a commitment that 'public funding for political parties will be tied to the level of participation as candidates those parties achieve.' Little attention was paid to this commitment at the time, beyond among women's organisations and activists who welcomed it as progress and pushed for more clarity on its implementation.

Within the first year of the Government's term it became clear that the vehicle through which the commitment would be delivered was the Electoral (Amendment) (Political Funding) Act. Steered by Phil Hogan TD and Minister at the Department of Environment, Community and Local Government, the Act reformed the process of political donations, reducing the figure politicians and parties can receive from individuals and corporations, introducing greater transparency and – with reference to women – requiring that all political parties in receipt of State funding field a minimum of 30% of candidates of either gender, or lose 50% of their State funding. Within seven years the proportion of candidates fielded rises to 40%. This became law on the last Dáil sitting the day before the 2012 summer recess. Women's organisations gathered to celebrate at an otherwise deserted Leinster House. The journey towards election 2016 had begun.

The Quota Alone is Not Enough

The quota, however, is just part of the story. The Joint Oireachtas Report and numerous other reports are clear that while quotas provide an immediate and impactful stimulus to increase women's political participation, they are not the entire solution. In tandem with quotas, training and mentoring for female candidates as well as concrete measures to make Parliaments more family friendly are key.

In 2011, in reaction to the election result, we founded Women for Election to inspire and equip women to succeed in politics by providing tailored training, mentoring and support programmes focused on contesting selection and election. Building on models used by the White House Project, EMILY's List and the Women's Campaign School at Yale, we sought to build a national movement of political women – from all parties and none – and to address the oft-heard lament from political parties that they simply cannot find the women.

In 2012, Women for Election formally launched in the Mansion House in Dublin, supported by all political parties and a group of independents. That Spring we began running INSPIRE, a one day training programme for women interested in getting involved in politics at any level: as a canvasser, a campaign manager or a candidate. In just one year, 350 women took part in INSPIRE in Dublin, Cork, Galway, Limerick and Athlone. Many of these women found Women for Election themselves – they had long harboured a desire to get involved in politics, but were unsure where to start, how to navigate the system – others came from political parties, and wanted to ensure they were best placed to win selections when the time came. Our experience in 2012 and 2013, as we ran INSPIRE up and down the country was of a mismatch: a media and political narrative that focused on women's lack of desire to get involved in politics, and the determination and drive among the hundreds of women we met to put themselves forward.

From Rhetoric to Reality: The Local and European Elections 2014

The focus in those years was the local and European elections, scheduled for May 2014. These elections, we believed, were a proxy for the general election that would follow shortly afterwards. Would parties use the opportunity the local elections provided to increase their pipeline of female candidates? Would they identify strong candidates, support them to run and win locally, with a view to fielding them in the general election when, with the new legislation, they would inevitably be seeking more women to contest?

The table below outlines the proportion of female candidates fielded by parties and the subsequent proportion of those elected that were women. Some parties introduced clear rules around candidate selection and identified constituencies where new female candidates at the general election would have a strong chance. Others chose not to apply rules at local level, and to run a much smaller proportion of women than the 30% national quota would require.

Table 1: Proportion of female candidates fielded by political parties at the local elections 2014 and subsequently elected

Party	Proportion of Female Candidates	Proportion of Women Elected
Fine Gael	23	21
Labour	30	35
Fianna Fáil	17	14
Sinn Féin	32	30
People Before Profit	40	43
Green Party	30	25
Anti-Austerity Alliance	29	33

On Election Day, 23rd of May 2014, a total of 196 women contested, making up 22% of all candidates, an increase from 16% in 2009. Of those 196 almost 100 were elected, 21% of the total, and a 33% increase on the 2009 number. Of those 100, more than half were Women for Election alumnae. At European level, women made up 37% of candidates, and 55% of those elected, a remarkable achievement for Ireland and one that ranks us 2nd in the European Parliament in terms of women's representation.

The local elections provided important learning. They showed clearly that when women run women win – 22% of all candidates were women, and 21% of all those elected were women. And – as would become apparent later – building a pipeline at local level makes the job of selecting candidates in advance of a general election easier. After the elections, it returned to business as usual for politics, with the issue of women's participation raising its head here and there during the latter half of 2014, but not generating the same level of interest or passion as it had when selections were at play.

Preparing for the 2016 General Election

That, of course, was short lived. In 2015, with speculation of an early election rife, parties and candidates began to prepare. Only at that point, halfway through 2015, did the reality of the gender quota, introduced into law in 2012, hit home for some. If we are to increase the number of women elected to the Dáil it is inevitable that we will reduce the number of men. This is not a suggestion that women are better than men or vice versa, but recognition of the evidence that shows that balanced decisions are better decisions and that all of us are better off when there is a mix of women and men around the table.

With selections underway in earnest, it became clear that parties, in some instances, would have to impose directives at selection conventions to ensure they reached the required 30% of female candidates. The first surprise came when Richard Bruton was added to a ticket in Dublin Bay North, when the Fine Gael selection – obliged to select one man and one woman – selected Cllr. Naoise O'Muiri and Stephanie Regan. Much was made of Connie Gerety Quinn's selection in Longford, where two male sitting councillors were instructed by Fianna Fail Fáil HQ not to contest the convention, and of Mary Fitzpatrick's selection for the same party in Dublin Central, which ultimately led to a court challenge by Brian Mohan, who was excluded from contesting, based on a party directive that the candidate must be female.

These examples, while generating significant hype, are few in number. In most cases, parties got on with selecting female candidates and discovered that there is indeed a wealth of capable, competent and determined women, keen to make their contribution to political life. As it stands, all parties will reach the 30% quota, and some will exceed it.

Table 2:

Party	Total Candidates	Female Candidates	Percentage
Fine Gael	86	26	30.2
Labour	36	13	36.1
Fianna Fáil	67	21	31.3
Sinn Féin	50	18	32
Green Party	35	12	34.3
AAA–PBP	31	13	41.9
Renua Ireland	19	4	21.1
Direct Democracy Ireland	9	0	0
Social Democrats	15	6	40
Workers' Party	5	2	40

The Quota in Action: A Changed Offering to the Irish Voting Public

Currently, in excess of 141 women are contesting the election of 465 declared candidates. That is 30.3%: double the percentage that contested in 2011. Of these women, at least 67 (85%) of those running for larger parties are either elected at local or national level, or have run before. These women are not novices; they are experienced vote getters and winners. For them, the quota has created an environment within their parties whereby they are supported to contest and win selection, and – for many of the hopefuls – election.

Already the quota is a success. There are more women contesting this election than ever before. Parties have moved from years of empty promises to seeking and finding strong, competent female candidates to contest. Politics has been opened up to a group that, in the past, were largely excluded. There is an increased focus – given the hard-fought nature of selections – on candidates' qualification and ability to do the job, which can only be a good thing for politics overall. And, most importantly, we voters will have much greater choice when we come to mark our ballot paper.

It is worthwhile to reflect, as we enter this election, why the quota was introduced: to right an historic imbalance. Ireland is one of the worst performers in the developed world in relation to women's representation in politics. We rank 86th out of 189 countries globally, alongside countries like Libya, Uzbekistan and North Korea. We are 24th out of 28 EU member states, and, in 2015, have just 15% women in our national Parliament – the highest number ever. Gender quotas are the only proven method of increasing women's representation in Parliaments within a reasonable timeframe. The quota has pushed parties to play their part, but the real choice remains with us, the voters. We will decide on Election Day whether the 32nd Dáil will reflect the values of equality that we will talk so much about in Ireland in 2016.

Some Old and Some New: Media in Election 2016

Larry Donnelly, Analyst, Irish and American Politics

An extraordinary amount has already been said and written internationally about both the ongoing changes to the manner in which news is provided by traditional media outlets and the part increasingly played by social media in disseminating information of all sorts to an ever-expanding audience. Of course, an in many ways transformed 'old' media and the infinite variety of perspectives available via 'new' media are having a significant impact on campaigns and elections, as well as on politics more generally.

Perhaps the one thing that political watchers across the ideological spectrum in Ireland can agree upon presently is that how the electorate will monitor events and educate itself in the coming weeks as the general election approaches will be quite different to how they did so in the past. Media outlets have been readying plans to cover the election 24 hours a day and 7 days a week with unprecedented resources dedicated to their online presence. Political parties, individual candidates, their supporters and interest and lobby groups have well-developed social media strategies in place.

What follows is not an attempt at the herculean task of assessing precisely how and just to what extent media coverage of the upcoming general election campaign will shape its contours or bear upon its outcome. Rather, four distinct and, it is submitted, crucial points are considered: 1) candidate strategy to maximise both a local/regional and national media profile; 2) the need for candidates to harness the power of social media, yet remain cognisant of its inherent limitations; 3) 'opinion formers' on a large and, just as importantly, small scale; and 4) the still central position and corresponding obligations of the national radio and television broadcasters and newspapers.

Local/Regional and National Media

A comment on Twitter last July on the day TDs Stephen Donnelly, Catherine Murphy and Róisín Shorthall formally launched their new party, the Social Democrats, captures in a nutshell why those who sit in or will be seeking seats in the Dáil must have an integrated strategy ensuring the best possible exposure and outreach in both local/regional and national media.

The tweeting voter in Deputy Donnelly's Wicklow/East Carlow constituency wanted to know why he was doing interviews on national media before sitting down to talk with Declan Meehan on Wicklow's East Coast FM. After all, the voter wondered, Deputy Donnelly's mandate to serve in the Dáil was given to him by the people in Wicklow and they deserved to hear directly from him first. The voter had a point, and Deputy Donnelly was on East Coast FM shortly thereafter. He was there for good reason. In fact, and as the JNLR figures regularly prove, broadcasters like Declan Meehan in Wicklow, Keith Finnegan in Galway and others around the country are just as respected and revered voices in their localities as are national radio stalwarts like Seán O'Rourke, Pat Kenny, George Hook and Mary Wilson.

Further underpinning the need for candidates to remain mindful of Tip O'Neill's prescient, albeit trite, 'all politics is local' maxim is a contradictory impulse in the electorate. When questioned or polled, Irish voters will typically lament the fact that TDs, in general, spend too much time on the 'parish pump' when they should be focused on matters of national interest. Indeed, this seemingly widespread view and a consequent desire for reform are at least partly behind the formation of two new parties in 2015, the aforementioned Social Democrats and Renua Ireland.

Yet at the same time, when it comes to their own localities, many of these same voters often call on their TDs and expect them to be completely in touch with all that is affecting daily life in the communities they represent. Recent polling – which reveals strong support for traditional, constituency and/or issue-oriented, 'ear to the ground' independents, on the one hand, and low levels of support for both Renua Ireland and the Social Democrats on the other – illustrates that the contradiction is alive and well.

Still, however, there is no doubt that having a national media presence is an asset for any politician. Voters take note of and even take pride in seeing and hearing the politicians they vote for and might know personally on TV or on RTÉ or Newstalk radio. In the coming weeks, candidates must pursue such opportunities, but not at the expense, whether actual or perceived (they are one and the same in a campaign), of appearances on regional radio stations and coverage in regional newspapers. As ever, the challenge – or more accurately, the trick – for candidates and their advisers will be how to achieve the ideal balance between the local and the national and do both well.

Social Media: Potential and Pitfalls

One of the defining features of last year's marriage equality referendum campaign was the Yes side's extensive use of social media, particularly Facebook and Twitter. Both platforms were employed to distribute information, rebut arguments proffered by their opponents and to develop messaging. Most importantly, though, Twitter and Facebook were utilised to organise canvasses, recruit volunteers and mobilise voters. The power of social media in this regard cannot be underestimated. Candidates in this election would be well-advised to emulate some of the tactics of the Yes side.

Equally, however, candidates would be foolish to depend too heavily on social media or to adopt the view that an apparent consensus on Twitter and Facebook is necessarily representative of broader public sentiment. Social media can be something of an echo chamber and dissenting viewpoints, especially those on the political right, can be shouted down and made to seem extreme, even though they might be shared by a substantial segment of the electorate. What's more, despite the ongoing growth in the number of social media users, there are many voters who are not active on Facebook or Twitter. Crucially, this latter group is likely to be older and far more likely to cast a ballot on Election Day.

Social media will be an effective tool for candidates in this election and will be utilised to a greater extent in the coming weeks than in any previous campaign. But it is no substitute for having a good ground game. What social media can do, as marriage equality campaigners will readily attest, is act as a speedy and comprehensive conduit to building the ground game necessary to win a seat in the next Dáil.

'Opinion Formers'

Cynics are fond of pointing out that many people don't really watch, read or listen to 'heavy' news and current affairs stories – either carefully or at all. They have a point. Although Ireland's news literacy is relatively high when compared with somewhere like the United States, a lot of people who will vote in this election won't be making decisions that are as informed as they ideally should be, and most of them would readily admit that.

Here is where the role of 'opinion formers,' not the media pundits who have the privilege of sharing their analysis with large audiences, but the tens of thousands of active consumers of both traditional and social media, is pivotal. Even though they are seldom discussed, in this country or elsewhere, these active citizens typically dictate, at least in part, how handfuls of their family and friends throughout Ireland ultimately decide to vote. (Hint: If you're reading these words, you probably are an 'opinion former.').

Collectively, these men and women are the lynchpin of the democratic societies in which they live. Candidates' media appeals must be directed at them. They do much of the homework for their family and friends and will determine the outcome of this general election.

National Broadcasters and Newspapers

In a recent column, the former editor of The Irish Times, Geraldine Kennedy, writes: 'It is going to be a challenging – indeed, a difficult and different general election – for The Irish Times to cover in a fair, balanced, proportionate and independent way in the newspaper and, for the first time seriously, across all digital platforms.' Her comment applies equally to all of Ireland's national news outlets in 2016.

It is worth noting that election coverage has been underway for some time now. In this regard, although it has had some bad moments, The People's Debate series undertaken by the Tonight with Vincent Browne programme on TV3 merits a mention. Televising the candidates (at least those who've been willing to set out their stalls) and their constituents in the same rooms across the country has been a useful exercise in democracy and has provided the broader viewing public with some valuable insights on just how difficult and thankless the job of being an elected representative can be.

The first part of the media's shared challenge identified by Ms. Kennedy – to cover the campaign in a fair, balanced, proportionate and independent way – raises myriad issues. Of course, 'fair and balanced,' the slogan of America's Fox News network, has become a loaded term, given that Fox's coverage of American politics and global events is often unfair and imbalanced. In Ireland, the allegation of biased media coverage is raised at times by politicians of every hue.

A quick perusal of Twitter will show that Sinn Féin supporters claim the 'southern media' is out to get the party; that the anti-water charges campaign feels that the 'media establishment' is opposed to it; that social conservatives are looked down upon by 'Dublin 4 media elites'; that Fianna Fáil has never been given credit for the good that it did in Government; that Fine Gael has been unjustifiably hammered for making the decisions necessary to get this country back from the brink; and that one Dublin-based Labour party councillor believes that his party's representatives are deliberately denied a voice on many TV and radio programmes.

It is not overly glib, however, to say that, if criticism comes periodically from all sides, then it is a signal that the Irish media does a reasonably good job of covering politics. Those who hold or stand for office must always be held to account and subjected to in depth questioning. And this will surely again be the case as the general election approaches.

On the other hand, criticism has been entirely warranted in the past where the requirement of balance has been interpreted so rigidly as to mandate the need for precisely equal speaking time, etc. It is vital that coverage be balanced; it is equally vital that the need for balanced coverage isn't taken to unreasonable extremes.

The second challenge Ms. Kennedy rightly observes relates to digital platforms. This time around, there will be real pressure on national media outlets to continually publish stories online, so that the electorate can keep up to date with events as they happen. The less frenetic news cycle in the past, which allowed additional time for reflection and double and triple fact-checking before publishing a story in a daily newspaper or running a package on TV or radio, is a luxury that is now well and truly gone.

Media outlets will have to satisfy the public's expectation for immediate delivery of news about the campaign and keep pace with their competitors, while simultaneously maintaining the highest journalistic standards. Inevitably in this environment, a journalist may get something wrong, yet the investment that outlets have made in their online presence and personnel, together with the capacity to very quickly remedy a mistake, militate against major blunders.

Moreover, now well-established news websites like TheJournal.ie and BreakingNews.ie, coupled with the growth in the numbers of online journalists at traditional media sources, have engendered a cadre of experienced 24/7 journalists in Ireland. In the main, online journalists have enriched the coverage of politics internationally. They are already doing likewise here and will perform an important service for Irish democracy in election 2016.

Conclusion

The Irish people will follow this year's general election in a different way than they ever have before. It is impossible to predict what impact, if any, the changes to the delivery of 'old' media and the new prism provided by 'new' media might ultimately have until things kick off in earnest. What can be said with certainty, however, is that the coverage will be impossible to escape in early 2016 – on TV, radio, online or in newspapers – for even those with the most inveterate aversion to campaigns and elections.

As such, the tasks and obligations lying ahead of politicians and journalists are immense. And they go well beyond what has been discussed briefly here. It will be fascinating to examine their performance in this substantially altered milieu after we, as citizens, have exercised our sacred right to vote and the dust has finally settled. And in this vein, it is crucial to remain eternally mindful that, leaving aside the nuances of modern political campaigns and changes to media coverage thereof, democracy is still all down to us.

To Debate or Not to Debate – The Leaders' Question

Dr. Brian Murphy, Lecturer in Communications, Dublin Institute of Technology

Charles Haughey once witheringly dismissed the importance of televised party leaders' election debates as 'a bit of theatre, a bit of a circus and a great media hype,' but nowadays such contests are an integral part of the Irish electoral process.

At the last general election, the first campaign debate between the leaders of Fianna Fáil, Fine Gael, the Green Party, Labour and Sinn Féin was the fourth most watched television programme on Irish television in 2011. It drew an average audience of 964,000 people. Only the Late Late Toy Show, the Eurovision Song Contest and the All-Ireland Football between Dublin and Kerry attracted a larger viewership.

In 2007, the general election campaign's only televised head-to-head between Taoiseach Bertie Ahern and the Fine Gael leader Enda Kenny saw over one million people tune in to a debate moderated by Miriam O'Callaghan. Meanwhile, RTÉ.ie had its biggest day of internet traffic ever, with over 1.5 million hits. In the same campaign, even a TV debate between the potential candidates for Tánaiste was watched by more than 580,000 people.

The notion that Irish people are growing increasingly apathetic about politics is not reflected in the mass TV audiences who engage with televised leaders' debates. Indeed, the strong appeal that election debates hold for Irish TV audiences is evident from the fact that in the 2011 General Election over 408,000 people watched at least part of a three-way debate conducted entirely in the Irish language between Eamon Gilmore, Enda Kenny and Micheál Martin. This extraordinarily high level of viewership was in spite of the fact that the census earlier that year highlighted that

Irish was only the third most spoken language in the country, after English and Polish.

For voters, televised leaders' debates are an attractive proposition because of their gladiatorial nature, their potential for drama and for their ability to test the mettle of those aspiring to high office. Such debates also give voters the opportunity to assess the merits of the various policies being proffered by the political parties from the luxury of their own living rooms and to arrive at a judgment on the competence of the rival leaders.

For party leaders, the televised leaders' debates have the potential to make or break their aspirations to be Taoiseach, especially as this prime time TV slot is undoubtedly the main point of political engagement for many undecided voters.

For Ireland's television stations, election debates mean guaranteed huge viewership figures and a consequent boom in advertising revenues. Put simply, leaders' debates are big commercial business.

Traditionally, leaders' debates have been the preserve of RTÉ, as the national public service broadcaster. However, since the advent in 1998 of TV3, the country's first commercial free-to-air television network, an alternative broadcasting forum has been available to host election debates.

During the 2002 General Election, Andrew Hanlon, TV3's director of news, confirmed that negotiations on a televised leaders' debate between the four main party leaders concluded unsuccessfully with Fianna Fáil saying 'No' to the idea. A subsequent attempt by TV3 to organise their own leaders' debate during the 2007 General Election also proved fruitless because of a failure by Fianna Fáil and Fine Gael to agree terms on the format of the debate.

Impetus was given to TV3's efforts to break RTÉ's stranglehold on leaders' debates by events in the United Kingdom in 2010. For the first time in British political history (and more than a quarter of a century after Ireland), the main UK party leaders – Gordon Brown, David Cameron and Nick Clegg – participated in a televised general election debate. Among the terms and conditions ironed out by the parties in taking this historic step was that there would be three debates hosted, in turn, by three separate UK broadcasting organisations, BBC, ITN and BSkyB.

Less than seven months later, during the 2011 Irish General Election, debates were hosted by three separate Irish broadcasting organisations, RTÉ (two debates), TG4 and TV3, though the latter channel's debate is best remembered for a controversial no-show. Micheál Martin and Eamon Gilmore did participate in the TV3 debate, but Enda Kenny, the overwhelming favourite to win the election, declined to take part. The Fine Gael leader said his decision was based on remarks made by TV3 broadcaster Vincent Browne the previous year about suicide.

Kenny's withdrawal from the TV3 debate was strongly criticised by Fianna Fáil. Micheál Martin remarked that 'as a leader of government you have to be able to deal with tough negotiations in many forums. Talking to former paramilitaries about peace, with other countries about treaties or multinational executives about investments – you have to face much tougher situations than a debate moderated by Vincent Browne.'

Browne himself claimed that he had been 'used as a ploy to get out of debates' by the Fine Gael leader and he offered to step back from being moderator, but even this move did not result in Kenny's participation in the TV3 debate.

A likely line of attack from the opposition parties in General Election 2016 will be the accusation that the Taoiseach is not accountable and has a track-record of dodging debates. This criticism has its roots not just in Kenny's 2011 TV3 absence, but also in his refusal in October 2013 to participate in a referendum campaign debate on his own proposal to abolish the Seanad. This latter decision ultimately backfired. In an incisive intervention, the Wicklow TD, Stephen Donnelly said he viewed Mr Kenny's refusal to debate as 'deeply, deeply suspicious' and he asked voters to 'imagine [if] David Cameron said I am going to abolish the House of Lords, but I am not willing to debate it on television. Imagine Barack Obama saying I am going to ask the American people to abolish the US Senate, but I am unwilling to debate that issue.'

Fine Gael had argued that 'there is no precedent for a Taoiseach being engaged in a referendum debate,' but it is hard to accept that its response would have been as tepid if, for example, Charles Haughey had sought to abolish a house of the national parliament, but declined to debate it. The Taoiseach's refusal to actually debate a proposal he had previously described as a personal 'leader's initiative' – and which would significantly have involved over 40 amendments to the Constitution – is believed to have weighed heavily on many voters' minds when they cast their ballot. The referendum to abolish the Seanad was defeated by just 42,500 votes.

Kenny's defenders will argue that no incoming Taoiseach has ever contested more TV debates in a single campaign than the current Fine Gael leader. Despite shunning TV3, Enda Kenny did engage in three televised campaign debates in the 2011 General Election. As Taoiseach, Kenny may have consciously chosen to run the risk of not debating the Seanad referendum, but as an experienced party leader he would have been astutely aware that precedent showed that such a strategy was unlikely to pay dividends in a general election. In the 1989 General Election, Taoiseach Charles Haughey severely miscalculated by going down this route.

Riding high in opinion polls, Haughey succumbed to the temptation to call a general election less than twenty-seven months after the previous election in pursuit of an elusive overall majority. Believing that a cautious approach to public debate was the best way to maintain his lead, Haughey ruled out any prospect that he would take part in a televised confrontation with the Fine Gael leader, Alan Dukes, before polling day. Haughey stuck doggedly to this position throughout the campaign.

In a press conference three days before the electorate cast their votes, Haughey argued that televised leaders' debates were 'an out-dated formula.' Haughey also suggested that it was 'a reasonable assumption to make' that he would never participate in this type of debate again – a prediction that was to prove wholly accurate, but possibly not in the way Mr Haughey imagined, as he was replaced by Albert Reynolds as leader of Fianna Fáil and Taoiseach in February 1992.

Haughey's unwillingness to debate Dukes was one of a number of factors that caused Fianna Fáil's support to decline in the course of the 1989 General Election. An Irish Times/MRBI opinion poll from the last week of the campaign showed that nearly two out of every three voters wanted to see a televised debate between Haughey and his Fine Gael opponent. The same poll showed that younger voters were most interested in seeing a debate and that even 41 of Fianna Fáil supporters disagreed with Haughey's stance of not debating. Fianna Fáil fell three seats short of an overall majority and, to remain as Taoiseach, Haughey was forced into coalition with the Progressive Democrats, ending Fianna Fáil's longstanding core value of single party government. Had Haughey, who had acquitted himself well in leaders' debates in previous campaigns, chosen to debate in 1989, the trajectory of late twentieth century Irish political history may well have been very different.

In an attempt to set the parameters for General Election 2016, Micheál Martin told his parliamentary party 'think in' in Sutton last September that he is 'absolutely' the only alternative Taoiseach to Mr Kenny. The Fianna Fáil leader said Fine Gael's 'fundamental strategy is to hide Enda Kenny as often as they can in order to propel themselves to victory.' Martin insisted that Kenny would have to take part in a 'no holds barred' televised debate with him 'so we can have a fulsome, energetic and active campaign where political leaders don't go for the soundbites or running for the organised PR opportunities.'

In the forthcoming election campaign, Fianna Fáil can be expected to push repeatedly for as many debates as conceivably possible. There is nothing new in this. Fine Gael pursued the same strategy in 2002 when the then party leader Michael Noonan demanded that Taoiseach Bertie Ahern face him in a number of debates. Fianna Fáil, however, would only agree to one debate. Tactically, it makes sense for parties lagging behind their main rivals in the polls to insist on more debates, as an opportunity for their leader to outshine or expose the frontrunner.

The number of televised leaders' debates can have a significant impact on a campaign, but so too can their timing. In 2002, at Ahern's insistence, his only head-to-head debate with Michael Noonan took place just three days prior to polling. Ahern had enjoyed a sizeable lead throughout the campaign and, by scheduling the only televised debate so late, he knew it would be difficult for Fine Gael to build momentum even if Noonan was perceived as the winner. Noonan attacked relentlessly in a fractious debate, but, as Mark Hennessy noted in the following day's Irish Times, he 'failed to land the killer punch.' Bertie Ahern was re-elected Taoiseach with an increased majority.

From the outset of televised leaders' debates in an Irish context, Fianna Fáil seems to have recognised that the later a debate occurs in a campaign, the less impact it will have. In February 1982, Charles Haughey's personal popularity ratings were over 20 behind those of Taoiseach Garret Fitzgerald and this made Fianna Fáil strategists nervous about a debate between the two party leaders, especially as campaign opinion polls showed Fianna Fáil at 47% and in reach of an overall majority. In consenting to a debate, Fianna Fáil stipulated that it had to be held just two days before polling. In a frank admission, Tony Fitzpatrick, a Fianna Fáil press officer, told the Irish Times that the debate 'would not be a significant factor in the election,' as the broadcast was 'far too late to have an effect.' He maintained that 'people have already made up their minds on how they are going to vote and they are hardly going to be influenced by how many times a man smiles on TV.'

In 2007, Fianna Fáil's approach was radically different. Bertie Ahern ultimately insisted upon a debate much earlier in the campaign. The campaign had opened in disastrous fashion for Fianna Fáil with media attention over the first ten days focusing predominately on questions about Ahern's personal finances. Going into the campaign, Fianna Fáil's preference had been for a late debate, but given the campaign's chaotic start, party strategists maintained that a 'circuit-breaker' was needed. The Ahern–Kenny clash took place on 17th May, a full week out from polling day. An Irish Independent Millward Brown–IMS poll published two days before the debate suggested that Fianna Fáil faced 'the doomsday prospect of losing 20 seats.'

After a hesitant debate opening, Ahern came out fighting and he successfully managed to undermine the costings of Fine Gael's election pledges. He also forced Kenny to retreat from party policy as enunciated by his own Justice spokesman, Jim O'Keeffe. A consensus emerged that Bertie Ahern was the debate's clear winner. This factor on its own did not decide the election, but it was a game-changer. A resurgent Fianna Fáil campaign was further boosted by Eoghan Harris's tour de force defence of Ahern in an influential Late Late Show debate and by some strong media performances from the Minister for Finance, Brian Cowen. However, without the momentum generated by his debate victory and the full week Fianna Fáil had to capitalise on this, it is unlikely that Bertie Ahern would have achieved his ambition to become the first Taoiseach since Eamon de Valera to win three successive terms in government.

Last October, details of RTÉ's proposals for General Election 2016 emerged in the Irish Times. According to Harry McGee, RTÉ will seek two distinct leaders' debates, one involving seven parties, the other confined to the four larger parties.

RTÉ's proposal is for the seven-leader debate to be held seven to twelve days after the election is called at the University Concert Hall in Limerick, in front of a live audience, representing the first time that an RTÉ leaders' debate will take place outside the confines of Montrose. RTÉ have suggested that Claire Byrne will host the Limerick debate and the leaders of Renua Ireland, the Anti-Austerity Alliance/People Before Profit Alliance and the Social Democrats will all be invited to participate alongside Fine Gael, Labour, Fianna Fáil and Sinn Féin.

RTÉ's second debate is planned for a week before polling day and is to be hosted by Miriam O'Callaghan. This proposed debate is to take place in RTÉ without an audience and is to comprise Enda Kenny, Joan Burton, Micheál Martin and Gerry Adams.

RTÉ's decision not to seek a one-on-one debate between the outgoing Taoiseach and leader of the opposition is likely to prove controversial. Micheál Martin has previously declared himself not to be a fan of multi-party debates, describing them as 'empty shouting matches.' In contrast, at the last election Fine Gael strongly supported the notion of a five-way debate, which their then Director of Elections Phil Hogan said 'reflected his repeated calls for a discussion of the issues between the leaders of all the main parties.'

At this point in time, it is unclear whether TV3's debate ambitions will again end up amounting to a political case of Hamlet without the Prince. In 2011, Enda Kenny's decision to rebuff TV3's invitation vastly reduced the significance of the Ballymount channel's election debate broadcast. However, Fine Gael's decision last year to reverse a party ban on its TDs participating in Vincent Browne's 'People's Debate,' a series of live debates from each constituency in the run up to the General Election, provides some grounds for optimism that the Taoiseach may take part in TV3's leaders' debate.

In Irish politics, the question of who should or should not take part in a leaders' debate has been a perennial one that for many years actually prevented televised debates from taking place. Even before the dawn of television in Ireland, American voters had been both entertained and informed by televised debates dating back to the landmark Kennedy–Nixon debates in 1960. By the 1970s, Irish politicians were becoming more cognisant of the power of television to appeal to voters. On the campaign trail in 1973, the leader of Fine Gael, Liam Cosgrave, said that it had been a feature of recent Irish elections and referenda that 'people made up their minds mainly by what they saw on television' and that his party had received 'professional advice' on how best to utilise the medium of television for electoral purposes. However, until the early 1980s, efforts to bring about an Irish version of US presidential-style head-to-head televised debates ran aground because of the quirks of the Irish two and a half party system. For example, in 1981, a protracted political wrangle put paid to RTÉ's efforts to bring about a leaders' debate between Charles Haughey and Garret Fitzgerald. Frank Cluskey, the Labour Party leader, insisted that he should be included in any such broadcast and, for tactical reasons, Fianna Fáil supported Cluskey's insistence on a three-way debate. In the end, Haughey, Fitzgerald and Cluskey were interviewed separately by a panel of journalists.

The first ever leaders' debate in February 1982 came about largely because of the good relationship between Michael O'Leary and Garret Fitzgerald in government. The Labour leader and Tánaiste chose not to push his party's claim to be represented in a leaders' debate in order to facilitate the Taoiseach's desire to debate Haughey. O'Leary's withdrawal set a longstanding precedent.

All of the main televised leaders' debates up until the last election were between the leaders of Fianna Fáil and Fine Gael.

The lasting legacy of the 'Gilmore for Taoiseach' posters may be to have increased the number of participants in the debating studio. This expansion has been further facilitated by the ongoing fragmentation in Irish politics. Labour is numerically the second largest party in the 31st Dáil, but at different stages opinion polls have shown both Fianna Fáil and Sinn Féin to be the second most popular party. Each of these parties can make a credible case for why their leader should participate in a one-on-one debate with the Taoiseach. Over the coming weeks of General Election 2016, we will hear a lot more in this regard.

Seat or Party Changes since 2011

On 10 June 2011 Brian Lenihan (Fianna Fáil, Dublin West) died. On 29 October 2011 Patrick Nulty (Labour) won the seat in a by-election. On 6 December 2011 Nulty resigned from Dáil Eireann. On 24 May 2014 Ruth Coppinger (Socialist Party, Dublin West) won the by-election arising from Nulty's resignation.

On 7 July 2011 Denis Naughten (Roscommon–South Leitrim) lost the Fine Gael party whip. He will contest the 2016 election as an independent.

On 1 December 2011 Tommy Broughan (Dublin North East) lost the party whip and he will contest the 2016 election as an independent in Dublin Bay North.

On 26 September 2012 Róisín Shorthall (Labour, Dublin North West) resigned from the Labour parliamentary Party. On 15 July 2015 she became co-leader of the Social Democrats with Stephen Donnelly (Independent, Wicklow) and Catherine Murphy (Independent, Kildare North)

On 31 August 2012 Clare Daly (Dublin North) resigned from the Socialist Party. She will contest the 2016 election as an independent.

On 13 December 2012 Colm Keaveney (Labour, Galway East) resigned the Labour party whip. On 3 December 2012 he joined Fianna Fáil.

On 21 December 2012 Shane McEntee (Fine Gael, Meath East) died and on 27 March 2013 his daughter Helen McEntee won the seat in a by election.

On 25 April 2013 Joan Collins (Dublin South Central) resigned from the People Before Profit Alliance. She will contest the 2016 election as an independent.

On 2 July 2013 Peter Matthews (Dublin South) Brian Walsh (Galway West) Terence Flanagan (Dublin North East) Lucinda Creighton (Dublin South East) and Billy Timmins (Wicklow) each lost the Fine Gael whip. Brian Walsh subsequently rejoined Fine Gael and will contest the 2016 election for the party. Peter Matthews will contest the 2016 election as an independent. On 15 March 2015 Terence Flanagan, Billy Timmins and Lucinda Creighton launched a new political party, Renua Ireland.

On 25 March 2014 Nicky McFadden (Fine Gael, Longford–Westmeath) died. On 24 May 2014 Gabrielle McFadden, her sister, won the seat in a by-election.

On 26 May 2014 Brian Hayes (Fine Gael, Dublin South West) resigned his Dáil seat on election to the European Parliament. On 10 October 2014 Paul Murphy (Socialist Party, Dublin South West) won the by-election to replace Brian Hayes.

On 26 May 2014 Luke 'Ming' Flanagan (Indpendent, Roscommon–South Leitrim) also resigned his Dáil seat having been elected to the European Parliament. On 10 October 2014 Michael Fitzmaurice (Independent) was elected to the seat.

On 30 October 2014 Phil Hogan (Fine Gael, Carlow–Kilkenny) resigned his seat on appointment to the European Commission. On 23 May 2015 Bobby Aylward (Fianna Fáil) won the resultant by-election.

On 26 September 2015 Eamonn Maloney (Dublin South West) resigned from the Labour Part. He will contest the 2016 election as an independent.

On 24 November 2015 Sean Conlan (Cavan–Monaghan) resigned from Fine Gael.

Election Day

The Length of the Dáil Term

The Constitution provides that the same Dáil shall not continue for a period longer than seven years. It also provides that a shorter period can be fixed by law. Section 33 of the Electoral Act 1992 currently provides for a maximum period of five years.

The Dissolution of the Dáil

The President, on the advice of the Taoiseach, may dissolve the Dáil at any time, and where a Taoiseach retains the majority support of the Dáil the President must assent to the Taoiseach's request. This is traditionally done by the Taoiseach making a statement in the Dáil that he proposes to go to Áras an Uachtaráin to seek dissolution. However, it should be noted that there is no legal restriction on where or when this announcement is made. Indeed, there is no legal requirement that the Taoiseach even announce in advance that he intends to travel to the Áras to seek a dissolution. There is also no requirement that his announcement and the request for dissolution should occur on the same day.

The Dissolution Date

Article 16.4.2 of the Constitution provides that the election of members to the new Dáil must take place not later than 30 days after dissolution. However, the Electoral Acts limit this further by requiring that the election take place not less than 17 days and not more than 25 days (excluding Sundays and bank holidays) after the dissolution. There are no legal restrictions on the day of the week on which polling can be held. The polling date will be designated by an order made by the Minister for the Environment and Local Government.

Polling Hours

The ministerial order will set out the hours of polling. By law the polls must be open for at least twelve hours. The law also provides that the earliest they can be opened is 8.00 a.m. and the latest they can be closed is 10.30 p.m. Of course there is nothing to prevent the government from amending this law prior to dissolution to extend the period for which polls can be open.

The First Meeting of the New Dáil

The Constitution provides that the proclamation issued by the President bringing about the dissolution must set out the date on which the new Dáil will meet. The new Dáil elects a Ceann Comhairle at its first meeting. However, there is no obligation on the new Dáil to select a new government at its first meeting. Indeed, three of the last six Dála have failed to select a government on their first meeting.

The Electoral System and the Counting of Votes

Proportional Representation with Single Transferable Vote

The Constitution provides that elections to the Dáil and Seanad and to the Office of President must be by proportional representation with single transferable vote: PRSTV. Legislation has provided that the same PRSTV electoral system is to be used for European and local elections. There have been two attempts to amend the Constitution by referendum to change the PRSTV electoral system for Dáil elections. Both of the proposed constitutional amendments were rejected. It is worth noting that a referendum would not be required to change the voting system for local or European elections. The enactment of reforming legislation would be sufficient, as it is a legislative rather than a constitutional requirement.

A consideration of the merits or demerits of PRSTV, and whether it achieves the objective of being truly proportionate or whether it gives rise to inefficiency and duplication in representation, is beyond the scope of this article, which is a work of electoral law rather than a political science treatise. For our purposes it is necessary only to examine the law governing the operation of the system, how ballot papers are marked, and how votes are counted in accordance with this electoral system.

Multi-seat Constituencies

The PRSTV electoral system is complicated, particularly since it operates in Ireland on the basis of multi-seat constituencies, i.e. where more than one member is elected for each constituency.

For the purposes of this Dáil election the country will be divided into 40 constituencies, with representation ranging from a minimum of three to a maximum of five seats. For European elections the country is divided into four constituencies: Dublin, Leinster and Munster, each with four seats, and Connacht/Ulster, which has three seats.

The presidential election involves the filling of just one seat, and in the context of the election it is of assistance to view the whole country as a large one-seat constituency. However, PRSTV really only operates in a presidential election when there are three or more candidates. The process in a two-candidate presidential race is similar to that which would prevail under a first-past-the-post system.

It should also be noted that PRSTV is used for all Dáil elections, although in the case of byelections the Dáil constituency where the vacancy occurs becomes a one-seat constituency.

Marking the Ballot Paper

While proportional representation systems are common throughout the world, our particular type of electoral system, with the single transferable vote, is somewhat rare.

The voter must indicate the order of his or her preference by writing the number '1' opposite the name of their first choice and, if they wish, the number '2' after their second choice, the number '3' opposite the name of their third choice, and so on. In this way the voter instructs the returning officer that when that vote is being counted, it should be transferred to the second choice candidate if the first choice candidate is either elected or eliminated. If the second choice candidate has also been elected or eliminated, the vote may be transferred to the third choice candidate, and so on.

Arrangements for the Count

The returning officer is responsible for conducting the count and making arrangements for it in every constituency.

For Dáil elections the ballot boxes are taken to a central counting centre in each constituency. Not less than four days before polling, the returning officer must give written notice to each candidate of the place where the count is to be held and the time at which it will commence. The returning officer is legally required to ensure that, where practicable, the count centre is accessible to persons with physical disabilities. For Dáil elections, the counting of votes begins at 9.00 a.m. on the day after polling.

Where two elections, or an election and a referendum, have been held on the same day, all ballot boxes will be opened and all ballot papers sorted before the count for either poll is conducted. Even though different ballot boxes may be used and different colour ballot papers are used for each poll, all ballot boxes will be open and sorted in order to ensure that the ballot papers for the different polls have not been mixed up.

The Electoral Act requires that, once begun, the count should so far as practicable continue unbroken, except for breaks for refreshments. The count should not continue past 11.00 p.m. or recommence before 9.00 a.m. unless the returning officer and candidates agree. In reality, returning officers will continue beyond 11.00 p.m. where the count is likely to be completed at a reasonable hour, or until a convenient point at which to adjourn has been reached.

At all times, including periods when counting is suspended, the returning officer must retain the ballot papers in his care 'under his own seal', and must ensure that they are not interfered with.

Agents for the Candidates at the Count

Candidates, or their election agents, are allowed to attend at the counting of votes to oversee the voting process. The returning officer decides how many agents each candidate may appoint to be present at the count. The candidate must notify the returning officer at least two days before polling of the names of the agents so appointed.

Although conducted 'in public' (before the media), access to the count is restricted to the returning officer's staff, Gardaí, and these duly appointed agents for the candidates, with others only being admitted with the express permission of the returning officer.

The returning officer is required by law to give the agents of the candidate all such reasonable facilities and information as are required to oversee the counting of votes and, in particular, facilities for satisfying themselves that the ballot papers have been sorted correctly.

Opening Postal Votes

As they are received, the returning officer puts the returned postal votes, which will be in the covering envelope provided, into the postal voters' ballot boxes. These are opened at some stage before the count for the constituency begins. Candidates are entitled to appoint agents on their behalf to be present at the opening of the postal ballots.

Each postal ballot box is opened and the number of envelopes is counted.

Each covering envelope is then opened in clear view of the attending agents. The receipt or declaration of identity is checked to ensure that it is signed. If the declaration of identity is not signed, or if the ballot paper is not accompanied by the required declaration of identity, it is deemed rejected. The returning officer can, however, accept votes as valid even if the ballot paper or declaration of identity is in the wrong envelope, the ballot paper is not in a sealed envelope, or the documents are not returned in the covering envelope.

The sealed envelopes are mixed and opened, and the ballot papers, still folded, are placed in a new ballot box. This ballot box is then sealed and is reopened on the morning of the count with all the other ballot boxes.

Opening the Ballot Boxes

In normal circumstances, each ballot box is opened and emptied in the presence of agents for the candidates.

As the votes are counted, they must be kept face upwards in order to prevent anyone from seeing the numbers printed on the back of the ballot papers and also so that they are open to scrutiny, and conveniently placed to assist tallypersons, who require a clear view of how the papers are marked. Candidates or their agents are not allowed to handle ballot papers during the count.

The next step is to ascertain the total number of ballot papers in each box in order to reconcile this with the number of ballot papers issued at the polling station, as notified in the account returned by the relevant presiding officer.

The ballot papers are mixed thoroughly and then sorted into bundles according to the first preference recorded for each candidate. At this stage, any ballot papers which may be invalid or spoilt are set aside for further scrutiny, and accepted or rejected as appropriate. The returning officer calculates the total valid poll by disregarding the spoilt or invalid ballot papers and counting the number of ballot papers in each bundle.

Spoilt or Invalid Votes

Section 118 of the 1992 Electoral Act defines an invalid vote in the following terms:

- Any ballot paper that does not bear the official mark. The official mark is embossed on the ballot paper and should be clearly visible from both sides.
- A ballot paper on which the number '1' or word 'one' or any other mark which might, in the opinion of the returning officer, clearly indicate a first preference is not placed at all or is not placed in such a way as to indicate a preference for one candidate. It follows therefore that even if a number or mark is theoretically capable of expressing a first preference, but is not put opposite, near or connected to a specific candidate it is impossible to determine who it is a vote for and so it is invalid.

- A ballot paper where the number '1' or word 'one' or any other mark which, in the opinion of the returning officer, expresses a preference is set opposite the name of more than one candidate. Again the difficulty of determining with clarity which candidate the preference is for renders the vote invalid.
- Any ballot paper which has anything written or marked on it (apart from an indicated preference) which, in the opinion of the returning officer, is calculated to identify the voter.

The returning officer must write 'Rejected' clearly on any ballot paper which he deems to be invalid. Where he admits a ballot paper about which there may be a doubt, he can write his reasons for admitting it on the paper, in such a way as not to interfere with the voting preferences on it.

It is important to note that the writing of something other than a mark or number or word designed to indicate a voting preference on the ballot paper does not of itself render the vote invalid. The writing, for example, of a political slogan or remark on the ballot paper does not render that vote invalid provided that it is not calculated to identify the voter, and that a clear voting preference is otherwise marked on the ballot paper.

While the clearest way to indicate a first preference is to mark the ballot paper with the number '1' or word 'one', any mark which, in the opinion of the returning officer, clearly indicates a preference for one and only one candidate will be counted as a first preference.

Transferable and Non-Transferable Ballot Papers

A transferable ballot paper is one on which, following a first preference, a second or subsequent preference is recorded in consecutive numerical order for a remaining candidate. A remaining candidate is one who has not already been deemed elected or eliminated.

Section 118 of the 1992 Electoral Act also defines what amounts to a non-transferable ballot as one of the following:

- A ballot paper on which no second or subsequent preference is recorded for a remaining candidate.

- A ballot paper on which the names of two or more candidates, whether remaining candidates or not, are marked with a mark which, in the opinion of the returning officer, indicates the same preference and are next in order of preference is deemed a non-transferable ballot paper. It follows therefore that if, on the second count, a ballot paper has the number '2' opposite two different candidates, it is non-transferable.
- A ballot paper where the candidate next in order of preference, whether remaining or not, is marked with a mark which, in the opinion of the returning officer, does not follow consecutively after some other mark on the ballot paper.
- A ballot paper that is void for uncertainty is non-transferable.

Calculating the Quota

The quota is the minimum number of votes necessary to guarantee the election of a candidate. The quota is ascertained by dividing the total valid poll by one more than the number of seats to be filled in that constituency and adding one to the result. Any fractional remainder is disregarded.

The calculation can be illustrated with the following example. If 1,000 valid votes are cast in a four-seat constituency, the quota is calculated as follows:

1,000 (votes) ÷ 4 + 1 (seats) = 200, so the quota is 201 (200 + 1)

Using this method in any constituency, only the same number of candidates as there are seats to be filled could reach the quota. In the above four-seat example, only four candidates could possibly reach the quota.

Deeming a Candidate Elected

Candidates are deemed elected in one of three circumstances:

- When at the end of any count the number of votes credited to any candidate is equal to or greater than the quota.
- When the number of remaining candidates equals the remaining number of vacant seats.

- When one seat remains vacant and the candidate has votes greater than the sum of all other remaining candidates plus any undistributed surpluses.

Distribution of Surpluses

A surplus is the total number of votes exceeding the quota, which a candidate has following his election. These surplus votes are transferred proportionately to the remaining candidates in the following way.

Surplus on the first count

Where a candidate exceeds the quota on the first count, all of the votes are 'original votes,' i.e. first preferences.

All the votes in the candidate's bundle are examined, and all those that are transferable (i.e. a subsequent preference is expressed thereon) are arranged into sub-bundles in accordance with the next available preference on them. If the number of transferable votes is equal to or greater than the surplus, then each remaining candidate will receive all the votes from the appropriate bundle of transferable papers.

Surpluses on second and subsequent counts

In this instance, the votes credited to a candidate are made up of 'original' votes and 'transferred' votes (i.e. his own first preferences and any transfers he has received), or only of transferred votes (if he got no first preferences).

The returning officer examines only those votes in the bundle of transfers last received by the candidate and arranges the transferable votes in that last bundle into further sub-bundles in accordance with the next available preference recorded on them.

If the surplus is exactly equal to the number of transferable votes, which is unlikely, the returning officer simply transfers each of the sub-bundles of transferable votes to the candidate for which the next available preference is stated.

If the surplus is greater than the total number of transferable papers, then the ballots in the sub-parcel are transferred directly, and the difference between the total number of transferable papers and the surplus is deemed non-transferable. .

If, as is more likely, the surplus is less than the total number of transferable papers, each remaining candidate will receive from the appropriate bundle of transferable papers a number of votes, calculated as follows:

Surplus x number of papers in bundle [Dan, check line] Total number of transferable papers

Order in which Surpluses Must Be Distributed

If two or more candidates exceed the quota on any one count, the larger surplus must be distributed first.

Where two or more candidates have surpluses from two different counts, then the surplus of the candidate who exceeded the quota in the earliest count is distributed first.

Where the surplus of the two candidates is exactly the same, the surplus of the candidate who got the most first preferences is distributed first. If the first preferences were equal, then lots are drawn as to which candidate's surplus is distributed first.

A returning officer must transfer the surplus of a candidate deemed elected in all cases except when the surplus, together with any other surpluses not transferred, is less than the number of votes the highest remaining candidate needs to reach the quota.

Elimination of Candidates

If no candidate has a surplus, or the surplus is insufficient to elect one of the remaining candidates or to materially affect the progress of the count, the lowest of the remaining candidates is eliminated and his ballot papers are transferred to remaining candidates according to the next preference indicated on them. If the lowest candidates have equal votes, then the one who got the lowest first preference vote is eliminated first. If they have equal first preference vote, then lots are drawn.

The returning officer can eliminate two or more of the lowest candidates together where the total number of votes for all those candidates and any surpluses not transferred is less than the votes of the next highest candidate.

The ability to eliminate candidates together is subject to the protection that one of them either already has or could not otherwise attain one quarter of a quota. This benchmark entitles them to retain their deposit and qualify for a reimbursement from the Exchequer of some election expenses.

Filling the Final Seats

When the number of remaining candidates is the same as the number of seats to be filled, the remaining candidates are deemed elected.

Where there is only one seat left to be filled and the highest remaining candidate has more votes than the total of all the other remaining candidates and any surpluses not transferred, the highest remaining candidate is deemed elected.

If any of the remaining candidates does not yet have one quarter of the quota, which is unlikely, then any further transfer of votes remaining to be done must be carried out in case they would give the remaining candidate enough votes to attain one quarter of the quota.

Recounts

It is important to clarify what is involved when a recount takes place in an election. A recount does not involve remixing all the ballot papers and restarting the counting of votes. It involves the re examination of all the bundles that are created by the original counts and rechecking to ensure they were counted and calculated properly. When recounting, the order of the papers in the bundles and sub bundles must not be disturbed unless it is necessary to do so due to the discovery of an error.

Where a significant error is discovered, which is likely to affect the result of the election, the returning officer must count all the papers afresh from the point at which the error occurred.

A candidate, or the election agent of a candidate, may at the conclusion of any count request a reexamination and recount of papers dealt with during that count and can request a complete reexamination and recount of all parcels once and once only. The returning officer is not obliged to, but may, grant more than one request for such a recount.

A returning officer may on his own initiative recount all or any of the papers at any stage of a count, as often as he wishes, until he is satisfied as to the accuracy of the count.

The returning officer has discretion to refuse any request for a recount, which in the returning officer's opinion is frivolous or vexatious, or when the parcel has already been re-examined or re-counted.

If, during the course of a recount being carried out at the request of a candidate, the request is withdrawn, it is at the returning officer's discretion whether or not to continue with the recount.

Challenging Decisions of the Returning Office

The returning officer has the final decision on the elimination of a candidate, the admissibility of a vote, or the allocation of transfers. Decisions of the returning officer, whether expressed or implied, are final, subject only to reversal on an election petition to the High Court questioning the election result.

Retention and Destruction of Ballot Papers

On the completion of the count, the returning officer must place in separate sealed packs:

- The counted ballot papers
- The ballot papers rejected at the counting of the votes
- The unused and spoilt ballot papers
- The counterfoils of ballot papers issued at polling stations
- The marked copies of the register of electors
- The ballot paper accounts
- The candidate nomination papers (valid and invalid)
- The authorisation to electors to vote at other polling stations

He marks each sealed pack with the election, the date of polling day and the constituency, and forwards them to the Clerk of the Dáil.

The Clerk of the Dáil retains all these documents for six months from the date of the poll at the election. The documents cannot be inspected by anyone except by order of the High Court. The High Court can only make such an order for the purposes of an election petition or where the inspection or production or the documents is required for the purpose of instituting or maintaining a prosecution for an offence under the Electoral Acts. If such an order is not made, or unless he has reason to believe that the papers will be required for such purposes, the Clerk of the Dáil, after the six months have passed, must arrange for all these documents (including the ballot papers) to be destroyed.

TREORACHA

1. Scríobh an figiúr 1 sa bhosca le hais an chéad iarrthóra is rogha leat, scríob an figiúr 2 sa bhosca le hais an dara hiarrthóir is rogha leat, agus mar sin de.
2. Fill an páipéar ionas nach bhfeicfear do vóta. Taispeáin cúl an pháipéir don oifigeach ceannais, agus cuir sa bhosca ballóide é.

INSTRUCTIONS

1. Write 1 in the box beside the candidate of your first choice, write 2 in the box beside the candidate of your second choice, and so on.
2. Fold the paper to conceal your vote. Show the back of the paper to the presiding officer and put it in the ballot box.

DOYLE – LIBERAL SOCIALISTS
MARY DOYLE, of 10 High Street, Knockmore, Nurse.

LYNCH – URBAN PARTY
JANE ELLEN LYNCH, of 12 Main Street, Ardstown, Shopkeeper.

MURPHY
PATRICK MURPHY, of 12 Main Street, Ballyduff, Carpenter.

Ó BRIAIN — CUMANN NA SAORÁNACH
SÉAMUS Ó BRIAIN, as 10 An tSráid Ard, Carn Mór, Oide Scoile.

O'BRIEN — NON-PARTY
EAMON O'BRIEN, of 22 Wellclose Place, Knockbeg, Barrister.

O'BRIEN – THE INDEPENDENT PARTY
ORLA O'BRIEN, of 103 Eaton Brae, Cahermore, Solicitor.

O'CONNOR — NATIONAL LEAGUE
CAROLINE O'CONNOR, of 7 Green Street, Carnmore, Engineer.

THOMPSON — RURAL PARTY
WILLIAM H. THOMPSON, of Dereen, Ballyglass, Farmer.

Ballot Paper Format for Election 2016

Carlow–Kilkenny

Outgoing Deputies:

John McGuinness (FF), Ann Phelan (Lab), John Paul Phelan (FG), Pat Deering (FG), Bobby Aylward (FF)

Bobby Aylward (FF) was elected in a by-election on 22nd May 2015 arising from the resignation of Phil Hogan (FG).

The Constituency:

This five-seater includes all of the county of Kilkenny and the county of Carlow except for an area in east Carlow which is in the Wicklow constituency. The boundaries of this constituency and the number of seats are unchanged since 2011.

	% Vote 1997	% Vote 2002	% Vote 2007	% Vote 2011	Swing 2011	Quotas 2011
Fine Gael	29.19	21.87	29.61	39.22	9.61	2.4
Labour	15.19	13.15	9.35	16.25	6.90	1.0
Fianna Fáil	42.19	50.20	47.70	28.10	–19.60	1.7
Sinn Féin	–	3.42	3.80	9,54	5.74	0.6
Green Party	5.52	8.15	7.96	2.81	–5.15	0.2
Others	7.94	3.20	1.59	4.08	2.49	0.3

2016 Candidates will include:

Pat Deering (FG), David Fitzgerald (FG), John Paul Phelan (FG), Ann Phelan (Lab), Bobby Aylward (FF), John McGuinness (FF), Jennifer Murnane O'Connor (FF), Kathleen Funchion (SF), Malcolm Noonan (GP), Conor MacLiam (AAA–PBP), Adrienne Wallace (AAA–PBP), Patrick McKee (Renua), Noel G Walsh (Ind)

In Brief:

It would have been challenging for Fine Gael to hold the three seats they won in 2011 even with Phil Hogan on the ticket. His replacement David Fitzgerald had a strong if unsuccessful run out in the 2015 by-election. After that by-election Fianna Fail has two sitting TDs in Kilkenny and should be able to retain them. Of the outgoing deputies Labour Junior Minister Anne Phelan looks most vulnerable not only to the strong tickets from the two large parties but also to Sinn Féin's Kathleen Funchion.

Fine Gael:

Fine Gael won three seats on 39 percent of the first preference vote in 2011. It since lost one of those seats in the 2015 by-election. It is running three candidates, one incumbent from Kilkenny and one from Carlow together with the by-election candidate who is Kilkenny-based.

Pat Deering lives at Ballyoliver, Rathvilly and has his constituency office in Carlow town. He has been a member of Dáil Éireann since 2011. In that election he polled 7,470 first preferences and took the last of the five seats. Prior to that he was a member of Carlow County Council from 2009 for the Tullow electoral area. He replaced his father Michael who had served on the council from 1991 to 2009. Pat polled 17.66% of the first preference vote in the 2009 council elections. He has been heavily involved in Carlow G.A.A. and has been Chairman of the County Board. As a dairy farmer he is particularly involved with agricultural issues.

David Fitzgerald is a member of Kilkenny County Council for the Kilkenny City West electoral area. In the 2014 local elections he polled 1,319 first preferences and took the fifth of the six seats in that area, having been elected to Kilkenny Borough Council in 2009. He was the Fine Gael candidate in the May 2015 by-election caused by Phil Hogan's appointment to the European Commission. In that by-election Fitzgerald polled 13,744 first preferences (20.6%) which was 4,828 votes behind Bobby Aylward (FF) on the first count and this margin grew slightly wider before the final count. Fitzgerald is the nephew of former Fine Gael TD Kieran Crotty who represented the constituency from 1969 to 1989. He was the youngest ever president of Kilkenny Chamber of Commerce and the Chairman of Kilkenny's winning Tidy Towns committee in 2014.

John Paul Phelan lives near Tullogher in County Kilkenny and has his constituency office in Thomastown. Although he has been a

Dáil Deputy since only 2011, he is now the party's senior politician in the constituency. He first ran for the Dáil in 2007 and got 6,494 first preferences but was 649 votes behind Mary White (GP) for the last seat. In the 2011 election Phelan topped the poll with 10,939 first preferences and took the third seat. He was a member of Seanad Éireann from 2002 to 2009 on the Agriculture panel. He was a member of Kilkenny County Council for the Piltown electoral areas from 1999 to 2002. He sits on the Joint Oireachtas Committee on Justice, Law and Defence. He is a delegate to the Parliamentary Assembly of the Council of Europe and a representative to the British–Irish Parliamentary Assembly.

Labour Party:

The former Ceann Comhairle Seamus Paterson held a seat for the party here for 46 years up to 2007. When he retired Labour ran two candidates who secured just 9.35%, of the vote between them, losing the seat. In 2011 the party again ran two candidates, Ann Phelan in Kilkenny and Des Hurley in Carlow. Together they polled 15.19% and Ann Phelan regained the seat.

Ann Phelan is based in Graignamanagh and has her constituency office in Kilkenny. She has been a Dáil deputy since 2011. She has been Minister of State at the Departments of Agriculture, Food and Marine and Transport, Tourism and Sport with Special Responsibility for Rural Economic Development and Rural Transport since July 2014. The 2011 election was her first time contesting for the Dáil, she polled 8,075 first preferences and with 2,447 transfers from her running mate Des Hurley (Lab) and 2,094 transfers from Kathleen Funchion (SF) Phelan took the first seat in the constituency. She previously served on Kilkenny County Council for the Thomastown local electoral area from 2004 to 2011.

Fianna Fáil:

The party won three seats here in 2007 but were left with only one after the 2011 election. Its vote in that election dropped by almost 20%. Bobby Aylward, who lost his seat in 2011, regained it in the 2015 by-election.

Bobby Aylward lives in Knockmoylan, Mullinavat and has his constituency office in Kilkenny. The family political base is in Piltown. He has been a Dáil Deputy from 2007 to 2011 and again since May 2015. In the 2007 Dáil election he polled 11,600 and took the second seat. In 2011 his vote fell to 6,762 and although he survived until the final count he was 1,876 behind Pat Deering (FG) for the last seat. He also works as a farmer. He was a member of Kilkenny County Council from 1992 to 2007 representing the Piltown electoral area. His brother Liam was a Dáil Deputy from 1977 to 2004 and was a regular constituency poll topper. Liam was a member of the European Parliament from 2004 to 2014. Their father, Bob Aylward, was a Fianna Fáil Senator from 1973 until his death in 1974.

John McGuinness is based in Kilkenny and has been a member of Dáil Éireann since 1997. He is currently chairman of the high profile Dáil Public Accounts Committee. He was a member of Kilkenny Corporation from 1979 to 2004 and of Kilkenny County Council from 1991 to 2004. He was Minister for State with special responsibility for Trade and Commerce from 2007 to 2009. In November 2010 he published a book about his experience as a Dáil Deputy and Minister of State entitled *The House Always Wins*. He has worked previously running the family haulage and other business interests. He has been Fianna Fáil's spokesperson on Small Business and Regulatory Frameworks throughout the present Dáil. His eldest son, Andrew is currently a Fianna Fáil member of Kilkenny County Council for the Kilkenny City East ward where he topped the poll with 1,373 first preferences in the 2014 local elections. John McGuinness was also previously a member of Kilkenny Borough Council from 1979 to 2003 and was a member of Kilkenny County Council from 2001 to 2003. John, like his father before him, is a former Mayor of Kilkenny City.

Jennifer Murnane O'Connor has been a member of Carlow County Council for the Carlow electoral area since 2002 when she was co-opted to replace her father Jimmy Murnane. In the 2014 local elections she topped the poll there with 1,530 first preferences. This is her second Dáil election outing. In 2011 she polled 4,428 and survived until the tenth count. She was also a member of Carlow Town Council and was an unsuccessful candidate for the Seanad in 2007 and 2011. The mother of four children recently helped to set up St Clare's Hospitality, a food kitchen that helps people in need.

Sinn Féin:

In the 2011 election the party ran two candidates. Kathleen Funchion and John Cassin and between them they got almost ten percent of the vote which was 0.6 of a quota. Funchion was its candidate in the 2015 by-election. She is its sole candidate for this general election.

Kathleen Funchion is a member of Kilkenny County Council for the Kilkenny City West electoral area. In the 2014 local election she polled 952 first preferences and took the last of the six seats. This is her fourth Dáil election. In the 2007 general election she polled 2,668 first preferences (3.8%). In the 2011 general election, as part of a two person ticket she herself polled 4,078. In the 2015 by-election she took 16.2% of the first preference vote. She is a workers' rights advocate with SIPTU. She is married to the Waterford Sinn Féin Senator and 2016 Dáil election candidate David Cullinane.

Green Party:

The party's former deputy leader, Mary White has decided not to contest again after she lost her seat in 2011 so the party has a new candidate.

Malcolm Noonan has been a member of Kilkenny County Council since 2009. In the 2014 local elections he polled 987 first preferences on the first count in the Kilkenny City West electoral area and took the third of the six seats. He was also previously a member of Kilkenny Borough Council. In the 2015 by-election he polled 5.3%. Married, with four children, he worked as a graphic designer in Dublin before returning to Kilkenny to set up a landscaping and gardening business. He has a BA in Rural Development and also works with Lifeline Kilkenny Suicide Prevention Forum. A musician and illustrator in his spare time, he has also chaired St Patrick's Day/Tradfest in Kilkenny. He is the Green Party's national spokesman on Environment, Community and Local Government.

Anti-Austerity Alliance – People Before Profit:

In the 2015 by-election the two candidates running this time attracted 4,571 votes (6.9%) between them, with MacLiam's votes transferring most strongly to Wallace and Sinn Féin's Funchion. Only half of Wallace's votes transferred after the fourth count and those went mostly to Funchion.

Conor MacLiam has been peripherally active in left wing politics since the 1980s. He came to national prominence when he began to campaign for health service reform after the delayed diagnosis and subsequent death of his wife, the late Susie Long. A member of the Socialist Party he ran under the Anti-Austerity Alliance banner in the 2015 by-election when he polled 2,194 votes (3.3%), and as a Socialist Party candidate in 2011 when his vote was 1,135 (1.54%)

Adrienne Wallace ran in the 2015 by-election on the People Before Profit ticket when she took 2,377 first preferences (3.6%). She has a BA in Humanities, English and Philosophy from St Patrick's, Carlow College. She believes politics in Ireland is suffering from 'a lack of female input', saying, 'Politics is everything, including the water in your tap and the money in your pocket. More women's voices need to be heard'. She is a bar worker in Carlow.

Renua Ireland:

Patrick McKeee has been a member of Kilkenny County Council for the Kilkenny City West electoral area since 2014. He joined Fianna Fáil as a student in 2006, rising rapidly through the party's youth organisation. He was a trainee solicitor when he was elected to Kilkenny County Council as a Fianna Fail candidate in the 2014 local elections. He polled 984 first preferences and took the fourth of the six seats. In March 2015 he resigned from Fianna Fáil to join Renua Ireland and become its candidate for the May 2015 by-election. In that contest he came in fourth, polling 9.5% of the first preference vote. At that time he expressed the view that the 'old, weak, party political system' was not capable of serving modern

Ireland. A gay man, he campaigned actively for the Yes vote in the 2015 marriage referendum.

Independents:
Noel G. Walsh of Kilkenny city has had two previous electoral outings in this constituency. In the 2011 general election he polled 119 first preferences, while in the 2014 by-election he doubled that to 243 (0.36%). He previously lived for several years in Gorey and (as Ger Walsh) ran in Wexford in 2004 where, as a Labour candidate in the 2004 local elections he polled 20 first preference votes. In 2009 he stood there as an independent in the county council elections and polled 171 (1.23%). He had intended to run in the 2007 general election but missed the deadline for nominations, having already spent a large sum on his campaign. In the past he has been involved in campaigns against household, property and water charges, picketing Phil Hogan's constituency office on one occasion. His by-election literature stressed improved care of the elderly and respect for the environment. He suggests that there should be as much support for needy Irish people as for immigrants. Away from politics he is a member of the Civil Defence and enthusiastic GAA and Irish Rugby supporter.

Cavan–Monaghan

Outgoing Deputies:
Caoimhghín O Caoláin (SF), Brendan Smith (FF), Joe O Reilly (FG), Sean Conlan (Ind), Heather Humphrey (FG).

Sean Conlan was elected as a Fine Gael candidate in 2011. In November 2015 he announced that he was leaving the party and that he would contest the 2016 election as an independent.

The Constituency:
This four-seater has been reduced from five seats in 2011. It comprises the counties of Cavan and Monaghan except for thirty–six electoral divisions in the west of County Cavan, with a population

of 13,183, which have been transferred to the Sligo Leitrim constituency since 2011.

	% Vote 1997	% Vote 2002	% Vote 2007	% Vote 2011	Swing 2011	Quotas 2011
Fine Gael	34.67	25.18	31.20	39.56	8.36	2.4
Labour	3.96	0.89	1.21	5.63	4.42	0.3
Fianna Fáil	38.44	34.95	37.77	20.15	−17.62	1.2
Sinn Féin	19.37	17.51	20.01	25.89	5.88	1.7
Green Party	–	1.78	3.62	0.74	−2.88	0.04
Others	3.21	19.33	6.18	8.03	1.85	0.5

2016 Candidates will include:

Heather Humphreys (FG), Joe O Reilly (FG), Brendan Smith (FF), Niamh Smyth (FF), Caoimhghin Ó Caoláin (SF), Kathryn Reilly (SF), Micheál Callaghan (GP), Michael McDermott (DDI), Sean Conlan (Ind), John Wilson (Ind)

In Brief:

With five sitting deputies contesting for five seats and Sinn Féin's Kathryn Reilly it is likely this will be a highly competitive constituency. Fine Gael will lose a seat. Fianna Fáil sees itself as having an outside chance of a second seat but again the reduction in seat numbers makes that unlikely. There will be much interest in whether former Fine Gael deputy Sean Conlan, who left the party last November and is contesting as an independent, can hold his seat. Another independent of interest will be the former Garda and prominent whistleblower, John Wilson, although he seems unlikely to feature in the final shake out for seats.

Fine Gael:

Fine Gael impressively won three seats with 40 percent of the first preference vote when this was a five-seater in 2011. The party had originally selected the three sitting deputies as candidates for the 2016 election. However, in November 2015 one of their Cavan deputies, Sean Conlan, resigned from the party and announced that he would contest as an independent. Fine Gael then announced it would not be replacing him on the party ticket and would run two candidates only. The reduction in the number of seats from five to four and a further improvement in the Sinn Féin vote together with Conlon's defection means the party will face a challenge to retain even two seats.

Heather Humphreys is based in Monaghan and has been a member of Dáil Éireann since 2011. She has been Minister for the Arts, Heritage and the Gaeltacht since July 2014. In the 2011 election she polled 8,144 votes on the first count and took the last of the five seats. Humphreys had been co–opted to replace Seymour Crawford on Monaghan County Council representing the Clones electoral area in 2003 and held the council seat comfortably in all elections until she was elected to the Dáil. She is a former Credit Union official. She is the only Presbyterian member of the outgoing Dáil.

Joe O'Reilly is based in Bailieborough in County Cavan. He has been a member of Dáil Éireann since 2011. He was the party's second candidate in the 2009 European elections in the North West constituency and polled 37,564 first preferences (7.6%) but was not in the running for a seat. In the 2011 Dáil election he polled 8,333 first preferences and won the third of the five seats. He also contested in 2007 and surprised many when he did not win a seat then. In 2007 this was effectively a four-seater because outgoing Ceann Comhairle Rory O'Hanlon was returned automatically. O'Reilly polled 9,550. He was one of two Fine Gael candidates with outgoing deputy Seymour Crawford. Crawford won a seat but O'Reilly was 1,965 votes behind Margaret Conlon for the last seat. O'Reilly is a former member of Cavan County Council representing the Bailieborough local electoral area. He was a member of Seanad Éireann from 1989 to 1992 and again from 2007 to 2011. He worked previously as a national school teacher. He also holds a masters degree in the History of International Relations from University College Dublin.

Labour Party:

This has never been a strong constituency for Labour. The last time a candidate made an impact for party here was in 1997 when

Ann Gallagher, later a senator, polled 2,359 first preference votes. Its candidate in 2002 and 2007 was Des Cullen, a member of Cavan Town Council who gained 0.9% of the vote in 2002 and 1.21% in 2007. The party's candidate for the 2011 Dáil election was Liam Hogan who polled 4,011 first preference votes, a share of 5.6% which saw him finish in 7th place. The party has no seats on either Cavan or Monaghan County Councils and at the time of going to press was having difficulty fielding a candidate in this constituency.

Fianna Fáil:

In 2007 the automatic return of Rory O'Hanlon as the outgoing Ceann Comhairle made it easier for the party to win two of the four contested seats, giving it three out of five overall. When O'Hanlon retired in 2011 it ran just two candidates in the five-seater, the other incumbents being Brendan Smith in Cavan and Margaret Conlon in Meath. In 2011 however the party's vote collapsed by almost 18 percent and Conlon lost her seat. For the 2016 election the party has selected two Cavan-based candidates, the incumbent Brendan Smith and Ballieborough councillor Niamh Smyth.

Brendan Smith is based in Cavan town and has been a Dáil Deputy since 1992. Before 1992 Smith was a long time constituency manager and political adviser to the former Tánaiste, John Wilson. Endorsed by Wilson as his successor, Smith topped the poll on his first outing in 1992 with 7,093, and again in 2002 with 10,679 first preferences and in 2007 when he polled 15,548 first preferences (23.6%). His personal vote crashed to 9,700 in 2011 but he took the second seat on Margaret Conlon's elimination. Smith was first appointed as Minister of State in the Department of Agriculture in Bertie Ahern's 2004 cabinet reshuffle, before becoming Minister for Children at the Department of Health and Children following the 2007 election. In 2008 he was appointed Minister for Agriculture, Fisheries and Food. He is currently the party spokesperson on Foreign Affairs and Trade and on Border Region Development.

Niamh Smyth has been a member of Cavan County Council for the Bailieborough–Cootehill electoral area since 2014. In the 2014 local elections she topped the poll in that electoral area and took the first seat. Fianna Fáil won three of the six seats there. She has worked both as a secondary school teacher and as an Arts Education Officer. She is President of the new Fianna Fáil Women's Network. Niamh comes from a long line of Fianna Fáil representatives in Cavan. Her grand uncle Paddy Smith was a TD for this constituency and was the longest serving minister in the history of the State with a total of 54 years in different posts. Several other male relatives have served as members of Cavan County Council before her, also for the Baillieborough area.

Sinn Féin:

Caoimhghín Ó Caoláin has been a member of Dáil Éireann since 1997. He was the sole Sinn Féin candidate in Cavan Monaghan for the 1997, 2002 and 2007 elections. A former senior bank official at Bank of Ireland, he is based in Monaghan town. In the 1997 election he topped the poll with 11,531 first preferences and became the first Sinn Féin TD to be elected since the party abandoned its policy of abstentionism. He again topped the poll in the 2002 Dáil election, this time with 10,832 first preferences. He stood in the 2007 election despite cardiac surgery early that year, finishing second in the poll behind Brendan Smith, with 13,162 first preference votes, an increase of over 2,000. Ó Caoláin was a member of Monaghan County Council for the Monaghan local electoral area from 1985 to 2004. He was Sinn Féin leader in Dáil Éireann from 1997 to 2011 and is currently party spokesperson on Health and Children.

Kathryn Reilly is based in Ballyjamesduff in County Cavan and has been a member of Seanad Éireann since 2011. She was the second party candidate in the 2011 Dáil election. Prior to that she was personal assistant to the then Louth Dáil deputy Arthur Morgan. In her first outing in 2011 she polled 6,539 first preferences, which was 9.2% of the poll. She was 521 votes behind Heather Humphries (FG) for the last seat. In April 2011 she was elected to Seanad Éireann on the Industrial and Commercial Panel thereby becoming the youngest ever member of that House and the youngest member of the current Oireachtas. Her portfolios within the party are European Union Affairs and Youth Affairs and she is also a member of the Joint Oireachtas Committee on EU Affairs.

Green Party:

Mícheál Callaghan from Ballinode studied Law at TCD and then took a masters in Environmental Law and Sustainable Development from Queen's University Belfast. This is his first election campaign. As a recent graduate he joined the Green Party because he believes its policies offer the best chance for a sustainable and prosperous future. He has served for two years as secretary of the Cavan–Monaghan Greens and in 2011 represented the Young Greens on the National Executive. He co–founded Transition Monaghan to create links between local organisations and sustainability champions as well as raising awareness of local sustainability issues. Mícheál is also an active member of Young Friends of the Earth Ireland and in late 2015 took part in activities around the UN Climate Change talks in Paris.

Renua Ireland:

The party had selected Mary Smyth, a counselling psychologist based in Monaghan town as its candidate but in December 2015 they deselected her arising from comments made by her on social media. At the time of going to print no replacement candidate had been announced.

Direct Democracy Ireland:

Michael (Mick) McDermott and his young family emigrated to Australia in 2011 in search of employment and while they were there heard that a government spokesman had called what he describes as the 'hardest decision of his life' a lifestyle choice. He is running this time to try and prevent others having to go through the same experience. An automotive technical sales demonstrator and trainer he is a member of Ballyjamesduff Community Council. Heavily involved in Cavan–Monaghan soccer he coaches children from 6 to 16 and helped to set up the local Hat Trick Football program, which caters for children with Aspergers, ASD and ADHD. He also spends time at Cavan Courthouse assisting those faced with eviction and founded Cavan Says No to Water Charges.

Independents:

Sean Conlan is based in Ballybay and has been a Dáil deputy since 2011. He was elected to Ballybay Town Council in June 2009 and to Dáil Éireann on his first attempt in 2011. In the 2011 election as a Fine Gael candidate he polled 7,864 first preferences and took the fourth seat, the second of Fine Gael's three seats, on the ninth count. Conlan is a former Chairperson of Young Fine Gael in University College Dublin where he gained a degree in Economics. He was a practising Solicitor and owner of Conlan's Bar in Ballybay at the time of his election to Dáil Éireann. He has been at the centre of a number of controversies since his election in 2011. He is the son of John Conlan who was a TD for Cavan from 1969 to 1977 and for Cavan–Monaghan from then until 1989. John Conlan was one time election agent to James Dillon. In November 2015 Sean Conlan resigned from Fine Gael insisting that the reason he was doing so was because of the North–South Interconnector and his opposition to Fine Gael's position on the proposal, which would see hundreds of pylons built across counties Cavan, Monaghan, Meath, Armagh and Tyrone. On the 2nd December 2015 he was charged with offences arising from an alleged assault in his family pub in August 2015. The trial of those charges has not yet come on for hearing.

John Wilson is a former member of An Garda Síochána. He first came to national prominence as a Garda whistleblower, highlighting irregularities in the application of penalty points for motoring offences. He has strong family connections to Fianna Fail. He is a nephew of the former Tánaiste John Wilson and brother of Senator Diarmuid Wilson. He has been active in the anti water charges campaign although he has withdrawn from formal participation in the Cavan Water Charges Opposition Group because some members of the group have suggested that there might be conflicts of interest with his election campaign. He is the first substitute for the European Parliament seat currently held by independent 'Ming' Flanagan in the North and West Constituency. In March 2014 he announced his intention to contest the election for Cavan County Council in the Cavan–Belturbet electoral area but in early May 2014 withdrew from that election after being diagnosed with bowel cancer from which he has now recovered.

CLARE

Outgoing Deputies:

Pat Breen (FG), Michael McNamara (Lab), Joe Carey (FG), Timmy Dooley (FF)

The Constituency:

This four-seater is unchanged since 2011. It includes the county of Clare except for a part of the county in the Parteen area, which is included in the Limerick City constituency.

	% Vote 1997	% Vote 2002	% Vote 2007	% Vote 2011	Swing 2011	Quotas 2011
Fine Gael	30.08	25.46	35.21	42.34	7.13	2.11
Labour	3.59	3.45	1.58	14.80	13.22	0.7
Fianna Fáil	50.36	45.38	44.03	22.11	–21.92	1.1
Sinn Féin	–	–	3.42	–	–	–
Green Party	3.59	5.83	5.07	1.99	–3.08	0.1
Others	12.37	19.87	10.69	18.76	8.07	0.9

2016 Candidates will include:

Pat Breen (FG), Joe Carey (FG), Michael McNamara (Lab), Timmy Dooley (FF), Michael 'Malty' McDonagh (FF), Michael McDonagh (FF), Clare Colleran Molloy (FF), Noeleen Moran (SF), Fergal Smith (GP), Ann Norton (Ind), Richard Cahill (Ind), Gerry Flynn (Ind)

In Brief:

It seems improbable that the outgoing government parties could again win three out of the four seats. The fall in the Labour vote nationally suggests that Labour's Michael McNamara will be in trouble, although he is known for his independent streak, which may save him. The Fine Gael seats look comfortable. This is a constituency that has been prone to independents, this time Ann Norton in Ennis is the one to watch.

Fine Gael:

The local constituency organisation was instructed by the national party to select two candidates and the two outgoing deputies were selected. The national executive then added a third candidate, Councillor Mary Howard.

Pat Breen lives in Lisduff, Ballynacally and has a constituency office in Ennis. He has been a Dáil deputy since 2002. He received 4,541 first preferences in 2002 (9.12%) and 7,036 (12.48%) in 2007. In the 2011 Dáil elections he polled 9,855 first preferences (17%). He is the Chairman of the Oireachtas Foreign Affairs and Trade Committee and is deputy leader of the Irish Delegation to the Council of Europe. He was previously the party's Deputy Spokesperson on Foreign Affairs with special responsibility for Human Rights and Overseas Development Aid. He was a member of Clare County Council from 1999 to 2004 for the Kilrush electoral area and was formerly an architectural technician.

Joe Carey lives in Clarecastle and has a constituency office in Ennis. He has been a member since 2007. In the 2007 Dáil election he polled 5,818 first preferences and narrowly beat independent James Breen for the fourth seat. In 2011 he increased that to 7,840 votes (13.5%) of the first preferences and won the third seat. Carey was a member of Clare County Council for the Ennis electoral area from 1999 to 2007. His father, Donal Carey, was a member of Dáil Éireann from 1981 to 2002 and a Minister for State from 1995 to 1997.

Mary Howard was elected onto Ennis Town Council in 2009 with 791 first preference votes, which was 17 over the quota, and to Clare County Council for the Ennis area in 2014 with 720 votes (5.59%) which gave her the final seat. She is deputy mayor of Ennis municipal district. Her family has always been Fine Gael – she is the daughter of the late Senator Michael Howard who was a Dáil candidate in 1969 and 1973 and served in the Seanad from 1977 to 1987 and from 1989 to 1997. She describes Irish politics as being 'far from family friendly' and says she is not a fan of gender quotas but sees them as one means of overcoming the hurdles. She says she loves her job because 'politics is about people'. When the two sitting male TDs were elected by the Clare convention it was widely expected that her name was the one that would be added by the party's national executive, and she has expressed frustration that the decision on who to run was delayed into the new year.

Labour:

Labour previously held a seat here briefly from 1992 when in that 'Springtide' election the colourful local psychiatrist Moosajee Bhamjee took the seat with 5,113 first preference votes, an 11.46% share. He retired from politics in 1997, leaving the party with no candidate in that election. The candidates in 2002 and 2007 polled 1,720 and 892 respectively. The party's fortunes in Clare changed again in 2011 when they selected Michael McNamara.

Michael McNamara is a farmer and barrister based in Scariff. He first stood as an independent in the 2009 European parliament elections in the North West constituency, polling 12,744 first preference votes which placed him ninth place in the three-seater. He joined the Labour party in advance of the 2011 general election and polled 8,572 first preferences (14.8%) as a candidate for the party, taking the second seat. He has been a member of the Oireachtas Committee on Agriculture, Food and the Marine and is a member of the Parliamentary Assembly of the Council of Europe. In May 2015 he voted against the government on the sale of Aer Lingus and lost the Labour Party whip but was readmitted in September 2015. In the same month he married Sarah Hillery, granddaughter of the late President Patrick Hillery and daughter of Dr John Hillery. who was a Fianna Fáil candidate in Clare in the 2011 general election. McNamara worked previously for RTÉ, as a human rights lawyer for the OSCE and as a consultant for the UN.

Fianna Fáil:

Dr John Hillery, the son of former President Dr Patrick Hillery and a former president of the Medical Council, was the party's candidate along with Timmy Dooley in 2011 polling 6,015 first preferences. In July 2015 he announced that he was withdrawing his name for consideration for 2016, citing the delay in deciding which candidates would be selected.

Clare Colleran Molloy has been a member of Clare County Council for the Ennis electoral area since 2014. She polled 584 first preferences and took the first seat in that area in the 2014 local elections. She practises as a barrister on the South West Circuit. She was also called to the bar in New York and Florida. She is sister of *Irish Daily Star* managing director Ger Colleran. She will be the first female candidate to stand for the party in Clare since Síle de Valera retired in 2006.

Timmy Dooley is based in Tulla and has a constituency office in Ennis. He was elected to Dáil Éireann on his first attempt in 2007, He is the Fianna Fáil spokesperson on Transport, Tourism and Sport. In the 2007 election he topped the poll with 10,971 (19.14%) first preferences. In 2011 Dooley's vote fell to 6,789, which was still 774 votes higher than John Hillery so that Dooley took the final seat. Dooley was a member of the Seanad on the Administrative Panel from 2002 to 2007 and was party spokesperson on Transport in the upper house. He had previously been a prominent member of Fianna Fáil's National Executive's Committee of Fifteen, the National Forum on Europe and before that of the party's National Youth Committee. Before his election to the Seanad he had worked in sales and marketing and in business development. He is also one of the party's Vice–Presidents, first elected to that position by delegates to the party Ard Fhéis.

Michael 'Malty' McDonagh is a first time candidate. He is the current chairman of the Clare County GAA board, and a retired member of An Garda Síochána. A native of Milltown Malbay, he has been a community activist for many years but has not previously sought election to a public office.

Sinn Féin:

In 2007, Sinn Féin ran Anna Prior in this constituency. In her first election she recorded 1,929 first preference votes, a 3.42% share, and finished in tenth position. It had no candidate in 2011. It has a new candidate on this occasion.

Noeleen Moran from Ballyvaughan ran unsuccessfully for Clare County Council in the 2014 local elections in the West Clare electoral area. She polled 1,023 first preferences and was in ninth place on the first count. She is the Sinn Féin county secretary and worked in both agriculture and tourism before obtaining a degree in Public and Social Policy and an LLM from the Irish Centre for Human Rights both from NUI Galway.

Green Party:

The party candidate in 2011, and prior to that, was local councillor Brian Meaney. He has since left the Green party and has joined Fianna Fáil. In March 2015 the party selected Roisín Garvey to contest the general election but she later withdrew.

Fergal Smith is the party's new candidate. He returned to the Clare coast in 2011 after several years of professional surfing around the world. Settling near Lahinch he founded the Moy Hill Community Garden with a group of friends. This 17-acre open garden has become a focal point for the community, and Fergal and the Community Garden were subsequently nominated for a young entrepreneur of the year award. He describes the project as being about education, community involvement and the provision of much needed services and products to the community.

Renua Ireland:

The party had announced no candidate for this constituency at the date of publication.

Fís Nua:

Niamh O'Brien grew up in O'Callaghan's Mills and is the only declared Fís Nua candidate as we go to press. In the 2014 local election she stood in the Killaloe LEA of Clare County Council where her 731 first preferences kept her in until the fourth count. With a degree in Law and Business Studies she works as a voluntary advocate for a family law organisation and in debt support. With a young son, she was a founder of Ireland's first women's shed. She is the leader of 'Clare Says No to Water Charges'.

Independents:

Richard Cahill describes himself as a campaigner to close the urban–rural divide. He was born in Dublin but his family moved to Clare when he was 13. He lives in Sixmilebridge and is married with five adult children. He hit the news columns during the 2014 European elections when he announced that he would not be putting up posters, saying that they were a waste of money, and that he didn't have money anyway. He worked as an electrician until being forced to retire after a spinal injury. In the 2014 European elections he stood in Ireland South, gaining 10,719 votes (1.63%). He was eliminated on the fifth count. He describes himself as having been 'a stay at home Dad, a homemaker, a self-employed small business owner, and a mature student.'

Ian Lynch was elected to Kilrush Town Council on the Fine Gael ticket in 2009 and in 2014 decided to leave the party and stand as an independent after he failed to be selected at the conventions. It had been suggested that he would get the nomination in 2019 but he said that he felt it was essential that the town and its hinterland be properly represented now. He feels that consecutive governments have stripped the county of its local services. In the 2014 local elections he took 1,218 first preference votes, just under two thirds of a quota. It was suggested that he might decide to run for Renua but says that he thinks that Clare people want a true Independent, but that the prospect is financially daunting. He said, 'the political system in Ireland is not set up for someone like me, a young person with a family.'

Ann Norton has been an independent member of Clare County Council for the Ennis electoral area since 2014. She polled 821 first preferences (6.4%) votes in that election and performed strongly in attracting transfers to take the fourth of the eight seats. She is a well-known disability campaigner and was Clare Person of the Year in 2013. She is a founder of Clare Crusaders, a clinic based in Barefield, Ennis that provides therapy and specialist treatments to 350 children with special needs in County Clare.

Cork East

Outgoing Deputies:

Sean Sherlock (Lab), David Stanton (FG), Tom Barry (FG), Sandra McLellan (SF)

Sandra McLellan announced in October that she would not contest the 2016 election.

The Constituency:

This four-seater, which stretches from Mallow in the northeast to Cobh in the southwest is unchanged from 2011.

	% Vote 1997	% Vote 2002	% Vote 2007	% Vote 2011	Swing 2011	Quotas 2011
Fine Gael	30.12	29.09	30.85	36.62	5.77	1.8
Labour	18.83	20.98	20.91	30.85	9.94	1.5
Fianna Fáil	36.44	41.31	37.97	16.94	–21.03	0.8
Sinn Féin	3.56	5.73	6.82	11.05	4.23	0.6
Green Party	–	2.48	2.92	1.11	1.81	0.06
Others	11.03	0.41	0.52	3.43	2.91	0.2

2016 Candidates will include:

Tom Barry (FG), Noel McCarthy (FG), David Stanton (FG), Sean Sherlock (Lab), Kevin O'Keeffe (FF), Barbara Ahern (FF), Pat Buckley (SF), Natasha Harty (GP), Ciara Leonardi Roche (AAA–PBP), Paul Bradford (Renua), Ken Curtin (SD), Claire Cullinane (Ind), Kieran McCarthy (Ind), Mary Linehan Foley (Ind)

In Brief:

The pattern for a long time in this four-seater was two Fianna Fáil seats and two seats for the Fine Gael–Labour combination. Fianna Fail lost both of its seats in 2011. It is likely to regain one of them. Sinn Féin also broke the traditional pattern by taking a seat in 2011. Its TD has had a low profile since and uncharacteristically there has been turmoil in the local Sinn Féin party organisation over candidate strategy for this election. Ultimately the sitting TD Sandra McLellan (SF) declared she would not contest, and although a strong candidate has been selected in Councillor Pat Buckley this makes its task of retaining the seat more difficult. There has been some controversy also in Labour over its candidate selection, which ultimately accrued to the benefit of Fine Gael. Councillor Noel McCarthy wanted to be on the ticket with Minister of State Sean Sherlock, and when that didn't happen he jumped to Fine Gael and is now its third candidate, making it more likely they will hold two seats and that Sherlock could be squeezed out. Indeed McCarthy may displace one of the sitting Fine Gael deputies. Much interest will focus also on the performance of one time Fine Gael deputy Paul Bradford, now contesting for Renua, and of the candidate for the Social Democrats, colourful tweeter Ken Curtin. Geography is important here with a strong divide between the Mitchelstown and Midleton ends of the constituency.

Fine Gael:

Tom Barry is based in Killmallock at the Mallow end of the constituency. He has been a Dáil deputy since 2011. On his first run for Dáil Éireann in 2011 his 5,798 first preference votes gave him 10.2%, which was enough to carry him over the line thanks to solid transfers from the second Labour candidate, John Mulvihill. Prior to that he was a member of Cork County Council for the Mallow electoral area. He was first elected to the council in 2009 when he gained the fourth seat in the Mallow electoral area with 1,666 votes (11.21%). Formerly a farmer and farm-based businessman, he cut back on his business interests in 2007 to spend more time on family and politics. In 2013 he attracted considerable unfavourable publicity, both nationally and internationally, after pulling a female party colleague onto his lap during a late night debate, an incident for which he apologised profusely.

Noel McCarthy is based in Fermoy and has been a member of Cork County Council for the Fermoy local electoral area since 2009. As a Labour Party candidate in the 2009 local elections he polled 2,063 first preferences (15.3%) and took the third of the four seats in the area. Unusually for a Labour party councillor his vote in 2014 increased, and did so dramatically. In the enlarged Fermoy electoral area for the 2014 local elections he topped the poll with 3,511 first preferences to take the first seat in the six seat electoral area on the first count. McCarthy was leader of the Labour group on Cork County Council when he resigned from the party in early 2015 saying that he was seriously considering the possibility of a General Election bid but that the party had 'made little effort to encourage him to run.' He said that he had 'become seriously disillusioned with the party hierarchy.' The following month he joined Fine Gael and was added to its ticket for this Dáil election. Born and reared in Cobh he has lived and worked in Fermoy for twenty years.

David Stanton is based in Midleton and has been a member of Dáil Éireann since 1997 He is currently Chair of the Oireachtas Committee on Justice, Defence and Equality. In the 1997 Dáil election, Stanton, as Paul Bradford's running mate, polled 5,117 first preferences for a vote share of 11.9%. While his first preference vote share continued to be less than that of Bradford in both 2002 and 2007, transfers gave him the single Fine Gael seat on both occasions. In 2011 he was joined on the ticket by Tom Barry and Stanton. His 10,019 first preferences were 17.6% of votes cast and he took the third seat just ahead of Barry. Stanton was previously party spokesperson on Social and Family Affairs and Equality, Assistant Chief Whip, spokesperson on Disability Issues and on Defence. He is Director of Midleton and District Day Care Centre Ltd. He is a former teacher and career guidance counsellor and was a commissioned officer in the Reserve Defence Forces.

Labour Party:

Sean Sherlock is based in Mallow and has been a Dáil deputy since 2007. He is currently Minister of State at the Department of Foreign Affairs and Trade with special responsibility for Trade Promotion, Development and North South Co–Operation. From 2011 to 2014 he was Minister of State for Research and Innovation. Before becoming a full time public representative he worked as a Brussels–based personal assistant to the Labour Party, formerly

Democratic Left, MEP Prionsias De Rossa. His father Joe Sherlock was a candidate in this constituency in every election from 1973 to 2007, first for Sinn Féin the Workers Party, then the Workers Party, then Democratic Left and, after the merger, for the Labour Party. Joe Sherlock was a member of Dáil Éireann from November 1981 to November 1982, from 1987 to 1992, and from 2002 to 2007. Sean replaced his father on Mallow Town Council and Cork County Council in 2003 and he was re–elected to both in June 2004. In 2007 Sean took his father's place on the general election ticket beside John Mulvihill. In that election the combined Labour vote was 11,249, with 7,295 going to Seán Sherlock (13.6%) and 3,954 going to John Mulvihill. Seán was elected in third place. In 2011 Sherlock and Mulvihill were again the two Labour party candidates. Sean Sherlock topped the poll with 11,862 votes (20.8%), which was more than 6,000 votes more than Mulvihil, a little less than 500 votes over the quota. He took the first seat.

Fianna Fáil:

The party won a total of 20,431 votes in 2007 but that shrunk to 9,642 votes in 2011. The party convention in 2015 was instructed by the national executive to choose just one candidate and selected Kevin O'Keeffe, a son of the former deputy Ned O'Keeffe, after his brother Cllr Ciarán O'Keeffe withdrew. The party nationally later added a second candidate, Barbara Ahern, a daughter of the former TD Michael Ahern.

Barbara Ahern was added to the ticket by the party national executive in November 2015. She is an accountant and tax advisor who at the time of her selection was based in Gibraltar. She is from Carrigtwohill in the south of the constituency and Midleton is the family's political base. Her father Michael Ahern was first elected to Dáil Éireann in February 1982 and held his seat in each election until 2011. He was Minister for Science 1992 to 1993. He was on the front bench between 1994 and 1997 and was a Minister of State from 2002 to 2008. Her uncle Maurice Ahern was a long time member of Cork County Council for the Midleton electoral area. Her grandfather Liam Ahern was a Senator from 1957 to 1973 and a TD from 1973 to 1974. Her great grandfather John Dineen was a Farmers Party TD from 1922 to 1927.

Kevin O'Keeffe is a member of Cork County Council for the Fermoy Electoral Area. This is his second time standing for the Dáil. When he ran in the 2011 Dáil election he got 5,024 first preference votes, which gave him 8.8% of the poll. He was 406 votes ahead of Michael Ahern and when the latter was eliminated there was a strong transfer to O'Keeffe but he was still short of the necessary votes for a seat. O Keeffe was first co–opted to Cork County Council to replace his father, Ned O'Keeffe in 1997. Since then Kevin has taken the first seat in the Fermoy electoral area at each of the local elections. In the 2014 local elections he polled 2,923 first preferences (16.6%) which was again a comfortable margin over a quota. Kevin previously worked in the insurance industry and, like his father, is a businessman and farmer. Ned O'Keeffe was a TD for this constituency from November 1982 to 2011.

Sinn Féin:

After much internal turmoil outgoing TD Sandra McLellan has decided not to contest the 2016 general election. A 'structural review' of the constituency organisation conducted by national figures in the party led to several expulsions and resignations including the resignation of Cobh-based Councillor Kieran McCarthy who is now contesting the 2016 election as an independent. In October 2011 McLellan confirmed she would not contest the election saying 'Over the period I have served as a TD, my efforts were consistently and persistently undermined by a small number in the constituency that called themselves members of Sinn Féin.' Sinn Fein's new candidate is Pat Buckley.

Pat Buckley has been a member of Cork County Council for the East Cork local electoral area since 2014. He polled 1,753 first preferences and took the third of the six seats in that electoral area in the 2014 local elections. He was previously a member of Midleton Town Council. In December 2014 he was given a three year driving ban after being stopped by Gardai with a high level of blood alcohol. He now campaigns against drink driving. He is a co–founder of the suicide support group, The Let's Get Together Foundation, after losing two of his brothers to suicide.

Green Party:
Natasha Harty is a member of the Allen family of Ballymaloe fame. After graduating in Economics from TCD she worked on the family farm and in other parts of the business before marrying a local farmer. Living on the downwind side of Cork harbour exposed to emissions from factories in Ringaskiddy and sewage discharge from Midleton, and led her to becoming involved with local environmental campaigns. She is an active member of the County Cork local currency network, Cork LETS.

Renua Ireland:
Paul Bradford is a member of Seanad Éireann and a former Fine Gael member of Dáil Éireann. He and his wife, the Dublin South East TD Lucinda Creighton, were expelled from Fine Gael in July 2013 after voting against the Protection of Life During Pregnancy Bill in 2013. They later joined with other former Fine Gael TDs similarly expelled to form the Reform Alliance parliamentary grouping and with some of those parliamentarians went on in March 2015 to establish the new political party Renua Ireland, which Lucinda now leads. Paul operates off a political base in Mallow. He became the youngest ever member of Cork County Council in 1985 at the age of 21 and was first elected to Seanad Éireann in 1987. He was first elected to Dáil Éireann for this constituency in 1989. He then became the party's Chief Whip. He was re–elected in 1992 and 1997 but lost the seat in 2002. He stood again as a Fine Gael candidate in 2007 but failed to regain the seat. In that election he polled 8,916 first preferences but was 299 votes behind Sean Sherlock (Lab) for the last seat.

Anti-Austerity Alliance – People Before Profit:
Ciara Leonardi Roche is from Cobh. She will be one of the youngest candidates in the 2016 election at 22 years old. She studied at Cork Institute of Technology and first became involved in politics over the water charges issue.

Social Democrats:

Ken Curtin is based in Cobh and has a long history of political activism on behalf of Fianna Fáil at local and national level. The married father of two used his political skills most recently as a Director of the Yes Equality Cork campaigning group in the May 2015 Marriage referendum. Immediately after the referendum he resigned from Fianna Fáil saying that the party's lack of activity in that campaign had been the last straw for him. Curtin has long been a high profile tweeter on political issues and is also known for an entertaining and colourful selection of ties. Having left Fianna Fáil he joined the newly formed Social Democrats and in October 2015 was announced as its Cork East candidate.

Independents:

Claire Cullinane is based in Cobh and has been a member of Cork County Council since 2014. She is one of the architects of The People's Charter. She also ran as an independent candidate in this constituency in the 2011 Dail Election receiving 510 first preference votes which amounted to 0.9% of the first preferences. In the 2014 local elections she polled 947 first preferences (6.3%) in the Cobh electoral area and took the sixth of the seven seats.

Mary Lenihan Foley is based in Youghal and has been a member of Cork County Council since 2014. She was a member of Fianna Fáil until before the 2014 local elections when she left the party when party headquarters decided the local candidate slate without running the expected convention. She was first elected to Youghal Town council in 1999 and had been mayor three times. Her father and grandfather had previously been members of the town council. In 2009 she was a Fianna Fáil candidate for the county council in the Midleton area but her 1,056 first preference votes (4.29%) were not enough to give her a seat. She contested the 2014 elections for Cork County Council as an independent under the People's Convention banner and took the fifth seat with 1,134 first preference votes (7.83%). She is married with five children and two grandchildren and is current Chairperson of the Southern Committee of Cork County Council. She is also a member of the Housing SPC and the Arts & Culture SPC.

Kieran McCarthy has been a member of Cork County Council since 2014. He was elected to the council as a Sinn Féin candidate in the Cobh electoral area in the 2014 local elections. He polled 2,471 first preferences and took the second seat. However, in 2015 an internal party investigation accused him of attacks on then TD Sandra McLellan. He was subsequently expelled from the party in June 2015 but a month later that expulsion was lifted. The row also led to the resignation of many Sinn Féin members in Cobh and Fermoy.

Cork North Central

Outgoing Deputies:

Jonathan O'Brien (SF), Kathleen Lynch (Lab), Dara Murphy (FG), Billy Kelleher (FF)

The Constituency:

This is a four-seater. It comprises in the main those parts of the city north of the Lee. In the redrawing of constituencies before the 2011 election the population of this constituency increased by over 8,500 roughly half of which came in from Cork East and the other half from Cork North West. Western areas have been moved to Cork North West this time, shrinking that part of the constituency slightly, although it has acquired a very substantial population from Cork South Central.

	% Vote 1997	% Vote 2002	% Vote 2007	% Vote 2011	Swing 2011	Quotas 2011
Fine Gael	30.16	20.38	27.57	26.22	–1.35	1.3
Labour	12.42	11.77	12.33	26.47	14.14	1.3
Fianna Fáil	35.53	41.48	35.74	15.14	–20.60	0.8
Sinn Féin	3.76	6.34	8.16	15.20	7.04	0.8
Green Party	3.04	2.56	3.55	1.01	–2.54	0.05
Socialist Party/ULA	–	2.07	4.01	9.21	5.2	0.5
Others	15.09	15.4	8.63	6.75	–1.88	0.3

2016 Candidates will include:

Dara Murphy (FG), Kathleen Lynch (Lab), Billy Kelleher (FF), Jonathan O'Brien (SF), Thomas Gould (SF), Oliver Moran (GP), Mick Barry (AAA–PBP), Ted Tynan (WP), Thomas Kiely (Ind), Aislinn Tongue (Ind)

In Brief:

The Labour seat in this constituency is under threat from Mick Barry who is running for the Anti-Austerity Alliance – People Before Profit. The existing Fine Gael seat looks comfortable. Fianna Fáil's Director of Elections Billy Kelleher will also hold its one seat in this constituency. Sinn Féin's Jonathan O'Brien topped the poll the last time and also looks safe.

Fine Gael:

In the 2002 election Fine Gael's Bernard Allen comfortably retained his seat but the party lost its second seat, which had been held by Liam Burke who retired at that election. The party vote was up significantly in 2007 to 27.6% but, because the constituency had been reduced from five to four seats, the party could not regain its second seat. In 2011 Dara Murphy and Pat Burton, who were both running for the first time, received 26.2% of the poll between them with Murphy narrowly taking the seat. Pat Burton has since decided to leave politics. Amid some controversy the sitting deputy and Minister of State Dara Murphy TD defeated Senator Colm Burke at the party's constituency convention of September 2015.

Dara Murphy is Minister of State with responsibility for European Affairs and Data Protection at the Departments of the Taoiseach and Foreign Affairs and Trade. He is based in the Gardiner's Hill area and is originally from Glanmire. In the 2011 Dáil election he polled 6,597 first preference votes (12.7%), which was 475 behind his running mate Pat Burton and it was only on the final count and the redistribution of Kathleen Lynch's surplus that he squeezed ahead of Burton. Murphy was Mayor of Cork for the year 2009–2010. He was member of Cork Corporation for the North East ward from to 2004 to 2011. He first ran for the council in 1999 getting 478 votes. In 2004 he increased that to 728 votes and took the sixth seat. In 2009 he polled 1,001 first preferences which was almost a quota and he took the second seat. He was elected a Vice President of the European People's Party, of which Fine Gael is a member, at its annual conference in Madrid in October 2015. He was managing director of Variety Supplies, a catering equipment company, established in 1992 supplying catering and hygiene products to hotels, bars, restaurants and hospitals.

Labour Party:

Kathleen Lynch has been a Dáil deputy from 1994 to 1997 and from 2002 to date. She is currently Minister of State at the Department of Health with special responsibility for Primary Care, Social Care (Disabilities & Older People) and Mental Health. She is based in Farranree and was a member of Cork City Council from 1985 to 2004, latterly for the Cork City North Central ward. She has contested seven previous Dáil elections, firstly as a Democratic Left candidate and then after the parties merged as a Labour party candidate. She was first elected as a Democratic Left TD in a 1994 by-election. She lost the seat in the 1997 election. She has contested as a Labour party candidate since 2002 when she took 11.77%, followed by 12.33% in 2007 and 14.7% in 2011. In 2011 Lynch had a running mate in the form of Blarney-based councillor John Gilroy. He polled 6,125 first preferences and Lynch polled 7,677, which was his highest vote ever for the party, except for the 1994 by-election. They had 1.3 quotas between them. This time Lynch will be the sole candidate.

In the week leading up to the party convention to select a candidate for this election Lynch refused to confirm whether she would stand again and missed the party's date for nominations for the convention. However, in the days before the convention she formally declared her candidacy, saying that she was 'anxious to discuss issues in relation to my own areas of interest, and to do that I needed to speak to both Joan Burton and Brendan Howlin, which I have done over the weekend'. John Gilroy, who had run with her in 2011, was expected to contest the nomination but instead offered his backing to Kathleen Lynch. She is the sister-in-law of Ciarán Lynch who is the party TD for Cork South Central and again a candidate in this election.

Fianna Fáil:

At the time of going to print Fianna Fáil had announced only one candidate for this election in the form of incumbent deputy Billy Kelleher.

Billy Kelleher lives in Glanmire and has his constituency office at Ballyhooley Road, Dillon Cross. He has been a Dáil Deputy since 1997. He is the party's spokesperson on Health. In November 2015 he was also appointed Fianna Fáil's Director of Elections for the 2016 election. This will be his fifth Dáil election. He came very close to being elected on his first attempt in 1992 when he lost out by just 23 votes. He was a Taoiseach's nominee to Seanad Éireann from 1993 to 1997. He unsuccessfully contested the 1994 by-election caused by the death of Labour's Gerry O'Sullivan. In the 1997 general election he polled 5,419 votes and in 2002 he polled 5,801 first preferences. His vote jumped to 9,456 when he topped the poll in 2007. In 2011 his 7,896 votes were only 15.1% of the total. He is a former member of Cork City Council for the North East Ward.

He was appointed Fianna Fáil's assistant chief whip in 2002 and was Minister of State with special responsibility for Trade and Commerce and then Minister of State with special responsibility for Labour Affairs from 2007 to 2009. He is a cousin of Liam Burke, a former Fine Gael deputy for this constituency. Kelleher is also a farmer.

Sinn Féin:

The party performance in this constituency in 2011 was spectacular. Don O'Leary had been the party's Dáil candidate here for ten years, from 1987 to 1997, without success. He took the party vote from 681 to 1,654, but never got above a 4% vote-share. In 2002 Jonathan O'Brien took over as the candidate and grew the vote to ultimate success in 2011. In this election O'Brien has a running mate.

Jonathan O'Brien lives in Farranree and has been a Dáil deputy since 2011. He took over from Don O'Leary as the party's candidate for the Dáil in 2002 and over that period he has grown his vote dramatically. In 2002 he polled 2,860 first preference votes (6.34%). In 2007 he increased his vote to 3,456 (8.16%). In 2011 he topped the poll, more than doubled his vote and almost doubled his vote share. He polled 7,923 first preference votes (15.2%) and took the first seat on the eighth count when he got half the transfers of Socialist candidate Mick Barry.

O'Brien had been a member of Cork City Council since 2000. He had been co-opted to replace Don O'Leary on Cork City Council in 2000. In 2004 he held the seat when he topped the poll in the Cork City North West ward with 1,150 first preferences, In the 2009 local elections he topped the polled again with 1,319 first preference votes. He was one of the founding members of the Coalition of Communities Against Drugs. He played football with Na Piarsaigh GAA Club and is a director of Cork City FC.

Thomas Gould is a councillor for Cork North Central Ward. In 2009 his 618 first preference votes (7.8%) were sufficient to give him the 5th seat in that electoral area. In 2014 he topped the poll with 1,828 votes (26.71%) easily taking the first seat. A resident of Cathedral Road, he is married with two children. He is a development officer with St. Vincent's GAA club and is the club's delegate to the county board. He has previously been a youth leader with Foróige and is a former director of Knocknaheeney youth centre.

Green Party:

The party has never run the same candidate in two successive elections in this constituency. In 2002 Nicholas McMurray polled just 1,155 first preferences. In 2007 the candidate was Chris O'Leary, a member of Cork City Council who is based in Mahon and polled 1,503 votes. In 2011 he left the Green Party for Sinn Féin but failed to get that Party's nomination. The 2011 candidate, Ken Walsh, took only 524 votes, 1% of the poll. The party has a new candidate again in 2016.

Oliver Moran is based in Montenotte. He is a 37-year-old software engineer with Laya Healthcare. He is one of the co-founders of Wikimedia Ireland, the user group which coordinates the development of Irish related expert content in Wikipedia. In the field of non-partisan politics he founded the campaign group Second Republic to work for citizen led reform. He was a partner in the start up of the SmartVote app but resigned when he decided to run as a Green Party candidate for Cork City Council in 2014. He polled 235 votes (4.9%) in the North East electoral area in the 2014 local elections.

Anti-Austerity Alliance – People Before Profit:

Mick Barry has been a Socialist Party member of Cork City Council since 2004 and in all his previous outings that is what it has said on the ballot paper. He stood under the United Left Alliance banner in the 2011 Dáil election and will run for Anti-Austerity Alliance – People Before Profit this time and that is what will be on his ballot paper. This will be his third time to contest a Dáil election. In the 2002 Dáil election he polled 936 first preferences, while in the 2007 Dáil election he almost doubled his vote to 1,700. In 2011 his 4,803 votes gave him 9.2% of the poll, which was a trebling of his 2007 vote. He was eliminated on the seventh count. He was first elected to Cork City Council in 2004, when he topped the poll in the Cork City North Central electoral area with 1,390 first preferences. In the 2009 local elections, he again topped the poll in the same electoral area with 2,096 first preferences. The Sinn Féin candidate led the poll in 2014 but his 1,462 votes (21.36%) were still enough to see him elected to the second seat on the first ballot. Barry is a member of the Cork Householders against Service Charges campaign and secretary of Cork Independent Workers Union Home Helps branch. He was jailed for failing to pay refuse charges in 2001 and is a founder member of the national Anti-Water Tax campaign that was launched in 2010.

Workers Party:

Timothy (Ted) Tynan has been the Worker's Party's candidate here since 2007 and before that stood for Sinn Féin the Workers Party. He began contesting Dáil elections in 1977. In the 2011 Dáil election he polled his highest Dáil vote ever with just 681, which gave him a 1.3% share. He was elected to Cork City Council for the North East ward in 1979. He regained his seat on that council in 2009 after a hiatus of twenty years when he took the fourth seat on the sixth count with 489 first preferences. In the 2014 local elections he polled 962 votes (20.09%) and took the second seat at the first count. He was jailed twice in the 1990s for failing to pay service charges and is also a member of the Householders Against Service Charges group. In Worker's Party politics Tynan is probably best known for strongly opposing then-party leader Pronsias de Rossa's attempts to reform the party structures in 1992.

Independents:

Thomas Kiely was born in Mallow and lives in Wilton. He describes himself as a candidate for The People's Convention, which does not appear on the ballot paper. He is a 33-year old qualified sheet metal fabricator who lost his job due to the recession and this and the needs of his autistic son prompted him to become politically active. He polled 463 votes (4.8%) in the Cork City South West electoral area in the 2014 local elections, missing out on the last seat for that area on Cork County Council by just two votes.

Aislinn Tongue was born in rural northeast Thailand and moved to Ireland in 2006, becoming an Irish citizen in 2009. Married, with two children, she is self-employed and lives and works in Cork city centre. She is a Buddhist but also worships in her local Catholic Church. Her platform includes the elimination of graft, a reduction in the number of councillors, improved immigration policies, empowering women to seek election without using gender quotas, an effectiveness based approach to renewable energy and rapid action on Cork's flood defences. She has never run for election before and sees this campaign as the first step on the ladder.

Cork North West

Outgoing Deputies:

Michael Creed (FG), Michael Moynihan (FF), Áine Collins (FG)

The Constituency:

This three-seater has been returned to its pre-2009 boundaries in the redraw of constituencies since 2011. Four electoral divisions, with a combined population of 5,048 at the last census, have been transferred back into this constituency from Cork North–Central.

	% Vote 1997	% Vote 2002	% Vote 2007	% Vote 2011	Swing 2011	Quotas 2011
Fine Gael	41.12	42.08	38.42	48.8	10.38	2
Labour	7.40	6.87	4.91	14.04	9.13	0.6
Fianna Fáil	46.50	50.06	53.05	24.90	–28.15	1
Sinn Féin	–	–	–	7.44	7.44	0.3
Green Party	–	–	3.63	1.42	2.21	0.06
ULA	–	–	–	3.329	3.39	0.1
Others	4.97	0.99	–	0.00	0.00	0

2016 Candidates will include:

Áine Collins (FG), Michael Creed (FG), Aindrias Moynihan (FF), Michael Moynihan (FF), Nigel Dennehy (SF), Cormac Manning (GP), Jason Fitzgerald (Renua), Diarmuid Flynn (Ind), Shirley Griffin (Ind), Steven O'Riordan (Ind), John Paul O'Shea (Ind)

In Brief:

Fianna Fail's vote in this constituency suffered one of the largest collapses in the country in 2011, falling from 53 per cent to 25 per cent. Fine Gael's vote rose by 10 per cent. Each of the parties will win a seat and Fine Gael are likely to retain its two seats. Fianna Fail's Aindrias Moynihan will mount a strong challenge for a seat, however, which could be strong enough to unseat his party colleague. Sinn Féin's vote share rose dramatically but it is still likely to be too far off a seat. Among the independents to watch is Diarmuid Flynn, of Ballyhea, who was a candidate in the 2014 locals and is running as part of the Independent Alliance.

Fine Gael:

Veteran Fine Gael deputy Frank Crowley lost his seat here in 1997, which was the first time Fine Gael had failed to win two seats since the constituency was created. The Fine Gael vote was actually up marginally in 2002, but the party still only won one seat, with the outgoing front bencher Michael Creed losing his seat to his party colleague Gerard Murphy, albeit by just 47 votes. Creed exacted political revenge in 2007, when he regained the seat at Murphy's expense, topping the poll with 10,516 first preference votes. In 2011, Fine Gael ran three candidates for the first time and took 48.8% of the vote and two seats. This time the party is running just the two incumbents.

Michael Creed is based in Macroom and was a member of Dáil Éireann from 1989 to 2002, and from 2007 to date. He topped the poll in the 2007 Dáil election with his 10,516 first preferences. In 2011 he topped the poll again with 10,112 first preference votes (22.1%) and again took the first seat. He was previously a member of Cork County Council for the Macroom electoral area, having first been elected in 1987. He topped the poll with 3,710 first preferences in the 2004 local elections before resigning his seat on re-election to Dáil Éireann in 2007. His son, also Michael Creed, is currently a member of Cork County Council for the Macroom electoral area. Michael Jnr topped the poll in the Macroom electoral area in the 2009 local elections, polling 4,655 first preferences (quota 4,282). In the 2014 local elections in the enlarged Blarney–Macroom electoral area Michael Jnr polled 3,406 (18.02%) and took the second seat behind Fianna Fáil's Aindrias Moynihan. Deputy Creed is the son of former TD and Minister of State Donal Creed, who served in the Dáil for 22 years. Donal Creed was a Dáil deputy for Mid–Cork from 1965 to 1981 and for Cork North West from 1981 to 1989.

During Michael Noonan's leadership, Michael Creed was front bench spokesperson on Education. He was also party spokesperson on Health from 1989 to 1993, Youth and Sport from 1993 to 1994 and Agriculture, Fisheries and Food from 2007 to 2010. Deputy Creed lost his position on Fine Gael's front bench after publicly supporting Richard Bruton's challenge to Enda Kenny's position as leader in 2010.

Áine Collins is based in the Mallow/Millstreet end of the constituency and has been a member of Dáil Éireann since 2011. She was a prominent member of the Fine Gael national executive at the time and won the party's nomination for the north of the constituency for that election after former deputy Gerard Murphy withdrew from contention. In 2011 her 7,884 first preference votes (17.2%) was almost three and half thousands votes ahead of the party's third candidate Derry Canty. She took the third seat over a thousand votes ahead of Labour's Martin Coughlan. A certified accountant who ran a financial services company at the time of her election, Collins is a member of the Dáil Public Accounts Committee and the Joint Committee on Jobs, Enterprise and Innovation. A native of Banteer she now lives in Millstreet.

Fianna Fáil:

Having won two of the three seats here for the first time in 1997 and comfortably held those two seats in 2002, Fianna Fail again retained the two seats in 2007 when Batt O' Keefe, who had transferred in from Cork South Central, won with Michael Moynihan. In 2011 the party's vote fell by more than 28 percentage points but Michael Moynihan, who polled more than three times the vote of his running mate Daithi O Donnabháin, held his seat.

Michael Moynihan is from Kiskeam near Mallow in the northern end of the constituency, which includes the urban centre of Kanturk. He has been a member of Dáil Éireann since 1997 when he topped the poll on his first attempt with 8,277 first preferences. In the 2002 Dáil election he again topped the poll, dramatically increasing his first preference vote to an impressive 10,540, which was comfortably over the quota. In 2007 his share of the first preference vote saw a slight decrease to 10,146, which at 21.76% was below just below the quota. In 2011 his 8,845 votes (19.3%) gave him the second seat in this constituency. He is a dairy farmer. He is a former National Chair of the party's youth wing, Ógra Fianna Fáil. He was Fianna Fáil's spokesperson on Agriculture and Food from April 2011 to July 2012. In July 2012, he was appointed as party spokesperson on Communications, Energy and Natural Resources. He also chairs the party's Constituency Committee, which was responsible for candidate selection and candidate strategy for the 2016 election.

Aindrias Moynihan has been a member of Cork County Council since 2003 when he was co-opted to replace his father Donal Moynihan. Donal was a Dáil Deputy for this constituency from November 1982 to 1989 and from 1991 to 2002. Aindrias was elected to the council on the first count in 2004 with 3,130 votes (25.24%) and on the 6th count in 2009 with 3,642 (17.01%). He topped the poll in impressive fashion in the 2014 local elections in the enlarged Blarney–Macroom electoral area. He polled 3,816 first preferences (20.19%), which was just over 1.4 quotas. Aindreas is currently chairman of the Macroom–Blarney Municipal District Committee of the council. He worked formerly as an electronics engineer.

Labour Party:

The party candidate in 2011 was Macroom urban district councillor Martin Coughlan who polled 6,421 first preferences. At the time of going to print the party had not announced a candidate for this constituency.

Sinn Féin:

In 2011 Sinn Féin ran a candidate in this constituency for the first time. Des O'Grady, who was based in the Ballincollig area, polled 3,405 first preferences (7.4%). He decided not to contest the Sinn Féin convention for this election when it was held in April 2015 but will act as director of elections for the new candidate instead.

Nigel Dennehy is a first time Dáil candidate. He is a 27-year-old community activist based in Rylane. He beat Ballincollig-based Mark Bodren at the party convention.

The Green Party:

In 2011 Mark Collins from Ballincollig was the party candidate but he came bottom in the poll with 651 votes (1.4%).

Cormac Manning is a 23-year-old from Ballincollig and is a first time candidate. He is currently studying Law and Irish at University College Cork. He was a prominent straight Yes campaigner in the May 2015 marriage equality referendum

Renua Ireland:

Jason Fitzgerald is a dairy farmer from Kanturk. His family have a suckler herd and when he lost his construction job in 2009 he decided to lease a dairy farm. He came into politics when the family's farm was included as part of hen harrier designated land, which he feels has made the land, and that of many other families, worthless. He describes the designated land situation 'for the sake of just 40 pairs of hen harriers' as 'nonsensical'. Married, with three small children, he says that small, marginal farmers are neglected.

Independents:

Shirley Griffin describes herself as a People's Convention candidate although this is not a registered political party. She contested the 2014 local elections for Cork County Council in the Ballincollig–Carrigaline electoral area and polled 472 first preferences (2.02%). She is originally from Dublin, where she worked as a PA/secretary, but now lives in Ballincollig with her husband and three children. She says that it was the imposition of the property tax and the difficulty of moving back into the workplace when her children had all started school that made her start taking an active political role.

Diarmuid O'Flynn is a founder of the 'Ballyhea says No' campaign, which has held weekly protests in the village against the state funded repayment to bank bondholders. He is a former sports writer with the Irish Examiner newspaper. O'Flynn stood as an independent candidate in the 2014 European election in the Ireland South constituency elections and polled 30,323 votes which was 4.61% of the first preferences. He survived until the tenth count. He is running as part of the Independent Alliance in this election.

He is currently parliamentary assistant to Luke 'Ming' Flanagan, Member of the European Parliament for the North and West Constituency.

Steven O'Riordan is from Millstreet and is a first time candidate. He is a film maker and disability advocate who came to national attention when he made the film No Limbs, No Limits about his sister Joanne O'Riordan. She was born with the condition Tetra-amelia syndrome and has successfully challenged disability stereotypes, nationally and internationally. Steven says he wants to give something back to the local people who have always supported his campaigns.

John Paul O'Shea is a native of Lombardstown in the east end of the constituency. He has been a member of Cork County Council since 2009. He is currently Mayor of County Cork, and the first independent mayor/chair of Cork County in the council's 116 year history. He stood in the Kanturk–Mallow electoral area, which lies partly in Cork North West, in the 2014 local elections polling 4,374 first preferences (20.53%). He first ran for the County Council in the Mallow electoral area in 2009 when he took the second seat with 1,859 votes (12.51%). He is chairperson of Laharn Community Action LTD, a board member of Mallow development partnership and a trustee of Dromahane Community Park.

Cork South Central

Outgoing Deputies:

Simon Coveney (FG), Jerry Buttimer (FG), Michéal Martin (FF), Michael McGrath (FF), Ciarán Lynch (Lab)

The Constituency:

This is now a four-seater, having lost a seat in the redraw of boundaries since the 2011 election. It includes all of what was previously the Cork city council administrative area south of the River Lee and most of the county council area of Carrigaline. The most recent boundary changes see it losing a chunk of Cork city, which in the last census had a population of 17,300 people. The areas transferred included Bishopstown and parts of Glasheen, the Mardyke and the city centre from South Central to North Central.

	% Vote 1997	% Vote 2002	% Vote 2007	% Vote 2011	Swing 2011	Quotas 2011
Fine Gael	30.57	19.49	28.41	34.70	6.29	2.1
Labour	8.92	5.94	9.25	18.53	9.28	1.1
Fianna Fáil	42.62	48.57	44.28	28.01	−16.27	1.7
Sinn Féin	–	3.75	5.11	8.20	3.09	0.5
Green Party	6.58	8.96	8.37	2.56	−5.81	0.2
Others	11.32	13.39	4.57	8.00	3.43	0.5

2016 Candidates will include:

Simon Coveney (FG), Jerry Buttimer (FG), Ciarán Lynch (Lab), Michéal Martin (FF), Michael McGrath (FF), Donnchadh Ó Laoghaire (SF), Lorna Bogue (GP), Fiona Ryan (AAA–PBP), Jim O'Connell (AAA–PBP), Mick Finn (Ind), Elizabeth Hourihane (Ind), Diarmuid Ó Cadhla (Ind)

In Brief:

With five sitting TDs and a strong Sinn Féin contender challenging for four seats where there were once five this will be a key constituency to watch. Agriculture and Defence Minister Simon Coveney is secure but will be tasked with bringing back his running mate Jerry Buttimer, whose chances of re-election are hobbled not only by the reduction in seats, but also by the fact that the redraw sees his base in Bishopstown moved out of the constituency. Although he took the second seat in 2011 the high profile chair of the Banking Inquiry Ciaran Lynch, who is the outgoing Labour deputy, looks very vulnerable. The party lost all of its councillors in this area in the 2014 local elections. This is the only Cork constituency where Fianna Fáil won two seats in 2011. The party has two comfortable quotas even in the four-seater and are set to hold their two seats, although a high profile casualty for them against the national trend can never be ruled out.

Fine Gael:

In 2007 the party ran outgoing deputies Simon Coveney and Deirdre Clune with local councillor Jerry Buttimer. The party's vote improved significantly on 2002, by no less than 9 percentage points, and Deirdre Clune returned to Dáil Éireann with Simon Coveney. Buttimer was eliminated on the fourth count. With all three running again in 2011, Buttimer and Coveney each had a 3% increase in their personal vote share while Clune's fell slightly and she was eliminated after the 10th count. Clune has since been elected to the European Parliament. In the reduced constituency the party is only running the two sitting deputies.

Simon Coveney is based in Carrigaline and has been a member of Dáil Éireann since 1998. He has been Minister for Agriculture, Food and the Marine since 2011 and also assumed the position of Minister for Defence in May 2014. Simon Coveney won the October 1998 by-election following the death of his father Hugh Coveney, who had been a TD from 1981 to 1987 and again from 1992 to 1998. Hugh Coveney held Ministerial office from 1993 to 1997. Simon held the Dáil seat comfortably in 2002. In 2004 he was elected to the European Parliament for the Ireland South constituency, which included all of Munster except Clare. In that election Coveney polled 118,937 first preferences, a 24.56% share. He resigned from the European Parliament to contest again for the Dáil in 2007. He polled 5,863 (9.9%) in that year's Dáil elections. He improved on that again in 2011 with 9,447 (14.8%) first preferences and took the third seat.

Simon Coveney was a member of Cork County Council for the Carrigaline electoral area from 1999 to 2003. During his period in the European Parliament, he held the position of human rights coordinator for the European People's Party. He was the Fine Gael spokesperson on Communications, Energy and Natural Resources from 2007–2010. In June 2010, Coveney was among a number of party frontbenchers to state that they had no confidence in their party leader, Enda Kenny. Despite Kenny's victory in a subsequent confidence motion, Coveney was re-appointed to the Front Bench in July 2010 as spokesperson for Transport. He was Fine Gael's campaign Director for the Marriage Equality Referendum in May

2015. He previously played rugby for Garryowen, Cork Constitution and Cross Haven. In 1997–98 he led the Sail Chernobyl Project, which involved sailing 30,000 miles around the world for charity.

Jerry Buttimer has been a Dáil deputy since 2011. He is based in Bishopstown and has a constituency office at Glasheen Road in Cork. In April 2012 Jerry Buttimer came out as the first openly gay Fine Gael TD, saying, 'I am a TD who just happens to be gay – it is just one little composition of the story that is me and I will continue to be the politician I was yesterday'. He is founder and chair of Fine Gael LGBT group and was a prominent campaigner in the May 2015 Marriage Equality referendum.

Buttimer had an impressive but unsuccessful Dáil election attempt in 2007 when he polled 5,180 first preferences, which was 8.77% of the total, In 2007 he successfully contested the Seanad election on Labour panel and became Fine Gael's Seanad spokesperson on Community, Rural and Gaeltacht Affairs. He also took the time to write about his experiences during the 2007 Dáil Election in his book *Candidate*, which was published by Gill & MacMillan in November 2007. In 2011 he increased his vote to 7,128 (11.1%). Buttimer was a member of Cork City Council from 2004 to 2007 for the Cork South West Ward.

Buttimer's Bishopstown base has been moved to Cork North Central in the redraw of the constituencies since 2011. There was some speculation that he might transfer constituencies but he has chosen to stay in Cork South Central. He was formerly a secondary school teacher and Director of Adult Education at Ballincollig Community School. He is a former Youth and Development Officer of Cork County GAA Board. His brother John Buttimer is a member of Cork County Council for the Cork City South West ward and topped the poll there in the 2014 local elections with 1,750 first preferences.

Labour Party:

Ciarán Lynch has been a Dáil Deputy since 2007. He is chairman of the Oireachtas banking inquiry. This is his third Dáil election. In 2007 he polled 5,466 first preferences and took the fourth of the five seats. In 2011 the Labour Party decided to run two candidates in this constituency for the first time. Lynch increased his personal vote to 8,481 votes (13.2%) and he was elected on the 10th count after the elimination of his running mate, Paula Desmond, who took 3,388 first preference votes (5.3%). Lynch was a member of Cork City Council from 2004 to 2007 for the Cork South Central ward, polling 1,226 first preferences. He was formerly an adult literary officer with Cork Vocational Education Committee. In the outgoing Dáil he has been the Labour party spokesperson on Housing and Local Government. He is a brother-in-law of the Labour party's Cork North Central Deputy Kathleen Lynch. Kathleen was a successful local election candidate in this area and also ran unsuccessfully for three Dáil elections in this constituency for Democratic Left before transferring in 1997 to Cork North Central.

Fianna Fáil:

In 1997 and 2002 Fianna Fáil won three of the five seats in this constituency. In 2002 its three candidates, Micheál Martin, Batt O Keefe and John Dennehy, polled 48.6% combined and the party held its third seat by just six votes. In 2007 John Dennehy was again a candidate along with Micheál Martin, and the third candidate was newcomer Michael McGrath. The party's other incumbent, Batt O'Keeffe, had followed his Ballincollig political base into the newly redrawn Cork North West Constituency. In 2007 Fianna Fáil lost that third seat. Michael McGrath proved an impressive newcomer beating Dennehy by more than 4,000 first preferences on the first count. In 2011 Michéal Martin was barely over the quota and McGrath took a second seat for Fianna Fáil at the 12th count with Fine Gael surpluses.

Micheál Martin has been the leader of Fianna Fáil since 2011. He was first elected to Dáil Éireann in 1989 on his second attempt and has been returned in each election since. He was Minister for Foreign Affairs from May of 2008 to 2011, having been Enterprise, Trade and Employment Minister from 2004 to 2008. Minister for Health from 2000 to 2004 and Minister for Education from 1997 to January 2000. As Minister for Health and Children in 2004, he introduced a ban on tobacco smoking in all Irish workplaces. He was a member of Cork City Council from 1985 to 1997 and Mayor of Cork for the year 1992–93. His brother Seán has been a member of Cork City Council in the Cork South Central ward since 1997 though he only took the last seat narrowly in 2014, with 640 first preference votes (10.39%). His brother Padraig was a first time candidate for Cork County Council in the Carrigaline local electoral area and polled 1,194 (quota 3,359), failing to get elected. Micheál Martin polled 11,226 first preference votes in the 2007 general election, which was a drop of 3,516 or almost 7% on his 2002 total, and in 2011 his personal vote fell again to 10,715 (16.7%). He was formerly a secondary school teacher and is author of *Freedom to Choose: Cork and Party Politics in Ireland 1918–1932*, a book based on his MA Thesis, which was published in 2009.

Michael McGrath has been a member of Dáil Éireann since 2011 and is the party spokesperson on Finance. He was first elected to Passage West Town Council in 1999 at the age of 22. He was a member of Cork County Council from 2004 to 2007. He topped the poll in the Carrigaline electoral area on his first attempt in 2004 with 3,951 first preferences. He qualified as a chartered accountant with KPMG and was previously Head of Management Information Systems in University College Cork. He is a member of the Joint Oireachtas Committee on Finance, Public Expenditure and Reform and also a member of the Committee of Inquiry into the Banking Crisis. In the 2007 Dáil election McGrath polled 9,866 first preferences. In the 2011 Dáil election he polled 7,221. His brother Seamus McGrath has been a member of Cork County Council local electoral area since 2009. Seamus polled 3,956 first preferences for in the Carrigaline electoral area. In 2014 in the enlarged Ballincollig–Carrigaline electoral area Seamus again topped the poll and took the first seat with massive 4,700 votes (20.13%), which was 2.2 quotas.

Sinn Féin:

In 2002 Tom Hanlon, a Passage West town councillor, polled just 2,063 first preferences for Sinn Féin. The party's candidate in 2007 was Cork City Councillor Henry Cremin who improved its vote slightly, bringing it to 3,020. Cremins had also been a candidate in the October 1998 by-election, which followed the death of Hugh Coveney. In 2011 the party candidate was former Green party councilor Chris O'Leary, who had contested the May 2009 local elections as an independent. O'Leary joined Sinn Féin in July 2010. In the 2011 Dáil election he polled 5,250 (8.2%) first preferences and held on until the last count, when he was 1,836 votes behind McGrath for the final seat. O'Leary, who is currently the Lord Mayor of Cork, attempted to be the candidate on this occasion but tied with Donnchadh Ó Laoghaire at a convention to pick the party candidate. The party then held a second convention at which O'Leary lost out to O' Laoghaire.

Donnchadh Ó Laoghaire has been a member of Cork County Council since 2014. He previously stood as the Sinn Féin Candidate in the 2009 Local Elections in the Carrigaline electoral area when at 20 years of age he polled 1,502 first preference votes (6.39%) and narrowly missed out on the last seat. In 2014 he polled 2,567 first preferences in the enlarged Ballincollig–Carrigaline electoral area and took the second seat behind Fianna Fail's Seamus McGrath. Ó Laoghaire is a law graduate from University College Dublin. He currently works for two Sinn Féin Senators as a Political Advisor. He has previously been National Organiser of Ógra Sinn Féin, the party youth wing. He is a Scout Leader with the 5th Cork Lough Scouts and a prominent member of St Finbarrs GAA club.

Green Party:

In 2011 the Green Party candidate was once again Dan Boyle. Then a high profile senator, Boyle won a Dáil seat here in 2002. Although the party's vote fell by only 0.6% in the constituency in 2007 Boyle lost the seat to the Labour party. In 2011 the vote fell further and he polled 1,640 (2.6%).

Lorna Bogue is the Green party's new candidate for the 2016 election and lives and works in Cork. She is the national chair of the Young Greens/Óige Ghlas. Aged 23 she is originally from Limerick and has a degree in Irish Music and Dance. She has pledged that if she is elected she will be donating €25,000 of her TD's wage per annum to community projects in the constituency.

Anti-Austerity Alliance – People Before Profit:

Two candidates will run under this banner in the 2016 election.

Fiona Ryan was selected as the AAA candidate in this constituency after the original candidate, Rose Leadbetter, was forced to withdraw for personal reasons. This is her first time to run for election personally but the 26 year old previously worked on the team that saw the Anti-Austerity Alliance's Marion O'Sullivan become the first elected woman in the North West Ward of Cork Council. She intends to focus her campaign on the repealing of the 8th amendment, ending property and water charges, and rent reversals and rent controls.

Jim O'Connell is a member of the Socialist Workers Party and campaigns on behalf of Right2Water. In 2013 he and others were arrested but released without charge during property tax protests inside a bank.

Independents:

Mick Finn has been a member of Cork City Council since 2014. He has run twice as an independent in the local elections in Cork City South Central ward. In 2009 his 923 first preference votes (13.23% share) gave him the fourth seat at the fifth count, but in 2014 he polled 1,437 first preference votes (23.33%), topping the poll just ahead of Sinn Féin's Fiona Kerins and taking the first seat. He ran for Dáil Éireann for the first time in 2011 when he took 2,386 first preference votes (3.7%). On that occasion he was eliminated after the 7th count, having failed to attract transfers from other independents. In 2007 he was parliamentary secretary to the constituency's then Fianna Fáil TD, John Dennehy. He holds a BA degree from University College Cork and a Diploma in Journalism from Dublin Institute of Technology.

Elizabeth Hourihane was born and raised in Passage West and is the founder of the National Citizens Movement but runs on this occasion as an Independent, not as a Direct Democracy candidate. In 2014 she contested the Carrigaline–Ballincollig electoral area of Cork County Council and in 2015 she ran in the Carlow–Kilkenny by-election when she polled 215 first preference votes. Now a grandmother, she went back to education 'during the boom time' and ultimately obtained a BCL from University College Cork. She is currently taking a High Court case against Irish Water but is focusing her campaign on the need to build a better infrastructure before admitting large numbers of refugees. She also campaigns for the reintroduction of the dual mandate in order to ensure that national strategies, particularly in the areas of housing and disability, are properly implemented at local level.

Diarmuid Ó Cadhla is Secretary and PRO at An Chomhdháil Phobail/The People's Convention. He is a software engineer and specialist in business solutions and is owner of the website TheFuture.ie, He has been active in various political forums for many years. He ran here in the 2011 Dáil election taking 508 votes (0.8%). He has a diploma in Business Studies and Marketing from Cork Institute of Technology and later completed a BA in Computer Science and Irish at University College Cork.

Cork South West

Outgoing Deputies:

Jim Daly (FG), Noel Harrington (FG), Michael McCarthy (Lab) 2016 Candidates will include: Jim Daly (FG), Noel Harrington (FG), Margaret Murphy-O'Mahony (FF), Michael McCarthy (Lab), Rachel McCarthy (SF), Michael Collins (Ind), Alan Coleman (Ind)

	% Vote 1997	**% Vote 2002**	**% Vote 2007**	**% Vote 2011**	**Swing 2011**	**Quotas 2011**
Fine Gael	44.18	32.33	36.00	48.54	12.54	1.9
Labour	6.75	9.13	9.64	14.31	4.67	0.6
Fianna Fáil	39.05	39.48	42.57	23.63	–18.94	0.9
Sinn Féin	–	5.85	5.06	7.33	2.27	0.3
Green Party	3.5	–	6.73	1.67	–5.06	0.07
Others	6.52	13.20	–	4.52	4.52	0.2

In Brief:

This sprawling constituency is one of only a handful that currently have only government TDs. That will change in this election. The Labour seat looks most vulnerable and there is even an outside chance that both Fine Gael and Labour might lose a seat. In 2011 Fine Gael had two quotas, and Labour just over half a quota. On current polling the government parties are down more than a quota combined. The local elections were particularly bad for the Labour party in Cork generally and in this part of the county in particular. The strongest challenge will come from Schull based independent councillor Michael Collins who polled almost 3,500 votes in the 2014 local elections and who seems likely to win a seat. Fianna Fáil will also mount a strong challenge to regain a seat here with their new candidate Murphy O'Mahony. However, their efforts are hampered by the fact that Alan Colman, a prominent Fianna Fáil councillor, having failed to be selected at the convention for this election, is running as an independent. Sinn Féin's new candidate Councillor Rachel McCarthy is also one to watch. Although the party only got one third of a quota in 2011, she was poll topper in the Bandon–Kinsale area in the 2014 local elections and could cause an upset.

Fine Gael:

In 2011 both of Fine Gael's long serving deputies, Jim O'Keeffe and P. J. Sheehan, retired and the party ran three candidates in their efforts to hold onto the two seats, Jim Daly, Noel Harrington and Kevin Murphy. Both Daly and Harrington were successful. Murphy does not run this time.

Jim Daly was born and raised in Drinagh and is now based in Clonakilty. He has been a member of Dáil Éireann since 2011. Prior to that he was a member of Cork County Council for the Skibbereen local electoral area. He was first elected to the county council in 2004, polling 1,481 first preferences (quota 2,271) to come in seventh on the first count. In the 2009 local elections he topped the poll in the same area with 2,739 first preferences, which was 440 above the quota, and won the first of the seven seats. Daly also ran unsuccessfully in the 2007 Seanad election on the Labour Panel. In the 2011 general election he had 8,878 first preferences (19.4%), which saw him elected on the fifth count with almost 2,000 transfers to spare.

Daly studied Gaeilge and Philosophy at NUI Maynooth and then qualified as a primary teacher at Mary Immaculate College. He went on to be principal of Gaelscoil Dr. Ui Shúilleabháin in Skibbereen. He was formerly the proprietor of the Courthouse Bar in Rosscarbery. In 2012 his GP spotted an unusual pimple on his cheek when he appeared on Tonight with Vincent Browne and persuaded him to get it checked out. It was found to be cancerous and he had the necessary medical procedure to have it removed. He has used the experience to highlight the need to watch out for skin cancers.

Noel Harrington lives in Castletownbere and has a constituency office in Bantry. He has been a member of Dáil Éireann since 2011. Harrington polled 6,898 first preference votes (15.1%) in the 2011 Dáil election and was elected on the sixth count on the redistribution of Jim Daly's surplus. He chairs the Internal party Committee on Social Protection and is a member of the Joint Committee on Transport and Communications and the Joint Committee on Public Service, Oversight and Petitions. He lives more than 360km from Leinster House, the furthest of any TD. He plays darts for the local Castletownbere team when he has time.

Prior to being elected to Dáil Éireann Harrington had been a member of Cork County Council for the Bantry local electoral area since 1999 when he was successful on his first attempt. In that election his 16.05% share of the vote was enough for the third seat. His tally has dropped in subsequent elections, however, going from 1,550 in 1999 to 1,474 in 2004 and 1,440 in 2009. He was Mayor of County Cork for 2008/2009.

Labour Party:

Michael McCarthy is based in Dunmanway and has been a member of Dáil Éireann since 2011. He first contested for the Dáil in 2002 at the age of 25. In that election he polled 3,442 first preferences, which was credible but far from being enough to make a Dáil breakthrough. He was subsequently elected to Seanad Éireann on the Labour panel and again contested the Dáil election in 2007, when he improved his vote slightly by half a per cent to 4,095 first preference votes, a 9.64% share. In 2007 he was again elected to Seanad Éireann. The 2011 election was his third attempt at election to Dáil Éireann and he was finally successful, his 6,533 votes (14.3%) giving him the third and final seat. He is Chair of the Oireachtas Committee on the Environment, Culture and the Gaeltacht and was a member of the Constitutional Convention.

McCarthy was previously a process operator with Schering Plough pharmaceutical company based in Bandon. He was a member of Cork County Council from 1999 to 2004 for the Skibereen electoral area. His sister Phyllis ran in his stead in the 2004 local elections, when she polled 829 votes but did not win a seat. His sister Norma Thomson was the Labour party candidate in the West Cork electoral area in the 2014 local elections but polled only 749 first preferences, which was less than a quarter of a quota. Their cousin is the former senator Michael Calnan, who was based in Dunmanway and was Labour's Dáil candidate in the 1997 election.

Fianna Fáil:

In 2011 Fianna Fáil ran two candidates in this constituency, outgoing deputy Christy O'Sullivan, who had previously been a popular independent candidate and who topped the poll for the party in 2007 with 10,333 votes, and Denis O'Donovan who was TD for Cork South West from 2002 to 2007. In 2011 O'Donovan polled above O'Sullivan with 5,984 first preference votes (13.1%). O'Sullivan's 4,803 votes (10.5%) did not transfer solidly enough to bring his party colleague home. Neither of the two will contest the seat in 2016. O'Donovan, who is currently Leas–Cathaoirleach of the Seanad, was expected to run but withdrew his candidature in favour of Margaret Murphy-O'Mahoney, saying that he thought the party's chances would be better with a single candidate.

Margaret Murphy-O'Mahoney is a first time candidate and is based in Bandon. She has been a member of Cork County for the Bandon–Kinsale elected area since 2014. In 2014 she ran for Cork County Council for the first time. She came fourth on the first count in the Bandon–Kinsale electoral area with 2,057 votes

(12.89%) and took the fifth seat – the second for Fianna Fail in that area. She has twice been Mayor of Bandon having first been elected to Bandon Town Council in 2004. She was the first ever female Mayor of Bandon in 2004/2005 and held that office again in 2010/2011. She describes her upbringing as being in a 'strong Fianna Fáil house'. Married, with two children, she worked in the Post Office and in the area of special needs before becoming a full time public representative. She is also an active member of St. Vincent de Paul. Soon after she was chosen as the party's candidate she put up large election posters around the constituency, not realising that that this is illegal until the election has been called. She quickly removed them on being informed of her error.

Sinn Féin:

Unusually, the party ran two candidates in this constituency in 2002, Ann O'Leary and Cionnaith Ó Suilleabháin, who polled 899 and 1,308 respectively. Ó Suilleabháin was the party's only candidate in 2007 and the party first preference vote was down as a result, but only slightly from 5.86% to 5.06%. The Sinn Féin candidate in 2011 was Paul Hayes, a 33-year-old member of Clonakilty Town Council. Hayes increased the Sinn Féin vote to 3,346 (7.3%) in 2011.

Rachel McCarthy is Sinn Féin's new Dáil candidate in 2016. She is based in Bandon and has been a member of Cork County Council since 2014. In the 2014 local elections she topped the poll in the Bandon–Kinsale area with 2,344 votes (14.68%). She had also run in 2009 for both Bandon Town Council and Cork County Council, taking the sixth seat in the former with 192 votes (7.54%) but failing to take a seat on the latter on that occasion when her 979 votes were less than a third of a quota. The thirty-two year old mother of two young children has a degree in Social Work from University College Cork. She is currently Chairperson of the South West Health Committee and is also a member of the Housing and Economic Development Policy Committees in Cork County Council. She is also a member of the West Cork Local Community Development Committee.

Green Party:

The high profile environmental activist Quentin Gargan was the Green party candidate in 2007. He finished sixth on the first count with 2,860 first preference votes, a 6.73% share. In 2011 the party's candidate was Kevin McCaughey, a last minute substitute for the better known Jennifer Sleeman who withdrew when it was realised that she had never taken Irish citizenship. McCaughey polled 765 (1.7%).

Johnny O'Mahoney is the new Green party candidate on this occasion. He was a candidate in the 2014 local elections in Cork City South electoral area when he took 123 first preference votes (2%). He has been an active member of the Green Party for several years and has been involved in the Cork Environmental Forum. He is well known in Cork through his career as a bookseller and barman and he has set up various sports clubs, being a cyclist, sailor and open water swimmer. He describes himself as a campaigner for social justice, including a fairer social welfare system and is involved in groups working on improving security in rural areas and in the campaign to reopen the West Cork railway.

Independents:

Michael Collins is based in Lowertown Schull on the Mizen Peninsula. He has been a member of Cork County Council since 2014 when he topped the poll and took the first seat in the Cork West electoral area with 3,409 first preferences (12.5%) He has been Chairperson of Goleen & District Community Council, a member of the board of the West Cork Development Partnership, and Vice-chair of West Cork Rural Transport. He is a farmer.

Alan Coleman is a dairy farmer in Riverstick and Kinsale and has been a member of Cork County Council for the Bandon area since 1991. This is his first time to contest a Dáil election. Coleman was a lifelong Fianna Fáil member and had originally been expected to contest again for the party's nomination at the convention for this election. However he withdrew his name before voting took place, saying that he had become disillusioned with the party, that there was no room for dissent, and he felt that delegates were being directed to vote for another candidate. He ruled out running for any other party but later declared he would stand in this Dáil election as an independent.

Coleman has a long track record in local politics in Bandon. He first ran in 1991 when got 916 votes (4.79%) and took the seventh seat on Cork County Council in that electoral area. In 1999 that increased to 1,758 (16.15%) for the third seat and he took the third seat again with a slightly increased vote of 2,216 (16.41%) in 2004. His votes increased significantly in the 2009 local elections when he polled 3,370 votes (25.65%). In 2014 he got 2,288 (14.33%) although Sinn Féin's Rachel McCarthy topped the poll on that occasion and Coleman had to settle for the second seat. Coleman was Mayor of County Cork in June 2015 and Fianna Fáil leader on the council when he made the decision to leave in June 2015. He was an unsuccessful candidate for Seanad Éireann on the Agricultural Panel in 2007 and 2011.

DONEGAL

Outgoing Donegal North–East Deputies:

Joe McHugh (FG), Charlie McConalogue (FF), Pádraig Mac Lochlainn (SF)

Outgoing Donegal South–West Deputies

Dinny McGinley (FG), Pearse Doherty (SF), Thomas Pringle (Ind)

In July 2014 Dinny McGinley announced that he would not contest this election.

The Constituency:

This is a new five-seater brought about by the amalgamation of the two three seat constituencies of Donegal North–East and Donegal South–West and the transfer of some South Donegal areas to the new Sligo Leitrim Constituency. Donegal had been two three seat constituencies since 1981. The new constituency comprises the county of Donegal except for an area in the south of the county including Bundoran, Ballyshannon and Ballintra which are now in the Sligo–Leitrim constituency. This area had a population in the last census of 8,779 and consists of Ballintra, Ballyshannon Rural, Bundoran Rural, Carrickboy, Cavangarden, Cliff, in the former Rural District of Ballyshannon, Ballintra in the former Rural District of Donegal and the towns of Ballyshannon and Bundoran.

2016 Candidates will include:

Joe McHugh (FG), Pat 'The Cope' Gallagher (FF), Charlie McConalogue (FF), Gary Doherty (SF), Pearse Doherty (SF), Pádraig Mac Lochlainn (SF), Paula Flanagan (GP), Thomas Pringle (Ind), Peter Casey (Ind), Niamh Kennedy (Ind), Tim Jackson (Ind), Dessie Shiels (Ind)

Donegal South-West

	% Vote 1997	% Vote 2002	% Vote 2007	% Vote 2011	Swing 2011	Quotas 2011
Fine Gael	22.97	25.42	23.00	19.85	–3.15	0.8
Labour	4.20	3.03	2.79	5.11	2.32	0.2
Fianna Fáil	38.04	42.09	50.53	22.52	–28.01	0.9
Sinn Féin	–	10.75	21.23	32.97	11.74	1.3
Green Party	4.2	–	1.48	1.22	1.22	0.05
Others	30.58	18.72	0.97	18.33	17.36	0.7

Donegal North-East

	% Vote 1997	% Vote 2002	% Vote 2007	% Vote 2011	Swing 2011	Quotas 2011
Fine Gael	18.87	21.01	22.60	31.61	9.01	1.3
Labour	5.48	2.81	1.82	10.79	8.97	0.4
Fianna Fáil	41.81	49.40	50.26	17.44	–32.82	0.7
Sinn Féin	8.11	9.93	17.47	24.47	7.00	1.0
Green Party	–	–	1.35	0.54	–0.81	0.02
Ind FF	21.06	16.85	–	–	–	–
Others	4.66	–	6.50	15.15	8.65	0.6

In Brief:

Notwithstanding the reduction of the number of seats in the county from six to five, Sinn Féin will be competing for an extra seat on top of the two it already holds in the county. Killybegs based independent Thomas Pringle appears vulnerable from this Sinn Féin challenge and also from the newcomer, independent Niamh Kennedy, who is also from Killybegs. Fianna Fáil is running a political big beast in the form of Pat 'The Cope' Gallagher along with its sitting deputy Charlie McConalogue. The party won 11 of the 37 seats in the 2014 local elections in Donegal and has high hopes of winning a second seat Dáil seat. Gallagher is likely to win a seat but it is more likely to be at McConalogue's expense than at that of one of the other sitting deputies. Dinny McGinley's retirement probably means Fine Gael will loose one of its two seats. In mid 2015 'Dragon' businessman Peter Casey announced he would contest in this constituency although he seems to have been quiet since. It looks like two Sinn Féin, one Fianna Fáil and one Fine Gael seat for sure and then Fianna Fáil, Sinn Féin, and two independents fighting it out for the fifth seat.

Fine Gael:

Dinny McGinley held a seat in Donegal South–West for 33 years. In the 2011 election he polled 8,589 first preferences. McGinley's absence and the reduction in seat numbers makes Fine Gael's job in holding their seat in that part of the county very difficult.

Joe McHugh is based in Carrigart in the Letterkenny end of the constituency and has been a Dáil deputy for the Donegal North–East constituency since 2007. He was appointed Minister of State with responsibility for Gaeltacht Affairs and Natural Resources at the Departments of Arts, Heritage and the Gaeltacht and Communications, Energy and Natural Resources. He was appointed to this position in July 2014. He responded to criticism of his poor skills in the Irish language on his appointment by sucessfully undertaking a refresher course at Oideas Gael in Glencolmcille.

This is McHugh's third Dáil election. In 2007 he was the party's sole candidate in Donegal North–East. He polled 8,711 first preferences (22.6%) and took the third seat ahead of Sinn Féin's Pearse Doherty, although the latter had a higher first preference vote. In the 2011 general election McHugh ran with a running mate, Councillor John Ryan from Burnfoot, who was based at the south end of the Inishowen peninsula. On that occasion McHugh polled 7,330 first preferences (19.3%) and his share of the transfers of Ryan's 4,657 votes saw McHugh take the second seat very comfortably. McHugh was a member of Seanad Éireann on the Administrative panel from 2002 to 2007 and a member of Donegal County Council for the Milford electoral area from 1999 to 2004. He previously worked as a geography and maths teacher and as a community development worker. He is married to the former Fine Gael deputy for Laois–Offaly Olwyn Enright, who did not contest the 2011 election for family reasons.

Fianna Fáil:

In 2007 the party's first preference vote share in both the Donegal constituencies was in excess of 50% and they won four of the six seats in the county. In 2011 the party's vote collapsed by 28 percentage points in Donegal South–West and 32 percentage points in Donegal South–West and newcomer Charlie McConalogue won their only seat in the county. This time he is joined on the party ticket by veteran politician Pat 'The Cope' Gallagher.

Pat 'The Cope' Gallagher, is from Burtonport and based in Dungloe. He was first elected to Dáil Éireann for the Donegal South–West Constituency at the 1981 general election and he retained the seat in every election until 1997. In 1995 he had been elected to the European Parliament for the Connacht–Ulster constituency. He did not contest the 1997 Dáil election. In 2002, however, he returned to domestic politics and regained his Dáil seat, thereby resigning his European parliament seat. Between 2002 and 2007 the party had lost the Donegal South–West Dáil seat to the TV deflector campaigner Tom Gildea. In 2007 Gallagher and the party's other incumbent Mary Coughlan retained the two seats. In 2009 Gallagher stood successfully again in the European elections for the North–West constituency. He lost his seat in the European Parliament in the 2014 elections and has now been selected by the party to contest this Dáil election.

While an MEP he continued to receive pension payments of €70,562 a year from his time as a TD and junior minister and he donated these to charitable causes. Pat Gallagher's nickname is inherited from his grandfather Paddy 'The Cope' Gallagher who founded Templecrone Co-operative in Dungloe in 1906. The business is still known as The Cope, and has several outlets in the North–West.

Charlie McConalogue was elected in Donegal North–East in the 2011 general election, when he polled 6,613 first preference votes there, his 17.4% of the vote giving him the third and final seat behind Mac Lochlainn of Sinn Féin and Fine Gael's Joe McHugh. This makes him the only sitting Fianna Fáil TD running in the new Donegal constituency and his chances will depend on local perceptions of how he has performed as a TD since he has no local track record as a county councillor. After taking a degree in economics, politics and history from UCD, during which time he was the students' union education officer, he became a political organizer at Fianna Fáil's party headquarters until the death of his father took him home to Donegal to manage the family farm. In Dáil Éireann he was the Fianna Fáil spokesperson on Children from April 2011 to July 2012, when he was appointed spokesperson on Education and Skills, a position he still holds.

Labour Party:

As of going to print the Labour Party had not announced a candidate for this constituency. In 2011 Frank McBrearty, then a Labour party candidate polled 2,209 votes in Donegal South–West. He was eliminated at the same time as the independent Seamus McCahill making it difficult to determine the breakdown of McBrearty's Labour transfers but they seem to have gone slightly more to independents and Fine Gael than to Fianna Fáil. In 2011 Jimmy Harte was the Labour candidate in Donegal North–East, where he polled 4,090 first preferences and survived to the last count, although he was 1,757 votes behind Charlie McConalogue (FF) for the last seat.

Sinn Féin:

In 2016 Sinn Féin will run three candidates in the new five-seater Donegal constituency. Deputies MacLochlainn and Doherty are joined by Councillor Gary Doherty. With the two deputies based in Buncrana and Gweedore respectively the party has balanced the ticket by selecting a candidate from the Finn Valley.

Gary Doherty has been a member of Donegal County Council for the Stranorlar electoral area since 2014. In that local election he polled 1,967 votes which was 1.29 quotas, and he took the first seat. Full time politics is a significant career change for Doherty who was previously best known as the bass player in Donegal band 'The Heads of State' although he does hold a degree in politics. He was selected as an additional candidate for this constituency in November 2015.

Pearse Doherty has been a member of Dáil Éireann for the Donegal South–West constituency since 2010. He was born in Glasgow, lived most of his life in Gweedore and has a constituency office in Derrybeg. He first ran for the Dáil in 2002, as part of a two man ticket with Ballybofey-based Tom Dignam. They polled 1,133 and 2,696 first preference votes respectively. Combined that gave them just under 11% of the first preference votes which was never enough to win a seat. In the 2004 European Parliament elections Doherty was the party's candidate in the Ireland North West Constituency, as a result of which he gained considerable local and national profile and polled 65,321 first preferences. In 2007 he was the party's only candidate in Donegal South–West for the Dáil election and while he dramatically increased the party's vote, getting 8,462 first preferences, he was more than a thousand votes behind Dinny McGinley (FG) for the last seat.

In 2010 Doherty brought a successful High Court action to force the then government to hold the by-election necessitated by Pat 'The Cope' Gallagher's return to the European Parliament in 2009. Doherty went on to top the poll in that by-election with 13,719 (quota 17,213) first preferences and took the seat comfortably on the fourth count. On his entry to Dáil Éireann he became the party's spokesperson on Finance. He has held that front bench portfolio ever since. In the 2011 general election he topped the poll by a huge margin, receiving 14,262 first preferences, which was a third of all votes cast. He was a member of Seanad Éireann from 2007 to December 2010 and a member of Donegal County Council for the Gweedore electoral area from 2004 to 2007. He holds a Certificate in Civil Engineering from Dublin Institute of Technology.

Padraig MacLochlann is based in Buncrana and has been a Dáil Deputy for the Donegal North–East constituency since 2011. He is the party's Dáil spokesperson on Justice, Equality and Defence and is Chairperson of the Oireachtas Public Services Oversight and Petitions Committee. He was the party's sole Dáil candidate in Donegal North–East in the 2002, 2007 and 2011 elections. In 2002 he polled 3,611 first preferences (9.9%), increasing the party vote by 2%. In 2007 he almost doubled it to 6,733 first preferences, a 17.47% share of the total, narrowly losing out to Niall Blaney, then of Independent Fianna Fáil, for the final seat. In the 2011 Dáil election he topped the poll in Donegal North–East with 9,278 first preferences (24.5%), which was just 202 short of the quota, and he took the first seat.

MacLochlann is a former member of Buncrana town council and of Donegal County Council, to which he was elected for Inishowen electoral area in 2004 and 2009. He is a former member of the national executive of the Irish National Organisation for the Unemployed. He is the only TD from a Traveller background and holds a diploma in social science.

Green Party:

The Green organisation in Donegal has always been separate from the main party, although affiliated to it. In November 2009 it broke away from the Green Party to form a separate organisation, Donegal Greens. The party's eventual candidate in Donegal North–East for the 2011 election was Hubert Murphy, who gained only 206 votes. The Donegal Greens decided not to run a candidate in Donegal South–West in 2011 and the national party ran John Duffy who received only 527 votes. There is a new candidate again in 2016.

Paula Flanagan has lived in Donegal since 2001. She has an MSc in Sustainable Development, and has worked within the community and voluntary sector for over 20 years, promoting community development through education and training. She has also worked in EU Peace Projects representing young people, women, refugees and the unemployed. She will focus her campaign on reforming local government to improve the roll out of national policy, on the strengthening of the community and voluntary sector, and on developing the green economy in Donegal, with an emphasis on renewable energy, green building and eco-tourism.

Independents:

Thomas Pringle is based in Killybegs and has been a Dáil Deputy for the Donegal South–West Constituency since 2011. He first stood for the Dáil in 2002 as an independent candidate and polled just 2,630 first preferences. In January 2004 he joined Sinn Féin and stood for that party in the Donegal County Council elections in May 2004, topping the poll in the Donegal local electoral area. He did not contest the 2007 Dáil election. In November 2007 he resigned from Sinn Féin. In 2009 he retained his seat on Donegal County Council as an independent, polling 1,501 first preferences (quota 2,498) and taking the second of the 5 seats. In the 2010 Dáil by-election he contested as an independent and polled 3,438, coming in fourth of the six candidates just above the Labour party's Frank McBrearty. When he was eliminated on the third count he had 3,763 first preferences, 1,276 of which were non transferable. Of the remainder more than two thirds transferred to Pearse Doherty. In 2011 Pringle polled 5,845 first preference votes (13.5%) and then attracted sufficient transfers from Pearse Doherty's large surplus to keep him ahead of both Fianna Fáil candidates for the rest of the count, so that he took the third seat. He was once an employee of Donegal County council and studied at Letterkenny Institute of Technology.

Peter Casey is a first time candidate. He will be familiar to many in Donegal and elsewhere as one of the 'Dragons' in the RTÉ television's version of *Dragons Den*. Based partly in Derry and partly in Atlanta, Georgia, he is the Executive chairman of his international recruiting organisation Claddagh Resources. The European headquarters of his business is in Buncrana. In 2014 he published a book about India's giant Tata organisation. At the time of going to press it is uncertain if he still intends to stand.

Tim Jackson from Stranorlar is 26. Together with a few friends in July 2015 he launched a Clean Up Politics campaign that has called on General Election candidates to promise to cut their salaries in half, and not claim unaccountable expenses. He has also called for an end to the public funding of political parties and a reduction in political pensions. In October 2015 he took to the road with a mobile billboard making the same demands. He previously founded the 'Homes From Donegal' charity to build homes in Africa for refugees displaced by war. In December 2015 he announced his own candidacy.

Niamh (McGilloway) Kennedy is based in Killybegs and has been a member of Donegal County Council since 2014. She topped the poll in the Donegal Electoral area in the 2014 local elections polling 1,738 votes, which was just 246 votes short of the quota, and she took the first seat. She had been an elected member of the Killybegs Community Council for many years and chair of the sponsoring group for the community employment schemes in the area. She is running under the Independent Alliance banner in this election. She runs Marine Fleet Electronics Ltd together with her husband and was previously employed in the fishing industry for over 21 years as a health and safety and administration manager.

Dessie Shiels is an independent councillor based in Letterkenny, where he took the ninth of the ten council seats for that electoral area in 2014 with 955 first preference votes (5.5%). He says that as the economic and administrative hub of the county Letterkenny needs a strong TD without a party bias. A solicitor, he emphasises the need to maintain and develop facilities at both Letterkenny Hospital and Letterkenny Institute of Technology and suggests that the latter should be developed into a university to better serve the development of business and industry in the county. He has a young family and is an active participant in several sports, including taking part in the Donegal marathon in October 2015.

Dublin Bay North

Outgoing Dublin North–Central Deputies:
Richard Bruton (FG), Aodhán Ó Ríordáin (Lab) Finian McGrath (Ind)

Outgoing Dublin North–East Deputies:
Terence Flanagan (Ren), Tommy Broughan (Lab), Seán Kenny (Lab)

Terence Flanagan was elected for Fine Gael in 2011 but will contest this election as a candidate for Renua Ireland.

Tommy Broughan was elected for Labour in 2011 but will contest this election as an independent.

Sean Kenny (Lab) has announced that he will not contest this election.

The Constituency:
This new five-seater is an amalgamation of the previous constituencies of Dublin North–Central and Dublin North–East with the exception of an area around Portmarnock and north of the M50.

Dublin North–Central

	% Vote 1997	% Vote 2002	% Vote 2007	% Vote 2011	Swing 2011	Quotas 2011
Fine Gael	26.03	17.00	25.55	37.77	12.22	1.5
Labour	9.37	10.49	7.27	22.52	15.25	0.9
Fianna Fáil	46.44	50.05	44.02	12.94	–31.08	0.5
Sinn Féin	–	5.74	3.78	5.52	1.74	0.2
Green Party	3.82	5.68	5.19	1.29	–3.90	0.05
Others	11.05	11.03	14.19	19.96	5.77	0.8

Dublin North–East

	% Vote 1997	% Vote 2002	% Vote 2007	% Vote 2011	Swing 2011	Quotas 2011
Fine Gael	18.90	15.36	22.94	29.47	6.53	1.2
Labour	17.25	16.23	15.16	34.35	19.19	1.4
Fianna Fáil	40.61	40.12	39.69	11.46	–28.23	0.5
Sinn Féin	5.93	10.24	13.34	12.03	–1.31	0.5
Green Party	3.57	5.65	6.73	1.89	–4.84	0.08
Others	13.0	12.4	2.14	10.80	8.66	0.4

2016 Candidates will include:

Richard Bruton (FG), Naoise Ó Muirí (FG), Stephanie Regan (FG), Aodhán Ó Ríordáin (Lab), Deirdre Heney (FF), Seán Haughey (FF), Micheál MacDonncha (SF), Denise Mitchell (SF), Donna Cooney (GP), David Healy (GP), John Lyons (AAA–PBP), Michael O'Brien (AAA–PBP), Terence Flanagan (Ren), Cian O'Callaghan (Soc. Dem.), Tom Darcy (DDI), Tommy Broughan (Ind), Paul Clarke (Ind), Jimmy Guerin (Ind), Finian McGrath (Ind), Averil Power (Ind)

In Brief:

This newly carved sprawling constituency is over-populated with incumbents and indeed with candidates generally. The new five-seater replaces the two previous three seat constituencies of Dublin North–Central and Dublin North–East. Labour did extraordinarily well in both of these three seat constituencies in 2012. They got more than a third of the vote in Dublin North–East, which was the only constituency where they polled higher than Fine Gael. Between the two Labour won three of the six seats. One of those three TDs elected in 2011 for Labour, Tommy Broughan, has since gone independent, and another, Sean Kenny is retiring. This leaves Minister of State Aodhán Ó Ríordáin as the party's only candidate, and while he will struggle to retain even that one seat he should manage to hang on. The independent Finian McGrath, who this time is part of the Independent Alliance, is also likely to hold his seat. Fine Gael's Richard Bruton should also hold on. After that anything could happen. Sinn Féin are running one candidate in Kilbarrack and another in Coolock and one of them could win a seat. Fianna Fáil is running two candidates, Sean Haughey and Deirdre Heney, both in the Clontarf end, while the former Fianna Fáil Senator Averil Power, now running as an independent, is also in contention.

Fine Gael:

It was something of a surprise when the constituency convention, which had been told to select one male and one female candidate, chose local councillor Naoise Ó Muirí rather than Minister for Jobs, Enterprise and Innovation Richard Bruton as the male candidate. Bruton's name was immediately added to the ticket by the party's national executive. It seemed that local party members believed that a three candidate strategy would give the best chance in the constituency and felt that if not selected Bruton was more likely to be added than Ó Muirí.

Richard Bruton has been the Minister for Jobs, Enterprise and Innovation since 2011 and has been a member of Dáil Éireann for the Dublin North–Central constituency since 1982. He lives in Griffith Avenue in Drumcondra. His performances have been strong in all recent Dáil elections. He finished second in Dublin North–Central in 2002, polling 5,159 in the then four-seater, for a 12.88% share. He topped the poll in 2007 with his 9,303 first preferences above the quota of 9,105 and a 25.55% share of the vote. In the 2011 general election he again took a quarter of the first preference votes, his 9,685 votes being only 9 short of a quota and again he took the first seat.

Bruton has served in various ministerial offices. He was a Minister of State at the Department of Industry and Commerce from 1986 to 1987. He was Minister for Enterprise and Employment in the 'Rainbow' Fine Gael–Labour government from 1994 to 1997 and party spokesperson on Finance and Deputy Leader of Fine Gael from 2002 to 2010. He lost both of these positions when he challenged Enda Kenny's leadership in July 2010. In the subsequent reshuffle he was reappointed to the front bench as party spokesperson on Enterprise, Jobs and Economic Planning, and he was again appointed a Minister when the Fine Gael/Labour coalition was formed in March 2011. He was briefly a Senator in 1981–1982. He was a member of Dublin City Council 1991–1994 and a member of Meath County Council from 1979–1981. Before entering politics he was a research economist and has worked for the Economic and Social Research Institute, tobacco company P.J. Carroll and Cement Roadstone Holdings. He is the brother of former Taoiseach John Bruton.

Naoise Ó Muirí has been a member of Dublin City Council since 2004. This is his second Dáil election. As a candidate with Richard Bruton in Dublin North–Central in 2011 he polled 4,959 first preferences (12.8%), and was only eliminated on the 7th and final count. He has been elected for the Clontarf electoral area at every election since 2004, when he polled 2,042 votes (9.86%) and took the last seat. In 2009 he also took the last seat even though his vote had increased to 2,677 (13.01%). He was Lord Mayor of Dublin in 2012. In the 2014 local elections he polled 1,943 first preferences and took the third of the six seats in the Clontarf electoral area. Ó Muirí is a fluent Irish speaker. He is a qualified engineer, is Managing Director at Zing Technology, and previously worked at technology companies Phoenix and Accenture.

Stephanie Regan lives in Raheny and is a first time Dáil candidate. She was an unsuccessful candidate in the 2014 local elections in the Beaumont–Donaghmede local electoral area where she polled 688 first preferences. She is a psychotherapist and has focused on issues such as the raising of the Dollymount sea wall and the dumping of dredged material from the Liffey in environmentally vulnerable areas of Dublin Bay. A somewhat acerbic exchange with Finian McGrath TD, after he referred to her in a radio interview as 'Little Miss Twitter', has also increased her profile. She is a sister of former Fine Gael Senator Eugene Regan, who was a candidate in Dun Laoghaire for the 2007 Dáil election.

Labour Party:

In 2011 Labour won three seats in this part of the city. Two of those seats were won in Dublin North–East, one by Tommy Broughan, who has since left the party and is contesting this election as an independent, and one by Sean Kenny, who is retiring at this election. The other seat was won in Dublin North–Central by Aodhán Ó Ríordáin who is the party's sole candidate in this new amalgamated five seat constituency.

Aodhán Ó Ríordáin has been a member of Dáil Éireann since 2011. Since 2014 he has been Minister of State at the Department of Justice and Equality and the Department of Arts, Heritage and the Gaeltacht with responsibility for New Communities, Culture and Equality. In April 2015 the post of Minister of State at the Department of Health, with responsibility for the National Drugs Strategy, was added to his existing ministerial duties.

He was a member of Dublin City Council from 2004 to 2011 In the 2004 local elections he stood in the North Inner City Area, polled 1,412 first preferences, and took the third of the five seats. In the 2009 local elections he transferred to the Clontarf ward where he polled 3,387 first preferences, just 44 short of the quota, and took the second of the five seats. He took a 16.45% share of the vote in that election. Prominent supporter Johnny Giles joined Éamon Dunphy at a constituency fundraiser for Cllr. O'Riordáin in December of 2010. In the 2011 general election Ó Ríordáin's 8,731 first preference votes were 0.89 of a quota and easily gave him the second seat.

Until his election to Dáil Éireann he was principal of St. Laurence O'Toole's Girls' Primary School in Sheriff Street where his experiences informed the 'Right to Read' campaign he initiated when Deputy Lord Mayor of Dublin in 2006. In 2011 in Dáil Éireann he became Vice Chair of the Committee on Education and Social Protection and a member of both the Finance, Public Expenditure and Reform Committee and the Good Friday Agreement Implementation Committee.

Fianna Fáil:

It had been expected that Senator Averil Power, who was the party's candidate in Dublin North–East in 2011, would be, or be among, the party's candidates in this constituency for the 2016 election. However, she resigned from the party in the days after the Marriage Referendum in May 2015, accusing the party of lack of commitment to the Yes campaign. She is running as an independent in the 2016 election. At a subsequent convention the party national executive issued a directive that only one candidate should be chosen and Clontarf councillor Deirdre Heney was selected. The former deputy Sean Haughey was then added to the ticket by the national executive.

Sean Haughey was a member of Dáil Éireann for Dublin North–Central from 1992 to 2011. His votes in the 1992, 1997, 2002 and 2007 Dáil elections were 8,202 (17.88%), 7,670 (17.77%), 7,614 (19.01%) and 9,026 (24.79%) respectively. In the 2011 Dáil election his vote fell to 5,017 (12.94%) and he was eliminated at the 6th count. He is currently a member of Dublin City Council for the Clontarf electoral area. In the 2014 local elections he polled 2,440 votes and took the second of the six seats.

Sean Haughey was Minister of State at the Department of Education and Skills and the Department of Enterprise, Trade and Employment in the 2007–11 Fianna Fáil government. He was previously, from December 2006, a Minister of State at the Department of Education and Science with special responsibility for Adult Education, Youth Affairs and Learning Disadvantage. He was a member of Dublin City Council from 1985 to 2004, in the latter period for the Artane local electoral area. He was a Dáil candidate in neighbouring Dublin North–East in the 1987 and 1989 elections. He was Lord Mayor of Dublin from 1989 to 1992. His father, the late Charles J Haughey who was Taoiseach and leader of Fianna Fáil, was a TD for Dublin North–Central until 1992. Sean Haughey is also the grandson of former Taoiseach Sean Lemass and his uncle Noel Lemass Jnr, and aunt Eileen Lemass, were also TDs

Deirdre Heney has been a member of Dublin City Council since 1999. She first took a seat on Dublin City Council for the Ballymun/Whitehall area in 1999 with 1,018 votes giving her the second seat. She ran for Dáil Éireann in 2002 alongside Haughey and then sitting TD Ivan Callelly, in the Dublin North–Central constituency polling 5,533 (13.82%) but failing to take a seat. In the 2004 local elections she moved to the Clontarf area and has represented it ever since with votes of 4,487, 2,728 and 2,175 in 2004, 2009 and

2014 respectively. She was called to the Bar in 2008 and works as a barrister. She worked previously for Aer Lingus and Aer Rianta before moving into political activism. She has been parliamentary assistant to Noel Ahern TD who was then a deputy for Dublin North West and has been a researcher and adviser to the Fianna Fáil front bench. She is a former Deputy Lord Mayor of Dublin.

Sinn Féin:

Sinn Féin will field two first time Dáil candidates in this new constituency. While the party currently has no TD in either Dublin North–Central or Dublin North–East it won just over 12 per cent in both constituencies in 2011. More importantly, the party did very well in the 2014 local elections in this part of the city. It won three of the nine seats in the Beaumont–Donaghmede electoral area and also won one of the six seats in the Clontarf local electoral area.

Mícheál Mac Donncha is based in Kilbarrack and has been a member of Dublin City Council since 2011. He was co-opted to the council in May that year to replace Killian Forde, who had defected to the Labour Party. In the 2014 local elections he held the seat comfortably. Mac Donncha polled 2,245 first preferences (10.29%) in the Beaumont–Donagmede electoral area which was just over the quota. He has been a prominent figure in Sinn Féin since he became editor of An Poblacht in 1990, a post he held until he became political advisor to Caoimhghín Ó Caoláin TD in 1997. He has been manager of the Sinn Féin group in the Dáil since 2002 and he was Cathaoirleach of the Dublin City Council Finance Committee from 2011 to 2014. In September 2015 he accused the organisers of Irish rugby of being 'West Brits' because Ireland's Call rather than Amhrán na bhFiann was played during the rugby world cup.

Denise Mitchell is a native of Coolock and has been a member of Dublin City Council since 2014. She stood for Dublin City Council in the Artane–Whitehall area in 2009 when her 931 votes saw her eliminated on the third count. In 2014 in Beaumont–Donaghmede she polled 1,982 first preferences (9.08%), which gave her the third of three Sinn Féin seats in that electoral area. She is a former shop steward. She also worked previously on campaigns for local councillor and regular Sinn Féin Dáil candidate Larry O'Toole over several elections.

Green Party:

Donna Cooney and David Healy will be the two Green Party candidates in this constituency. In 2011 Cooney was the candidate in Dublin North–Central and Healy the candidate in Dublin North–East.

Donna Cooney was previously membership secretary for Bronwen Maher who was a regular party candidate in Dublin North–Central in local and national elections between 1991 and 2009. Maher failed to hold her Dublin City Council seat as an independent in 2009 and subsequently moved to the Labour Party. Cooney was co-opted to the former Dublin Corporation in 1996 on the resignation of Siabh O'Neill. She first ran for the Dáil in 1997 when she polled 1,332 first preferences (3.57%). In 2011 she took only 501 votes in Dublin North–Central (1.29%). She campaigned unsuccessfully for Dublin Corporation, and its successor Dublin City Council, first in Donaghmede in 1999 (963 votes, 7.5%) and 2004 (1,127 votes, 7.51%) and then in Clontarf in 2009 (616 votes, 2.99%) and 2014 (943 votes, 4.94%). The mother of four is a resident of Clontarf and along with her political work has been a self-employed artist, a games designer, and a teacher. She is the grand niece of Elizabeth O'Farrell, the nurse who delivered the surrender note in the Easter Rising.

David Healy has been a member of Fingal County Council since 2014. In that election he polled 1,206 (6.78%) first preferences in the Howth–Malahide local electoral area to take the seventh of the eight seats. He was previously a member of the council for the Howth electoral area from 1991 to 1999. He first ran for Dáil Éireann in Dublin North–East in 1992 when he polled 795 votes (1.99%). He ran again in 2002, more than doubling that vote to 1,656 (5.65%), and he increased it again in 2007 to 2,349 (6.73%). In the 2011 Dáil elections he polled just 792 votes (1.89%). He was policy advisor to Environment Minister John Gormley in the 2007–2011 coalition government. He is a member of the Planning and Strategic Infrastructure SPC of Fingal County Council. He is fluent in Irish and Esperanto and is currently policy and advocacy officer with Oxfam Ireland.

Anti-Austerity Alliance–People Before Profit:

Michael O'Brien is a Socialist Party activist and has been a member of Dublin City Council for the Beaumont–Donaghmede area since 2014. In the 2014 local elections, O'Brien represented the Anti-Austerity Alliance at the launch of a transfer pact between five left wing political groupings. In those elections his 906 votes (4.15%) gave him the seventh seat in that electoral area. In August 2014, he was one of those arrested while participating in a protest against the Greyhound waste collection company. He has been a Socialist Party and trade union activist for 23 years.

John Lyons is based in Whitehall and is a Socialist Workers Party activist. He has been a councillor for Beaumont–Donaghmede since 2014. In the 2014 local elections he polled 2,313 (10.6%) first preferences which was 131 over the quota and took the third seat. In the 2011 general election he polled 1,424 first preferences (3.67%). In September 2014 he was arrested during a water meter installation protest.

Renua Ireland:

Terence Flanagan is based on the Old Malahide Road and has been a member of Dáil Éireann since 2007. He was expelled from Fine Gael in 2013 and later joined Renua Ireland when the party was founded in July 2015. As a member of Fine Gael, Flanagan was co-opted to replace Richard Bruton on Dublin City Council for the Artane ward in 2003. In 2004's local elections he took the second seat in the area, with 2,594 votes giving him an 18.53% share of the vote. He was added to the Dáil election ticket in Dublin North–East in late 2006 and in the election in May 2007 the party vote was up 7.6% on that obtained in 2002, Flanagan came in 954 votes ahead of running mate Brody Sweeney and took the second of the three seats with 4,483 first preferences (a 12.83% share). In 2011 he was the only Fine Gael candidate in Dublin North–East and he topped the poll with 12,332 first preference votes (29.47%) which was just over the quota.

In July 2014 he was one of six Fine Gael parliamentarians who were expelled from the party after voting against the Protection of Life During Pregnancy Bill 2013. The group subsequently formed the Reform Alliance in September 2013, and in March 2015 Flanagan was among those from this group who formed Renua. On the day of the launch Flanagan made headlines when he was interviewed by RTÉ's Drivetime radio show without preparation and was unable to answer questions about the party's policies. A party spokesperson later explained the bad interview as a 'brain freeze' brought on by the physical and medical exhaustion arising from the effort involved in launching the party. Flanagan is a graduate of Dublin Business School and he previously worked in the banking industry as an accountant.

Social Democrats:
Cian O'Callaghan has been a member of Fingal County Council since 2009. He was first elected to the council as a Labour party candidate in the Howth–Malahide area in 2009, when he polled 2,256 first preference votes (10.14%). He went on to become leader of the Labour party group on the council. He left the Labour Party in 2013, saying that the party had left its previous centre-left position. He ran as an independent in the 2014 local elections, topping the poll in the Howth–Malahide area with 2,868 first preferences (16.12%) and taking the first seat.

Before becoming a full time public representative O'Callaghan worked in a variety of professional roles in policy analysis including in the areas of Housing, Mental Health, and Criminal Justice Reform. He obtained qualifications in Healthcare Economics and Social Policy after completing a Masters in Politics in University College Dublin. He is a voluntary member of the Dublin North–East Drugs Task Force and a member of the Audit Committee of Fingal County Council.

Direct Democracy Ireland:
Tom Darcy is a former property developer who became embroiled in a long running Supreme Court case when he represented himself in a repossession battle with AIB bank. He stood for Direct

Democracy Ireland in the 2014 European Elections in the Dublin area he gained 4,022 votes (1.14%). He is a leading member of the self-styled 'Reformed Land League'.

Independents:

Tommy Broughan has been a Dáil deputy for the Dublin North–East constituency since 1992. On that occasion he and Sean Kenny both won seats for the Labour party in the 'Spring Tide' in Dublin North–East. In 2002 Broughan was the only Labour candidate and he comfortably held his seat. He polled 3,447 in 1997 and 4,758 in 2002. In 2007 he was again the only Labour candidate and his first preference vote was down slightly. Although he was placed third on the first count he benefited dramatically from Sinn Féin transfers. When Larry O'Toole was eliminated on the fourth count Broughan got more than 45% of his available transfers and took the first seat. In 2011 Sean Kenny was again on the ticket with Broughan, who got 10,006 votes (23.92%) and took the first of two Labour seats in Dublin North–East. Later in that year he voted against the government's amendment to extend the bank guarantee and was expelled from the Labour parliamentary party. In April 2014 it was announced that he and supporters would form a 'Social Democratic Union'. By December 2015 this had not been registered as a political party and it seems he will contest the election as an independent.

Broughan was a member of Dublin City Council for the Donaghmede electoral area from 1999 to 2004. He is based in Howth and is a former teacher. From 2002 to 2007, Broughan was a noted critic of Pat Rabbitte's leadership, particularly his decision to form an electoral pact with Fine Gael. He was appointed party spokesperson on Transport in September 2007 but lost that position and the party whip in July 2010 when he abstained in a Dáil vote on the Wildlife (Amendment) Bill 2010. He was reinstated to the Parliamentary party in October 2010.

Paul Clarke ran as an independent candidate in the Dublin North–Central constituency in the 2011 Dáil election. On that occasion he polled 331 votes. In the 2014 local elections he ran unsuccessfully as an independent under the banner of 'the People's Convention' in the Beaumont–Donaghmede electoral area and polled 833 votes (3.82%), which saw him surviving to the 13th count. On that occasion he campaigned for popular involvement in decision-making and on a pro-life platform. He is Business Development Manager at Webify.com.

Jimmy Guerin has been a member of Fingal County Council for the Howth–Malahide electoral area since 2014. In the 2009 local elections he narrowly failed to be elected in his home Howth–Malahide electoral area with 1,814 votes (8.15%). On that occasion he had expected to be a Fianna Fáil candidate and ran as an independent when he failed to get the nomination. He ran as an independent again for the Dáil in 2011 on a very local platform and polled 1,285 votes (3.1%). In the 2014 Fingal County Council elections he credited his sons with running a very efficient social media powered campaign on his behalf. He polled 1,779 (10%) votes in that election, and he took the fourth of the seven seats. He is a former Sunday Independent journalist and media/print consultant. Jimmy Guerin is the brother of the late Veronica Guerin, the Sunday Independent crime correspondent who was murdered in June 1996.

Finian McGrath is based in the Griffith Avenue area and has been an independent member of Dáil Éireann since 2002. McGrath cut his political teeth with Tony Gregory in the inner city campaigns of the 1980s. He was an unsuccessful candidate for Dublin City Council in 1991, and for the Dáil in 1992 and 1997. He had his first electoral breakthrough when he was elected to Dublin City Council, for the Clontarf electoral area, in the 1999 local elections. McGrath took the second seat in that election with 1,861 first preferences. He first won his Dáil seat in 2002, standing on an 'Independent Health Alliance' ticket, polling 3,781 (9.44%) first preferences. He increased that to 5,169 in 2007, going from a 9.44% to a 14.19% share in the process. In 2011 he increased his personal vote again to 5,986 votes (15.44%), taking the third seat almost 5,000 votes ahead of Fine Gael's Ó Muirí.

McGrath not only attracts left-wing and republican votes but also transfers from more traditional parties. It was Seán Haughey's transfers that took him over the line in 2011. He was one of the nominators of Martin McGuinness for the 2011 presidential election campaign. In 2012 he resigned from the chair of the Dáil Technical Group when Mick Wallace rejoined. In March 2015 McGrath was one of the five TDs and two Senators who formed the Independent Alliance, a banner under which they and other non-incumbent independents in many constituencies will contest this election.

Averil Power has been a member of Seanad Éireann since 2011. She made her political debut as a Fianna Fáil candidate in the 2009 local elections when she obtained 1,659 votes (7.46%) in the Howth–Malahide area of Fingal County Council but did not get a seat. She was the sole Fianna Fáil candidate in Dublin North–East for the 2011 Dáil election when she polled 4,794 (7.5%) and was eliminated on the eighth count. She was subsequently elected to the Seanad on the Industrial and Commercial Panel and from 2011 until 2015 she served as the Fianna Fáil Seanad spokesperson on Education and Skills.

She grew up in a council estate, and was the first person in her family to sit the Leaving Certificate and to go to college. She obtained a degree in Business, Economics and Social Science from Trinity College, where she was also elected to the positions of Education Officer (2000–01) and then President (2001–02) of TCD Students' Union. She also holds a Diploma in Legal Studies from the Honorable Society of King's Inns and is a graduate of the Boston College Political Leadership Programme. She unsuccessfully contested the election for President of the Union of Students in Ireland in March 2002. She worked as a Special Adviser to Mary Hanafin as Minister for Education. She is married to Irish Independent Editor Fionnan Sheahan.

In May 2015 Power, who had been a leading campaigner in the Marriage Referendum, left Fianna Fáil saying the party was out of touch with the needs and concerns of ordinary people and that what she described as its 'cynical and cowardly approach to the marriage referendum was the last straw'.

Dublin Bay South

Outgoing Deputies:

Ruairi Quinn (Lab), Lucinda Creighton (Ren), Eoghan Murphy (FG), Kevin Humphreys (Lab)

In July 2014 Ruairi Quinn announced his resignation as Minister for Labour and that he would not be seeking re-election in 2016.

Lucinda Creighton resigned as Minister for European Affairs when she lost the Fine Gael whip in July 2013. She sat as an independent until March 2015 when she and others founded a new party, Renua Ireland.

The Constituency:

This is a four-seat constituency, formerly Dublin South–East that has been renamed and slightly redrawn since 2011. Five electoral divisions of Kimmage C and Terenure A, B, C and D with a population of 12,563 have been transferred to this constituency from Dublin South Central.

	% Vote 1997	% Vote 2002	% Vote 2007	% Vote 2011	Swing 2011	Quotas 2011
Fine Gael	27.38	16.06	18.65	35.52	16.87	1.8
Labour	16.67	12.43	16.65	25.36	8.71	1.3
Fianna Fáil	25.79	27.03	28.72	11.23	–17.49	0.6
Sinn Féin	–	7.39	4.72	3.64	–1.08	0.2
Green Party	11.71	16.23	13.84	6.79	–7.05	0.3
Others	18.44	20.85	17.41	17.46	0.05	0.9

2016 Candidates will include:

Eoghan Murphy (FG), Kate O'Connell (FG), Kevin Humphreys (Lab), Jim O'Callaghan (FF), Chris Andrews (SF), Eamon Ryan (GP), Annette Mooney (AAA–PBP), Lucinda Creighton (Renua), Glenna Lynch (SD)

In Brief:

All four deputies elected here in 2011 were from the government parties, although Lucinda Creighton has since left Fine Gael and formed a new party, Renua Ireland. Much attention will focus on whether she will retain her seat. On current polling she should. However, Fine Gael is mounting a determined effort to unseat her and if Fine Gael's vote improves nationally, on current poll data there will be a multiplier on that surge in Dublin South East which could see Kate O'Connell join their outgoing deputy Eoghan Murphy in the next Dáil. Labour have already acknowledged that they have lost one of their two seats by running only one candidate. Kevin Humphreys will struggle to hold even that one, especially against a strong challenge from former Fianna Fáil deputy, Sinn Féin's candidate Chris Andrews, who is also in the eastern part of the constituency. The Green Party leader, and former Dublin South TD Eamon Ryan has transferred into this constituency and is likely to win a seat. The final line up will include Eoghan Murphy for sure, and then probably Ryan and Creighton, with a four way fight between O'Connell (FG), Andrews (SF), Humphreys(Lab), and possibly Fianna Fáil's Jim O'Callaghan for the last seat. As of now Humphreys (Lab) looks best placed to win it.

Fine Gael:

This was the constituency of former leaders John A. Costello and Garret FitzGerald and has traditionally been a Fine Gael stronghold. Garrett FitzGerald was a deputy here from 1969 to 1992. However, Fine Gael's vote collapsed in this constituency in the 2002 election. The then deputy Frances Fitzgerald's vote went from 5,501 in 1997 to just 3,337. The party had just 0.8 of a quota split between two candidates and lost the seat. The party's new candidate for the 2007 election was Lucinda Creighton. She polled an impressive 6,311 votes on her first outing, just 458 votes short of the quota and took the second seat. In 2011 she had 6,619 first preference votes, a poll topping 19%. She lost the whip in 2013 and founded Renua in 2015, leaving her running mate of 2011, Eoghan Murphy TD, as the party's lead candidate in 2016 and he has a new running mate.

Eoghan Murphy has his constituency office in Ranelagh and has been a member of Dáil Éireann since 2011. He was elected to Dublin City Council on first attempt in the 2009 local elections. He topped the poll in the Rathmines–Pembroke local electoral area, with 2,637 first preferences, 125 votes above the quota. In the 2011 Dáil election his 5,783 votes (16.6%) gave him the third seat. A foreign affairs specialist before entering politics, he was a speechwriter at a United Nations-affiliated organisation in Vienna responsible for monitoring nuclear weapon testing. While he occasionally speaks against government policy on some economic issues and is a strong advocate of political reform he has a loyal voting record with the government. He is a prominent user of social media and not only holds traditional clinics but also hosts regular coffee mornings in cafes around the constituency. He says he is still gutted that his entry in Young Scientist of Year 1996 was rejected.

Kate O'Connell owns and runs a pharmacy in Rathgar. She is the only female Fine Gael member of Dublin City Council. She was elected to the council on her first attempt in the 2014 local election when she polled 1,615 votes (12.6%) in the Rathgar–Rathmines electoral area and took the second seat behind the Green Party's Patrick Costello. She gained notoriety in February 2015 by voting against the City Council's plan to develop a 30 bed hostel for the homeless at the former Longfield's Hotel on Fitzwilliam Street, but subsequently explained that she thought the building should be sold so that the council could use the money to make better provision at a lower cost elsewhere. She has also spoken publicly about how her experience of discovering during pregnancy that her son had very little chance of surviving after birth influenced her belief in the importance of informed choice and psychological and medical support for those in a similar position.

Labour Party:

In 2011 the party ran two candidates here, Ruairi Quinn and local councilor Kevin Humphreys. Although the party had only 1.3 quotas on the first count they both won seats. Quinn first contested Dublin South East in 1973, taking a seat in the first election of 1982 and holding it until now. This time Humphreys is the party's sole candidate.

Kevin Humphreys has been a member of Dáil Éireann since 2011. He has been Minister of State with responsibility for Employment, Community and Social Support at the Department of Social Protection since July 2014. Raised in Ballsbridge and Ringsend and coming from a family that worked for generations in Boland's Mill, he and his family now live in Sandymount. In the 2011 Dáil election Labour polled 25.4% with Humphreys taking 3,450 first preferences (9.9%). He was a member of Dublin City Council from 1999 to 2011. In his last local election campaign in 2009 he topped the poll in the South–East Inner City electoral area with 2,598 first preferences, which was 705 votes above the quota. In 2011 Humphreys was appointed Convenor of the Oireachtas Committee on Finance, Public Expenditure and Reform, and became a member of the Oireachtas Committee on the Environment, Culture and the Gaeltacht until he was appointed a minister for state.

Fianna Fáil:

Chris Andrews, who won a seat for Fianna Fáil in 2007 and lost it again in 2011, has since defected to Sinn Féin. In 2007 his running mate was Jim O'Callaghan who is the party's sole candidate on this occasion.

Jim O'Callaghan lives in Ranelagh and has a constituency office in Portobello. He has been a member of Dublin City Council since 2009. He ran in the Pembroke–Rathmines electoral area in 2009 and polled 1,356 votes (7.71%). In 2014 he ran in the enlarged Rathgar–Rathmines electoral area and polled 1,056 (8.24%). He had previously run unsuccesfuly in the 2004 local elections in Rathmines when he had 902 votes (8.18%). He ran unsuccessfully for Seanad Éireann in 2002. In the 2007 Dáil election, as part of a two-man ticket, O'Callaghan polled 3,120 first preferences (9.22%). He is a Senior Counsel and legal advisor to the Fianna Fáil front bench. He studied law at University College Dublin and Cambridge. He has played rugby for both universities and for London Irish, Wanderers and Leinster at senior level. He also represented Ireland at Under 21 level and now coaches underage rugby.

He co-edited Law and Government: A Tribute to Rory Brady. On Dublin City Council he is the Vice Chair of the South East Area Joint Policing Committee and a member of Arts, Sports and Culture Strategic Policy Committee. He is a member of the committee organizing the council's plans for commemorating the centenary of the 1916 Easter Rising.

Sinn Féin:

The party's candidate in 2011 was Ruadhán Mac Aodháin who polled only 1,272 (3.6%). Its candidate this time is the former Fianna Fáil TD Chris Andrews.

Chris Andrews is a former Dáil Deputy and is a member of Dublin City Council for the Pembroke–South Dock electoral area. He was a Fianna Fáil member of Dáil Éireann from 2007 to 2011. In the 2007 election he topped the poll with 6,600 first preferences (19.5%). In 2011, however, he polled 3,922 first preferences, the party vote overall collapsed from 28.7% to 11.2% and he lost his seat. In 2011 he was revealed as the person behind a Twitter account @brianformerff which had been used to attack party leader Micheál Martin and other senior party figures as well as his Dublin South–East running mate Jim O'Callaghan. He resigned from Fianna Fáil the same week claiming his resignation was due to the party's lack of direction, rather than to the Twitter revelation. In 2013 he announced that he had joined Sinn Féin. He stood for Sinn Féin in the Pembroke–South Dock electoral area in the 2014 Dublin City Council elections, topping the poll with 2,081 votes (15.07%), 1.36 quotas.

For Fianna Fáil he was a member of Dublin City Council for the Pembroke electoral area from 1999 to 2004. In the 2004 election he polled 1,225 but he lost his council seat. In late 2005 he was co-opted back on to the council to fill a vacancy in the South West Inner City ward. He unsuccessfully contested the 2002 Dáil election polling 3,449 (10.6%), his transfers giving Eoin Ryan the seat on the seventh count.

Chris Andrew's late father Niall Andrews was a Dáil deputy for the neighbouring Dublin South constituency from 1977 to 1987 and a member of the European Parliament for the Dublin constituency from 1984 to 2004. Chris Andrews is also a cousin of the party's former Dun Laoghaire deputy, Barry Andrews, and nephew of former deputy and Minister for Foreign Affairs, David Andrews. His grandfather was the late Todd Andrews.

Green Party:

The last Green Party TD for Dublin South East was the former party leader, John Gormley, who lost his seat in 2011. This time the current leader Eamon Ryan has switched to contest here in Dublin Bay South.

Eamon Ryan is leader of the Green Party and a former Dáil deputy. He narrowly missed out on election to the European Parliament in 2014 when he was pipped to the third and final seat in the Dublin constituency by Fine Gael's Brian Hayes by 1,238 votes. The former party leader John Gormley held a Dáil seat here from 2002 to 2011, peaking at 16.2% in 2002. Gormley's vote collapsed to 2,370 (6.8%) in 2011. Ryan first stood for Dáil Éireann in Dublin South in 2002, taking the final seat with 5,222 first preference votes. In 2007 he increased that to 6,768 (11.1%) but in 2011 he polled only 4,929 (6.8%) and although he proved transfer friendly he went out on the 7th count. He was Minister for Communications, Energy and Natural Resources in the Fianna Fáil–Green coalition government from 2007 to 2011. He has a degree in Commerce from University College Dublin and ran two cycling business before becoming a full time politician.

Anti-Austerity Alliance – People Before Profit

Annette Mooney is a candidate for People Before Profit for whom she was also the Dáil candidate in 2011. A registered nurse she worked as a community nurse in the constituency before becoming a secondary teacher. The mother of three children has helped organize campaigns against water charges and the property tax and for rent controls. In the 2011 Dáil election she polled 626 first preference votes (1.8%). She has promised that if elected in 2016 she will take only the average industrial wage and will donate the rest of her Dáil salary to promoting public awareness in the constituency.

Renua Ireland:

Lucinda Creighton is the leader of Renua and has been a member of Dáil Éireann since 2007. She lives in the Sandymount area. She was elected to Dáil Éireann as a Fine Gael candidate on her first attempt in 2007. She then became the party spokesperson on European Affairs and she enjoyed a relatively high profile for a new deputy although there were often reports of tensions between her and party leader Enda Kenny. She was Magill magazine's 'Politician to Watch' in 2006. In the 2011 Dáil election, again as a Fine Gael candidate, she topped the poll in Dublin South East with 6,619 first preferences (19%) and was made Minister of State for European Affairs. She resigned that position and lost the party whip in March 2013. She then sat as independent until September of that year when she, with other former Fine Gael deputies, formed an informal grouping called the Reform Alliance. In March 2015, with some of these former Fine Gael deputies, she founded the Renua Ireland political party. Originally an opponent of same-sex marriage she changed her views and announced she would vote Yes in May 2015.

She is married to Senator Paul Bradford, a former Fine Gael deputy who is Renua's candidate in Cork East for this election. She holds a BCL and masters degree in law from Trinity College Dublin. She was called to the bar in 2005 and is also a qualified attorney-at-law in the State of New York where she interned on Democratic Party campaigns. She and Bradford have a young daughter. Creighton's first electoral outing was in the 2004 local elections when as a Fine Gael candidate she took the first seat in the Pembroke ward of Dublin City Council with 1,567 votes (16.46%).

Social Democrats:

Glenna Lynch is based in Donnybrook and is a first time candidate. She is an interior designer and became a national figure during the RTÉ Frontline Presidential Election debate in November 2011 when she questioned the business ethics of independent candidate Sean Gallagher, who was leading in the polls at the time. The following day Gallagher implied to the Today With Pat Kenny radio programme that she was from someone else's campaign team and said he was 'tired of people being wheeled out with agendas.' Lynch phoned in to say that she had no political allegiance.

She has since said that she voted Fianna Fáil 'until a couple of elections ago' but became disillusioned. Since then she has taken part in various political campaigns. She was a substitute candidate for independent MEP Nessa Childers, formerly of Labour and the Green Party, in the 2014 European election and she was active in the Democracy Matters campaign which successfully opposed the Seanad Abolition referendum in 2012. She also considered joining the Independent Alliance and attended its think-in in Tullamore but decided that the grouping had not yet decided 'what it wanted to be.'

Dublin Central

Outgoing Deputies:

Paschal Donohoe (FG), Joe Costello (Lab), Maureen O'Sullivan (Ind), Mary Lou MacDonald (SF)

The Constituency:

This constituency has been reduced from four seats to three seats following the transfer of the electoral divisions of Ashtown A and B and part of the Phoenix Park electoral division, with a population of 13,256, to Dublin West, and the electoral divisions Botanic A, B and C and Drumcondra South C with a population of 11,506 to Dublin North–West.

	% Vote 1997	% Vote 2002	% Vote 2007	% Vote 2011	Swing 2011	Quotas 2011
Fine Gael	14.51	11.06	9.53	19.94	10.;41	1.0
Labour	8.49	12.17	12.57	28.28	15.71	1.4
Fianna Fáil	42.83	39.58	44.45	14.85	–29.60	0.7
Sinn Féin	6.65	14.61	9.19	13.08	3.89	0.7
Green Party	3.51	4.31	5.76	1.97	–3.79	0.1
Others	24.02	18.27	18.51	21.88	3.37	1.1

2016 Candidates will include:

Paschal Donohoe (FG), Joe Costello (Lab), Mary Fitzpatrick (FF), Mary Lou McDonald (SF), Ian Noel Smyth (GP), Mary Diana O'Dwyer (AAA–PBP), Gary Gannon (SD), Cormac McKay (DDI), Éilis Ryan (WP), Christy Burke (Ind), Andrew Kelly (Ind), Cieran Perry (Ind), Maureen O'Sullivan (Ind)

In Brief:

Four sitting deputies into three seats does not go. Sinn Fein's Mary Lou McDonald will be safe, after that anything could happen. Pascal Donohoe is the most vulnerable Fine Gael Minister in the country. Although Labour had a quota and a half to Fine Gael's one quota it may actually be the smaller coalition party who will lose out here. The constituency has returned an independent TD since February 1982 but Maureen O Sullivan, who succeeded to Tony Gregory's seat. will face her toughest test ever. This constituency was once Bertie Ahern's heartland although it is now significantly reorientated from the Drumcondra end. If there is a new deputy it is likely to be Fianna Fáil's Mary Fitzpatrick, but on balance that seems unlikely. The newcomer to watch is Gary Cannon, elected as an independent councillor in 2014 but running for the Social Democrats in this election. It will also be interesting to see how Christy Burke, now independent, does this time around having had a high profile as Lord Mayor. One for Sinn Féin is certain and the other two are likely to go to Fine Gael and Maureen O Sullivan.

Fine Gael:

Paschal Donohoe is originally from the Cabra area and now lives in Phibsborough. First elected to Dáil Éireann in 2011, he has been the Minister for Transport, Tourism and Sport since July 2014. Donohoe has been the party candidate in this constituency since 2007. The late Jim Mitchell held a seat for Fine Gael in this part of the city from 1977 to 2002. In 2007 Donohoe, then a councillor, stood as the party's new Dáil candidate and got 3,302 first preferences, being eliminated on the fourth count. He then successfully contested the Seanad Election on the Administrative Panel. He was again the party's candidate for the Dáil in the 2009 by-election and, although he polled 6,439 first preferences, came in second place to the Gregory-organisation's candidate Maureen O'Sullivan. In the 2011 Dáil election he topped the poll only 20 votes short of the quota with 6,903 first preferences (19.9%). He was appointed Minister of State for European Affairs following the resignation of Lucinda Creighton in 2012, and was promoted to his current cabinet post in 2014. O'Donohoe was a member of Dublin City Council for the Cabra–Glasnevin electoral area from 2004 to 2007. He previously worked as a sales and marketing manager. He has a degree in Politics and Economics from Trinity College Dublin.

Labour Party:

Joe Costello has been a member of the Oireachtas since 1989. He first won a Dáil seat in Labour's 'Springtide' election of 1992. He lost the seat in 1997, won it back in 2002 and held it comfortably in 2007. He retained it even more comfortably in 2011 when as part of a two candidate ticket he got 6,273 votes (18.1%) and took the second seat. He was a member of the Seanad from 1989 to 1992 and from 1997 to 2002 on the Administrative Panel. He is a former member of Dublin City Council for the North Inner City electoral area, where he was succeeded by his wife Emer Costello, who was subsequently Lord Mayor of Dublin 2009/10. She was co-opted to replace Proinsias de Rossa in February 2012 on his resignation from the European Parliament and subsequently unsuccessfully contested the 2014 European Parliament election.

Joe Costello was Minister of State for Trade and Overseas Development at the Department of Foreign Affairs and Trade from 2011 to July 2014 and he is currently a member of the Dáil Public Accounts Committee. He is a former teacher and a former president of the Association of Secondary Teachers of Ireland. He is also a former chairman of the Irish Prisoners Rights organisation.

Fianna Fáil:

In all elections from 1981 to 2007 former Taoiseach Bertie Ahern topped the poll with a local constituency operation that had a reputation for unrivalled efficiency. In 2007 Ahern had almost two quotas, with 12,734 first preferences, and his running mates Mary

Fitzpatrick and Cyprian Brady had 1,725 and 939 votes respectively. Cyprian Brady took the final seat however with a solid transfer from Ahern and became the candidate with the smallest share of first preferences ever to be elected to Dáil Éireann. He had 2.7% of the first preference vote. In the 2009 by-election the candidate was Bertie Ahern's brother Maurice who took just 12% of the vote. In 2011 Brady and Fitzpatrick were the party candidates. Fitzpatrick got twice as many votes as Brady but together they got only 15 percent of the vote, which was one third of what the party got here in 2007. This time Fitzpatrick is Fianna Fáil's only candidate.

Mary Fitzpatrick is based in Cabra and has been a member of Dublin City Council since 2004. This will be her third Dáil election. In 2011 she came within a thousand votes of winning a seat when she polled 3,504 first preferences (4.7%). In 2007 she polled 3,504 first preference votes.

In 2004 when she was elected to the Dublin City Council in the Cabra–Glasnevin electoral area she polled 1,848 first preferences (quota 3,027). In 2009 she dramatically improved on that performance, polling 3,088 first preferences, topping the poll and taking the first seat. The surge in support for her, on a day when Fianna Fáil was suffering setbacks city and countrywide, is attributable to voter reaction to perceived antagonism directed towards her by the Ahern camp.

Her father, Dermot Fitzpatrick, a local GP in the Navan Road end of the constituency, was a Dáil Deputy from 1987 to 1989 and from 2002 to 2007 and a Senator from 1997 to 2002. Like her father she has an obvious voter base in the Navan Road end of the constituency and it is this area that has been re-allocated to other constituencies in the redraw of the constituency boundary since 2011. With a degree in Italian and German she was one of those who emigrated in the 1980's, working in France, Germany, Italy and the USA before returning to Ireland in 1998. She is married and has three children.

Sinn Féin:

In 2002 Sinn Féin's long standing candidate in this constituency, Councillor Christy Burke, had passed the baton to the party's then

Cabra councillor Nicky Kehoe. Although Kehoe was hemmed in somewhat by Fianna Fáil's decision to run another Cabra councillor, Dermot Fitzpatrick, he still managed to poll an impressive 4,979 first preference votes. This more than doubled the Sinn Féin vote and Kehoe came very close to winning the fourth seat, but was beaten by Dermot Fitzpatrick by just 74 votes. Since 2007 the party candidate has been Mary Lou McDonald.

Mary Lou McDonald is Vice President of Sinn Féin and has been a member of Dáil Éireann since 2011. She is the party's Dáil spokesperson on Public Expenditure and Reform. She unsuccessfully contested the Dublin West constituency for Sinn Féin at the 2002 general election, polling 8.02% of the first preference votes. She was elected as MEP (Sinn Féin's first in the Republic of Ireland) for the Dublin constituency in the 2004 European election with 60,395 first preferences, which represented 14.32% of the vote.

When she first ran for the party in this constituency in the 2007 election McDonald polled 3,182 first preferences, which represented a drop in the party support in the constituency of more than five and a half percentage points. In 2009 she lost her seat in the European Parliament to the Socialist Party's Joe Higgins. She was again the Sinn Féin candidate for the 2011 Dáil election when her 4,526 first preference votes (13.1%) saw her take the final seat ahead of Fianna Fáil's Mary Fitzpatrick.

McDonald is a member of the Dáil Public Accounts Committee and a member of the Sinn Féin Ard Chomhairle. Married with two children, she lives in the part of the constituency that has been recently moved to Dublin West. She was originally a member of Fianna Fáil, which she left in 1998.

Green Party:

The Green Party has never held a seat in Dublin Central. The party's candidate in 2002, Tommy Simpson, polled just 1,469 votes. In 2007 their candidate was Patricia McKenna, the former Member of the European Parliament. She managed to increase the party vote only slightly to 1,995. McKenna left the Green Party in May of 2009 as a result of policy differences stemming from the party's participation in government with Fianna Fáil. The party ran David

Geary as its candidate in the 2009 by-election, and he polled 819 first preference votes. In 2011 Phil Kearney polled 683 votes. There is a new candidate in 2016.

Ian Noel Smyth stood in the Beaumont/Donaghmede ward of Dublin City council in the 2014 local elections, gaining 442 first preference votes (2.03%) and being eliminated on the 9th count. He lives in Drumcondra with his wife and four children and is a practicing architect and urban designer. His campaign is focused on future proofing homes, incentivising businesses to increase employment and to move to energy saving and energy creation, and encouraging banks to support homes and businesses to move to more sustainable practices.

Anti-Austerity Alliance – People Before Profit:

Diana O'Dwyer is running as a candidate for the first time but has been a Socialist Party activist for almost ten years. She is Joe Higgins's Banking Inquiry researcher and also helps to research housing policy and budget statements for the Anti-Austerity Alliance. She was one of those who took part in the ROSA (for Reproductive rights, against Oppression, Sexism and Austerity) bus and train trips to Belfast in 2014/15

Social Democrats:

Gary Gannon has been a member of Dublin City Council for the North Inner City Ward since 2014. The 2014 local election was his first electoral contest and he polled 741 first preference votes (7.2%) and took the sixth of the eight seats in the ward. He has no background in politics or family connections. He has worked with early school leavers to get them back into education and employment. He hit the headlines during the 2014 local election campaign when one of his supporters spotted a rival independent removing his posters. Gannon persuaded him to return the poster so that it could go up again. He came late to education, spending a year in the Trinity College Dublin Access programme before going on to do a degree in History and Political Science and then to youth work. He interned in Leinster House with Sinn Féin Senator David Cullinane but decided to run as an independent for Dublin

City Council in 2014. He joined the Social Democrats shortly after they were founded in July 2015.

Workers Party:

Malachi Steenson was the party candidate here in both the 2009 by-election and in 2011 general election. He polled 519 votes in the former and 274 in the latter. In 2016 the party has a new candidate.

Éilis Ryan is a member of Dublin City Council for the Inner City North ward. She took the 8th seat in this electoral area in 2014 with 628 first preferences (6.09%). Before becoming a full time public representative she worked in the field of overseas aid and human rights in various countries including Peru and East Timor. She is well known in the Dublin area as a musician.

Independents:

Christy Burke has been an independent member of Dublin City Council since 1999. He was the Sinn Féin candidate at all Dáil elections in this constituency from February 1982 to 1997 with the exception of November 1982. In all he ran for Sinn Féin in seven Dáil elections with his highest share of the vote the 13.27% he achieved in the 2009 by-election. His total of 3,770 first preferences in that Dáil by-election placed him fourth. Four days later he resigned from Sinn Féin, citing difficulties with party headquarters. He stood as an independent candidate for the 2011 Dáil election. His 1,315 votes (3.8%) largely transferred to Mary Lou McDonald when he was eliminated after the second count.

He has been a member of Dublin City Council since 1999 for the North Inner City Ward. In the most recent 2014 local elections he polled 1,238 votes (12.01%), which was 1.08 quotas and he took the second seat. He was a high profile Lord Mayor of Dublin 2014–2015 but declined to live in the Mansion House. He has been a long time campaigner on homelessness and other issues in the inner city.

Andrew Kelly is one of several local postmasters running to highlight the number of post office closures and the potential future loss of local services. He is from Cabra and is involved in many local organisations. He has been a scout leader in Phibsborough for 22 years, coaches rugby in Glasnevin and was a former chairman of Christ The King girls' school, Cabra.

Cieran Perry has been an independent member of Dublin City Council since 2009. He contested his first Dáil election as an independent candidate in 2007 and polled 952 votes. In 2009 he contested the local elections for Cabra–Glasnevin and came in third on the first count with 2,510 first preferences (quota 2,837). He had previously missed out on a council seat in that area in 2004, polling 1,753. He next contested the 2011 Dáil election and polled 2,394 votes (4.03%) and was eliminated on the fourth count. He ran again in the Dublin City Council elections in the re-organised Cabra–Finglas ward in the 2014 local elections topping the poll and taking the first seat with 2,268 (13.47%). Much of his support base has, however, moved to Dublin West or Dublin North–West in the redraw of this constituency since the 2011 election. He is currently Deputy Lord Mayor of Dublin and is a shop steward with the Unite trade union.

Maureen O'Sullivan was born and raised in the East Wall and is a graduate of University College Dublin. She has been a member of Dáil Éireann since June 2009, when she was selected by the 'Gregory organisation' to be their candidate in the by-election following Tony Gregory's death. Gregory first won his Independent seat here in 1982 and he retained it in every subsequent election. Prior to contesting the by-election O'Sullivan had been co-opted to the seat that the organisation held on Dublin City Council when long time Gregory lieutenant Mick Rafferty stepped down in September 2008. She comfortably retained the seat in the 2009 local elections, topping the poll in the North Inner City electoral area with 2,859 first preferences (quota 1,700). In the 2009 by-election she polled 27% of the vote on the first count and benefited from transfers across the board, including almost a third of Fianna Fáil's transfers, to comfortably win the seat. In the 2011 election she took the third seat with 4,139 votes (12.0%). She is a member of the Technical Group in Dáil Éireann, a grouping which allows independents and minor parties to gain access to more speaking time without their having to align their policies. O'Sullivan worked as a secondary school teacher in St Mary's Baldoyle for 35 years prior to her election to Dáil Éireann.

DUBLIN FINGAL

Outgoing Deputies:

James Reilly (FG), Brendan Ryan (Lab), Clare Daly (Ind), Alan Farrell (FG)

Clare Daly, then of the Socialist Party, was elected under the United Left Alliance banner in 2011. She has since left the Socialist Party and is expected to run as a non-party candidate in this election.

The Constituency:

This is now a five-seater. It is a renamed and substantially redrawn version of what used to be the Dublin North constituency with an extra seat. It includes all of the area which was in Dublin North in 2011 with the addition of Swords Forrest and Kilsallaghan from Dublin West, and Balgriffin and Turnapin from Dublin North–East. The additional territory had a population transfer of 26,840 at the time of the last census.

	% Vote 1997	% Vote 2002	% Vote 2007	% Vote 2011	Swing 2011	Quotas 2011
Fine Gael	18.98	11.81	14.03	31.39	17.36	1.6
Labour	13.64	14.47	9.62	26.37	16.75	1.3
Fianna Fáil	38.65	38.24	42.09	15.47	–26.62	0.8
Sinn Féin	–	3.07	2.66	–	–	–
Green Party	13.64	16.60	16.67	8.48	–8.12	0.4
Socialist Party	7.22	12.52	8.92	15.22	6.30	–0.8
Others	7.87	3.29	6.00	3.06	–5.94	0.2

2016 Candidates will include:

Alan Farrell (FG), James Reilly (FG), Brendan Ryan (Lab), Darragh O'Brien (FF), Lorraine Clifford–Lee (FF), Louise O'Reilly (SF), Joe

O'Brien (GP), Terry Kelleher (AAA–PBP), Barry Martin (AAA–PBP), Gerry Molloy (Renua), Clare Daly (Ind), Roslyn Fuller (Ind), Tony Murphy (Ind)

In Brief:

The redraw reintegrates Swords into this constituency which benefits both Clare Daly (Ind) and Darragh O'Brien (FF). Clare Daly would have been safe anyway given her strong profile locally and nationally. The additional seat also means Fine Gael should hold its two seats and even Labour, which might otherwise have been vulnerable could hold on. This is Fianna Fáil's best chance of a seat gain in the capital, with former deputy Darragh O'Brien, who is currently party leader in Seanad Éireann, almost certain to return to the lower house. Sinn Féin has only an outside chance of winning a seat. It looks therefore like two Fine Gael, one Fianna Fáil, Claire Daly and one Labour.

Fine Gael:

James Reilly is based in Lusk and has a constituency office in Balbriggan. He has been a Dáil deputy since 2007. He is the Minister for Children and Youth Affairs and also Deputy Leader of Fine Gael. In the 2007 election he polled 7,667 (14.03) and took the fourth seat. He was immediately appointed to the front bench as spokesman on Health and replaced Richard Bruton as the party's deputy leader after the latter's failed 2010 rebellion against Enda Kenny's leadership. In the 2011 Dáil election Reilly topped the poll and won his seat at the first count. His vote of 10,718 (20.6%) was 308 above the quota. He was Minister for Health from March 2011 to July 2014. Now Minister for Children and Youth Affairs he retains responsibility for Public Health and anti-smoking policy. He is a medical doctor and had a large GP practice in the constituency for 25 years, being a former president of the Irish Medical Organisation. He served on the former Eastern Health Board and was Chairman of its Community Care Committee and its Mental Health Committee.

Alan Farrell is based at the Swords end of the constituency and has been a Dáil deputy since 2011. He polled 5,310 first preference votes (10.8%) in that election and took the final seat in what was then a four-seater. He was elected to Fingal County Council in 2004 in the Malahide electoral area with 971 votes (8.24%) and in the larger Howth–Malahide electoral area in 2009 with 2,739 (12.31%). He was Mayor of Fingal in 2009. He was previously a member of the Fingal County Enterprise Board and the Fingal Development Board. He is a member of the Joint Oireachtas Committee on Justice, Equality and Defence and the Joint Oireachtas Committee on Finance, Public Expenditure and Reform. He owns and operates an estate agency in his home town of Malahide.

Labour Party:

In 2011, Labour ran a second candidate, Swords based Cllr Tom Kelleher. With Swords then divided between two constituencies for the 2011 election it was never likely that Kelleher would take a seat. Nonetheless he gained a creditable 3,205 first preference votes (6.5%) and on his elimination his vote divided fairly evenly between Swords-based United Left candidate Clare Daly, Fine Gael's Alan Farrell, and the Green Party's Trevor Sargent. Brendan Ryan is the only candidate on this occasion.

Brendan Ryan is based in Skerries and has been a Dáil deputy since 2011. His brother Sean Ryan was a Dáil Deputy for this constituency from 1989 to 1997 and from 1998 to 2007. Brendan first contested in the 2007 election but that year the party's vote fell by almost five percentage points by comparison to 2002. Brendan Ryan polled 5,256 first preferences in that election and he was 1,173 votes behind James Reilly on the last count. Ryan contested the subsequent Seanad Election on the Administrative Panel taking the second of the seven seats and was party spokesperson on Education, Science, Transport and Defence in the upper house from 2007 to 2011. In 2011 when he again contested for the Dáil he polled 9,809 votes (19.9%), which put him just 61 short of a quota and he took the second seat. He was Labour Party spokesperson on Enterprise, Trade, Employment, Transport and Education in the outgoing Dáil and a member of the Committee on Jobs, Social Protection and Education. Originally from the Donabate/Portrane area he has lived in Skerries since 1970. He holds a masters degree in food science and business.

Fianna Fáil:

In 2011 Fianna Fáil ran two candidates, Darragh O'Brien and Michael Kennedy, in Dublin North and their combined vote at 15.4 per cent was down dramatically on the party's vote here in 2007 which was in excess of 42 per cent.

Darragh O'Brien is a former Dáil deputy and currently the party leader in Seanad Éireann. He was elected to Dáil Éireann on his first attempt in 2007, when as part of a three man ticket he polled 7,055 first preferences (12.91%). In the 2011 election as part of two man ticket he polled 4,115 (8.3%) and was beaten by Fine Gael's Alan Farrell for the final seat by more than a thousand votes.

O'Brien is a former Vice Chair of the Dáil Public Accounts committee. He was elected to Seanad Éireann on the Labour panel in 2011. He was previously a member of Fingal County Council in the Malahide electoral area of Fingal County Council. He was co-opted to the seat vacated by the sitting deputy GV Wright in 2004 on the introduction of the dual mandate ban and was re-elected to the council in the 2004 local elections. He is a former finance and pensions manager with Friends First.

Lorraine Clifford-Lee is a solicitor. She is originally from Waterford though now resident in Portmarnock. She unsuccessfully contested the Dublin City Council ward of Pembroke–South Dock, which is in the Dublin Bay South constituency, in the 2014 local elections. In that election she received 747 votes (5.41%) and was eliminated at the 10th count. She is a member of the party's Ard Comhairle and according to Michael Moynihan TD, chairman of Fianna Fáil's National Constituencies Committee, has been added to the ticket to 'boost female participation in the party at all levels.' Her addition has caused considerable controversy in the constituency organisation, where some had hoped the second candidate would be Swords Councillor Darragh Butler who has consistently been Fianna Fáil's best performer in Fingal local elections and is a close friend and supporter of Darragh O'Brien. Clifford-Lee is married to the political editor of The Irish Mail on Sunday John Lee.

Sinn Féin:

Louise O'Reilly is a surprise Sinn Féin candidate in 2016 in this constituency. The party ran no candidate here in 2011. It had been expected by some that Councillor Phillip Lynam, who topped the poll in the 2014 local elections in the Swords area would be the one to run, but he has said he prefers to focus on local issues, though he also admitted that gender balance played a role in the decision. O'Reilly is a SIPTU Trade Union official from Crumlin but has been involved in negotiations on behalf of the union with Aer Lingus so will be known to many in the Fingal constituency. In 2007 the party's candidate was Matt McCormack, a River Valley-based trade union activist and Eircom employee who polled 1,454 first preferences, a 2.66% share. Mick Davis, the party's candidate in 2002, received 1,350 votes (3.1%).

Green Party:

Trevor Sargent was the Green Party TD for Dublin North from 1992 until he retired from politics after his defeat in 2011 when his 4,186 (8.5%) was the lowest he had received since that initial success. Much of his vote was personal. He was a former school principal. In 2007 the party ran a second candidate, Joe Corr, a member of Fingal County Council for the Balbriggan area. He polled 1,659 in that Dáil election. The party has a new candidate on this occasion.

Joe O'Brien lives in Skerries. He grew up on a small farm in Cork. He has postgraduate qualifications in social policy and sociology from University College Cork and Trinity College Dublin and he works as a Policy Officer for the social care agency Crosscare. In the local elections of 2014 he polled only 804 votes (4.91%) in the Balbriggan electoral area but proved to be transfer friendly and came close to being elected.

Anti-Austerity Alliance – People Before Profit:

Terry Kelleher is an Anti-Austerity Alliance candidate and a member of the Socialist Party. He is a former Balbriggan Town Councillor. He is also a Civil and Public Service Union trade unionist. He has been prominent in the anti-water charges campaign in the

Balbriggan area. He ran in the 2009 local elections for both Fingal County Council and Balbriggan Town council when his 882 votes (4.98%) were insufficient to get him elected to the county council, but he was elected to the Town Council with 363 votes (7.98%). In the 2014 local elections he was a candidate in the Balbriggan area and got 571 first preferences but survived to the seventh count before being eliminated.

Barry Martin is a People Before Profit candidate, He is from Rush and has been a member of Fingal County Council since 2014. In the 2014 local election he polled 840 first preference votes (5.13%) in the Balbriggan electoral area and he took the last of the seven seats.

Renua Ireland:

Gerry Molloy is a GP based in Malahide. He is on the specialist register in General Practice and is an Aviation Medical Examiner, providing medical services to companies and staff in Dublin Airport since 1997. He has been involved in a number of charities providing medical services to the sick and disabled, including accompanying Across in Ireland (a charity providing holidays to the physically disabled) on over-ground trips to Germany and acting for several years as a Medical Officer for Lourdes Pilgrimages.

Independent:

Clare Daly has been a Dáil deputy since 2011. She contested every Dáil election in this constituency since 1997 as a Socialist Party candidate. She resigned from the Socialist Party in 2012 and this time describes herself as an independent socialist. The change of label is unlikely to make any difference to her vote, which is personal. Daly was active in campus and national politics when studying for her accountancy degree at Dublin City University and followed that with SIPTU activism in the catering section of Aer Lingus. She was elected to the Labour Party's Administrative Committee as a youth representative but was expelled in 1989 with Joe Higgins and other 'Militant' left wing members.

When standing for the Socialist Party in the 1997 Dáil elections Daly polled 2,971, which was just over 7% of the vote, and in the 1998 by-election she increased that to an 8.15% share. In 1999 she became a member of Fingal County Council for the Swords electoral area, polling 1,287 first preference votes (14.14%), and taking the third seat. In the 2002 Dáil elections she polled an impressive 5,501 first preferences (12.5% of the vote) placing her fifth in what was then a four-seater. In 2004 she topped the poll in the County Council elections and took the first seat with 2,763 votes (16.51%). In 2007 her Dáil vote fell in both numbers and share to 4,872 (8.92%). In the 2009 local elections, however, she topped the poll in Swords, this time with 1.23 quotas and a vote of 3,192 (20.48%). In 2011, with the electorate turning against not only Fianna Fáil but the previously popular local Green TD Trevor Sargent, her time had come and she polled 7,513 first preference votes (15.22%) which put her more than 3,000 votes ahead of Sargent. She took the third of the four seats. This time her position is further strengthened by the fact that her Swords Forrest base has been returned to the constituency.

Roslyn Fuller was born in Canada and describes herself as an author, lecturer, law expert and commentator. She organized the Irish Bodypainting Competition until 2014. She holds a PhD in International Law from Trinity College Dublin, and a law degree from Georg-August Universitaet, Germany. She has lectured in law at Trinity College Dublin, NUI Maynooth, and Griffith College. She is the author of the textbook *International Law: An Irish Perspective* (Round Hall, Dublin) as well as the recently published *Beasts and Gods: How Democracy Changed its Meaning and Lost its Purpose* (Zed Books, London, November 2015). She co-founded the Irish Writers' Exchange which produces literature from new Irish authors and promotes integration through culture and literacy in socially disadvantaged schools. She says that her community activities primarily centre around education, immigration and Anti-Austerity (water charges).

Tony Murphy has been an independent member of Fingal County Council since 2014. In the 2014 local elections he took the second of the eight seats in the Balbriggan electoral area polling 1,404 first preferences (8.58%). He was a member of Fine Gael and was originally on the four person party ticket in Balbriggan for the 2014 local elections. However, in February 2014 he announced he would run as an independent instead after party headquarters imposed a fifth candidate onto the ticket. Murphy is a well-known businessman and chamber of commerce member in Balbriggan and his family have been involved with a wide range of community organisations over the years. On Fingal County Council he works with the major parties, saying that he believes that is the best way to deliver change.

Dublin Mid–West

Outgoing Deputies:

Joanna Tuffy (Lab), Frances Fitzgerald (FG), Robert Dowds (Lab), Derek Keating (FG)

In September 2015 Robert Dowds announced he would not run in this election.

The Constituency:

This is a four-seat constituency, the boundaries of which remain unchanged since the 2011 general election. It includes Saggart, Rathcoole and the area west of the M50 between the Naas Road and the Liffey, covering the Clondalkin–Ronanstown, Brittas and Lucan areas and also the Palmerstown area.

	% Vote 2002	% Vote 2007	% Vote 2011	Swing 2011	Quotas 2011
Fine Gael	11.51	12.00	30.93	18.93	1.5
Labour	9.01	10.91	30.75	19.84	1.5
Fianna Fáil	32.06	33.00	11.80	–21.20	0.6
Sinn Féin	6.52	9.27	11.84	2.57	0.6
Green Party	12.33	10.83	3.47	–7.36	0.2
Others	28.58	23.99	11.20	–12.79	0.6

2016 Candidates will include:

Frances Fitzgerald (FG), Derek Keating (FG), Joanna Tuffy (Lab), John Curran (FF), Eoin Ó Broin (SF), Lorraine Hennessy (WP), Gino Kenny (AAA/PBP), Anne-Marie McNally (Soc Dem), Paul Gogarty (Ind), Francis Timmons (Ind)

In Brief:

Francis Fitzgerald (FG) will hold her seat. Sinn Fein's Eoin Ó Broin, who lost out narrowly in 2011 will win a seat this time. Labour won two seats here in 2011 and has acknowledged that one of those is already lost by running just a single candidate. Joanna Tuffy will struggle even to retain that seat. The second Fine Gael seat is also vulnerable. The colourful former Green Party TD Paul Gogarty is contesting this time as an independent and is in contention for a seat. So too is the former Fianna Fáil deputy John Curran. It will be one definite Fine Gael seat, one Sinn Féin seat, and then a fight between Gogarty, Curran, Tuffy and the outgoing Derek Keating (FG) for the last two seats. Gogarty and Curran have the advantage at this stage. The other left wing candidate to watch is the AAA/PPB standard bearer Gino Kenny.

Fine Gael:

Frances Fitzgerald is Minister for Justice and Equality and has been a Dáil Deputy for this constituency since 2011. She was previously a Dáil Deputy for Dublin South East from 1992 to 2002. She took the second seat there in 1992 with 4,332 and in 1997 with 5,501. In 2002 her vote in Dublin South East dropped to 3,337 and she lost that seat. Before the 2007 election she transferred across the city to become the party's candidate in the newly drawn constituency of Dublin Mid–West. Although at 4,480 first preferences, her vote was impressive for a first-time candidate in the area, both Joanna Tuffy (Lab) and Paul Gogarty (GP) overtook her in subsequent counts and the Progressive Democrats' Mary Harney kept ahead of her, so Fitzgerald did not win a seat on that occasion. After her unsuccessful Dáil challenge in 2007, she contested the Seanad Election on the Labour Panel where she took the eighth of the eleven seats. She was then appointed Fine Gael leader in the Upper House.

In the 2011 election Harney had retired from politics, Paul Gogarty was suffering from the collapse of the Green vote, and Fianna Fáil's vote had imploded. Meanwhile Fitzgerald had solidified her support base in the constituency and in 2011 she took 7,281 first preference votes, which was 17% of the total and gave her the second seat. In March 2011 she was appointed Minister for Children and Youth Affairs and in May 2014 she became Minister for Justice and Equality. Before becoming a full time public representative she was a social worker and lectured on that subject at TCD. She was Chair of the National Women's Council of Ireland from 1988 to 1992.

Derek Keating has been a member of Dáil Éireann since 2011. He is a former FÁS Community Employment Scheme supervisor at St Mary's Parish Centre, Lucan. He was a member of Fianna Fáil during the 1980s but later joined the Progressive Democrats where he was director of elections for Tom Morrissey in the Castleknock local electoral area at the 1991 local elections. In 1998, following the constituency boundary revision which created the new constituency of Dublin Mid-West, he left that party and stood as an independent in the 1999 South Dublin County Council elections for the Lucan electoral area, polling 1,113 votes to take the last of the four seats. In 2004 he increased his vote to 3,680, taking the first seat. He ran as an independent in Dublin Mid–West in 2007, gaining 2,701 first preference votes (7.23%). On the 8th of July 2008 he joined Fine Gael and retained his council seat as a Fine Gael candidate in the 2009 local elections with an impressive 4,146 first preferences, 1,571 votes above the quota. In 2011 he joined Frances Fitzgerald on the ticket, taking 5,933 votes (13.89%), which gave him the fourth and final seat ahead of sitting TD John Curran of Fianna Fáil. He is a member of the Oireachtas Education Committee and was previously a member of the Oireachtas Committee on Health and Children.

Labour Party:

Joanna Tuffy has been a Dáil Deputy since 2011. She was formerly a member of South Dublin County Council for the Lucan electoral area from 1997 to 2003. She first stood for the Dáil in 2002. In that election she got a first preference vote of just 2,563 votes, crucially almost 1,000 votes behind Paul Gogarty (GP). She never closed that gap. In the 2007 Dáil election she increased her vote to 4,075 (10.9%), which was enough to win her the extra seat that had been created in the constituency, comfortably ahead of Frances Fitzgerald. In the 2011 Dáil election Tuffy topped the poll, her personal vote share increasing to 17.5% while her running mate Robert Dowds picked up another 13.2% to give the Labour Party 30.7% of the poll and a second seat. Dowds won 5,643 first preference votes, which gave him the fourth seat in the constituency. In September 2015 Dowds announced he would not run in 2016, saying that he thought Joanna Tuffy had a better chance than he did of holding the one seat the party was likely to win.

Tuffy was a member of Seanad Éireann from 2002 to 2007 on the Administrative Panel and publicly opposed her party's decision to campaign for the abolition of the Seanad. Her father Eamon Tuffy was co-opted to South Dublin County Council in 2003 to replace her when the dual mandate was abolished. He succeeded in holding the seat in 2004 and 2009 but lost it in 2014 when he polled only 507 votes.

Fianna Fáil:

John Curran was a member of Dáil Éireann from 2002 to 2011. After long serving and controversial deputy Liam Lawlor resigned from the party in 2000, Fianna Fáil ran two new candidates, both young businessmen, in 2002. Des Kelly ran in the Lucan end and John Curran in the Clondalkin end. Curran proved by far the stronger of the two, topping the poll with 5,904 first preferences and taking the first seat. He comfortably held it in 2007, topping topped the poll with 8,650 votes when another Lucan-based businessman, supermarket-owner Luke Moriarty, was his running mate. In 2011 Fianna Fáil opted for a one-candidate strategy and Curran ran alone. However, his 5,043 first preference votes, 11.8% of the total poll, never looked like being enough to see him through and he was eliminated on the seventh of the nine counts.

In 2008 Curran was appointed Minister for State at the Department of Community, Rural and Gaeltacht Affairs with special responsibility for Drugs Strategy and Community Affairs, in May 2009 he became Minister of State at the Departments of Community, Rural and Gaeltacht Affairs; Education and Science; and Justice, Equality and Law Reform with special responsibility for Integration and Community, and in March 2010 he was appointed Government Chief Whip. He was a member of South Dublin County council from 1999 to 2004 for the Clondalkin electoral area. Since he lost his seat in 2011 he has been working as a Dublin organiser for Fianna Fáil. He is a businessman and a prominent GAA activist in the Clondalkin area.

Sinn Féin:

The party candidate in 2007 was then-26-year-old Joanne Spain, a former journalist for An Phoblacht who also worked as a Sinn Féin press officer and on her first outing polled 3,462 first preferences (9.3%). In 2011 it ran Eoin Ó Broin and he is the candidate again this time.

Eoin Ó Broin is a member of South Dublin County Council for the Clondalkin local electoral area. He was co-opted to the council after the resignation of Cllr Mathew McDonagh in 2013. In the 2014 local elections Ó Broin held the seat comfortably, topping the poll with 2,992 votes, which was almost two quotas. His running mate Jonathan Graham got 2,306 first preferences and the party won two seats in the Clondalkin electoral area and would have won a third if they had another candidate. Ó Broin was also the party's candidate here in the 2011 Dáil elections in which he improved the party vote 2.5% and polled 5,060 first preferences which, with transfers, was only 552 votes behind Fine Gael's Derek Keating for the fourth seat on the final count. Ó'Broin previously contested local and Dáil Elections in the Dun Laoghaire constituency with little impact.

Ó Broin is a leading Sinn Féin strategist. He holds a MA from Queens University Belfast, is a political theorist, and is author of *Matxinada: Basque Nationalism and Radical Basque Youth Movements*, and *Sinn Féin and the Politics of Left Republicanism*. He is a former National Organiser of Ógra Sinn Féin and worked as Director of European affairs for the party from 2004 to 2007. He is also the editor of Left Republican Review and has had articles published in An Phoblacht, Magill, Village Magazine and the Irish Times. He was a member of Belfast City Council from 2001 to 2004. His partner Lynn Boylan MEP (SF) topped the poll in the 2014 European elections in the Dublin Constituency.

Green Party:

Paul Gogarty held this seat for the Green Party from 2002 to 2011. He has since left the party and will stand as an independent. At the time of going to press the party says that it intends to run a candidate in this constituency but could not confirm a name.

Anti-Austerity Alliance – People Before Profit:

Gino Kenny has been a member of South Dublin County Council since 2009. He first stood for election to the South Dublin County Council as a Socialist Workers Party candidate in 2004, polling 1,044, a 7.36% share, and failing to take a seat. In 2007 he stood for the Dáil as a People Before Profit candidate. On that occasion he obtained 1,058 votes (2.83%). He contested the local elections again in 2009 and got 1,137 which was a slight drop in vote share to 7.27%, however better transfers gave him the fifth seat with 1,137 first preferences. In 2014 he polled 1,696 votes (12.01%), which took him just over the quota on the first count and he won the fourth seat. He ran in the 2011 Dáil elections under the United Left Alliance banner. On that occasion he polled 2,471 first preference votes (5.8%) and survived to the 6th count. He works as a part time home care assistant in Clondalkin and lives in Neilstown.

Social Democrats:

Anne-Marie McNally lives in Lucan and is a first time candidate. She is Communications Coordinator & Policy Strategist to Catherine Murphy TD. She previously worked as Communications & Fundraising Manager for Dolphin House Community Development Association and as a community journalist. She has a Masters Degree in Political Communication from Dublin City University.

Workers' Party:

The Workers' Party has been represented in this constituency in the last two Dáil elections by Mick Finnegan, a trade union activist. In 2007 he received 366 first preference votes and in 2011 his 694 votes were 1.6% of the total. This time they have a new candidate.

Lorraine Hennessey is a community activist and part time shop assistant in Ballyfermot. A lone parent with a teenage son, she was active in setting up Balgaddy Working Together and campaigns on housing issues. In 2009 she stood for election to South Dublin County Council in Ballyfermot, got 433 votes (3.07%), and was eliminated at the 8th count.

Independents:

Paul Gogarty is a former Dail Deputy and current member of South Dublin County Council. He is based in Lucan. He joined the Green Party in 1989 and ran unsuccessfully for the party in Castleknock in the 1991 local elections. He first ran for Dáil Éireann in Dublin West in 1992 polling 906 first preferences. In the April 1996 by-election he increased that to 1,286 and he upped it again to 1,732 in the 1997 general election. In the 2002 Dáil election he polled 3,508 first preferences (12.3%) and took the third seat. He was the only Green Party deputy who did not serve as a Minister or Minister of State at some point in the Fianna Fáil/Green coalition of 2007–2011, although he was Chair of the Oireachtas Committee on Education and Science. In the 2011 Dáil election his vote collapsed and he polled only 1,484 votes (3.5%) and lost his deposit. Following this event he announced his retirement from politics and allowed his membership of the Green Party to lapse.

He decided to return to politics in 2014 and considered rejoining the Green Party, but eventually decided to run in the local elections as an independent. He is campaigning as part of the Independent Alliance although this does not appear on the ballot paper. He was elected to South Dublin County Council in the Lucan electoral area with 1,221 first preferences (8.71%), which gave him the fourth seat. He had previously held a seat on the council in the Lucan area from 1999 to 2003. In the 1999 local elections he topped the poll in Lucan with 1,238 first preferences (14.73%) and took the second seat. Before his election to Dáil Éireann he worked as a journalist.

Francis Timmons is an independent member of South Dublin County Council for the Clondalkin electoral area. He polled 682 first preference votes (4.83%) and took the fifth of the eight seats. He holds a degree in Social Care and Disability and has multiple qualifications in teaching both young people and adults, as well as a diploma in Health Service Management. In South Dublin County Council he is a member of the Arts, Culture, Gaeilge, Heritage and Libraries committees and he is currently chair of the Clondalkin Area Council. As a volunteer he is or has been involved with many organisations in the area, focusing on young people and people with disabilities.

Dublin North–West

Outgoing Deputies:

Róisín Shortall (Soc Dem), Dessie Ellis (SF), John Lyons (Lab)

Róisín Shortall was elected a Labour party deputy in 2011. In September 2012 she resigned from the party and sat as an independent. In September 2012 she was one of the founders of the Social Democrats.

The Constituency:

This continues to be a three seat constituency. Since 2011 four electoral divisions, consisting of Botanic A, B and C and Drumcondra C, with a total population of 11,506 have been transferred into this constituency from Dublin Central.

2016 Candidates will include:

Noel Rock (FG), John Lyons (Lab), Paul McAuliffe (FF), Dessie Ellis (SF), Cathleen Carney Boud (SF), Caroline Conroy (GP), Andrew Keegan (AAA–PBPA), Róisín Shortall (SD), Cormac McKay (DDI), Jimmy Dignam (WP)

	% Vote 1997	% Vote 2002	% Vote 2007	% Vote 2011	Swing 2011	Quotas 2011
Fine Gael	15.60	7.96	9.96	16.75	6.79	0.7
Labour	21.21	16.79	20.30	43.15	22.85	1.7
Fianna Fáil	47.04	47.54	48.84	11.79	–36.75	0.5
Sinn Féin	–	18.28	15.74	21.68	5.94	0.9
Green Party	4.16	2.32	2.75	1.00	–1.75	0.04
Others	11.99	7.11	2.41	5.62	3.21	0.2

In Brief:

This is another constituency where Labour won two seats in 2011 but faces a challenge to hold even one. John Lyons will have been helped by his local and national campaigning in the marriage referendum, although he faces strong competition of various shades. Sinn Féin has a seat here and will hold it, although his running mate Cathleen Carney Boud could replace its outgoing deputy Dessie Ellis. Róisín Shortall left Labour in 2012 and is now one of the leaders of the Social Democrats. She too will hold her seat. On balance therefore, it is likely to continue to be one seat for Sinn Féin, one for Labour and one for the Social Democrats here, though the Sinn Féin face may change. There has been no Fine Gael seat here for almost two decades and there is unlikely to be one after this election. If it does win a seat it will be at the expense of Labour's John Lyons. Fianna Fáil had two seats here until 2007 but has had none since 2011 and although its new candidate Paul McAulife will do well, it difficult to see it getting a seat in this three-seater given its current poll figures in the capital.

Fine Gael:

Fine Gael has been without a seat in this constituency since 1997 when incumbent TD Mary Flaherty lost her seat. In 2011 it had a two candidate strategy with councillor Bill Tormey and Clontarf businessman Gerry Breen who between them managed a combined vote of 16.7%. The party is running a new candidate in 2016.

Noel Rock has been a member of Dublin City Council for the Ballymun electoral area since 2014. He first stood for election in the 2009 local elections in the Artane electoral area. On that occasion his first preference vote of 1,284 (7.9%) was enough to keep him in the race until the eighth count but he failed to win a seat. In 2014 he moved to the Ballymun electoral area, where his 1,247 votes (7.27%) and transfers from the elimination of Tormey in the tenth count and Breen in the thirteenth count took him over the line to win the third seat.

Rock was raised by his mother and grandparents in Glasnevin and Ballymun and holds a degree from Dublin City University. He did an internship with then Senator Hilary Clinton and later had a press position in the European Parliament. He worked for a while in a cloud computing company. He has been parliamentary assistant to Senator Catherine Noone. Before the 2014 local elections he pledged that he would return his allowed unvouched expenses if elected and he keeps a counter of the money returned on his website. He will probably be Fine Gael's youngest candidate in 2016.

Labour Party:

Róisín Shorthall was elected on the Labour ticket here in all elections from 1992 to 2011. She resigned from the Labour Party in 2012 and in July 2015 launched the Social Democrats. The Labour party's only contestant in 2016 will be John Lyons TD, who took the final seat here in 2011.

John Lyons has been a member of Dáil Éireann since 2011. He was previously a member of Dublin City Council. He was co-opted to the council in February 2008 to replace university lecturer and trade union activist Mary Murphy. In the 2009 local elections Lyons topped the poll in the large Ballymun–Finglas electoral area polling 3,721 first preferences, which was 929 votes above the quota. His 22.22% share of the vote, added to his running mate's, made Labour the highest polling party in the area at 31.56% in those local elections. In the 2011 general election Lyons polled 4,799 first preferences (14.63%) and attracted transfers from across the board to win the last seat.

He is a former deputy principal at St Vincent's secondary school Glasnevin. He has focused on issues such as youth unemployment in Dáil Éireann and is Vice-Chairperson of the Oireachtas Committee on Jobs, Enterprise and Innovation and Deputy Whip of the Labour Party. He has a BA and HDip from NUI Maynooth and studied special education at Trinity College. He is gay and was one of the leading campaigners for the party in the Marriage Equality referendum in May 2015.

Fianna Fáil:

Fianna Fáil held two seats here from 1997 to 2011 with Noel Ahern and Pat Carey. It polled 49% of the vote in 2007 but this collapsed to 11.8% in 2011 and the party lost both seats. This time the party has a new candidate.

Paul McAuliffe has been a member of Dublin City Council for the Ballymun electoral area since 2009. He first ran for the Progressive Democrats in the 2004 local elections in his native Finglas. On that occasion his 1,031 votes (7.16%) were not enough to win him a seat. In the 2009 local elections he ran as a Fianna Fáil candidate in the Ballymun–Finglas electoral area and polled 1,144 votes (6.83%) which kept him in the race long enough to pick up enough transfers from his two Fianna Fáil running mates and independent Conor Sludds to take the final seat. In 2014 the electoral area was once more Ballymun and he improved his vote to 1,490 votes (8.69%), which was enough to give him the fifth of the seven seats.

McAuliffe is the Leader of the Fianna Fáil group on the City Council and is Chairperson of the Council's Enterprise and Economic Development policy committee. He studied Business and Resource Management at the National College of Ireland, graduating in 1999.

Sinn Féin:

After many attempts as the party sole candidate for the Dáil in this constituency Dessie Ellis finally won a seat here in the 2011 elections. On this occasion he is joined by a running mate.

Dessie Ellis has been a member of Dáil Éireann since 2011. He was first elected to political office on Dublin City Council for the Finglas electoral area in the 1999 local elections when he polled 2,278 first preference votes. He was then the party's candidate in the 2002 Dáil election when he polled 4,781, which was almost three quarters of a quota, leaving him 39 votes ahead of Labour's Róisín Shortall on the first count. However, Ellis did not do as well on transfers and he was 1,331 behind Shortall on the sixth and final count.

In the 2004 local elections Ellis topped the poll with 4,300 first preference votes, again in the Finglas electoral area, where this time the quota was 2,882. His vote in that local election was more than twice the nearest candidate. In the 2007 Dáil election he surprisingly failed to get elected. His vote was a disappointing 4,873 which was a drop of just over 2.5% on his 2002 share. In the 2009 local elections he polled 3,263 first preferences in the enlarged Ballymun–Finglas electoral area, which was 471 votes above the quota and he took the second seat behind Labour's John Lyons. In the 2011 Dáil election Ellis won 7,115 votes (21.7%). That figure was only 1,088 short of a quota but it took until the eighth count for him to make up the votes to take the second seat. In Dáil Éireann he is Sinn Féin spokesperson on Housing and Transport and a member of the Transport and Communications Committee and of the subcommittee on Transport, Tourism and Sports.

Cathleen Carney Boud is a member of Dublin City Council for the Ballymun electoral area. She is based in Ballygall in the Santry/Whitehall end of the constituency and is originally from Glasnevin. She studied law at Trinity College Dublin. In the 2014 local elections she and party colleague Noeleen Reilly each took more than a quota in the Ballymun electoral area with Reilly topping the poll with 2,540 (14.82%) at the Ballymun end, while Carney Boud took 2,328 votes (13.58%). After some internal party controversy Carney Boud rather than Reilly was selected by the party to run in this election with Ellis. Eamonn Nolan, the chair of Sinn Féin's Dublin Cúige (province) stepped down from that role for a while in spring 2015 after a formal complaint that he had favoured Carney Boud.

Green Party:

The party's first time candidate in 2002 was Eugene O'Brien who polled a poor 607 first preference votes. In 2007 the party ran

Declan Fitzgerald, whose 853 first preference votes were a 2.75% share. In 2011 Ruari Holohan was chosen to contest at the last minute when the previous candidate Rachel Pearson withdrew, but he could only gather 328 votes (1%). This time the party has a new candidate.

Caroline Conroy is based in Glasnevin. She holds degree in Business Studies obtained from Dublin City University while working full time as a human resources manager. She ran in the local elections in 2014 in Ballymun, garnering 738 votes (4.3%) and surviving until the thirteenth count. She is married with three children

Anti-Austerity Alliance – People Before Profit:

Andrew Keegan has been a member of Dublin City Council for the Ballymun electoral area since 2014. He took the 6th seat there with 642 votes (3.74%) and was elected on the final count. He stood previously for the Dáil in 2011 but polled just 677 votes (2.06%). He is a construction worker.

Social Democrats:

Róisín Shortall is based in Whitehall and was first elected to Dáil Éireann in 1992. She is currently joint leader of the Social Democrats. She was one of the few Labour deputies elected for the first time in 1992 to retain her seat in 1997. Having received 4,084 first preferences in 1997, Shortall increased that to 4,391 in 2002. In 2007 she increased it again to 6,286 first preferences, which was 20.30% of the first preference vote. She proved remarkably successful at attracting transfers in both 2002 and 2007, and importantly proved almost three times better at it than Sinn Féin's Dessie Ellis. In 2011 she polled 9,359 first preference votes (28.5%), which was 1,156 over quota and which ensured that Labour took the third seat ahead of Fine Gael. In the 2011 Fine Gael/Labour coalition she was Minister of State for Primary Care from 2011 until she resigned from the position and the party in 2012, criticising how the prioritisation of primary care centres had been carried out by her senior Minister, Fine Gael's James O'Reilly.

Shortall was chairperson of the Eastern Health Board from 1996 to 1998 and was a member of Dublin City Council from 1991 to 2003. She, along with former independent TDs Stephen Donnelly and Catherine Murphy, announced the formation of the Social Democrats on July 15th 2015. Deputy Shortall is based in Whitehall, has a degree in economics and politics and is a former primary school teacher at St Joseph's School for the Deaf in Cabra.

Workers Party:
Jimmy Dignam is a first time candidate. He is based in Ballymun and works in west Dublin with a fruit and vegetable delivery company based around cooperative principles. He is a keen supporter of Bohemians FC.

Direct Democracy Ireland:
Cormac MacKay is a carer from Drumcondra where he looks after an 85 year old friend while studying for a QQI award in Health Care. He ran in the Ballymun electoral area in the 2014 City Council elections, polling just 162 votes (0.94%). His personal platform on that occasion was making the Council and its staff more accountable and better spending prioritisation. He hopes to run for the post of directly elected Mayor of Dublin one day. Leaving school at 16 despite good Junior Cert results because he preferred the world of work he moved to Australia at the age of 19 and has also worked in London and Toronto, and has both shop floor and management experience with a wide range of companies. He plays hockey with St Brendan's Phoenix Park.

Dublin Rathdown

Outgoing Deputies:

Shane Ross (Ind), Alex White (Lab), Olivia Mitchell (FG), Peter Mathews (Ind), Alan Shatter (FG)

Peter Mathews (Ind) was elected as a Fine Gael candidate in 2011 but left the party in 2013 and will contest the 2016 election as an independent.

In September 2015 Olivia Mitchell (FG) announced that she would not be contesting the 2016 election.

The Constituency:

This three-seat constituency replaces the previous Dublin South constituency which had five seats. The constituency comprises the same area as Dublin South except that the divisions of Cabinteely–Loughlinstown (part east of Carrickmines–Kiltiernan road), Foxrock–Carrickmines Foxrock–Torquay and Stillorgan–Leopardstown have been returned to the neigbouring Dun Laoghaire constituency, while Ballyboden, Edmondstown, Firhouse–Ballycullen, Firhouse–Knocklyon, Rathfarnham–Ballyroan, Rathfarnham–Butterfield, Rathfarnham–Hermitage, Rathfarnham–St. Enda's and Rathfarnham Village are transferred to Dublin South–West.

	% Vote 1997	% Vote 2002	% Vote 2007	% Vote 2011	Swing 2011	Quotas 2011
Fine Gael	29.09	19.78	27.26	36.35	9.09	2.2
Labour	10.60	9.49	10.43	17.98	7.55	1.1
Fianna Fáil	38.62	36.64	41.33	9.42	–31.91	0.6
Sinn Féin	–	3.93	3.01	2.64	–0.37	0.2
Green Party	6.10	9.45	11.06	6.78	–4.28	0.4
Others	15.59	20.71	6.9	26.84	19.94	1.6

2016 Candidates will include:
Alan Shatter (FG), Josepha Madigan (FG,) Alex White (Lab), Mary White (FF), Sorcha Nic Cormaic (SF), Catherine Martin (GP), Nicola Curry (AAA–PBP), Peter Mathews (Ind), Shane Ross (Ind)

In Brief:
With four high profile TDs contesting for three seats at least one of them will be unsuccessful and indeed, apart from Shane Ross, none of the incumbents are safe. Along with Dublin West this is the constituency most likely to see a ministerial casualty. Alex White will struggle. Labour had just over a quota here and the sharp drop in their support in Dublin will be magnified in this volatile constituency. After Ross there will certainly be one Fine Gael seat, although outgoing deputy and former minister Alan Shatter faces a very strong challenge from his running mate Councillor Josepha Madigan. The third seat is likely to be between Labour's Alex White, Fianna Fáil's Senator Mary White, who has a habit of confounding pundits, and whoever is the second Fine Gael candidate. There is no room for two independents in this three-seater and Peter Mathews seems certain to lose out. Much could depend on how well the Green Party's Catherine Martin can hold on to the strong personal vote of party leader Eamon Ryan, and where her transfers go.

Fine Gael:
Josepha Madigan has been a member of Dun Laoghaire–Rathdown County Council for the Stillorgan electoral area since 2014. She is a family law solicitor. She has published both *Appropriate Dispute Resolution*, a handbook for family lawyers, and *Negligent Behaviour*, a novel about corruption in Ireland's 'Tiger Years'. Educated at Trinity College Dublin, she is married and has lived all her life in the Stillorgan area. In her first local election in 2014 she received 1,350 first preference votes (13.68%) and took the second seat. She is Leas-Cathaoirleach of the County Council. Josepha Madigan is a member of the Dundrum Environment, Culture, Housing and Community Committee and of the Dundrum Planning and Enterprise, and Transportation and Water Services Committees.

Alan Shatter was first elected to Dáil Éireann in 1981 and held his Dáil seat at each election from 1981 until 2002. Fine Gael once held three seats in this constituency but in the 2002 election the party's vote share fell to 19.78%, which meant that it could not even win two seats. Alan Shatter's vote fell from his 8,094 in 1997 to 5,368 in 2002. Olivia Mitchell's vote was two hundred more than that and in the end she took the party's one seat by 657 votes. In 2007 Shatter regained the seat when the party recovered 7.4% of the vote lost in 2002 to bring it to 27.3%. In 2011 Shatter and Mitchell were again the candidates along with Peter Mathews and the party increased its share to 2.18 quotas. The surplus from Shane Ross, along with many of the votes of the Green Party's Eamon Ryan, gave three seats. Shatter's personal vote was 7,716 (10.62%) which was enough to take the final seat.

He was a member of most of Fine Gael's frontbenches in the 1980s and 1990s as spokesman on issues such as Justice, Health and law reform. In 2011 he became Minister at both the Department of Justice and Equality and the Department of Defence. Although a reforming Minister in both departments, in May 2014 he resigned in the wake of the Guerin report and controversies about the handling of various policing and justice controversies. As a back bencher or opposition front bencher he was the author of a number of private member bills, which were enacted in the area of family law. A former solicitor, he was a member of Dublin County Council and later of South Dublin County Council between 1979 and 1999. He has suffered the loss of much of his base in the Rathfarnham area to the Dublin South West constituency. He was selected at the party convention only just ahead of Cllr Neale Richmond who ran Olivia Mitchell's campaign in 2011. Shatter has written two books, *Shatter's Family Law in the Republic of Ireland*, (Buttersworth) and *Laura* (Poolbeg, 1990) a novel.

Labour Party:

Labour's Eithne Fitzgerald famously polled more than 17,000 first preferences when she won a seat for the party here in 1992. However, she lost the seat when she fell victim to the backlash against Labour in 1997. She contested the Dáil again in the 2002 election but polled just 9.5% of the vote with 5,247 first preference votes. In 2007 Labour ran two new candidates, Aidan Culhane and Alex White. Together they did no more than hold the party's vote share.

Alex White is based in Rathfarnham and has been a member of Dáil Éireann since 2011. He has been Minister for Communications, Energy and Natural Resources since July 2014. He is a Senior Counsel and worked previously as a radio producer with RTÉ. He was the party candidate in the 2009 by-election in this constituency and was odds on favourite to win it until Fine Gael announced the candidature of high profile RTÉ Economics Correspondent George Lee. Lee won the seat in the by-election but White was second with 19.8% of the first preference vote. In the 2011 General Election White, as one of two Labour party candidates with Aidan Culhane, polled 8,524 votes (11.7%), almost twice those of his running mate, and took the second of the five seats in the constituency. In 2011 he was appointed chairman of the Joint Oireachtas Committee on Finance, Public Expenditure and Reform. In 2012 he became Minister of State for Primary Care following the resignation of Róisín Shortall. After the resignation of Eamon Gilmore in 2014 he stood for the party leadership, losing to Joan Burton. In 2015 he was made Minister for Communications, Energy and Natural Resources. He was a member of Seanad Éireann on the Cultural and Educational Panel and Labour leader in the Seanad from 2007 to 2011. He was a member of South Dublin County Council for the Terenure–Rathfarnham electoral area from 2004 to 2007. He was Director of the Labour party campaign in the May 2015 Marriage Equality referendum.

Fianna Fáil:

Fianna Fáil's Seamus Brennan and Tom Kitt took the first two seats here in 1997, 2002 and 2007. In the 2009 by-election, Seamus Brennan's son Shay came in third with just 17.8%. In 2011 Maria Corrigan, who had been the party's third candidate in 2002 and 2007 was the sole candidate and polled just 6,844 votes (9.4%). Shay Brennan contested the party selection convention for this election but lost out to Senator Mary White.

Mary White is based in Dundrum and has been a member of Seanad Éireann on the Industrial and Commercial Panel since September 2002. She holds a degree in Economics and Politics from University College Dublin and a Higher Diploma in Architectural Technology from Dublin Institute of Technology. She founded Lir Chocolates with her business partner Connie Doody in 1987. Mary White is a former chair of The President's Award – Gaisce, and has served on several state boards including the Higher Education Authority, the National College of Art and Design and An Bord Bia. In 2008 she announced that she would contest the Presidency but in 2011 decided not to seek the Fianna Fáil nomination for that office. She is married to Padraig White, former Chief Executive of the IDA. She has run a high profile campaign in the constituency against inheritance tax.

Sinn Féin:

In 2002 the Sinn Féin candidate was Deirdre Whelan who polled 2,172 first preference votes and was eliminated on the fourth count. In 2007 they ran two candidates – Sorcha Nic Cormaic, a primary school teacher in Dundrum and former member of Sinn Féin Ard Comhairle, and Shaun Tracey a party press officer. Together they polled 1,843 votes (3.0%). Tracey was the candidate in the 2009 by-election, when he had a marginal increase in the party vote share with 1,705 (3.3%). In 2011 Nic Cormaic was the candidate and the party vote share fell slightly to 2.6% although the actual vote was slightly increased at 1,915.

Sorcha Nic Cormaic has been a member of Dun Laoghaire–Rathdown County Council for the Dundrum electoral area since 2014. She finally gained a seat in Dundrum in 2014 with 1,161 first preferences (8.68%). She was previously an unsuccessful candidate in the 2004 local elections when she polled 1,876 votes (6.44%) in the Terenure–Rathfarnham electoral area and in the 2009 local elections when she stood in the Rathfarnham electoral area and polled 551 first preferences (3.18%). She has studied Classical Civilisation and Philosophy in University College Galway and gained an H.Dip Ed from University College Dublin. She is on the Dublin and Dun Laoghaire Education and Training Board.

Green Party:

Dublin South was the first constituency to elect a Green Party TD when Roger Garland won a seat here in 1989. He lost it in 1992. Ten years later that party took a Dáil seat seat here again when Eamon Ryan was elected in 2002. He retained the seat more comfortably than expected in 2007 but in 2011 his vote share fell by 5 percentage points and he lost his seat. In 2016 he will contest Dublin Bay South so the party's deputy leader will run as the candidate in this constituency, where she polled over 2,000 votes in the 2014 local elections.

Catherine Martin has been a member of Dún Laoghaire–Rathdown Council for the Dundrum electoral area since 2014. She is the deputy leader of the Green party at national level. She ran in the local elections for the first time in 2014 and her 1,068 votes (7.98%) gave her the fifth seat. She is also the Green Party's education spokesperson. She has been a teacher of English and Music at St Tiernan's school, Dundrum, for the last 15 years. She is on the board of the Dublin and Dun Laoghaire Education and Training Board and the Dublin Mid–Leinster Regional Health Forum and also serves on the Dun Laoghaire–Rathdown County Sports Partnership.

Anti-Austerity Alliance – People Before Profit:

Nicola Curry is based in Nutgrove. She began her career in politics as the chairperson of Ballyogan Environment Group. She stood in the 2011 Dáil election as a member of the People before Profit Alliance (PBPA) and the United Left Alliance (ULA) in 2011 and polled 1,277 votes (1.76%), being eliminated on the third count. In the 2014 local elections she polled 604 votes (6.76%) in the Glencullen–Sandyford electoral area but was eliminated on the eighth count. She is a working mother, having returned to adult education at University College Dublin to achieve a degree in social science and subsequently an MA in the same subject. In the 2011 general election she learned the dangers of political campaigning when her hand was bitten by a dog as she was putting a leaflet through a letterbox.

Independents:

Peter Mathews was the third Fine Gael candidate in Dublin South in 2011, achieving 9,053 votes (12.5%) and taking the second of three Fine Gael seats, ahead of Alan Shatter. In July 2013 he was expelled from the Fine Gael parliamentary party when he voted against Protection of Life During Pregnancy Bill 2013. In September of that year he and other former Fine Gael parliamentarians formed the Reform Alliance, However, when most of his colleagues went on to establish Renua Ireland, Mathews was not a member of the new party and announced that he would contest this election as an independent.

Mathews was educated at Gonzaga College and University College Dublin and joined the ICC bank in 1979. He left the bank in 1999 to set up a consultancy specialising in property deals. He is a chartered accountant and was a member of the Progressive Democrats when they were founded, but left the party shortly afterwards. Married, with four adult children, he lives in Mount Merrion and continues to be a frequent commentator on banking and economic matters for the print and broadcast media.

Shane Ross has been a member of the Dáil since 2011. Prior to that he represented the University of Dublin (Trinity College Dublin) constituency in Seanad Éireann from 1981 to 2011, becoming the longest serving member of Seanad Éireann. Between 1991 and 1999 he represented Fine Gael on Wicklow County Council and he also ran unsuccessfully for Fine Gael in Wicklow in the 1992 Dáil election. He took the Fine Gael whip in the Seanad from 1993–1997. He lost his deposit as an independent in the 1984 European Elections in Dublin. In the 2011 Dáil election he ran as an independent, topping the poll with 17,075 votes (23.5%), which was almost 5,000 votes over the quota. He was the largest single vote getter in the country in that election. More recently, with other independent deputies Finian McGrath and John Halligan, he has been one of the leaders of efforts to organize independent candidates for the 2016 in under the Independent Alliance banner.

Dublin South–Central

Outgoing Deputies:

Catherine Byrne (FG), Eric Byrne (Lab), Michael Conaghan (Lab), Aengus Ó Snodaigh (SF), Joan Collins (Ind)

In June 2015 Michael Conaghan (Lab) announced that he would not contest this election.

The Constituency:

This constituency has been reduced from five to four seats with the transfer of the districts of Kimmage C and Terenure A, B, C and D with a population of 12,563 to the renamed Dublin Bay South constituency.

	% Vote 1997	% Vote 2002	% Vote 2007	% Vote 2011	Swing 2011	Quotas 2011
Fine Gael	24.95	16.94	14.39	23.48	9.09	1.4
Labour	21.91	19.72	21.13	35.41	14.28	2.1
Fianna Fáil	34.43	34.32	33.08	9.50	–23.58	0.6
Sinn Féin	4.77	12.70	10.15	13.36	3.21	0.8
Green Party	3.95	5.22	5.80	1.99	–3.81	0.1
United Left	–	–	–	12.91	12.91	0.8
Others	10.19	11.1	15.46	3.36	–12.10	0.2

2016 Candidates will include:

Catherine Byrne (FG), Eric Byrne (Lab), Catherine Ardagh (FF), Aengus Ó Snodaigh (SF), Máire Devine (SF), Oisín Ó hAlmhain (GP), Bríd Smith (AAA–PBP), Michael Gargan (Renua), Joan Collins (Ind), Paul Hand (Ind), Richard Murray (Ind)

In Brief:

It is striking in this constituency that Sinn Féin are the only party running two candidates. Catherine Byrne is from Inchicore so unaffected by the moving of districts at the east side of the constituency. At the time of going to press she was the only Fine Gael candidate, which seems like a wise course. She will hold her seat. This is yet another constituency where Labour won two seats in 2011 but has already acknowledged that one of those seats is gone by running just one candidate. Outgoing deputy Eric Byrne has run a dozen times in Dáil elections and has never managed to retain his seat. This time, however, he seems well placed to do so. Outgoing deputy Joan Collins, describing herself this time as an Independent Socialist, and Brid Smith of People Before Profit, are also very strong, Sinn Féin's Aengus Ó Snodaigh will definitely retain his seat. It looks like one Sinn Féin, one Fine Gael and then Eric Byrne, Joan Collins and Brid Smith fighting for the last two seats.

Fine Gael:

Catherine Byrne was reared in Inchicore and now lives on Bulfin road. She has been a Dáil Deputy since 2007. She ran with then deputy Gay Mitchell in the 2002 election when she received 2,012 first preferences and didn't get elected. She was also the party's candidate in the 1999 by-election in this constituency, when she finished third with 4,037 votes. She was a member of Dublin City Council from 1999 to 2007, representing the South–West Inner City area. In the 2004 local elections she topped the poll with 1,971 first preferences, which was 22.64% of the vote, and took the second seat. In 2007's general election she took the fourth seat with 4,713 first preferences. In 2011 the party, perhaps surprisingly, ran three candidates in this traditionally left wing constituency and although the party as a whole had a 23.5% vote share it was not until the twelfth count that Byrne, who polled 5,604 first preferences (11%) won her seat after her two party colleagues had been eliminated. She was Lord Mayor of Dublin in 2005/2006.

Labour Party:

In 2011, in the absence of Mary Upton, the party ran three candidates, Eric Byrne, her nephew Henry Upton and Cllr. Michael Conaghan. Byrne was only 131 votes short of a quota, topping the poll by a substantial margin with 8,357 votes (16.4%). Conaghan came home when Upton was eliminated. Neither runs this time around with Conaghan saying that he thinks there is only one seat here for Labour.

Eric Byrne has been a member of Dáil Éireann from 1989 to 1992, from 1994 to 1997, and again since 2011. This will be his twelfth time to contest a Dáil election. He was a Democratic Left TD from 1989 to 1992. He lost the seat in the 1992 election but regained it in the 1994 by-election. He narrowly lost his seat, after a marathon 10-day recount against Ben Briscoe, in 1997. Under the terms of the Labour and Democratic Left merger pact he contested the seat for the Labour Party alongside Mary Upton in the 2002 election and again with Upton in 2007 but failed to be elected on either occasion. He was ultimately successful in regaining the seat in 2011. 2016 will be Byrne's twelfth Dáil election in the area where he first ran in 1977 with Sinn Féin the Workers' Party. He was a member of Dublin City Council for the Crumlin area from 1985 to 2011. He topped the poll in the Crumlin/Kimmage electoral area in the 2004 local elections with 4,045 first preferences, where the quota was 3,359. In the 2009 local elections he again topped the poll in the same electoral area, polling 3,652 first preferences, again well above the quota of 2,883. He is a member of of the Joint Committee on Foreign Affairs & Trade, the Joint Administration Committee and the Joint Committee on European Affairs.

Fianna Fáil:

Fianna Fáil ran just one candidate here in 2011. In December 2010 one of its sitting deputies, Seán Ardagh, announced his intention to retire and argued that the party should run just one candidate. The party candidate was the other incumbent Michael Mulcahy, who polled 4,837 votes (9.5%). He lost out to Sinn Féin's Aengus Ó Snodaigh for the last seat on the final count. In 2015 Seán Ardagh's daughter Catherine Ardagh was selected to be the party's only candidate after the National executive had issued a directive to the local organisation that it must select a female candidate.

Catherine Ardagh is a member of Dublin City Council for the Crumlin–Kimmage electoral area. She is a solicitor based in Crumlin village. In 2009 she ran for Dublin City Council in the

Inner City South–West ward, where she gained 719 votes (8.7%), which was not enough to give her a seat. In the 2014 local elections, however, she polled 857 votes (7.56%) and took the fifth of the six seats. Her father Seán Ardagh was a TD for this constituency from 1997 to 2011.

Sinn Féin:

This is one of a handful of constituencies where the party is running two candidates with some real prospect of challenging for a second seat.

Aengus Ó Snodaigh has been a member of Dáil Éireann since 2002. He is currently Sinn Féin's Chief Whip in Leinster House and their spokesperson on Social Protection. Before contesting the 2002 general election he was the party candidate in the 1999 by-election in this constituency. He took 5,591 (12.7%) of the first preference when he first won the seat in 2002. In 2007 the party's share fell back to 10.15% and he polled 4,825 first preferences but he retained the seat. His position strengthened again in 2011 to 13.4% when he took 6,804 first preference votes.

Ó Snodaigh was also an unsuccessful Dáil candidate in the neighbouring Dublin South East constituency for the 1987 election. He previously worked as a journalist with An Phoblacht and as an officer with Bord Na Gaeilge. On 30 May 2010, he was one of three Irish politicians who were prevented from leaving Cyprus by authorities to join an ill-fated flotilla carrying aid to the blockaded Gaza Strip. In 2012 RTÉ revealed that, before a limit was set on TDs use of Dáil ink cartridges, Ó Snodaigh had used €50,000 worth in 2007 and 2008 which he had said were needed to inform his constituents of legislative changes and protests.

Máire Devine is a surprising choice by the party to run in this constituency since she is a member of South Dublin county council for the Tallaght Central electoral area, which is in the Dublin South–West constituency. She had hoped to be the party's candidate in that constituency for the 2014 by-election but the party ran her council colleague Cathal King instead. Devine was co-opted to Dublin South County Council in 2011 when Seán Crowe regained his Dáil seat. In 2014 she topped the poll in the Tallaght Central electoral area with 2,874 votes (24.45%). She has a degree in Politics and History and a post graduate qualification in Management. She has also qualified and now works as a mental health nurse.

Green Party:

The party candidate in 2002 was Kristine McElroy who polled 2,299 votes. The party's candidate in 2007 was Tony McDermott, then a member of South Dublin County Council for the Terenure/ Rathfarnham area. He polled 2,756 votes for a 5.8% share of the first preference vote. The party has a new candidate in 2016.

Oisín Ó hAlmhain was born in Terenure and lived in Inchicore. He was also the party's candidate in the 2011 election. He was then 22 years of age and polled 1,015 (2.0%) first preferences. He is a great nephew of former President Cearbhall Ó Dálaigh. Oisín is a hospital pharmacist by profession. Married, with three children, he is regularly seen with various hands on community groups around the city, working on area clean ups and similar activities.

Anti-Austerity Alliance – People Before Profit:

Bríd Smith has been a member of Dublin City Council since 2009. She comes from a long republican socialist tradition. Her maternal grandfather was a shop steward during the 1913 Lockout and fought in the Four Courts in 1916, while her protestant working class bus driver father was a strong trade unionist who became involved in the republican movement during the 'Troubles'. She herself contested her first national election in 1997 when, running for the Socialist Workers Party in this constituency, she gained just 218 votes (0.54%). In 2002 she increased that to 617 (1.4%). In the 2004 Dublin City Council elections she stood in the Ballyfermot electoral area and got 1,094 (11.76%) and although this was almost half a quota she failed to attract enough transfers to take a seat. The general election of 2007 saw her running under the People Before Profit banner with a substantial increase in her vote to 2,086 (4.39%) and the changed political climate of 2009 finally gave her a local authority seat in Ballyfermot–Drimnagh with 2,269 (18.8%). She did not run in the 2011 General Election although she was Director of Elections for the party. She was the People Before Profit candidate in the European elections of 2014, when she garnered 23,875 (6.77%). The Socialist Party candidate and outgoing MEP Paul Murphy, who lost his seat, accused Smith of splitting the left wing vote in the European elections. On the same day Smith retained her local authority seat with a slightly decreased 2,031 (13.82%).

Renua Ireland:
Michael Gargan has no previous political experience. He is the owner of a computer repair business in Kimmage. He has not previously campaigned for any party. His special issues in this campaign include the bringing in of 'Three strikes' sentencing, the introduction of a €500 million tax credit for childcare for working families and the use of private pension funds to create social housing. At the launch of the Renua manifesto he was one of the five candidates who declared their support for a change to the 1983 amendment to the Constitution.

Independents:
Joan Collins is based in Inchicore and has been a member of Dáil Éireann since 2011. In that election she stood for the United Left Alliance polling 6,574 first preferences (12.9%) and taking the fourth of the five seats. However, in 2013 she left that grouping and, with Clare Daly, founded United Left. She now describes herself as an Independent Socialist. Collins was a member of Dublin City Council from 2004 to 2011. In 2004 as an independent candidate on an anti-bin charge platform, she polled 2,777 first preferences (quota 3,359) and took the fourth of the five seats in the Crumlin–Kimmage electoral area. In the 2009 local elections, as a People Before Profit candidate, she polled 2,512 first preferences (quota 2,883) and took the second of the four seats in the reduced area. She was also an independent candidate for Dublin South Central in the 2007 Dáil elections, polling 2,203 first preferences for a 4.63% share. During her time as a City Councillor Collins continued to work as a clerk with An Post and was active in the Communications Workers Union. In September 2015 she

was charged with offences alleged to have taken place at a protest against the installation of water meters. She denies the charges and the trial is still pending.

Paul Hand is an independent member of Dublin City Council for the Ballyfermot–Drimnagh electoral area. He first ran in the local elections in 2014 when his 1,300 first preference votes (8.84%) won the fourth of six seats in that area. Raised in Bluebell by his mother after his parents separated he is particularly active in campaigning for the provision of social and affordable housing. He and his brothers had difficulty finding affordable accommodation after their family home was sold in 2015 after the death of their mother.

Richard Murray is a first time candidate. He and his wife have lived in the constituency for nearly 30 years and have a young family. He has been exploring new ways to fund his campaign. An attempt at crowd funding in 2015 failed when only €20 of the €10,000 he was seeking was pledged. In December 2015 he used a sponsored walk to raise election funds and awareness. In his election pledges he says that he is seeking the establishment of a Corruption Assets Bureau to specifically target and seize assets of corrupt politicians, bankers, and state figures. He promises that if elected he will donate €40,000 to local community groups and initiatives.

Dublin South–West

Outgoing Deputies:

Pat Rabbitte (Lab), Seán Crowe (SF), Eamonn Maloney (Ind), Paul Murphy (AAA)

Brian Hayes (FG) was elected for this constituency in 2011 but resigned his seat when he was elected to the European Parliament in 2014. Paul Murphy (AAA) was elected in the resulting by-election in October 2014. In July 2015 Pat Rabbitte announced that he would not contest the 2016 election.

Eamonn Maloney was elected for the Labour Party in 2011 but in September 2015 announced he was leaving the party and would contest this election as an independent.

The Constituency:

This constituency is now a five-seater having gained an extra seat in the redraw of constituencies since 2011. It comprises the southern part of South Dublin county council. An area of the former Dublin South, with a population of 39,311 has been added including Ballyboden, Edmondstown, Firhouse–Ballycullen, Firhouse–Knocklyon, Rathfarnham–Ballyroan, Rathfarnham–Butterfield, Rathfarnham–Hermitage, Rathfarnham–St.Endas, and Rathfarnham–Village with a population of 39,311.

	% Vote 1997	% Vote 2002	% Vote 2007	% Vote 2011	Swing 2011	Quotas 2011
Fine Gael	15.50	12.65	20.04	27.77	7.73	1.4
Labour	21.89	19.80	19.99	36.27	16.28	1.8
Fianna Fáil	29.94	38.68	39.27	10.77	–28.50	0.5
Sinn Féin	8.90	20.29	12.16	17.17	5.01	0.9
Green Party	3.14	3.14	3.71	1.02	–2.69	0.05
Others	20.63	5.45	4.83	6.99	2.16	0.3

2016 Candidates will include:

Colm Brophy (FG), Anne-Marie Dermody (FG), Karen Warren (FG), Pamela Kearns (Lab), Mick Duff (Lab), John Lahart (FF), Seán Crowe (SF), Sarah Holland (SF), Francis Noel Duffy (GP), Paul Murphy (AAA), Sandra Fay (AAA), Ronan McMahon (Ren), Stephen Sinclair (DDI), Deirdre O'Donovan (Ind), Declan Burke (Ind), Peter Fitzpatrick (Ind), Eamonn Maloney (Ind), Katherine Zappone (Ind)

In Brief:

What was previously mostly Tallaght and its environs has a significantly changed demographic with the addition of much of Rathfarnham, Ballyboden and the more middle class end of Firhouse. With both Pat Rabbitte and Brian Hayes not contesting this time around, and Eamonn Maloney having left Labour to run as an independent there is no outgoing government TD contesting even though the government won three seats here in 2011. Paul Murphy looks safe. Sinn Féin is certain of at least one seat although Seán Crowe may not necessarily occupy it. There is also likely to be a Fine Gael seat, which will be closely fought for by Colm Brophy and a well-resourced campaign from the party's newcomer Anne Marie Dermody. Maloney, now an independent, high profile Senator Katherine Zapponne and Fianna Fáil's John Lahart will fight for the last seat.

Fine Gael:

Brian Hayes was elected to the Dáil in 1997, when he topped the poll on his first attempt, but in 2002, in a dramatic turn around in his fortunes, his first preference vote dropped from 6,487 to 4,654 and he lost the seat. He regained his Dáil seat in 2007 with 8,436 first preferences. He retained it comfortably in 2011 with 9,366 first preference votes (19.9%) and in 2014 was elected to the European Parliament. In 2014 the party lost the seat in the subsequent by-election. Fine Gael's candidate in that contest was Senator Cáit Keane, who received only 2,110 first preferences (8.8%). The party is running three candidates in the 2016 election, two of them first timers.

Colm Brophy has been a member of South Dublin County Council since 2008. He was a candidate for the party in Dublin South Central in the 2011 Dáil election, where as one of three candidates he polled 3,376 first preferences (6.63%) but failed to win a seat. Much of his local electoral base has since been redrawn into Dublin South–West. Brophy first ran for office for Fine Gael in Ballybrack in 1991 when his 684 votes were not sufficient to get him elected. He was co-opted in the Terenure–Rathfarnham electoral area of South Dublin County Council in January 2008 and then ran successfully in 2009 in Tallaght Central electoral area, his 3,085 votes (12.98%) giving him the second seat. He was also unsuccessful in that year's Seanad elections on the Industrial and Commercial panel. In the 2014 local elections he won a seat in the Templeogue–Terenure electoral area with 1,552 votes (9.28%).

Brophy is a businessman from Kilmacud. He is the former president of Young Fine Gael and current president of the Association of Irish Local Government. He is leader of the Fine Gael group on South Dublin County Council, where he chairs the Transport Strategic Planning Committee. He is also a member of the County Enterprise Board and a director of South Dublin Tourism. In 2012 he was appointed by then Environment Minister Phil Hogan to the board of the Housing Finance Agency.

Anne-Marie Dermody is a solicitor and has been a member of South Dublin County Council since 2011. She was first active in Fine Gael as a student at University College Dublin where she studied civil law. As a solicitor she specialises in the areas of banking, commercial, property and employment law, including property purchase, disposal and security reviews as well as debt management and recovery. She and her family live in Butterfield Avenue. Her three boys attend Ballyroan Boys' National School and Colaiste Eanna. She was co-opted onto South Dublin County Council in 2011 for the Rathfarnham ward and was re-elected there in 2014, with 1,634 first preference votes (13.22%), which gave her the second seat, the first of two Fine Gael seats in that ward. She was recently nominated to the board of the charity Goal.

Karen Warren is based in Bawnville in Tallaght and was added to the ticket by the party national executive in a move to balance the locations of the other two candidates, who are both from the predominately middle class east of the constituency. A former member of South Dublin County Council, she was Brian Hayes's running mate in the 1999 local elections in the Tallaght Central electoral area, polling just 420 votes (4.65%). In the 2004 local elections as the party's sole candidate she took the 4th seat there with 1,624 votes (10.44%), becoming Deputy Lord Mayor in 2005. In 2009 she fought in the Tallaght South electoral area polling 1,655 votes (10.87%), leaving her in sixth place in the five-seater, with party colleague Brian Lawlor taking the one Fine Gael seat. 2014 saw her in Tallaght Central where her vote was just 632 (5.38%). She is a former student at Assumption College, Walkinstown and works in the Oireachtas as administrative assistant to the Chathaoirleach Senator Paddy Burke.

Labour Party:

Labour is without both of its 2011 candidates for the 2016 contest. The party's long time local deputy and former leader Pat Rabitte is retiring. Their first term deputy Eamon Maloney has gone independent. Together they polled more than 36 per cent of the vote in 2011, which was 1.8 quotas. Even if the party's vote share had held up nationally it would have struggled to hold its second seat without them. Now, with polls showing Labour's support halved across Dublin and Maloney running against them, Labour could lose both seats. The party nationally decided that it would run two candidates in this election, a strategy with which Maloney disagreed and he did not contest the party convention. Some time later, however, he announced that he would run as an independent. The party's new candidates for this election are both local councillors,

Pamela Kearns has been a member of South Dublin County Council since 2009. She was also the party's candidate in the October 2014 by-election. Her first political outing was in 2009, when she ran in the Tallaght Central electoral area where she won the fifth seat with 2,643 first preference votes (11.12%). She was the county's Deputy Mayor in 2011. In the 2014 local election she stood in the Templeogue–Terenure electoral area, again taking a seat with a vote of 1,426 (8.52%). In the 2014 Dáil by-election she polled 2,043 votes (8.5%). Married, with two adult children, she owns and operates a pre-school service in Templeogue. Her husband has a small business in the same area. She is a former student at CBS James's Street and she coaches soccer in Templeogue United Football Club.

Mick Duff has also been a member of Dublin South County Council since 2009. He first contested a local election in 2009, when he polled 3,125 votes in the Tallaght Central electoral area and took the first seat with 3,125 first preference votes (13.15%). He was one of three new Labour councillors elected for that electoral area in 2009 and he was made Mayor on his first appearance in the council chamber. As the lead group on South Dublin County Council at the time they agreed to forgo their conference expenses, diverting them to the provision of an emergency hostel in Tallaght, which opened in 2013. In the 2014 local election he was re-elected to the county council polling 982 first preferences (8.4%). Duff has worked in the Tallaght Drugs Task force since 1998. Originally from Inchicore he is married with four children.

Fianna Fáil:

Fianna Fáil comfortably had two seats in this constituency in 2002 and 2007, with both Conor Lenihan and Charlie O'Connor. In 2007 their combined vote was 16,355, but in 2011 their combined vote was less than a third of that at 5,059 and the party failed to take even one seat. Conor Lenihan has since moved on from politics and while Charlie O'Connor contested the party conventions he lost out to John Lahart.

John Lahart has been a member of Dublin South County Council since 1999. He was also the party's candidate in the 2014 by-election. In that by-election he polled 2,077 (8.6%). A native of Ballyroan, Lahart joined Fianna Fáil at the invitation of the late Seamus Brennan in 1983. He qualified as a Post-Primary teacher in 1988, working as a teacher until 1992. From 1992–1994 he worked for Tom Kitt TD, who was Minister of State at the Department of the Taoiseach. In 1995 Lahart returned to teaching and received a Masters degree from Mater Dei in 1996. In 1999 he competed in the South County Dublin local election for the first time in Terenure–Rathfarnham, taking the 5th seat with 1,978 first preference votes (9.77%). In 2000 he returned to the Oireachtas as Special Advisor to Minister Tom Kitt, firstly as Minister of State and then as Government Chief Whip. In 2004 Lahart topped the poll there with 3,828 votes (13.14%), just over the quota. He was over the quota again in the newly shaped Rathfarnham in 2009 with 3,605 (20.81%). In the local elections in May 2014 he polled 1,972 (15.95%), which was 1.12 quotas.

In 2007 Lahart obtained a degree in Counselling and Psychotherapy and left his government post to develop a private practice in Rathfarnham. In 2012, following the changes to constituency boundaries he moved to Dublin South–West. During the May 2014 local election campaign he became embroiled in controversy when one of his canvassers was alleged to have made anti-semitic remarks on a doorstep. Councillor Lahart immediately distanced himself from them and removed the canvasser from his campaign, calling on the householder to make a personal unreserved apology both for the remarks and for the distress they had caused. The apology was accepted.

Sinn Féin:

Seán Crowe is based in Tallaght and was a member of Dáil Éireann from 2002 to 2007, being re-elected in 2011. He was also the party candidate in Dáil elections here in 1989, 1992, and 1997. In addition, he was the party candidate in the 1999 European elections in the Dublin area, when he finished seventh. He polled 3,725 first preferences in 1997's Dáil election, but almost doubled that to 7,446 in 2002 in a stunning poll-topping performance which put him 100 votes over the quota on the first count. In 2007 his vote fell a whopping 8 percentage points and he lost his seat. 2011 saw his vote up again to 8,064 (17.2%). In the 2014 by-election Sinn Féin came close to taking a second seat in the constituency when Tallaght South councillor Cathal King topped the poll with 7,288, a 30.3% vote share. Paul Murphy of the Anti-Austerity Alliance proved more transfer friendly, however, and pipped King in the final count.

Crowe was a member of Dublin South County Council for the Tallaght South electoral area from 1999 to 2004. He stood again for the county council in the Tallaght Central electoral area in 2009, after being co-opted to replace Mark Daly. In that local election Crowe polled 2,715 first preferences and took the third of the six seats. He is currently party spokesperson on Foreign Affairs, Trade, and Defence. Originally from Rathfarnham, he has lived in Tallaght since 1988. He is a former member of the party's Ard Comhairle, and was the head of the Sinn Féin delegation to the Forum on Peace and Reconciliation.

Sarah Holland has been a member of South Dublin County Council since 2014. She polled 1,614 first preferences (13.06%). Originally from Belfast, but now living in Rathfarnham with her partner and daughter, she is the currently Mayor of South County Dublin. Her Rathfarnham base balances Crowe's in Tallaght.

Green Party:

The party vote in this area has never been enough to stand a realistic chance of gaining a seat, hovering consistently at about 3%. The highest vote share so far was achieved by Elizabeth Davidson in 2007 with 1,546 votes (3.7%).

Francis Noel Duffy has been a member of South Dublin County Council for the Rathfarnham electoral area since May 2014. He took the sixth and final seat in Rathfarnham ward with 944 votes (7.64%) in those local elections. He was the party candidate here in 2011 when he got 480 votes (1.0%), while in the 2014 by-election his vote actually fell to 447 although the percentage rose to 1.9% in the very low turnout. Originally from Carrickmacross he is currently the Deputy Mayor of South Dublin. Duffy is an architect, specialising in domestic projects and he lectures in the Dublin School of Architecture, DIT. In 2006 he produced a series of portraits of forgotten women of 1916, 'Women Rising Up'. He is married to Green Party Deputy Leader, Catherine Martin and coaches at Ballyboden Wanderers GAA Club.

Anti-Austerity Alliance – People Before Profit:

Paul Murphy has been a Dáil Deputy since the October 2014 by-election. He says that he became a Socialist while still a student at St Killian's, the German school in Clonskeagh, as he became conscious of events such as the WTO protests in Seattle. He graduated at the top of his class in University College Dublin where he studied law. He then began an as yet uncompleted PhD entitled 'Does Socialist Law Exist?' He held various jobs before becoming a full time politician and activist, listing barwork, a job in Tesco and tutoring at UCD among these 'small jobs'. He worked for Joe Higgins as a political advisor when Higgins was an MEP and after Higgins was elected to Dáil Éireann in 2011 Murphy replaced him in the European Parliament. He contested the European elections in 2014 as a Socialist Party candidate. He polled 29,953 on that occasion but failed to retain the seat. In 2014 Murphy contested the

Dublin South–West seat left vacant by Brian Hayes' election to the European Parliament and came in second on the first count with 6,540 (27.2%), eventually taking the seat on the eighth count.

Murphy has been a high profile campaigner against the property tax and against water charges. He was charged in September 2015 with the false imprisonment of Labour Tanaiste Joan Burton and her assistant after their car was blocked by anti water charge protesters for over two hours after leaving a graduation event at the adult education centre An Cosán in Tallaght on Saturday November 15th 2014. Murphy denies the charges and the case has not yet come on for hearing. In 2015 Murphy paid the property tax on his former home in Ballinteer so that he could sell it to move to a new home in Tallaght.

Sandra Fay is from Jobstown and teaches Business Studies at St Mark's Community School. One of the Jobstown water protestors, she described it on RTÉ's Claire Byrne Live as 'a great protest' and has said she would do it again. She has not previously run in any election.

Renua Ireland:

Ronan McMahon has been an independent member of South Dublin County Council since 2014. He was unsuccessful in an attempt to be selected as a Fine Gael candidate in the Templeogue–Terenure ward of South Dublin County Council before the 2014 local elections. Instead he ran designated as a non-party candidate on the ballot paper, but describing himself as independent Fine Gael and using the Fine Gael party colours on his election literature. His 2,299 votes (13.74%) were more than 750 ahead of the official Fine Gael candidate and gave him the second seat. He contested the 2014 by-election in Dublin South–West as an independent, where his 2,142 votes (8.9%) were 32 ahead of Fine Gael's Cáit Keane. He has since joined Renua.

McMahon was born and bred in Bohernabreena. He pledged to remain an independent when he was elected in 2014. He says, 'I thought I'd go in as an independent, full of gung-ho, and effect change. But I must say I find it very difficult as an independent to effect change.' He went on to say that he believes that Renua is a new type of party with new opportunities. He is the owner of Snap Printing in Tallaght, a qualified accountant, and one of the founders of Knocklyon Credit Union. Ronan is the son of former Fine Gael TD and senator Larry McMahon, who successively represented Dublin County South, Dublin County Mid, and Dublin South–West in the 1970s and early 1980s.

Direct Democracy Ireland:

Stephen Sinclair, originally from a tenement in the city centre, was brought up in Crumlin but has lived in Tallaght for over 25 years. At sixteen he had to leave school to help support his family and completed an apprenticeship with Aer Lingus just in time to be laid off in 1981. Emigrating in search of work he lived in several countries before returning to employment within the health service in Ireland. He is a qualified paraglider and hanglider, a sports shooter and a former all Ireland gymnastics champion and qualified coach. He sees political involvement as an inevitable progression, 'standing beside friends and fellow citizens in the rain to prevent evictions or water meter installations'. Although not arrested he was one of those who delayed Joan Burton at Jobstown in November 2014.

Independents:

Declan Burke was only 21 when he ran in the 2014 local elections in the Tallaght Central Ward of South Dublin County Council, where he lives with his brother and parents. He gained 524 votes (4.46%) under the Peoples Convention banner, and in the 2014 Dublin South–West by-election he polled 681 (2.83%). A signatory to The People's Contract he is committed to direct democracy.

Peter Fitzpatrick is a 35-year-old from Kingswood Heights in Tallaght. Married, with one little girl, his entire education has been in Tallaght, where he obtained a degree in Computer Science from IT Tallaght in 2002. He later obtained a Postgraduate Diploma in software development and website design. In 2014 he and his brother in law founded the Our Children's Health campaign, mounting daily protests outside the Taoiseach's office over a six month period. As a result he was appointed to the National Clinical Advisory Group as a patient representative. He has stepped aside from this role for the duration of this election campaign. After a year as a web designer he qualified as a landscape designer but had to change track again when the recession hit and says it revealed to him how little support there is for the self-employed in the social welfare system. In 2010 he became a special needs assistant in a secondary school, working in that field until 2012, when a cap was put on the number of jobs available as part of the austerity cut backs. He now works in an IT/Finance role for the Iveagh Trust. He promises that, if elected, he will donate at least €20,000 per annum of his salary as a TD to non-political charities within the constituency.

Eamonn Maloney has been a Dáil Deputy since 2011. He was first elected for the Tallaght South electoral area of South Dublin county council in 1999. In the 2009 local elections he topped the poll there with 2,344 first preferences, just 193 below the quota, and took the second seat. He first ran as an independent in the 1987 Dáil election in the area and, after a poor display then, failed to get a seat in Tallaght Old Bawn for Labour in the 1991 local elections. Since then he has run successfully for Labour on three occasions in local elections, boosting the party vote each time. Originally from Donegal, Maloney was elected Mayor of South Dublin County Council in June of 2009, having previously served in that role also from 2006–07. Running with Pat Rabbitte as the second Labour candidate in 2011 he took the final seat in the then four-seater, with 4,165 first preference votes (8.9%). In July 2015 Maloney announced that he would not contest the seat again and was thanked by party leader Joan Burton for the work he had done for the party and for the personal support he had given her. In September 2015 he said that he had resigned because the party had decided on a two candidate strategy and that he would be running as an independent. Several members of the party organisation in the constituency left with him and will work on his campaign.

Maloney is a former factory worker who has experienced life on the dole and is author of a local history book, 'Tallaght: A Place in History', which was published in 2009. When he was elected in 2011 he decided not to accept any expenses for carrying out his

Dáil duties and he is the only TD who does this. He is the brother of former Labour senator and Donegal Dáil candidate and local representative Sean Maloney, who in 1999 left Labour for Fine Gael, standing for that party unsuccessfully in Donegal North–East in 2002

Deirdre O'Donovan lives in Knocklyon and has been a member of Dublin South County Council for the Rathfarnham electoral area since 2014. She is part of the Independent Alliance grouping. Like many independents her involvement in politics developed from her membership of residents associations and parents' groups. She says that she was further galvanized by the sharp drop in her family income as a result of the recession. Standing in the Rathfarnham ward of Dublin South County Council in the 2014 local elections she gained 1,517 first preference votes (12.27%), which gave her the fourth of the six seats. On the council she is Chairperson of the Rathfarnham/Terenure/Templeogue Area Committee, Chairperson of the Joint Policing Committee, and a member of the Regional Health Forum and the Environment SPC.

Katherine Zappone has been a Taoiseach's nominee to Seanad Éireann since 2011. She and her wife Anne Louise Gilligan founded An Cosán, an organisation which offers adult education and other services to women from disadvantaged areas. They operated these facilities from their own home originally and An Cosán now provides these facilities from a purpose built premises in Jobstown. An Cosán is Ireland's largest community education organisation. In 2006 Zappone and Gilligan launched a high court case seeking to have their Canadian marriage recognised in Ireland but lost in the High Court. Zappone is an opponent of water charges but described herself as 'deeply disappointed' in the interpretation placed by Paul Murphy TD on the events that occurred after An Cosán's graduation ceremony when Tanaiste Joan Burton and her assistant were blockaded in their car by protesters, saying that what she saw was 'one of the most traumatic things I've ever experienced since I've been a politician.' The first openly lesbian member of the Oireachtas she has been a long time campaigner for civil rights. She holds an MA from the Catholic University of America and an MBA from University College Dublin. She was born in Washington State and is a feminist theologian. She says her experiences on the doorstep in the marriage equality campaign, as well as her experiences in the Seanad, have led her to stand as an independent candidate.

Dublin West

Outgoing Deputies:

Leo Varadkar (FG), Joan Burton (Lab), Joe Higgins (SP), Ruth Coppinger (SP)

Brian Lenihan (FF), who was elected in 2011, died in July 2012. The resultant by-election was won by Patrick Nulty (Lab), who resigned the seat in 2014. The by-election which resulted from his resignation was won by Ruth Coppinger (SP)

In April 2014 Joe Higgins (SP) announced that he would not contest the next general election.

The Constituency:

This continues to be a four seat constituency but the boundaries have been substantially redrawn since 2011. That part of the Airport electoral division north of the M50, that part of the Dublin electoral area north of the M50 and an area in Kilsallaghan and Swords-Forrest (with a population of 17,291) have been transferred from Dublin West to Fingal in the redraw. On the other hand the areas of Ashtown A, Ashtown B, and that part of the electoral division of Phoenix Park situated north of a line drawn along Chapelizod Road, Conyngham Road and Parkgate Street, with a population of 13,256 have been moved from Dublin Central into Dublin West.

2016 Candidates will include:

Catherine Noone (FG), Leo Varadkar (FG), Joan Burton (Lab), Jack Chambers (FF), Paul Donnelly (SF), Roderic O'Gorman (GP), Ruth Coppinger (AAA-PBP), Geoff Boyle (Ind), TJ Clare (Ind), David McGuinness (Ind), Lorna Nolan (Ind)

	% Vote 1997	% Vote 2002	% Vote 2007	% Vote 2011	Swing 2011	Quotas 2011
Fine Gael	16.94	12.32	20.39	27.19	6.80	1.4
Labour	12.11	12.71	17.06	28.99	11.93	1.4
Fianna Fáil	33.19	34.63	37.45	16.59	−20.86	0.8
Sinn Féin	5.00	8.02	4.78	6.11	1.33	0.3
Green Party	4.32	2.49	3.78	1.42	19.03	0.07
Socialist Party	16.21	21.48	14.91	19.03	5.87	1.0
Others	12.23	8.35	1.63	0.66	−0.97	0.04z

In Brief:

Although at one point during the current Dáil the Labour party held two of the four seats here, they now have one and the Tánaiste Joan Burton could lose her seat. Health Minister Leo Varadkar will hold his seat. If Fine Gael have a very good day, he could even bring his running mate Senator Catherine Noone into Dáil Éireann with him. The Socialist Party now have two seats after the second by-election but are running one candidate and its leader Joe Higgins is not contesting. Its other incumbent, deputy Ruth Coppinger, is running this time as part of the Anti-Austerity Alliance – People Before Profit grouping and will comfortably hold her seat. Sinn Féin's Paul Donnelly, who was runner up in the 2014 by-election, also looks set to win a seat. Even after Brian Lenihan this constituency represents Fianna Fáil's best chance of a seat gain apart from Fingal. It has opted for a new candidate in Councillor Jack Chambers who is mounting a high profile and well resourced campaign. However, the fact that Councillor David McGuinness, who was its standard bearer in the two by-elections, is running as a member of the Independent Alliance skews the pitch for Fianna Fáil. The bottom line is that the outcome here depends on how Labour performs in the campaign. As of now it is likely to be one Fine Gael, one Socialist, one Sinn Féin and a battle between Joan Burton (Lab), Jack Chambers (FF) and perhaps even Catherine Noone (FG) for the fourth seat.

Fine Gael:

Leo Varadkar is based in Carpenterstown and has been a member of Dáil Éireann since 2007. He has been the Minister for Health since July 2014. He began in politics as a member of Fingal County Council for the Castleknock electoral area. He had been co-opted onto the county council to replace Senator Sheila Terry in 2003. Varadkar then retained the seat in spectacular fashion in the 2004 local election, when he topped the poll with 4,894 first preferences, which was just under two quotas, making him the most successful candidate in the country in that election. In the 2007 general election he replaced Senator Terry as Fine Gael candidate for the Dáil and increased the party support by more than eight percentage points. He got 6,928 votes (20.4%) and took the second seat. In the 2011 Dáil election Joan Burton topped the poll but Varadkar still managed a strong 8,359 votes, (19.7%) and was only 136 votes less than the quota. When the coalition government was formed Varadkar was named Minister for Transport, Tourism and Sport, and in 2014 he replaced Dr James Reilly as Minister for Health.

Varadkar is a medical doctor who worked previously at Blanchardstown hospital. In January 2015, in advance of the Marriage Equality referendum campaign he spoke for the first time publicly about being gay, saying that it does not define him. He is the first openly gay cabinet minister. His Indian born father was a general practitioner in the Castleknock area. He was one of a number of front-benchers who supported a motion of no confidence in Enda Kenny as leader of Fine Gael in June of 2010.

Catherine Noone was a member of Dublin City Council from 2009 to 2011 for the South-East Inner City electoral area, which is in Dublin Bay South, where her 1,234 first preferences (13.04%) gave her the fourth and final seat. She was elected to the Seanad in April 2011 on the Industrial and Commercial Panel. She is the Fine Gael Seanad spokesperson on European Affairs. Originally from a County Mayo Fine Gael background, she studied law at National University of Ireland, Galway and is a practising defence litigation solicitor. She is a fluent Italian speaker, having studied at Verona University. In July 2015 she suggested that candidates should be capped at 400 posters each.

Labour Party:

In 2011 Labour ran a second candidate with Joan Burton, Patrick Nulty, then a member of Fingal County Council for the Mulhuddart electoral area. He failed to be elected on that occasion, with a vote of 2,686 (6.3%), but in the 2011 by-election caused by the death of the Brian Lenihan, Nulty took the seat with a poll topping 8,665 (24.3%). Always seen as something of a left-wing rebel within the party he lost the whip when he voted against the 2012 budget. In 2014 he resigned from Dáil Éireann after The Sunday World made him aware that they were publishing the story that he had sent inappropriate Facebook messages to a 17-year-old female, and to two other adult women. There will be no second candidate in 2016.

Joan Burton has been Tánaiste and Labour party leader since 2014 and Minister for Social Protection since 2011. She was first elected to Dáil Éireann in 1992, but lost her seat in 1997 when her vote share was almost halved to 12.1% from 22.6% in 1992. As a result of the redrawing of constituencies and the decision of Austin Currie to move to Dublin Mid-West, she regained her seat in 2002, polling 3,810 first preferences. In 2007 she improved her vote to 5,799 and in 2011 she topped the poll with 9,627 (22.7%), which 1,132 over the quota.

Burton was brought up in Ballymun. She was a member of Dublin County Council from 1995 to 1999 for the Mulhuddart electoral area and of Fingal County Council from 1999 to 2004 for the Castleknock electoral area. She was Minister of State at the Department of Social Welfare from 1992 to 1994 and then at the Department of Foreign Affairs with responsibility for Overseas Development from 1995 to 1997. A chartered accountant, she is a former lecturer in finance at the Dublin Institute of Technology. She was an unsuccessful candidate for the Labour Party leadership in October 2002, became Deputy Leader in 2007, and defeated Alex White for the post on the resignation of Eamon Gilmore in 2014.

Fianna Fáil:

The party has a single candidate strategy in 2016. In recent national elections they ran a two candidate ticket in this area, with the late

Brian Lenihan Jnr and David McGuinness being the candidates in 2011. McGuinness managed only 623 (1.5%) in 2011, when Lenihan took the fourth seat with 6,421 (15.1%). McGuiness was Fianna Fáil candidate in the by-election in October 2011 caused by Lenihan's death. He came second on that occasion, polling 7,742 (21.7%), but the seat went to the Labour Party's Nulty. In the 2014 by-election he polled 5,053 (17.5%). McGuinness was defeated at the party's constituency convention in 2015 by fellow Fingal County Councillor Jack Chambers. McGuiness subsequently resigned from Fianna Fáil and will contest this seat as an independent in 2016.

Jack Chambers has been a member of Fingal County Council since 2014. He topped the poll in the Castleknock ward in that election with his 2,693 (18.61%) votes being almost one and a half quotas. In 2015 he became Deputy Mayor of Fingal. Chambers holds a degree in Law and Political Science from TCD and is currently studying medicine at the Royal College of Surgeons of Ireland. He has used Lenihan's old constituency office in Laurel Lodge as his headquarters since he began his county council campaign. His family is originally from Mayo but he was born in Galway and brought up in Castleknock.

Sinn Féin:

Paul Donnelly has been a member of Fingal County Council since 2014. He was also the party's candidate for the 2011 general election and the 2011 and 2014 by-elections. In 2008 he was co-opted to replace Felix Gallagher on Fingal County Council but in the 2009 local elections failed to retain the seat. He polled 1,517 first preferences and finished sixth in the five-seater Castleknock ward. In the 2011 Dáil election he improved the party vote considerably with 2,597 votes (6.1%). He was its candidate in the two by-elections as well, winning 3,173 first preferences in the 2011 by-election (8.9%) and topping the poll in the 2014 by-election with 6,056 (20.9%) but being rapidly overtaken by the Socialist Party's Ruth Coppinger, who won the seat ultimately on Donnelly's transfers. Donnelly stood in the Mulhuddart ward of Fingal County Council for the 2014 local elections and topped the poll with a massive 3,201 votes (27.26%), which was 2.45 quotas.

Donnelly is Sinn Féin group leader on Fingal County Council. He is a Project Worker with the School Completion Programme in Coolock. He was raised in the North Inner City, is married with four children, and has lived in Clonsilla for nearly 20 years.

Green Party:

Roderic O'Gorman is originally from Mulhuddart, but now lives in Blanchardstown village and has been a member of Fingal County Council for the Castleknock electoral area since 2014. This will be his third time contesting for Dáil Éireann. After ten years of campaigning in local and national elections he finally won a seat on Fingal County Council in the Castleknock ward in 2014, when his 1,393 first preference votes (9.96%) placed him third in the poll. He first ran in the 2004 local election, gaining only 666 votes (5.2%) and in 2009 improved on that to 1,9238 (9.18%) but did not win a seat. In the 2007 Dáil election he polled 1,286 for a 3.78% share of the vote. The collapse in the Green vote in 2011 saw him drop to 605 votes (1.42%) but at the by-election in the same year his vote improved to 1,787 (2.76%) and it increased a little more in the 2014 by-election to 1,856 (2.87%), although he went out after the second count in both by-elections.

O'Gorman is the Chair of the Green Party. He lectures in the school of Law and Government at Dublin City University, where he is programme chairperson for the BA in Economics, Politics and Law degree. He was involved with the Legal Education for All Programme (LEAP), which helps adults who left the education system early to study law. He was one of only four openly gay candidates in the 2011 Dáil election. (The others were David Healy in Dublin North-East, Dominic Hanigan in Meath East and John Lyons in Dublin North-West)

Anti-Austerity Alliance – People Before Profit:

Socialist Party leader and Dublin MEP Joe Higgins represented this constituency in Dáil Éireann from 1997 to 2007 and again from 2011 to date. He had also been an unsuccessful candidate in the 1992 general election, polling 1,407, and was runner up in the 1992 by-election, when he polled 6,742 first preferences. He polled 6,442 to take the first seat in 1997 with 16.21% of the vote. However, he lost his Dáil seat to Fine Gael in the 2007 election. He contested the European elections in the Dublin constituency in 2009, when he was elected with 50,510 first preferences to take the last of the three seats. In 2011 he returned to Dublin West, his 8,084 votes (19.0%) giving him the third of the four seats. In April 2014, in the lead in to the by-election, he announced that he would not contest the next Dáil election although he will remain in politics in another capacity.

Ruth Coppinger lives in Mulhuddart and has been a member of Dáil Éireann since she won the 2014 by-election. In that contest she won 5,977 (20.6%) of the first preferences. Prior to that she had been a member of Fingal County Council for the Mulhuddart electoral area. In 2003 she was co-opted to the council to replace Joe Higgins. In the 2004 local elections she was elected in her own right, taking the first seat with 1,848 (14.72%). She took that first seat again in 2009, this time topping the poll with 1,705 (12.86%). In the 2011 Dáil by-election she was second in the poll with 7,542 (11.66%). In the 2014 local elections, standing under the banner of the Anti-Austerity Alliance, she took the second seat in Mulhuddart behind Sinn Féin's Paul Connelly with 2,568 votes (21.87%), which was 1.97 quotas. She worked previously as a secondary school teacher.

Independents:

Geoff Boyle has been postmaster in Blanchardstown village for 12 years, and is seeking election as part of the Community and Post Office Candidates group. The group's slogan is 'Your Community, Your Post Office, Your Choice'. It is a movement of independent candidates, all of whom are practicing postmasters or postmistresses and are seeking to protect the post office network. The group advocate the development of a wider role for Post Offices including electronic transaction accounts that could be used not only for social protection payments but services such as motor tax, drivers licence renewal, payment of hospital charges, payment of State examination fees and many others of the ideas set out in the interim report of the Post Office Business Development Group which was chaired by the business man Bobbie Kerr. Mr Boyle is active in many community organisations but has not previously run in any election.

T.J. Clare is a primary school teacher based in Blanchardstown village. He describes himself as a Strong Left Independent Community Activist. He ran unsuccessfully as an independent in the Castleknock electoral area in the 2014 local elections polling 473 first preference votes (3.38%). Originally from Dun Laoghaire, he moved to Athy as a child, returning to Dublin when he was 18. Now 26, he has lived in the Dublin West Area since he completed his B. Ed at St. Patrick's College of Education. He was heavily involved in the Yes Equality Campaign in Dublin West and in the Right2Water Campaign in the constituency. He has a special interest in educational disadvantage, psychology and Gaeilge and campaigns strongly for smaller class sizes.

David McGuinness, originally from Sheephill Park, has been a member of Fingal County Council since 2009. At the time of that election he was just 24 years of age. He polled 1,203 votes and took the fourth of the five seats in the Mulhuddart electoral area for Fianna Fáil, thereby becoming the party's youngest councillor in the country at the time. He expected to be on the Fianna Fáil ticket in Dublin West this time around, having been its candidate in both the 2011 and 2014 by-elections and the second candidate with Brian Lenihan in the 2011 general election. Following his defeat in February 2015 at the party convention by fellow councillor Jack Chambers he left Fianna Fáil saying, 'There's no doubt about it. There's a class divide in Fianna Fáil and I'm clearly on the wrong side of the tracks.' He will now stand for the Independent Alliance. He polled 623 (1.5%) in 2011, polled 7,742 (21.7%) in the 2011 by-election and 5,053 (17.5%) in the 2014 by-election. In the 2014 local elections he polled 1,360 first preferences, which was 55 votes above the quota in the Mulhuddart electoral area and he took the fifth of the eight seats. He is a music and history teacher and a graduate of Trinity College Dublin.

Lorna Nolan, who has been a member of Fingal County Council for the Mulhuddart electoral areas since 2014, is contesting this Dáil election under the Independents Alliance banner. She polled 355 votes (3.02%) in that area in the 2014 local elections and took the final seat. She has lived in Dublin 15 for the past 18 years with her two children. She is one of the founders of Suicide Awareness Dublin 15 and currently works there on a voluntary basis. Nolan is also working on rebuilding the Fingal Disability Network. In October 2014 she recruited several of her fellow councillors from all groupings to take part in the Focus Ireland 'Shine a Light' sleep out to raise funds for the charity.

Dún Laoghaire

Outgoing Deputies:
Eamon Gilmore (Lab), Sean Barrett (FG), Mary Mitchell O'Connor (FG), Richard Boyd Barrett (AA)

As the outgoing Ceann Comhairle Sean Barrett will be automatically returned in the 2016 election assuming he decides to contest, which he is expected to do.

Eamon Gilmore (Lab) announced in June 2015 that he would not contest this election.

The Constituency:
This remains a four seat constituency. The electoral divisions of Cabinteely–Loughlinstown, Foxrock–Carrickmines, Foxrock–Torquay and Stillorgan–Leopardstown, with a population of 13,762, have been added from Dublin South.

2016 Candidates will include:
Sean Barrett (FG), Mary Mitchell-O'Connor (FG), Marie Bailey (FG), Carrie Smyth (Lab), Cormac Devlin (FF), Mary Hanafin (FF), Shane O'Brien (SF), Ossian Smyth (GP), Richard Boyd Barrett (AAA–PBP), Frank Cronin (Renua), Carol Hunt (Ind)

	% Vote 1997	% Vote 2002	% Vote 2007	% Vote 2011	Swing 2011	Quotas 2011
Fine Gael	30.96	15.04	23.56	34.57	11.01	1.7
Labour	21.52	22.68	16.00	30.38	14.38	1.5
Fianna Fáil	25.83	30.29	34.87	15.23	−19.64	0.8
Sinn Féin	–	4.03	2.20	–	–	–
Green Party	5.09	9.33	7.72	3.80	−3.92	0.2
AAA–PBP	–	–	–	10.95	10.95	0.5
Others	15.58	19.64	15.65	5.07	−10.58	0.3

In Brief:

Assuming the Ceann Comhairle Sean Barrett stands again, then Fine Gael are guaranteed his seat in this four-seater and will also win a second in what will be for the purpose of the election a three-seater. Even in that scenario Richard Boyd Barrett also looks safe. Former Tánaiste Eamon Gilmore, who has been elected here since 1989, is not re-contesting and the party is likely to lose the seat. If so, former Minister Mary Hanafin, who is likely to be the stronger of the two Fianna Fáil candidates, could make a Dáil return, although a third seat for Fine Gael cannot be ruled out.

Fine Gael:

In 2011 the party paired Sean Barrett with then popular local councillor Mary Mitchell O'Connor and between them they received 1.72 quotas, giving them the second and third seats behind Labour's Eamon Gilmore. This time with Barrett automatically re-elected they are running local councillor Mary Bailey with the sitting deputy Mitchell O' Connor

Mary Mitchell O'Connor is based in Cabinteely and was elected to Dáil Éireann on her first attempt in 2011. In that election she polled 9,087 votes (16.03%). She was a member of Dún Laoghaire–Rathdown County Council prior to that. She was first elected to the county council in 2004 as a Progressive Democrats candidate. She contested as a Fine Gael candidate in the 2007 local elections when she polled 2,031 first preferences, which was just 532 votes short of the quota and gave her the third of six seats. She holds a Masters degree in Education and Management from NUI Maynooth. She was principal of The Harold School, Glasthule from 1999 to her election to the Dáil. She is Chairperson of the Internal Fine Gael Education Committee. In Dáil Éireann she serves on the Committee on Health and Children, the Select Sub-Committee on Children and Youth Affairs and the Select Sub-Committee on Health.

Marie Bailey has been a member of Dún Laoghaire–Rathdown County Council since 2004. In that year's local elections she took the fifth seat in what was then the Ballybrack ward with 2,055 first preferences (12.15%). Her local election vote in 2009 was just short of a quota in 2009 with 2,298 (16.4%). In 2014 in the enlarged Killiney–Shankill electoral area her vote share fell but she still managed to take the second seat with 1,087 (9.23%). She is the daughter of John Bailey, who was a Fine Gael Dáil candidate in the 2002 elections and who is also a member of Dún Laoghaire–Rathdown County Council. He has topped the poll in the Dún Laoghaire electoral area in two out of the last three local elections.

Marie Bailey is married, with two children. She previously worked for Aer Lingus in ground staff, but had to leave that position because her life long migraine problems required her to work more regular hours. Finding exercise essential to the management of the condition she regularly addresses migraine support groups on its management. She is the former chair of the Transportation Strategic Policy Committee and County Development Board of Dún Laoghaire–Rathdown County Council.

Labour Party:

With the party winning 30.3% of the poll the Labour Party's Ivana Bacik should have had a better chance of taking the final seat here in 2011 instead of People Before Profit's Richard Boyd Barrett. The opportunity was missed because of poor vote management. She is not contesting the 2016 Dáil election. Former party leader Eamon Gilmore was always a strong vote getter, having been first elected to the Dáil as a Workers Party deputy in 1989. He had a core 7,000 to 8,000 first preference votes in every general election since. His retirement at this election presents the Labour party with a real challenge to retain its seat.

Carrie Smyth has been a member of Dún Laoghaire–Rathdown County Council for the last twelve years. She was co-opted to the council in the Ballybrack ward when her father resigned due to ill health in 2003. She held that seat in 2004 (1,998 votes, 11.81%) and 2009 (2,210 votes, 15.77%) taking the second seat behind party colleague Denis O'Callaghan on that occasion. In 2014, with the ward re-organised as Killiney–Shankill, and People Before Profit topping the poll by a large margin, her 1,220 votes (10.86%) gave her the fourth seat and O'Callaghan the sixth.

Smyth is from a local family. She grew up in Dalkey and Shankill and now lives in Killiney with her husband and two dogs. She has worked most of her life in St Michael's Hospital, Dún Laoghaire. She was Cathaoirleach of Dún Laoghaire–Rathdown Council for the year 2013–2014 and has served on the Dún Laoghaire and Dublin Education Training Board, the Dún Laoghaire Harbour Company, Dún Laoghaire–Rathdown Social Development and Inclusion Committee and the Loughlinstown, Shankill and Ballybrack Local Policing Forum.

Fianna Fáil:

The party's national executive directed that only one candidate should be selected at convention to contest this election. There had been speculation that there would also be a directive that the candidate selected would have to be female but this did not emerge. Cllr Cormac Devlin won the convention ahead of fellow councillor Kate Feeney and former deputy minister and now councillor Mary Hanafin. The party's National Constituencies Committee subsequently decided to add Hanafin. Devlin has said that the decision 'dramatically reduces' Fianna Fáil's chance of getting back either of the two seats it lost here in 2011.

Cormac Devlin has been a member of Dún Laoghaire–Rathdown County Council since 2004. He was then 23 and in the local elections that year polled 1,776 votes (9.8%) in the Dún Laoghaire electoral area and took the second of the six seats. In the 2009 local elections his vote fell to 1,331 (7.42%) but he took the fifth seat. In the 2014 local elections the number of seats in that ward increased to eight and Devlin again took the second seat, this time with 1,253 first preferences (8.37%). He is currently the Fianna Fáil group deputy leader and whip on Dún Laoghaire–Rathdown Council. He is Chair of the Dún Laoghaire Area Committee and Chair of the council's Environment, Climate Change and Energy SPC. He holds a BA in Public Management from the Institute of Public Administration and is married with three children. In 2012 the Standards in Public Office Commission (SIPO) ruled that he and a Fine Gael colleague should have not been allowed to claim his college fees as expenses and he repaid the sum of €910 which he had claimed for repeat fees.

Mary Hanafin was a Dáil Deputy from 1997 to 2011. In 1997 she polled 5,079 votes (9.36%). In 2002 she came close to a quota and took the first seat with 8,818 (16.44%). In 2007 she topped the poll with 11,884 votes (20.24%) and again took the first seat. She was Minister for Education and Science from 2004 to 2008, Minister for Social and Family Affairs from 2008 to 2010, and Minister for Tourism, Culture and Sport from then until the end of the Dáil term. She briefly added Minister for Enterprise, Trade and Innovation to that portfolio after the resignation of Batt O'Keeffe in January 2011. In 2011 she again ran with the party's other outgoing deputy Barry Andrews. Together they had won 20,471 votes in 2007 but that fell to 8,632 combined in 2011 and the party lost both seats. Hanafin's own vote dropped by more than half to 5,090 votes (8.98%) and she was eliminated on the eleventh count. She was a late addition to the party ticket in the Blackrock electoral area for the 2014 local elections, in controversial circumstances where party headquarters asked her to run and then reversed its decision but only after it had issued Hanafin with a certificate of party affiliation. Hanafin proceeded to lodge her nomination papers and polled 1,501 (14.45%) first preferences in that election. Both she and the party's other candidate in that ward, Kay Feeny, were elected.

Hanafin was born and raised in Thurles. She has a BA from NUI Maynooth. She was formerly a secondary school teacher at the Dominican College Sion Hill in Blackrock. She is the daughter of former Senator Des Hanafin and her brother John Hanafin is also a former Senator. She does not draw any expenses as a councillor because she is in receipt of a ministerial pension.

Sinn Féin:
Shane O'Brien from Ballybrack has been a member of Dún Laoighaire–Rathdown county council since 2014. He is 29 years old. He ran as Shane Connolly O'Brien at the start of his campaign for the Killiney–Shankill ward of Dún Laoghaire–Rathdown County Council in 2014 and uses both forms of his name. In the 2014 local election he polled 1,504 votes (12.77%) and won the fifth of the eight seats. He is a member of a number of committees on the council including the Corporate Policy Group and Regional Health Forum. He is Chairman of Loughlinstown, Ballybrack and Shanganagh Men's Sheds. He says he is running in the general election to 'help give young people a voice', explaining that, 'Young people are simply under-represented in Dáil Éireann.' In April 2015 the Journal.ie named him one of 'The 30 hottest young politicos in Ireland right now'.

Green Party:
Ciarán Cuffe held a seat for the party here from 2007 to 2011. In the 2011 Dáil election, however, his vote share of 3.8%, at 2,156 first preference votes, was sharply down on the 7.7% he received in 2007 and the 9.3% of 2002. Although he has stayed in politics, successfully campaigning for Dublin City Council in the Inner City North ward, he decided not to run again in Dún Laoghaire. In 2016 the party's candidate will be Ossian Smyth.

Ossian Smyth is based in Monkstown and has been a member of Dún Laoghaire–Rathdown County Council since 2014. In that election he polled 1,068 votes (7.14%) and took the fifth of the eight seats. He is a Technical Project Manager in Saint Vincent's Hospital and volunteers as a mentor at a local CoderDojo, teaching young people computer programming and other computer skills. He is also an unpaid adviser to the European Parliament Green Energy Experts group, the Green Party Spokesperson for Communications, Energy and Natural Resources, and a member of the Dublin Cycling Campaign.

Anti-Austerity Alliance – People Before Profit:

Richard Boyd Barrett is based in Glenageary and has been a member of Dáil Éireann since 2011. He has been running in local and national elections since 2002, originally for the Socialist Workers Party. In 2011 he took the final seat here as a People Before Profit candidate with 6,206 (10.9%). In the 2007 Dáil election he polled 5,233 first preferences votes (8.91%), an increase of over 4,500 from 2002 when he had secured 876 votes for the Socialist Workers Party. In the 2009 local elections he ran for Dún Laoghaire–Rathdown County Council in the Dún Laoghaire local electoral area, polling 4,091 votes, which at 22.81% of the poll was an impressive 1.60 quotas.

Boyd Barret was raised by adoptive parents in Glenageary. He has a Masters degree in English Literature from University College Dublin and has been active in left-wing politics since university. He only takes a small proportion of his Dáíl salary, donating the remainder to People Before Profit and various other campaigns.

Renua Ireland:

Frank Cronin is originally from Cork but now lives in Sandycove. He is new to party politics. He is a former chief executive of Newstalk radio, the Sunday Tribune newspaper and Setanta Sports and now runs IPC Digital Media. He is running because he feels that the Dáil has enough retired teachers already and needs more business people. Locally he thinks that a strategic plan needs to drive new start up businesses for Dún Laoghaire, make Dalkey a cultural town and Blackrock a vibrant food town.

Independent

Carol Hunt is a journalist and columnist with the *Irish Independent* and she is running as part of the Independent Alliance. She describes herself on Twitter as 'Journalist. Feminist. Passionate about social justice'. She is married, with two children. She holds a degree in political philosophy from Trinity College Dublin, where she won the Wray prize. She says she has always been strongly interested in politics: 'If you don't like the political system get involved. Change it.'

GALWAY EAST

Outgoing Deputies:

Michael Kitt (FF), Paul Connaughton Jnr (FG), Ciarán Cannon (FG), Colm Keaveney (FF)

Colm Keaveney who won a seat for the Labour in 2011 resigned from the party in June 2013. In December 2012 he joined Fianna Fáil and will contest for them in this election.

Michael Kitt (FF) announced in September 2015 that he would not contest this election.

The Constituency:

This constituency is now a three-seater having lost a seat in the redrawing of boundaries since 2011. 32 electoral divisions in Ballinasloe Urban, the former Ballinasloe No. 1 Rural District, the former Glennamaddy Rural District, the former Mount Bellew Rural District, and the former Tuam Rural District with a total population of 20,52 have been transferred to the new Roscommon–Galway constituency.

	% Vote 1997	% Vote 2002	% Vote 2007	% Vote 2011	Swing 2011	Quotas 2011
Fine Gael	31.17	31.52	39.13	42.87	3.74	2.1
Labour	7.92	–	3.13	13.21	10.08	0.7
Fianna Fáil	48.60	46.77	39.69	18.04	–21.65	0.9
Sinn Féin	–	3.70	3.21	6.13	2.92	0.3
Green Party	–	2.07	1.89	0.68	–1.21	0.03
Others	12.30	15.94	12.96	19.07	6.11	1.0

2016 Candidates will include:

Paul Connaughton Jnr (FG), Ciarán Cannon (FG), Lorraine Higgins (Lab), Colm Keaveney (FF), Anne Rabbitte (FF), Annemarie Roche (SF), Sean Canney (Ind), Michael Fahy (Ind)

In Brief:

This constituency has been substantially redrawn and has been reduced from four seats to three seats. There is in reality a four way fight here for the three seats between Connaughton (FG), Cannon (FG), Colm Keaveney (FF) and the independent Sean Canney. Labour lost its seat to Fianna Fáil when Colm Keaveney switched parties and he is well placed to retain it for his new party. The party's other outgoing deputy Michael Kitt is retiring. Fine Gael have two seats but may lose one this time. While Connaughton was stronger than Cannon on the last occasion, a large chunk of the Connaughton base has been transferred out of Galway East to the Roscommon–Galway constituency since 2011. Sean Canney polled almost 6,000 votes in 2012 and this time contesting as part of the Independent Alliance he is more likely to win a seat, even though the constituency is now a three-seater.

Fine Gael:

The party ran four candidates in the 2011 election, each of them a first time candidate. Paul Connaughton replaced his father when the latter retired and he ran with former PD leader Ciarán Cannon, former Deputy Mayor of Galway County, Council Tom McHugh, and then Mayor of County Galway Jimmy McClearn. The four of them had 42.8% of the votes between them and the party won two of the four seats.

Paul Connaughton Jnr was elected to Dáil Éireann on his first attempt in 2011. He replaced his father, also Paul Connaughton, who had run for the party in every general election since 1972 and had been a Dáil deputy from 1981 to 2011. In the 2011 election Paul Jnr polled 7,255 first preference votes (12.2%) and took the second of the four seats. At that time he was 27 years old and a youth worker with Foroige. When the dual mandate ban was introduced in 2003 it was Paul Connaughton's sister Sinead, a teacher at Athenry Vocational School, who was co-opted to the seat on Galway County Council for the Tuam electoral area vacated by their father. In 2004 she comfortably held the seat with 2,030 first preferences. She decided not to run again in 2009 for personal reasons and Paul Connaughton Jnr therefore stood in the Ballinasloe electoral area in 2009 topping the poll with his 2,563 votes (18.8%), which was 1.13 quotas. The recent boundary changes mean that much of the Connaughton family heartland around Mountbellew has been moved to the newly named Roscommon–Galway constituency. It remains to be seen whether enough survives to keep the family seat.

Ciarán Cannon is based in Athenry and has been a Dáil deputy since 2011. Shortly after his election he was made Minister of State for Training and Skills and he held that post until the 2014 re-shuffle. He was appointed to the Seanad in 2007 for the Progressive Democrats by the Taoiseach, Bertie Ahern and he briefly led the party from the Seanad in its final phase. When the Progressive Democrats were wound up in November 2009 he joined Fine Gael. In 2004 he was elected as a Progressive Democrat to Galway County Council in the Loughrea electoral area with 1,307 votes (7.56%). As the Progressive Democrats candidate in Galway East in the 2007 general election, he polled 3,321 first preferences (5.95%) and was eliminated on the fifth count. Before becoming a full time politician, he was Chief Executive Officer of Irish Pilgrimage Trust. He and his wife run The Gate Lodge, a pub in the centre of Athenry. He is active in several initiatives to encourage young people to coding and other computer skills. He is founder of Excited – The Digital Learning Movement.

Labour Party:

In 2011 Labour ran two candidates in this constituency for the first time, Colm Keaveney and Lorraine Higgins. Together they won 13.2% of the vote and Keaveney took the fourth and final seat. He since left the Labour party and after a time as an independent joined Fianna Fáil.

Lorraine Higgins is based in Athenry and has been a member of Seanad Éireann since 2011. As one of two candidates for the party in 2011 she polled 3,577 votes, which was 677 votes behind Keaveney, and she was eliminated on the 5th count. She unsuccessfully contested the Seanad election in April 2011 on the Industrial and Commercial panel. She was subsequently nominated to the Seanad by An Taoiseach, Enda Kenny, in May 2011. In the Seanad she is the Labour Party spokesperson on Reform and Foreign Affairs. In 2014 she ran as the Labour Party candidate in the Ireland North and West constituency in the 2014 European elections where she polled 31,951 (4.94%), which saw her eliminated on the second count. She first ran as an independent in the 2009 local elections for Galway County Council. On that occasion she polled 809 first preferences and was eliminated on the sixth count. She holds a BA Degree in Political and Social Science and History from NUI Galway and qualified as a barrister at Kings Inns in 2005. She has taught Contract Law at Griffith College Dublin.

Fianna Fáil:

Anne Rabbitte has been a member of Galway County Council for the Loughrea electoral area since 2014. In the 2014 local elections she topped the poll in that area with 1,729 first preferences (10.64%). She described the campaign experience as follows; 'It was a long and arduous road that tested me in every way imaginable– but I emerge stronger for it and it was with great pride and gratitude that I took my seat as councillor in June 2014.' The party national executive mandated that one female candidate and one male candidate be selected at the convention to choose candidates for this Dáil election. Rabbitte was the only female candidate and was therefore selected unopposed.

On the council she chairs the Galway and Roscommon Education and Training Board and the Finance Committee of that board. She also sits on the Joint Policing Committee and the Strategic Policy Committee for Environment, Water services and Fire/Emergency services, as well as numerous committees for the Loughrea and Athenry areas. She works as a financial adviser. Locally she sits on the Portumna Camogie Club, Portumna Scouts, St Brendan's N.S. Parents Association and Portumna Tidy Towns Task Force Committee and is involved in Portumna FitTowns committee which was launched in Portumna in January 2015 to encourage the whole community, young and old, to get out and get active.

Colm Keaveney has been a Dáil deputy since 2011. His electoral career has been characterised by a gradual building up of the Labour base in this constituency and a volatile and ultimately terminal relationship with the party leadership and ultimately the party itself.

In 1999 Keaveney failed to be elected in the Tuam electoral area with 837 votes, although he did gain election to Tuam town council on the same day. He polled 1,923 votes for Galway County Council in 2004, taking the second seat in the Tuam electoral area. As the Labour candidate in Galway East for the 2007 Dáil election he polled 1,747 first preferences, being eliminated on the fourth count. In August 2007 he left the Labour party and sat as an independent on both local authorities but he rejoined in 2008 following discussions with the party leader. In the 2009 local elections he ran as a Labour candidate again in the Tuam electoral area, where he polled 2,519 (quota 2,347). He was elected for Labour in the 2011 Dáil election with 4,254 votes (7.18%). Elected to the chair of the Labour Party, in December 2012 he voted against the government on the issue of the cutting of Respite Care allowances in the Social Welfare Bill. In June 2013 he resigned from the Labour Party and in December of 2013 he joined Fianna Fáil. He is the Fianna Fáil spokesperson on Mental Health and Special Needs in Dáil Éireann.

Keaveney worked as a SIPTU trade union official and is a former president of the Union of Students in Ireland. He grew up working in his father's bar but is now teetotal, saying alcohol and politics don't mix.

Sinn Féin:

Annemarie Roche was born in England of Irish parents and lives in Loughrea. She has a BA in Public and Social Policy and an MA in Public Advocacy and Activism from NUI Galway. Her platform in this election includes the need for social housing in East Galway, the provision of affordable childcare in East Galway and the refurbishment and restoration of Loughrea Town Hall and Cinema building as a civic centre for the promotion of Loughrea's cultural heritage.

Green Party:

The party has said that it will run a candidate here in 2016 but at the time of writing no name had been released. The candidate in 2011 was Ciarán Kennedy who polled 402 votes (0.7%).

Independents:

Seán Canney, from Belclare, is running under the Independent Alliance banner. Cannery was a strong candidate in the 2011 Dáil election and has been a member of Galway county council for the Tuam area since 2004 with 1,483 first preference votes (8.19%). In 2007 he was campaign manager for his brother-in-law, Fianna Fáil County Councillor and later independent TD Paddy McHugh. In 2009 he was comfortably re-elected there, topping the poll with 3,273 votes (17.43% and 1.39 quotas). He stood as an independent in the 2011 Dáil election and polled 5,567 (9.4%) first preferences and was in contention until the end of the sixth count, when his votes transferred almost evenly across the surviving candidates. Since then he was re-elected comfortably to the County Council, again topping the poll in the Tuam area this time with a massive 3,171 first preferences (17.03%) which was 1.7 quotas in an area which had been enlarged from seven to nine seats. He was Mayor of Galway County Council in 2007–2008.

In 2011 Canney attracted considerable attention by suggesting the amalgamation of Galway City and County Councils, saying that this would save more than €2,000,000 a year. He is active in promoting the improvement of road, rail and electronic communications in the area. He is one of seven children from a family farm and is a quantity surveyor and lectures at GMIT. He is married with three children and takes an active part in many community organisations.

Michael Fahy, a farmer from Ardrahan is the longest serving councillor on Galway County Council. He was first elected to the council for the Loughrea electoral area in 1979 on a Fianna Fáil ticket and he continued to sit for Fianna Fáil until 2004 when he resigned from the party. In February 2007 he was prosecuted on charges of fraud, false accounting, and attempting to make a personal gain or cause a loss to the Galway council in respect of the erection of more than a mile of fencing on his land. He was convicted by a jury on all charges and was sentenced to 12 months in prison and fined €75,000. However, after serving almost eight months in jail, the Court of Criminal Appeal overturned the conviction and ordered a re-trial. At his re-trial in 2008, Mr Fahy was convicted of one charge of obtaining the benefit of €7,055 from Galway County Council by false pretences. That conviction was overturned by the court of criminal appeal in 2011.

He is sometimes referred to as Michael 'Stroke' Fahy. He acquired the nickname in the 1970s from a local journalist after he persuaded the Fianna Fáil national executive to add his name to the local election ticket when the local party had declined to nominate him. He remained on the county council during his term of imprisonment since, notwithstanding the fact he was serving the prison sentence, his case was still under appeal.

Fahey was previously a Dáil candidate in 1987 as an independent in the Galway West constituency where his local base then was. In that election he polled 3,139 votes (5.95%). In local elections he topped the poll for Fianna Fáil in 1991, 1999 and 2004 and as an independent he topped it again in 2009 with 2,247 (12.28%). In the 2014 local elections his vote fell to 1,437 (8.84%) but he still retained his seat.

In an interview with the *Galway Advertiser* Michael Fahy said he believes the General Election is wide open. 'Nobody's seat is safe, especially following the boundary changes, it is going to make things very interesting. I have never seen a greater opening for the people of South Galway. There has not been a TD based in this area since before Frank Fahy departed to Galway West.'

Galway West

Outgoing Deputies:

Éamon Ó Cuív (FF), Derek Nolan (Lab), Brian Walsh (FG), Noel Grealish (Ind), Seán Kyne (FG),

In November 2015 Brian Walsh (FG) announced that, on medical advice, he would not contest this election.

John O'Mahony (FG), the outgoing Dáil deputy for Mayo, will contest the 2016 election in this constituency.

The Constituency:

This continues to be a five seat constituency but has been renamed and substantially redrawn. It includes the city of Galway and the western part of county Galway. The following areas in County Mayo have been transferred to Galway West. The Former Ballinrobe Rural District, consisting of Ballinrobe, Cong, Dalgan, Houndswood, Kilcommon, Kilmaine, Neale and Shrule and from the Former Claremorris Rural District Garrymore, with a total added population of 10,306.

	% Vote 1997	% Vote 2002	% Vote 2007	% Vote 2011	Swing 2011	Quotas 2011
Fine Gael	22.21	16.90	20.40	30.72	10.32	1.8
Labour	10.07	10.54	11.05	12.35	1.30	0.7
Fianna Fáil	45.94	41.33	37.15	20.95	−16.20	1.3
Sinn Féin	2.51	5.62	2.96	6.28	3.32	0.4
Green Party	3.44	4.43	5.49	1.85	−3.64	0.1
Others	15.83	21.19	22.97	27.84	4.87	1.7

2016 Candidates will include:

Sean Kyne (FG), Hildegarde Naughton (FG), John O'Mahony (FG), Derek Nolan (Lab), John Connolly (FF), Mary Hoade (FF), Éamon Ó Cuív (FF), Trevor Ó Clochartaigh (SF), Seamus Sheridan (GP),

Tommy Holohan (AAA–PBP), Nicola Daveron (Renua), Niall Ó Tuathail (SD), James Charity (Ind), Catherine Connolly (Ind), Mike Cubbard (Ind), Noel Grealish (Ind), Fidelma Healy-Eames (Ind), Seona O'Fegan (Ind), Tommy Roddy (Ind)

In Brief:

While the decision of outgoing deputy Brian Walsh to retire from the Dáil on health grounds is a setback for Fine Gael, it still has a strong ticket with Mayo deputy John O'Mahony transferring across to join its other sitting Galway deputy and will hold its two seats. One time Progressive Democrat and now independent Noel Grealish is also likely to hold his seat. Éamon Ó Cuív will hold his seat and there is unlikely to be a second Fianna Fáil seat. One time Labour member and now independent councillor Catherine Connolly came extremely close to winning a seat in 2011 and will win one this time, probably at the expense of the outgoing Labour deputy Derek Nolan.

Fine Gael:

The last three elections saw Fine Gael's vote share grow steadily in this constituency from 16.9% in 2002, through 20.4% in 2007 to 30.7% in 2011. It should hold these two quotas notwithstanding the early retirement of one of its sitting deputies.

John O'Mahony has been a Dáil deputy for the Mayo constituency since 2007. He is based in Ballaghderreen. He was manager of the Mayo GAA county football team when he won a Dáil seat on his first attempt in 2007. He got 6,869 first preference votes (9.62%), which gave him the third of five seats in Mayo and he was appointed party deputy spokesperson on Sport. In 2011 he took the fourth Fine Gael seat in Mayo with 8,667 votes (11.7%). The constituency boundaries report published in 2015 provided for the reduction of the Mayo constituency from five seats to four and also provided for the transfer of a large area of county Mayo into Galway West. In April 2015 O'Mahony confirmed his decision to transfer constituencies citing the fact that about 8,000 voters in South Mayo, where he had received considerable support in the past, had been moved into Galway West.

In the current Dáil O'Mahony has been a member of the Joint Oireachtas Committee on Education and Science and the Joint Oireachtas Committee for Arts, Sport, Tourism, Community, Rural and Gaeltach Affairs. He chairs the Joint Oireachtas Committee on Transport and Communications. Married, with five daughters, he is from Kilmovee and is a former teacher. He won All-Ireland football titles playing for Mayo Minors and Under 21s in 1971 and 1974 respectively. He has managed the Mayo, Galway and Leitrim GAA county football teams. He won two All-Ireland championships with Galway in 1998 and 2001, guided Leitrim to the Connacht Championship in 1994 and steered his native county to the 1989 All-Ireland final.

Seán Kyne is from Moycullen and was first elected to Dáil Éireann in 2011. Prior to that he had been a member of Galway City Council for the Connemara electoral area since 2004, with 864 first preference votes (5.18%). He was also a candidate for the party in the 2007 Dáil election but then polled just 1,912 votes (3.47%) and was eliminated on the sixth count. He contested the Seanad elections on the agricultural panel that year, also unsuccessfully. Standing in Connemara again in the local elections of 2009 he increased his vote to 1,927 (11.7% and 0.9 quotas) and took the second seat. In the 2011 general election he polled 4,550 first preferences (7.5%) and took the final seat in Galway West with a very close margin of just 17 votes ahead of Catherine Connolly (Ind).

In the outgoing Dáil Kyne was a member of the Joint Oireachtas Committee on Jobs, Social Protection and Education and the Joint Oireachtas Committee on European Union Affairs. He holds an MSc in Agricultural Science from University College Dublin and worked as a REPS consultant for 11 years. In October 2015 he published an autobiography called *Keeping the Faith*.

Hildegarde Naughton is a primary school teacher from Oranmore and has been a member of Seanad Éireann since 2013. She was nominated to the Seanad Éireann by An Taoiseach Enda Kenny following the resignation of Dr Martin McAleese. Prior to that she was a member of Galway City Council, having been elected for the Galway City West ward in 2009 with 1,061 first preference votes (12.07%). She also contested the 2011 Dáil election and polled 3,606 first preferences (5.9%), being eliminated on the 6th count. She was Mayor of Galway for 2011 to 2012. As mayor there was controversy when she used her casting vote to refuse David Norris permission to speak to the council when he was seeking a nomination for the presidential election in 2011. Her father was a member of the Fine Gael National Executive.

She has a BA in French and Economics and an MA in French from NUI Galway and she trained as a primary school teacher at Mary Immaculate College, Limerick. In 2007 she was co-ordinator of the Galway City and Council People in Need telethon which raised over €300,000 for local charities. A classically trained soprano, she won the Association of Irish Musical Societies award as best actress for her portrayal of Eliza Doolittle in 2008.

Labour Party:

President Michael D. Higgins long held a seat here for the Labour party. He was first elected to Dáil Éireann in 1981. He was re-elected in February 1982 but lost his seat in the November 1982 election. He regained his seat in 1987 and held it until 2011. The seat was then won by Derek Nolan who is again the party's sole candidate.

Derek Nolan is based in Riverside, Galway and was elected to Dáil Éireann on his first attempt in 2011. He topped the poll with 7,489 votes in that election and took the second seat. He joined the Labour Party when he was 19 years old and studying in NUI Galway. His first electoral outing was in 2004 when he unsuccessfully stood in Galway City No 1 (East & North) Ward and got 440 votes (4.5%). In 2009 he was successful in the Galway City East Ward, polling 995 (11.31%). He holds an LL.B. in Corporate Law from NUI Galway. He was a trainee solicitor when he stood for the Dáil in 2011. He is a member of the Dáil Public Accounts Committee.

Fianna Fáil:

Neither Frank Fahey nor Michael Crowe, who contested the seat for Fianna Fáil in 2011, put themselves forward at the constituency convention in 2015 so long time deputy Éamon Ó Cuív has new running mates on this occasion.

John Connolly is a schoolteacher based in the Bearna area. He was backed for the nomination by former candidate Michael Crowe, who contested in 2011. Connolly was a city councillor from 2004 to 2009 in the Galway City No 2 (West Ward), where he gained 887 votes (16.75%). In 2009 he failed to take a seat in Galway City Central, polling 599 votes (11.59%). He did not contest the 2014 local election.

Éamon Ó Cuív has been a Dáil deputy since 1992. He was also an unsuccessful candidate in the 1989 election. The 2011 election was the first time he did not top the poll since 1997. This time he was in second place with 7,441 votes (12.3%), only 48 behind Labour's Derek Nolan. In 2007 Ó Cuív became Minister for Social Protection (and held various other reassigned ministries after January 2010). He was Minister for Arts, Culture, Heritage and the Islands from 2002 to 2008. He was previously a Minister of State at the Department of Agriculture with responsibility for rural and western development from 2001 to 2002 and Minister of State at the Department of Arts, Culture and the Gaeltacht from 1997 to 2001. He was a member of Seanad Éireann from 1989 to 1992. After the 2011 election he was made Fianna Fáil spokesperson on Communications, Energy and Natural Resources and in August 2011 was made deputy leader of Fianna Fáil. He resigned both positions after criticising leader Micheál Martin in February 2012. In July 2012 Ó Cuív was reappointed to the Fianna Fáil front bench as spokesperson on Agriculture and Food, and on Community Affairs.

Ó Cuív worked formerly as the manager of a gaeltacht co-operative in Corr Na Móna. He was a member of Galway County Council for the Connemara electoral area from 1991 to 1997. He is a grandson of former President, former Taoiseach and former Leader of Fianna Fáil Éamon de Valera. He is a cousin of Síle de Valera, who was previously a Dáil deputy for the neighbouring Clare constituency.

Mary Hoade is a native of Headford and has been a member of Galway County Council for the Oranmore electoral area since 1992. She first contested the local elections in 1999 when she got 571 votes (5.28%) but failed to be elected. In 1992 she was successful in the Oranmore electoral area with 1,314 votes (15.77%). In the 2004 local elections, again in the Oranmore area, she topped the poll and took the first seat with 2,567 votes (21.71%). In 2009 boundary changes necessitated her move to the Tuam, taking a council seat there with 1,864 votes (9.33%). She took the fourth seat in Tuam in 2014 with 1,886 first preference votes (10.13%), just four votes over the quota. In 2014 she was elected Mayor of Galway. She has a very strong presence in the east of the constituency. She gave up full time employment in 2003 to pursue a career in politics. She was an unsuccessful candidate for Seanad Éireann in both the 2002 and 2007 Seanad Elections.

Sinn Féin:

In the 2007 General Election the Sinn Féin candidate Ann Marie Carroll polled just 1,629 first preferences here.

Trevor Ó Clochartaigh who is based in An Cheathru Rua is again the party candidate for this Dáil election. In 2011 he improved the party vote to 3,808 (6.3%). He first stood unsuccessfully as a Labour candidate for Galway County Council in the Connemara local electoral area in 2004, polling 619 votes (3.71%). In 2009 he was the Sinn Féin candidate in the same electoral area. On that occasion his 893 votes (5.42%) were not enough to take a seat. As Sinn Féin candidate for the 2011 Dáil election he polled 3,808 votes (6.28%). He was elected to Seanad Éireann in 2011 on the Agriculture Panel.

Ó Clochartaigh was born and brought up in the United Kingdom. His parents came from Connemara and he is a native Irish speaker. He took a degree in Commerce at NUI Galway and then pursued a career in Irish language theatre and subsequently in television as a manager and director and as a producer. He is the Sinn Féin spokesperson on the Irish Language, Rural Affairs, and the West.

Green Party:

Seamus Sheridan is a businessman based in the Rahoon area. This is his first Dáil election. In the 2014 local elections he polled 479 votes (7.53%), missing a seat by 45 votes on the final count in

Galway City Central electoral area. He is a frequent commentator on food and agriculture issues in the domestic and international media. He has been the Green Party's spokesperson on Agriculture, Food and the Marine since the retirement of Trevor Sargent in 2011. He has been a key figure in the development of the Irish artisan food industry, and in particular in the development of the Irish artisan cheese export market since he set up his first cheese stall in Galway market in 1995. Seamus Sheridan has served on and chaired many boards and voluntary groups both in Galway and nationally dealing with food education, agriculture and tourism including the North/South Ministerial body 'Safefood' which promotes awareness and knowledge of food safety and nutrition on the island of Ireland.

He has a long record of supporting the arts and sport in Galway and trains local youth teams in football and hurling. He and his wife, a primary teacher, have three children. In November 2015 he published *Sheridans Guide to Cheese.*

Anti-Austerity Alliance – People Before Profit:

Tommy Holohan is from Claddagh and now lives in Knocknacarra. In the 2014 local elections he polled 393 first preference votes (4.57%) in the Galway City West electoral area but he did not get elected. Speaking at his adoption meeting for this election Holohan questioned Government claims about an upturn in the economy. 'What little recovery there is for low and middle income people is built on the back of severe exploitation in the form of JobsBridge type scams and low paid precarious work with little or no real job security', he said.

Holohan is an expert on the history of old Claddagh and has proposed the establishment of a maritime museum on Claddagh quay. He took up marathon running in his 40s and this year completed his eighteenth consecutive New York City marathon at the age of 63. He has run for a number of charities but now runs for Croí, the heart and stroke charity. He hopes his two sons will join him when he runs his twentieth New York marathon.

Renua Ireland:

Nicola Daveron is a first time candidate with no previous political background. A Galway native, she has lived in Renmore and Salthill. She attended NUI Galway where she studied economics, legal science, history and classical civilisation and obtained a Bachelor of Arts degree and a Higher Diploma in Education. Ms Daveron has worked in teaching, construction and the fashion industry. Currently she is a solicitor in Galway in general practice with a special interest in the mortgage arrears cases. She intends to prioritise Galway Hospital, flooding, rural and urban crime and traffic congestion in her campaign.

Social Democrats:

Niall Ó Tuathail was raised in Dangan Heights. He studied Management Science and Information Systems at Trinity College Dublin. After university he travelled, including undertaking a 6000km bicycle trip from France to Kyrgyzstan. He then joined the international consultancy group McKinsey & Company for whom he worked in London and Lisbon. He started a software design business called Mobile Clipboard in 2014, which is based in Galway and serves clients in Dublin, London and Lisbon. He became frustrated with Irish politics during the bank guarantee and bailout, and moved back to Ireland to have an impact on the 2011 election. He ran the canvass for first time independent Stephen Donnelly in his successful candidacy in Wicklow for the 2011 election and did the same for the independent David Hall in the Dublin West by-election in 2014. Ó Tuathail lives in Galway City with his Portuguese partner and young son.

Independents:

James Charity is a barrister based in Corrandulla. He has been a member of Galway County Council for the Oranmore electoral area since 2014. In that local election he polled 1,424 (11.12%) first preferences as an independent. He has a BA in Arts (Legal Science, Sociology and Politics) from NUI Galway and subsequently took an LL.B and Master of Laws degree from NUI Galway and studied at King's Inns. He says he has a keen personal and professional understanding of the difficulties faced by many sections of the community who have been affected by the economic downturn. In May 2015 he joined Renua and was named as that party's candidate for Galway West, but in July 2015 he left it again citing differences with Lucinda Creighton over water charges.

He is a voluntary director of the Galway Citizens Information Service and believes that in a society where the basic tenets of equity and fairness appear to be under sustained and constant threat, it is imperative that the community have access to adequate resources to ensure they can protect and, where necessary, vindicate their rights as citizens of the State. In his personal time he is a keen follower of Gaelic football, hurling and soccer.

Catherine Connolly is originally from Shantalla and has lived in the Claddagh since 1988. She is a member of Galway City Council for the Galway City West ward. In the 2014 local elections she polled 1,513 first preferences, which was well over the quota of 1,229. She has also contested two previous Dáil elections as an independent and came very close to winning a seat in 2011. A practicing barrister on the Western circuit, she previously worked as a Clinical Psychologist with the Western Health Board in Ballinasloe, Galway City and Connemara.

She first won a seat on the council in 1999 when she stood for the Labour Party and polled 457 votes (11.14%) in what was then the Galway City No 2 (West Ward), which gave her the first seat. She ran again for Labour in 2004, this time in the Galway City No 3 (South Ward) where she took the third seat with 1,265 votes (15.7%). She was Labour Mayor of Galway for the year 2004–5. Her sister Collette Connolly ran in her stead in the Number 2 ward in the 2004 local elections, also as a Labour Party candidate. Catherine had hoped to be a candidate for Labour in the 2007 general election, but the party decided that Michael D. Higgins would be the sole Labour candidate. She then left the party and stood as an independent in the 2007 election, polling 2,006 first preferences (3.64%). In 2009 she ran again as an independent for Galway City Council in the Galway West ward, taking the second seat with 1,180 votes (13.43%). She also stood again in the Galway West Dáil election of 2011 when she more than doubled her 2007 figure to

4,766 (7.9%), and enforced a complete recount before finally conceding the last seat to Fine Gael's Seán Kyne by a margin of 17 votes.

Mike Cubbard has been a member of Galway City Council for the Galway City Central electoral area since 2014. He stood as an independent candidate in the 2009 local elections, polling 474 first preferences (9.17%). He stood also as an independent candidate in the 2011 Dáil election when he polled just 853 (1.41%) and was eliminated after the first round. In the 2014 local elections he topped the poll with 850 votes (13.36%) in Galway City Central. He is now 25 years of age, comes from a long established Claddagh family and works for Aviva Insurance in Knocknacarra. He is under 16 coach at Galway Hibernians/Foyle in Bohermore and Crestwood. He says his interests are 'soccer and current affairs' and that it is time that youth and dynamism is injected into Dáil Éireann.

Noel Grealish is based in Carnmore near Oranmore and has been a member of Dáil Éireann since 2002. He was elected to Dáil Éireann as a Progressive Democrat candidate on his first attempt in 2002 taking the seat previously been held firstly for Fianna Fáil and then for the Progressive Democrats by Bobby Molloy for over 30 years. Grealish was a member of Galway county council for the Oranmore electoral area from 1999 to 2004. He was the Progressive Democrat spokesman on Rural Planning and also served as the chairman of the parliamentary party. He was re-elected at the 2007 general election with 10.54% of the first preferences. Grealish was Deputy Leader of the Progressive Democrats from May 2007 to the March 2009. Since the Progressive Democrats party was wound up in November 2009 Grealish has stood as an independent. In the 2011 Dáil election he polled 6,229 first preferences (10.3%) and took the fourth of the five seats. In the outgoing Dáil he is part of the Technical Group, a group of independent TDs who work together to maximize their speaking time and other benefits that would normally only accrue to political parties. He has confirmed that he will not join the Independent Alliance. Originally from Carnmore, he is also a company director.

Fidelma Healy Eames is based in Oranmore and has been a member of Seanad Éireann since 2007. She was a Dáil candidate for Fine Gael in Galway West in the 2002, 2007 and 2011 elections. In 2002 she polled 1,320 first preferences. In 2004 she was elected to Galway county council for the Oranmore electoral area with 1,632 first preferences, holding the seat until she was elected to the Seanad on the Labour panel in 2007. In the 2007 Dáil election she polled 3,904 votes (7.09%) and in 2011 she polled 5,046 (8.32%). In the Seanad she was Fine Gael Spokesperson on Social Protection from 2011 until she was expelled from the party in 2013 after voting against the Protection of Life During Pregnancy Bill 2013. She subsequently joined the Reform Alliance, which comprised other Fine Gael TDs and Senators who voted against the same bill. She did not, however, go on to join Renua, deciding instead to contest this election as an independent. Married and living in Oranmore, she grew up on a family farm in Moylough and was a primary teacher and lecturer at Mary Immaculate before becoming a full time politician. She also owns her own business, FHE Education and Training Providers.

Seaona O'Fegan is running as a candidate for the Irish Postmasters Union. She took over the running of Barna village post office from her mother-in-law, Noreen O'Fegan, in 2003, and took over the Fr Griffin Road Post Office in Galway in December, 2014. She is the mother of four children between 17 and 23 years old and she aims to secure election on a platform of 'better services for communities.' She has said that her campaign will not be just about the post offices, but will also focus on investment, education, health services, transport, and employment.

O'Fegan says, 'Through my work as a postmistress, I listen to the concerns and needs of people. What I hear is a need for greater Government support for vibrant communities. A key part of maintaining and developing better services in communities is the Post Office as a front office for essential public and commercial services in villages, towns, and cities – where people can collect welfare, pay bills, do financial transactions, and carry out government or local authority business.' She is a previous secretary of the Galway/Tuam branch of the Irish Postmasters' Union.

Tommy Roddy is based in Salthill. In the 2014 local elections he stood unsuccessfully for Galway City Council in the Galway

City West electoral area polling 270 first preference votes (3.14%). A long time community activist, Mr Roddy volunteers with Youth Work Ireland and with shOUT! LGBT Youth Project. He also facilitates delivering mental health modules to transition year students. He is the PRO for ALâ Participatory Theatre Galway and is involved with Fr Griffin's/Éire Óg GAA Club and St Patrick's Scout Group.

Kerry

Outgoing Deputies:

Kerry North: Jimmy Deenihan (FG), Arthur Spring (Lab), Martin Ferris (SF)

Kerry South: Brendan Griffin (FG), Tom Fleming (Ind), Michael Healy-Rae (Ind)

The Constituency:

This new five-seat constituency has a population of 145,502 and its boundaries are aligned to the geographical county boundaries. Kerry has not previously been electorally united since 1937. This new constituency was brought about by the merger of the two previous three seat constituencies of Kerry South and Kerry North and the redrawing of those parts of County Limerick that had been in Kerry North into the Limerick constituency.

Kerry North–Limerick West

	% Vote 1997	% Vote 2002	% Vote 2007	% Vote 2011	Swing 2011	Quotas 2011
Fine Gael	24.29	22.09	32.30	40.77	8.47	1.6
Labour	29.90	22.40	10.90	20.08	9.18	0.8
Fianna Fáil	26.31	30.15	31.30	11.47	–19.83	0.5
Sinn Féin	15.91	24.24	20.43	20.35	–0.08	0.8
Green Party	–	–	1.90	0.52	–1.38	0.02
Others	3.6	1.13	3.17	6.81	3.34	0.3

Kerry South

	% Vote 1997	% Vote 2002	% Vote 2007	% Vote 2011	Swing 2011	Quotas 2011
Fine Gael	13.77	17.66	25.09	32.63	7.54	1.3
Labour	14.05	14.48	13.48	11.10	–2.38	0.4
Fianna Fáil	31.79	44.64	40.65	13.33	27.32	0.5
Sinn Féin	–	–	3.52	–	–	–
Green Party	–	–	1.89	0.90	–0.99	0.04
Others	40.39	23.22	15.35	42.03	26.68	1.7

2016 Candidates will include:

Jimmy Deenihan (FG), Brendan Griffin (FG), Grace O'Donnell (FG), Arthur Spring (Lab), John Brassil (FF), Norma Moriarty (FF), Martin Ferris (SF), Michael Fitzgerald (GP), Brian Finucane (AAA–PBP), Tom Fleming (Ind), Michael Healy-Rae (Ind), Kevin Murphy (Ind), Michael O'Gorman (Ind)

In Brief:

The merger of the two three seat constituencies into one means there are only five seats to go around and there are six outgoing deputies contesting. Fianna Fáil will also mount a strong challenge to win a seat. Sinn Féin's Martin Ferris will win a seat. Fine Gael's Jimmy Deenihan is likely to be the stronger of the party's two outgoing deputies and seems almost certain of winning a seat. His party colleague Brendan Griffin will have a tougher task. Labour's Arthur Spring, based in Tralee, is likely to lose his seat in this new larger constituency. Of the independents, Michael Healy Rae is likely to be the strongest locally in south Kerry and more likely than others from the south to attract support this time in the northern half of the county. It looks therefore like one Sinn Féin seat, at least one Fine Gael seat, one Fianna Fáil seat, a seat for Healy Rae (Ind) and a battle between two other southern based candidates, Tom Fleming (Ind), the outgoing independent and Brendan Griffen (FG) for the last seat.

Fine Gael:

The party will run three candidates in this new five-seat constituency.

Jimmy Deenihan is based in Listowel, which is in the far north of this new constituency. He has been Minister of State at the Departments of An Taoiseach and Foreign Affairs with special responsibility for the Diaspora since July 2014. Prior to that he was Minister for Arts, Heritage and the Gaeltacht from 2011 to 2014. He was first elected to Dáil Éireann in 1987 and he has retained his seat in each subsequent election. In 1987 his first preference vote was 10,087, in 1997 it was 8,689 and in 2007 it was 12,697. In 2011 his vote was 12,304 (27%), which was 900 over the quota. He was a Minister of State at the Department of Agriculture and Forestry from 1994 to 1997. He was a member of Kerry County Council for the Listowel electoral area from 1985 to 1994 and from 1999 to 2004. Deenihan formerly worked as a teacher. He was captain of the All-Ireland winning Kerry senior football team in 1981, holds five All-Ireland inter-county GAA football medals and received a GAA All-Star award in 1981. He was a Taoiseach's nominee to the Seanad in 1983.

Brendan Griffin lives in the parish of Keel, in the foothills of the Sliabh Mish Mountains on the Dingle Peninsula. He was elected to Dáil Éireann for Kerry South on his first attempt in 2011, unseating his party colleague Tom Sheehan. He topped the poll in that constituency with 8,808 votes (19.8%). He was a member of Kerry County Council from 2009 to 2011. He first stood for election in the Dingle local area in 2004, when he polled 1,044 (12.67%) and failed to be elected. In 2009 he increased his vote to 2,038 (21.93%) to top the poll and take the third seat. He was Jimmy Deenihan's parliamentary assistant for three years before the redrawing of the constituency boundaries.

Shortly after his election he was criticised for hiring his wife Róisín as his secretarial assistant and his cousin Tommy Griffin as his parliamentary assistant. Griffin only takes half of his salary as a TD. At first he gave the other half directly back to the exchequer and then in 2012 he began to donate half of his salary to pay for a third teacher in a small rural Kerry school. Before his election to

Dáil Éireann he published a novel, Secrets of a Moonlit River, written at night after closing time at his pub, the Castle Inn in Castlemaine. He has made several public attacks on the whip system and on Irish Water but has been a loyal voter with the government.

Grace O'Donnell is a businesswoman and a former member of Tralee town council and Mayor of Tralee. She was elected to Tralee town council in 2009 with 491 votes (5.2%), serving as mayor in 2011. However, she failed to win a seat a seat on Kerry county council in 2014 with 657 votes (4.11%). She was added as a candidate by the Fine Gael national executive after the local organisation had selected the two sitting deputies at convention. She has said she would be naïve not to realise she was added because of gender quotas but that she has a strong track record and is a very credible candidate. She is the co-founder of Kare4Kidz which was established in 2011 and is an active member of the Kerry businesswomen's network.

Labour Party:

Labour suffered an electoral trauma in Kerry North in 2002, when former party leader and three-time Tánaiste Dick Spring lost his seat. When Spring retired from politics Terry O'Brien, a member of Kerry County Council for the Tralee electoral area, took his place for the 2007 elections. In 2011, however, Arthur Spring, a nephew of Dick Spring, was the candidate and the party regained the seat.

Arthur Spring is based in Tralee and was first elected to Dáil Éireann in 2011. In the 2011 Dáil election he polled 9,159 first preferences (20.1%) to take the second seat. At that time he was Mayor of Tralee Town Council and Vice-Chairperson of Kerry County Council, having topped the poll in the Tralee electoral area in 2009 with 3,155 votes (18.10%), which was 1.45 quotas. He had previously worked as a personal assistant to Dick Spring, who was his campaign manager in 2011. After a career in Finance Arthur returned to Tralee where he set up a juice bar business. His uncle Dick Spring was a TD for this constituency from 1981 to 2002 and his grandfather Dan Spring was the local TD from 1943 to 1981.

Fianna Fáil:

The party is running two new candidates in 2016.

John Brassil is a pharmacist from Ballyheigue. He has been a member of Kerry County Council for the Listowel electoral area since 1999. In the 1999 local elections he polled 1,298 (9.57%) of the first preference vote. He was an unsuccessful Seanad candidate in 2002 on the Cultural and Educational Panel, He was re-elected to Kerry County Council in 2004 with 1,755 votes (10.96%), taking the second seat. He was again re-elected in 2009 with 2,036 votes (12.44%) for the fifth seat. In 2014 he topped the poll with 1,912 (12.96%), which was 67 votes over the quota. He is the current Cathaoirleach of Kerry County Council and a former Chairman of Shannon Development. In his spare time the 51-year-old father of three follows Munster Rugby and his local GAA. After studying to be a civil engineer and working in that field for a number of years he qualified as a pharmacist and took over the family business in Ballyheigue. He defeated former Fianna Fáil TD for North Kerry, Tom McEllistrim, to win the selection convention.

Norma Moriarty is from Waterville and has been a member of Kerry County Council for the Kerry South and West electoral area since 2013 when she was co-opted to replace Paul O'Donoghue, brother of former Ceann Comhairle John O'Donoghue. In the 2014 local elections she polled 1,512 first preferences (7.3% and took the seventh of the nine seats. She was added to the ticket by the party's national executive after the local organisation had selected Brassil at convention. Moriarty says that while she is conscious of the role gender quotas played in her selection she is glad of the opportunity which might not otherwise have come her way. She did not put herself before the party selection convention but instead made a written submission to party headquarters when it became clear that there was an opportunity for a female candidate from the south of the constituency. She is an English and Learning support teacher, is from a farming and small business background, and has been involved in community and sporting activities locally for almost twenty years.

Sinn Féin:

Martin Ferris is based in Ardfert and has been a member of Dáil Éireann for Kerry North since 2002. He had run unsuccessfully in the 1997 Dáil election, when he polled 5,671 votes. He increased that to 9,496 first preferences in 2002. He was re-elected with a somewhat reduced vote, dropping back to 8,030, in 2007. In 2011 he took the third seat with 9,282 first preference votes (20.3%). He was the party's candidate in the Munster constituency in the 1999 European elections, polling 29,060 first preferences. From 1999 to 2004 he was a member of Kerry county council for the Tralee electoral area. Ferris was also a member of Tralee town council from 1999 to 2004. His daughter Toiréasa Ferris was co-opted to his county council seat in 2003 and in the 2004 local election she polled 2,343 first preference votes, taking the first seat. She improved on this to take 1.38 quotas for the first seat in 2009. In the European elections of that year she was the Sinn Féin candidate for the South constituency and received 64,671 first preferences. In the 31st Dáil Ferris is the Sinn Féin spokesperson on Agriculture and Rural Development, and also on the Marine and Natural Resources. He has served terms of imprisonment for IRA activity including one in Portlaoise Prison from 1984 to 1994.

Green Party:

Tom Donovan was the Green Party candidate in Kerry North in 2011, polling 239 votes (0.5%), while Oonagh Comerford polled 401 votes (0.9%) in Kerry South.

Michael Fitzgerald, from Castlegregory, has worked for many years in the areas of education and tourism and is a strong believer in wide consultation with local communities prior to finalizing major initiatives which impact on them.

Anti-Austerity Alliance – People Before Profit:

Brian Finucane, a native of Ballylongford was the People Before Profit candidate in the Listowel electoral area in the 2014 local elections. He polled 390 (2.64%) on that occasion. He was a member of the campaigns against household and water charges in 2011 and was the founder of the People Before Profit Listowel branch which has evolved into PBP Kerry. He had earlier campaigned against cuts to cancer patients' medical cards, charges for septic tanks, and the universal social charge, amongst other issues. Brian also founded, and is the current PRO of, the Right2Water Kerry campaign.

Kerry Independent Alliance:

Michael Gleeson, a former teacher from Killarney, played senior football for Kerry from 1969 until 1972. He first ran for Killarney Town Council in 1991 when he was an unsuccessful Labour candidate. He ran for the Dáil in Kerry South as an independent in 1997 when he was eliminated on the first count with 1,388 votes. Running for the South Kerry Independent Alliance, the forerunner of his present party, in 1999 he was successful in both the Killarney Town Council and the Kerry County Council election. His 1,478 votes (10.31%) gave him the fifth seat in the Killarney area. He has held that seat ever since and exceeded the quota in 2009 and 2014 with 2,536 (13.46%) and 2,139 (11.69%) respectively. He ran for the South Kerry Independent Alliance in the 2011 general election and on that occasion his 4,939 votes (11.13%) saw him maintain his challenge for the second or third seat until the fourth count when independents Fleming and Healy-Rae pulled away from the pack. He has throughout his political career emphasized the need for long term planning and budgeting if local authorities are to be effective.

Independents:

Tom Fleming is from Scartagin Village and has been a member of Dáil Éireann for Kerry South since 2011. He was a Fianna Fáil candidate in the 2002 and 2007 elections but he left the party in January 2011 when it decided to run only a single candidate in that year's election. Standing as an independent, and strongly criticising the social welfare provisions in the 2010 Budget, he took the second seat with 6,416 first preference votes (14.5%). He was a member of Kerry county council for 20 years in the Killarney electoral area and was chairman from 2000 to 2001. He was the fourth generation of his family to serve on the council. In Dáil Éireann he is a member of the Joint Administration Committee and the Committee on Jobs, Social Protection and Education. He is a publican.

Henry Gaynor, from The Spa, Tralee, is a services operator at the Kerry Ingredients factory in Listowel. He is married with two children and his slogan is 'Different in many ways.' He says that the event that brought him into political activism was the bank guarantee. That led to a letter writing campaign to local and national media 'exposing the rot in the system.' He then joined various protest groups including Tralee/Ballyhea says No before deciding to run for election. He is opposed to the introduction of gender quotas in politics believing that it is 'possible the rough and tumble of politics might not suit them' (letter to *The Kerryman*).

Michael Healy-Rae was elected to Dáil Éireann for Kerry South on his first attempt in 2011. With a first preference vote of 6,670 (15.0%) he took the third and final seat. He replaced his father Jackie Healy-Rae who had been an independent TD for South Kerry since 1997. Michael has represented Killorglin on Kerry County Council from 1999 to 2011, increasing his share of the poll on each occasion, and topping it with 3,198 votes (21.28%) in 2009. Michael's nephew Johnny was co-opted to the county council and topped the poll in 2014 with almost one and a half quotas. Michael's brother Danny has also been a member of Kerry County Council since 2003. The latter topped the poll in the Killarney electoral areas in 2009 and 2014 local elections.

Unlike some of the other independents Michael Healy-Rae has not been a member of the Technical Group in the Dáil. He worked previously in the family plant hire business and had a shop and petrol pumps business. He has said on many occasions that the rules on drinking and driving should be relaxed in rural areas.

Michael 'Pixie' O'Gorman is from Bedford and was also an independent candidate in the Listowel Electoral Area for the 2014 local election. He polled 802 (5.44%) votes and was eliminated on the ninth count He is running on a Right2Change and Right2Water platform and is a founder member of the Tralee Says No anti-bank bailout campaign. He is a stonemason and married father of two. He is one of the founders of the Kerry Save Our Woods environmental campaign.

Kevin Murphy, is a community activist from Killarney. He also supports the Right2Change policy principles which have grown out of the Right2Water movement. He was a key figure at local anti-water and Anti-Austerity protests in 2015, including a high profile march in February, which gathered at the Market Cross in Killarney and ended up at the INEC where the Labour Party Conference was being held.

KILDARE NORTH

Outgoing Deputies:
Bernard Durkan (FG), Emmet Stagg (Lab), Catherine Murphy (SD), Anthony Lawlor (FG)

Catherine Murphy was elected as an independent in 2011. On 26th September 2012 she was one of the founders of a new party, the Social Democrats.

The Constituency:
This remains a four seat constituency and there has been a small adjustment to the boundary with Kildare South since 2011. This involved the transfer of Kilpatrick and Windmill Cross in the Former Edenderry No. 2 Rural District and of Robertstown and Timahoe South in the Former Naas No. 1 Rural District with a total population of 4,698 to Kildare South.

	% Vote 1997	% Vote 2002	% Vote 2007	% Vote 2011	Swing 2011	Quotas 2011
Fine Gael	26.19	17.54	21.22	33.29	12.07	1.7
Labour	19.00	21.38	17.44	29.24	11.80	1.5
Fianna Fáil	34.86	43.21	39.50	14.52	–24.98	0.7
Sinn Féin	–	–	2.44	5.65	3.21	0.3
Green Party	4.44	5.99	4.90	1.77	–3.13	0.1
Others	15.49	11.88	12.32	15.53	3.21	0.8

2016 Candidates will include:

Bernard Durkan (FG), Anthony Lawlor (FG), Emmet Stagg (Lab), James Lawless (FF), Frank O'Rourke (FF), Réada Cronin (SF), Maebh Ní Fhállúin (GP), Ashling Merriman (AAA–PBP), Catherine Murphy (SD), Brendan Young (Ind)

In Brief:

The Social Democrats' Catherine Murphy will retain her seat. After that the question is whether the government parties can retain their three seats. Fine Gael had 1.7 quotas in 2011 and won two seats while Labour had 1.5 quotas and won one. On that basis the second Fine Gael seat looks more vulnerable than the Labour seat. Fianna Fáil is mounting a strong challenge to win back a seat in this constituency. It has selected two high profile councillors from different ends of the constituency and could take a seat. John Lawless is likely to be the stronger of its two candidates. Overall it looks as if Murphy is safe, and Fine Gael will win one seat. Emmett Stag should hold on with Fianna Fáil fighting it out with Fine Gael for the fourth seat, with Fianna Fáil more likely to take it.

Fine Gael:

Fine Gael took 1.66 quotas here in 2011, an improvement of half a quota on its 2007 performance.

Bernard Durkan, who is based in Maynooth, was first elected to Dáil Éireann in 1981. He lost his seat in February 1982, regained it in November of that year and has held it in each election since. He polled 5,340 first preferences in 2007 for a personal quota of 0.6. In 2011 he topped the poll, almost doubling his vote to 10,168 first preference votes (19.9%). He served as a Minister of State in the Department of Social Welfare with responsibility for Information and Consumer Services from 1994 to 1997, and was the party's Chief Whip from June 2002 to October 2004. He was a member of Kildare County Council for the Celbridge electoral area from 1976 to 1994 and was chairman of the council for the year 1986–87. He is Vice-Chairman of the Joint Oireachtas Committee on Foreign Affairs and Trade and a member of the Joint Committee on European Affairs. He was a member of Seanad Éireann from February to November 2002. Originally from Mayo, he formerly worked as an agricultural contractor

Anthony Lawlor is based in Kill and has a constituency office in Naas. He has been a Dáil deputy since 2011. He was previously a member of Kildare County Council to which he was co-opted in 1998 on the death of his mother Patsy Lawlor, who had been an independent member of the council. He stood as an independent in the 1999 local elections when he took the first seat in the Naas electoral area with 1,209 votes. He did not seek re-election in 2004. In the 2009 local elections he stood for Fine Gael and topped the poll in the Naas local electoral area with 2,113 votes, one vote ahead of his Fine Gael running mate. In the 2011 Dáil election he polled 6,882 first preferences (13.4%) to take the final seat on the elimination of the Labour Party's John McGinley. In Dáil Éireann he is a Member of the Jobs, Enterprise and Innovation Committee and he is Chair of the internal Fine Gael European and Foreign Affairs Committee.

He has a degree in Agricultural Science from University College Dublin and has an H.Dip in Education. He taught briefly in Naas and then for two years in Vanuatu with Volunteers Serving Overseas before becoming a full time farmer. He is heavily involved in local sporting organisations.

Labour Party:

In the 2011 election Labour ran two candidates, long time incumbent Emmet Stagg and Leixlip councillor John McGinley. Together they won almost 15,000 votes and 1.46 quotas. This time Stagg will contest on his own.

Emmett Stagg, who is based in Straffan, has been a member of Dáil Éireann since 1987, firstly for the five seat Kildare constituency and since 2002 for this three seat Kildare North constituency. He was a Minister of State at the Department of Environment with special responsibility for Housing and Urban Renewal from 1993 to 1994 and was Minister of State at the Department of Transport, Energy and Communication with responsibility for Nuclear Safety, Renewable Energy, Gas and the Oil Industry from 1994 to 1997. He was chairman of the Labour Party from 1987 to 1989. He has been Chief Whip since 2002. He was a member of Kildare County

Council for the Celbridge electoral area from 1978 to 1993 and was chairman of the council for the year 1981–82. He formerly worked as a medical laboratory scientist, having studied at the College of Technology, Kevin Street in Dublin.

Fianna Fáil:

Fiánna Fáil won two seats in 2007, notwithstanding the fact that both its candidates, Charlie McCreevy and Michael Fitzpatrick, were based in the Naas area. Áine Brady won the by-election when McCreevy became European Commissioner in 2009. Both she and Fitzpatrick lost their seats in 2011 when the party vote collapsed by almost two thirds. Together they polled 7,436, which was just over three quarters of a quota. The party is running two first time candidates in 2016.

James Lawless is based in Sallins and is a member of Kildare County Council for the Naas electoral area. He was an unsuccessful candidate in the 2009 local elections when his 971 votes (7.39%) failed to win him a seat. He did a lot better in 2014, topping the poll and taking the first seat with 2,123 votes (16.15%) which was 1.61 quotas, his surplus ensuring the success of the other two Fianna Fáil candidates running with him.

He has B.A. and M.Sc. degrees in Maths and Finance from Trinity College Dublin and has also trained as a Barrister at the Kings Inns. He has worked in IT and in financial services and currently works in regulation, with a particular focus on data protection, corporate governance and consumer protection. He is married, with two children, and commutes daily. He enjoys most sports, especially GAA, and is also a regular participant in 5k and 10k runs around Kildare

Frank O'Rourke lives in Celbridge and has been a member of Kildare County Council for the Celbridge electoral area since 2011. He was co-opted to the council in early 2011 following the resignation of Paul Kelly from the party and the council when he was appointed to the District Court. O'Rourke ran in the reorganised Celbridge–Leixlip electoral area in the 2014 local election and topped the poll with 1,814 votes (15.31%). He is married with a daughter and although originally from Leitrim he has lived in

Kildare for over 20 years. He has been involved in politics since he was very young, joining the Sligo IT Cumann in 1989. He became active in Kildare Fianna Fáil as soon as he moved there and acted as Director of Elections for Kildare North in the 2007 elections. He is Head of Operations at Irish Tar and Bitumen Suppliers where he has worked since 1997.

Sinn Féin:

Martin Kelly polled 2,896 votes (5.7%) in 2011 and a third of his votes transferred to independent Catherine Murphy. This time the party has a new candidate.

Réada Cronin is based in Maynooth and has been a member of Kildare County Council since 2014. In that local election she was the second placed candidate on the first count with 1,291 votes (10.5%) in the large Maynooth electoral area and she took the third of the nine seats. She is a mother of four and was a founding member of the campaign against 12 hour cutbacks to Kildare ambulance service.

Green Party:

J.J. Power, the son of Fianna Fáil TD Paddy Power and brother of Séan Power TD, was the candidate here in the 2005 by-election when he polled 1,547 votes. Shane Fitzgerald was the party's candidate in 2007 and 2011. In the former election he polled 2,215 votes (4.9%) but in the latter his support fell to 905 votes, which was just 0.1 of a quota.

Maebh Ní Fhállúin is the new candidate here. She is from Leixlip where she was involved in Irish language and music organisations, GAA and Leixlip Musical and Variety Group. With a first degree in Finance and Computing from DCU she became station manager at Raidió na Life and followed that with a career in various media. She then pursued a Masters in Public Health from the London School of Hygiene and Tropical Medicine and returned to Ireland in 2014 to work as a health policy specialist for the Royal College of Physicians of Ireland. She is an advocate for health issues such as tackling obesity and is committed to protecting the environment. She is a fluent Irish speaker and a proponent of Irish culture.

Anti-Austerity Alliance – People Before Profit:

Ashling Merriman of the Socialist Workers Party is a Nurses' Aid and has worked in Naas hospital. She writes on health issues in the Socialist Worker. She is active in the Right2Water campaign. Ashling also fundraises for the Simon Community.

Social Democrats:

Catherine Murphy was first elected to Dáil Éireann in 2005. In that by-election she polled 5,985 first preferences, which represented 23.64% of the vote, and attracted enough transfers from all the eliminated candidates to win the seat. In the 2007 Dáil election she polled 5,188 votes (11.5%), which proved insufficient to retain her seat. She recaptured the seat, however, in 2011 when she polled 6,911 first preferences (13.5%). She sat in the Technical Group in the Dáil and was its chief whip. Murphy is a former member of the Workers Party, Democratic Left and the Labour Party. She was a member of Kildare County Council from 1991 to 2005, latterly as an independent member. She was also a member of Leixlip town council from 1994 to 2004. In 2014 she launched the Social Democrats and is joint leader of the party with deputies Stephen Donnelly and Róisin Shortall. Catherine Murphy was selected as TD or parliamentarian of the Year by various media commentators at the end of 2015, primarily for her work seeking an investigation into certain transactions between the Irish Bank Resolution Corporation, the former Anglo Irish Bank, and Siteserv.

Independents:

Brendan Young is based in Celbridge and has been a member of Kildare County Council for the Celbridge–Leixlip electoral area since 2014. He ran under the Community Solidarity label in the 2014 local elections and won 738 vote (6.23%) which gave him the fifth of seven seats. He sits on the Environmental and Water SPC of Kildare County Council. In the 1980s he had to leave Ireland to find work as a fitter in the United Kingdom and he subsequently qualified as a teacher. He has been prominent in calling for parties and independents on the left to work more closely together.

Kildare South

Outgoing Deputies:

Martin Heydon (FG), Jack Wall (Lab), Seán Ó Fearghaíl (FF)

In July 2015 Jack Wall (Lab) announced that he would not be contesting this election.

The Constituency:

This is a three-seat constituency with some minor changes since 2011. This involved a population of 7,186 in the former Athy No.1 Rural District, consisting of Ballybrackan, Churchtown, Harristown, Kilberry, Kildangan and Monasterevin which has been transferred from Kildare South to the Laois constituency.

	% Vote 1997	% Vote 2002	% Vote 2007	% Vote 2011	Swing 2011	Quotas 2011
Fine Gael	26.49	17.76	17.17	33.33	16.16	1.3
Labour	20.25	18.52	20.68	27.82	7.14	1.1
Fianna Fáil	37.59	46.43	50.37	21.71	–28.66	0.9
Sinn Féin	–	–	–	6.03	6.03	0.2
Green Party	–	3.70	6.18	1.37	–4.81	0.05
Others	15.66	13.58	5.60	9.75	4.15	0.4

2016 Candidates will include:

Martin Heydon (FG), Fiona McLoughlin-Healy (FG), Mark Wall (Lab), Seán Ó Fearghaíl (FF), Fiona O'Loughlin (FF), Patricia Ryan (SF), Declan Crowe (Ind)

In Brief:

Were it not for the use now of candidate photographs and logos there would be an obvious risk of confusion here with a Fine Gael candidate and a Fianna Fáil candidate having almost identical names. Fine Gael will win a least one of the seats and Fianna Fáil will win another. The key question is whether Labour newcomer

Mark Wall can hold onto the seat long held by his father Jack Wall, who is retiring. There is a real possibility that Fine Gael will take the seat from him. Fine Gael's Fiona McLoughlin-Healy may be stronger than outgoing deputy Martin Heydon and together they are likely to be strong enough to win two seats. Unlike many of his colleagues on the Fianna Fáil front bench Seán Ó Fearghail has a strong running mate in Councillor Fiona O'Loughlin who may even threaten his seat.

Fine Gael:

This was the scene of one of Fine Gael's biggest and most surprising losses in 2002, when former leader and outgoing frontbencher Alan Dukes lost his seat. The party's vote dropped by 9% between 1997 and 2002, and by a further 0.59% in 2007, when Alan Gillis and Richard Daly were the candidates.

Martin Heydon has been a member of Dáil Éireann since 2011. He is also a farmer and is from the Athy end of the constituency. He trained at Kildalton Agricultural College. In the 2011 Dáil election he topped the poll with 12,755 votes (33.3%), one third over the quota. He was previously a member of Kildare County Council, representing the Athy electoral area, having been first elected there in June 2009, with a vote of 1,980 (17.32%), which gave him the third seat. In Dáil Éireann he is a member of the Joint Oireachtas Committee on Agriculture and chairs Fine Gael's Internal Agricultural Committee. He is also a member of the British Irish Parliamentary Assembly.

He says of himself, 'I love all sports, especially horse racing and GAA and am an active member of my local football club, St Laurence's, previously serving as Secretary for seven years.' His wife is a pharmacist and she captained the Kildare Ladies All-Ireland winning team in 2004.

Fiona McLoughlin-Healy is a member of Kildare County Council for the Kildare–Newbridge electoral area. In the 2014 local elections she topped the poll there with 1,786 first preference votes (12.45%), which gave her a quarter of a quota to spare. She originally trained as a nurse in University College Hospital Galway and then went on to volunteer in an orphanage in Romania, an experience she says fanned the flames of her interest in issues of equality and justice and its impact on children and their ability to succeed. She returned to NUI Galway to complete a degree in Law and Politics and then completed an MSc in PR, Communication and Advertising at Ulster University. Her property sales website Privateseller.ie was shortlisted for a Golden Spider award. She has been a finalist in the Network Ireland Entrepreneur Of The Year awards and for the IAA's Net Visionary awards. She is a frequent contributor to TV3's Midday show. She is married to Bernard Healy, a GP based in Newbridge. They have three children, the inspiration behind the introduction of her Food Rebels Programme in three Newbridge crèches.

Labour Party:

Mark Wall has been a member of Kildare County Council for the Athy electoral area since 2009. In that local election he topped the poll and took the first seat with 3,284 votes (28.72%). In the 2014 local elections his vote share was almost halved when he got 1,531 votes (15.01%) but he was again over the quota. Mark is the son of outgoing TD Jack Wall. Jack Wall was an unsuccessfull candidate in the 1992 five seat Kildare constituency, with Emmett Stag. He was first elected to Dáil Éireann in 1997 when this new three-seater was created. Although the Labour vote was down almost two percentage points in 2002, Jack Wall managed to hold the seat by just 187 votes and in 2007 he increased the party vote share by 2.16% to take the third seat comfortably, exceeding the combined Fine Gael vote. In 2011 he polled 10,645 first preferences (27.8%). Now 70 years old, he has decided to retire and his son Mark will replace him on the ballot paper.

Mark is currently the Cathaoirleach of Athy Muncipal District council and is a former Mayor of County Kildare. He is married, with two sons and completed his third level education at IT Carlow, where he studied business to Certificate level and then marketing to Diploma level. In 1996 he joined Smurfit Irish paper sacks where he started as a Sales intern and finished as Quality Manager in 2006. He then moved to the Oireachtas as parliamentary assistant to his father. He is the first Chairperson of the new

Kildare–Wicklow Education and Training Board and is involved in many areas of youth work. He coaches both football and hurling up to Under 14 levels.

Fianna Fáil:

From 2002 to 2011 Fianna Fáil ran the same two candidates in this constituency, Sean Ó Fearghail and Sean Power, and held two seats. The Fianna Fáil vote rose by 8.84% between 1997 and 2002. In 2007 it rose by a further 3.94% to 17,425 which was more than 50% of the total poll with the same two candidates each receiving just over a quota. In 2011, however, the party vote collapsed by more than half in this constituency and Power and Ó Ferghail got less than a quota between them and only Ó Fearghail was elected. In 2016 Power is replaced on the ballot by Fiona O'Loughlin.

Fiona O'Loughlin has been a member of the Kildare County Council for the Kildare–Newbridge electoral area since 1999. In the 2014 local elections she polled 1,786 first preferences (12.45%), topping the poll and taking the first seat. She worked previously as a primary school teacher and now says that she is combining her role as a Public Representative with ensuring that the very positive legacy of the 2003 Special Olympics World Games Host Town Programme lives on in our communities and towns. At the constituency selection convention for this election the party national executive had directed they should only select one candidate and she was defeated by Seán Ó Fearghail. She has since been added to the ticket since the party takes the view that with an original base in Rathangan and living in Newbridge she will complement Ó Fearghaíl's strongest polling areas, which are Athy and Kildare town.

Seán Ó Fearghail lives in Kildare and has his constituency office in Athy. He has been a member of Dáil Éireann since 2002. He is the Fianna Fáil Chief Whip and spokesperson on Constitutional Reform, Arts and Culture, and Defence. He unsuccessfully contested the 1987, 1989 and 1992 Dáil elections and came very close to winning a seat in 1997, when he was just 439 votes behind Labour's Jack Wall on the last count. In 2002 he polled 4,503 first preferences and took the second seat. In 2007 his 8,731 votes were

25.2% of the poll and gave him 1.10 quotas. In the 2011 Dáil election that support was reduced to 4,514 votes (11.8%). He was a member of Kildare County Council for the Kildare electoral area from 1999 to 2004. He ran unsuccessfully for Seanad Éireann on the agricultural panel in 1997 but was elected to the upper house in a by-election in June 2000 and served there until he was elected to Dáil Éireann in 2002. He was the Fianna Fáil party whip and spokesperson on Foreign Affairs and Trade from April 2011 to July 2012. He comes from a farming background and previously worked for Dublin Corporation.

Sinn Féin:

Patricia (Tricia) Ryan is based in Monasterevin. The recent redrawing of the constituency has placed her on its boundary. She was selected at a convention of the local party organization in February 2015. Jason Turner from Newbridge was the party candidate in 2011 and polled 2,308 first preferences which was one fifth of a quota.

Greens:

Vivian Cummins, based in Athy, was the party's candidate in 2011. He polled just 523 (1.4%) votes. Although the party has said that it intends to run a candidate here in 2016 no one had been selected at the time of writing.

Independents:

Local councillor Willie Crowley (Ind) was due to run for the Independent Alliance. He was sadly killed in a hit and run road incident in December 2015.

Declan Crowe is a construction worker. He is a founder of the Athy Against Water Charges and Kildare Action For Change. He was an independent candidate in the Kildare–Newbridge electoral area in the 2014 local elections for Kildare County Councils, polling 373 first preferences (2.59%). The father of two ran a low budget campaign for the County Council, making his own posters on the kitchen table. Anti-Water Charges protester Lorraine Hayden had originally indicated she might contest the Dáil election for the National Citizens Movement but is now supporting his campaign.

Laois

Outgoing Deputies for Laois–Offaly:

Charles Flanagan (FG), Marcella Corcoran Kennedy (FG), Barry Cowen (FF), Brian Stanley (SF), Seán Fleming (FF)

Barry Cowen and Marcella Corcoran Kennedy will contest in the Offaly constituency in the 2016 election.

The Constituency:

This new three-seat constituency consists of all of the administrative county area of Laois combined with six electoral divisions formerly in the Kildare South constituency. These areas are from the former Athy No. 1 Rural District. Ballybrackan, Churchtown, Harristown, Kilberry, Kildangan and Monasterevin electoral divisions had a combined population of 7,186 at the time of the last census.

Laois–Offaly

	% Vote 1997	% Vote 2002	% Vote 2007	% Vote 2011	Swing 2011	Quotas 2011
Fine Gael	28.38	23.02	27.36	33.75	6.39	2.0
Labour	11.61	2.53	2.38	7.82	5.44	0.5
Fianna Fáil	49.85	51.30	56.38	26.72	–29.66	1.6
Sinn Féin	–	4.11	5.11	10.83	5.72	0.6
Green Party	–	0.82	1.14	0.41	–0.73	0.02
Others	10.17	18.21	7.63	20.40	12.77	1.2

2016 Candidates will include:

Thomasina Connell (FG), Charlie Flanagan FG, John Whelan (Lab), Sean Fleming (FF), Brian Stanley (SF), Sinead Moore (GP)

In Brief:

Notwithstanding the fact that Laois has now broken off from Offaly and the constituency includes a little bit of South Kildare, this is the constituency most likely to see no change in either party representation or personnel. Fine Gael, Fianna Fáil and Sinn Féin will each win a seat. Charlie Flanagan (FG) is unlikely to be deposed by his running mate, and both Sinn Féin and Fianna Fáil are running their sitting deputies as the only candidate. Labour's challenge for a seat will inevitably be weaker this time than in 2011.

Fine Gael:

Charles Flanagan lives and has a constituency office in Portlaoise. He has been Minister for Foreign Affairs and Trade since July 2014. He was first elected to Dáil Éireann for the Laois–Offaly constituency in 1987 and held his seat until 2002. He then regained it in 2007 and was comfortably re-elected in 2011. In that year he topped the poll with 10,427 first preferences (14.1%). and took the first seat. He was a member of Laois County Council from 1984 to 2004, originally in the Tinnahinch electoral area and then, from 1999, in the Portlaoise electoral area. He did not contest the 2004 local election. A practising solicitor for many years, as a backbencher and opposition front bencher he has published draft bills and amendments in a range of legislative areas. He was leader of the Fine Gael delegation to the Constitutional Convention in 2013–14. He was chairperson of the Fine Gael parliamentary party from June 2011 to May 2014. He was born and raised in Mountmellick. His father, Oliver J. Flanagan, was a member of Dáil Éireann from 1943 to 1987.

Following the resignation on 7 May 2014 of Alan Shatter as Minister for Justice and Minister for Defence, Flanagan was appointed Minister for Children and Youth Affairs. Then, when Frances Fitzgerald was made Minister for Justice and Equality in July 2014, Flanagan was appointed Minister for Foreign Affairs and Trade, in succession to Eamon Gilmore.

Thomasina Connell is a solicitor from Ballybrittas. In November 2015 she was added to the ticket in Laois by the Fine Gael National Executive. She has been actively involved in Fine Gael in the constituency for several years and says she has a particular understanding of its needs both from her experience as a solicitor and as someone who grew up in a farming community.

Connell has served on the Criminal Law Committee for the Dublin Solicitors Bar Association and was Editor of the Criminal Law sector of the Parchment Magazine. She previously worked for the Northern Ireland Bureau in Washington D.C. She has also been active in the Dunamase and Cill Dara Riding Clubs, and Foróige, and is a supporter of Courtwood GAA Club.

Labour Party:

The party last held a seat here in 1992, when Pat Gallagher was elected to Dáil Éireann on the back of the 'Spring Tide' and, although he had developed a strong local base, he lost out for the fifth seat in 1997. He has since left politics and gone on to be County Manager or County Chief Executive in several counties. John Whelan, who was the party candidate in 2011, is again the candidate for this election.

John Whelan is based near Portlaoise and has been a member of Seanad Éireann on the Labour panel since 2011. He has been a journalist for more than 30 years and is a former Chairman of the Midlands Branch of the National Union of Journalists and a former member of the NUJ National Council. He previously worked as Editor of the Leinster Express in Portlaoise, the Offaly Express in Tullamore, the Leinster Leader in Naas and as Group Managing Editor of the now defunct Voice group of newspapers. His selection in 2011 was controversial and led to several high profile members in the area resigning from the party and joining the Socialist Party or Sinn Féin. In the election, however, he got 5,802 first preferences (7.8%) and was in contention until the final count when he lost out to Fianna Fáil's Sean Fleming, although Fleming had 1,825 votes to spare.

Whelan is a founder of the Portlaoise Jazz Festival, the Mountmellick Mardi Gras and the Laois Arts Festival, as well as being involved with local sporting organisations. Two weeks before the 2011 election he published his first novel The Buddha of Ballyhuppahaun under the pseudonym of Johnny Renko.

Fianna Fáil:

The party had originally intended to run two candidates in this constituency. The sitting deputy Seán Fleming and Catherine

Fitzgerald, a Fianna Fáil councillor in the Portlaoise electoral area were selected at the party convention in July 2015. However Fitzgerald later withdrew from the ticket and the party has decided not to replace her.

Sean Fleming is a native of the Swan and lives in Castletown. He has been a member of Dáil Éireann since 1997. In that election he was the second candidate along with the then outgoing deputy John Maloney. Fleming, on his first attempt, polled 5,481 (9.4%) and the party won two seats in Laois with Brian Cowen also holding his seat in the Offaly part of the constituency. In 2002 Fleming increased his personal vote and vote share to 7,091 (11.2%) but took only the fifth and final seat while in 2007 he took the third Laois–Offaly seat with 8,064 (11.3%). In 2011 he retained his seat in Dáil Éireann with a greatly reduced 6,024 first preference votes (8.1%). He was a member of Laois County Council for the Borris-in-Ossory area from 1999 until 2003. He formerly worked as an accountant and was employed as finance director for Fianna Fáil at party headquarters until his election to Dáil Éireann in 2007. He was chairman of the Oireachtas Committee on Finance and the Public Service from 2002 to 2007 and on the Committee on Environment and Local Government from 2007 to 2011. He has been the party's spokesperson on Public Expenditure and Reform since 2011.

Sinn Féin:

Brian Stanley is based in Port Laois and has been a member of Dáil Éireann since 2011. He is the party's spokesperson on the Environment. In the 2011 Dáil election he recorded 8,032 first preferences (10.83%) in Laois–Offaly. He was also the party's candidate in that five seat constituency for the 2002 Dáil election when he won 2,600 first preferences which was just over 4% of the vote. He increased this to 3,656 (5.1%) in 2007. Stanley was a member of Laois County Council for the Portlaoise local electoral area from 2004 to 2011. He is a former Mayor of Portlaoise and a member of Portlaoise town council from 1999 to 2011. He has served on Sinn Féin's Ard Comhairle.

Green Party:
Sinead Moore comes from a small farm in Coolbanagher where her father taught her and her siblings that they were custodians of the land. With a degree in theology from All Hallows and a teaching diploma from Trinity College Dublin she lives in Mulhuddart and teaches in Rush, County Dublin. As a teacher she worked with Trócaire in Kenya as a visiting teacher in 2012. With her students she has worked with the Young Social Innovators programme to set up a Foróige Youth Club in their school, as well as a bereavement support group and a business partnership between the school and a slum in Nairobi. She is the mother of two teenage children and a qualified football coach and computer teacher. Moore set up support for a Congolese charity with Intel, and has joined two Toastmasters clubs to improve her communication and leadership skills.

Limerick City

Outgoing Deputies:
Michael Noonan (FG), Kieran O'Donnell (FG), Willie O'Dea (FF), Jan O'Sullivan (Lab)

The Constituency:
This four-seater, once known as Limerick East, has undergone some boundary changes in the redraw of constituencies since 2011. 10 of 19 electoral divisions that had been transferred out of the constituency into Kerry North in 2009 have been returned, thereby removing the breach of the county boundary. The territory re-drawn back into the constituency had a population at the last census of 11,197.

2016 Candidates will include:
Michael Noonan (FG), Kieran O'Donnell (FG), Jan O'Sullivan (Lab), Willie O'Dea (FF), Maurice Quinlivan (SF), James Gaffney (GP), Cian Prendiville (AAA–PBP), Sarah Jane Hennelly (SD)

	% Vote 1997	% Vote 2002	% Vote 2007	% Vote 2011	Swing 2011	Quotas 2011
Fine Gael	26.51	27.84	25.52	43.29	17.77	2.2
Labour	15.94	9.26	10.33	20.29	9.96	1.0
Fianna Fáil	39.72	39.95	48.69	21.44	–27.25	1.1
Sinn Féin	–	–	4.21	8.59	4.38	0.4
Green Party	1.61	1.83	2.62	1.13	–1.49	0.06
Others	16.11	21.12	8.62	5.25	–3.37	0.3

In Brief:

Michael Noonan and Kieran O'Donnell have held two seats for Fine Gael here since 2007. It had well over two quotas in 2011 and will retain the two seats. Labour's Jan O'Sullivan had a bare quota in 2011 and will struggle to hold her seat. The biggest threat to her is from Sinn Féin, who did worse than expected in 2011 but had a very good local election here in 2014. Maurice Quinlivan may unseat Jan O'Sullivan this time. Fianna Fáil once had three of the five seats in the former Limerick East constituency but at the time of going to print are running only one candidate. Willie O'Dea will be comfortably re-elected and it seems that his party has given up on even building for a second seat.

Fine Gael:

Limerick East was a key target for Fine Gael in the 2007 election and, despite the drop in its vote, it managed to take the two seats it sought. Fine Gael has traditionally played second fiddle to Fianna Fáil in this area and did not exceed it in vote share until the Fianna Fáil collapse of 2011, when Fine Gael's share was 43.3%, more than two quotas, although it still took until the fifth count for Michael Noonan's surplus to bring O'Donnell home. This was notwithstanding the fact that then Limerick City mayor Kevin Kiely, who ran as an independent having failed to get the party's nomination, also polled 2.6% of the poll.

Michael Noonan has been Minister for Finance since March 2011. He was first elected to Dáil Éireann in 1981 and has held the seat on each occasion since. He was leader of the party from February 2001 until he resigned the leadership on the evening of the election count in June 2002. He was Minister for Justice from 1982 to 1986, Minister for Industry and Commerce from 1986 to 1987, Minister for Health from 1994 to 1997 and Minister for Energy from January to March 1997. He was a member of Limerick County Council from 1974 to 1981 and from 1991 to 1994. Noonan achieved the quota on the first count in 1997 and 2002, but failed to do so in 2007. In fact, his vote-tally fell from 10,092 in 1997 to 9,451 to 2002 and 7,507 in 2007. In 2011, however, almost one in three Limerick city voters voted for him and he polled 13,291 first preferences (30.8%). Noonan served as chairman of the Dáil Public Accounts Committee from 2004 to 2007. He was brought back onto the Fine Gael front bench in July 2010 as Finance spokesman after Richard Bruton's failed leadership heave against Enda Kenny. He is now 72 years of age and is a former secondary school teacher.

Kieran O'Donnell is based in Monaleen and has been a member of Dáil Éireann since 2007. He took the fifth seat on that occasion with 5,094 first preferences, a 10.32% share. In 2011 his 5,405 votes (12.5%) gave him the second seat, thanks to Noonan's surplus. O'Donnell was a member of Limerick County Council for the Castleconnell electoral area, where in the 2004 local elections he polled 1,163 first preferences. He took the fourth of the seven seats in that election. He contested the 2002 Seanad election for the party unsuccessfully on the Agricultural Panel. In October 2007, O'Donnell was appointed party deputy spokesperson on Finance with special responsibility for Freedom of Information, Procurement Reform and the Office of Public Works. He assumed the Finance portfolio briefly at the time of Richard Bruton's challenge to Enda Kenny's leadership in late June 2010, although he also later publicly supported that challenge. A qualified chartered account who had his own practice for many years, O'Donnell is the current Vice-Chairperson of the Public Accounts Committee and a member of the Oireachtas Finance Committee. He has a particular interest in disability issues. His uncle, Tom O'Donnell, was a member of Dáil Éireann for this constituency from 1961 to 1987, and also a government Minister and a member of the European Parliament.

Labour Party:

Jan O'Sullivan is based in Corbally and has been a member of Dáil Éireann since 1998. She has been Minister for Education since July 2014. In 1998 she won the by-election caused by the death of the popular Democratic Socialist turned Labour TD Jim Kemmy. O'Sullivan had previously run unsuccessfully as the Labour party's second candidate in the 1992 and 1997 Dáil elections and was also a former Democratic Socialist Party member before the two parties merged. In 2002 she polled 4,629 votes and she won re-election again in 2007 with an increased first preference total of 5,098. She was narrowly defeated by Joan Burton in the contest for the Labour party's deputy leadership in 2007. In 2011 her 6,353 first preferences (14.7%) gave her the fourth and final seat by a very substantial margin. In 2011 Labour ran a two candidate strategy for the first time since 1997. Limerick City Councillor Joe Leddin joined O'Sullivan on the ticket, giving Labour a combined 20.3% of the first preferences. She is the party's sole candidate on this occasion.

In Dáil Éireann O'Sullivan was Labour spokesperson on Equality and Law Reform from 1997 to 2002 and was appointed the party's spokesperson on Education and Science in 2002. In the present Dáil she has been successively Minister of State for Trade and Development, Minister of State for Housing and Planning and, since July 2014, Minister for Education and Skills. She was a member of Seanad Éireann from 1993 to 1997 and was leader of the Labour group in the upper house for that term. She was a member of Limerick City Council from 1985 to 2001. She formerly worked as a pre-school teacher, and when her children were small combined running a play-group in her house with political work in the evenings.

Fianna Fáil:

Fianna Fáil was the largest party in the old Limerick East constituency by vote-share in all but one of the elections from 1948 to 2011, taking two seats in the majority of elections. Willie O'Dea has held a seat here for 24 years and indeed took the first seat on all occasions from 1989 until 2011.

Willie O'Dea is based in Kilteely and has been a member of Dáil Éireann since February 1982. He is currently the party spokeperson on Social Protection. This will be his twelfth time to compete for the Dáil. He was also an unsuccessful candidate in the 1981 Dáil election. He topped the poll dramatically in 2002, having nearly five thousand votes above the quota and polling 3,723 first preferences more than the then Fine Gael leader Michael Noonan. In 2007 O'Dea again topped the poll, this time with a hugely increased vote of 19,082, a share of 38.65%. However, in 2011 his vote tumbled to 6,956 (16.1%), and he took the third of the four seats.

Formerly an accountant, barrister and college lecturer, O'Dea was a Minister of State at the Department of Justice from 1992 to 1993 and in the Departments of Justice and Health from 1993 to 1994. He was appointed Minister for Defence in September 2004, having previously been a Minister of State at the Department of Education, Science and Technology from 1997 to 2002 and at the Department of Justice, Equality and Law Reform 2002 to 2005. In February 2010 he resigned after making what he admitted were 'false and defamatory' accusations about the brother of Sinn Féin's Maurice Quinlivan. He writes regularly for the Sunday Independent and occasionally for other newspapers. In December 2015 he accused TV presenter Vincent Browne of the 'shameless bullying' of Limerick City Green Party candidate James Gaffney during the recording of the local episode of The People's Debate.

Sinn Féin:

Maurice Quinlivan is originally from Ballynanty Beg and has lived in the Thomondgate area of Limerick City since 2009. As the unsuccessful Sinn Féin candidate he polled 2,081 first preferences (4.2%) in 2007 and 3,711 (8.6%) in 2011. In the 2004 local elections Quinlivan was an unsuccessful candidate for Limerick city council in the Limerick No.1 Ward where he polled 568 first preferences when the quota was 1,092. He was first elected to Limerick City Council in 2009, polling 888 first preferences. In the 2014 local elections he improved on that performance considerably. He topped the poll in the Limerick City North electoral area for the new Limerick City and County Council polling 2,456 votes (24.5%) which was almost twice the vote of the candidate in second place. He has served as secretary of the party's Munster executive and was a member of the Sinn Féin Ard Comhairle. He was formerly the manager of a travel agency

Green Party:

The Green Party vote in the old Limerick East constituency was 2.62% in the 2007 election when Patricia (Trish) Forde Brennan, former chair of the National Parents Council was its candidate. In Limerick City in 2011 that fell back to 490 votes (1.1%) with Sheila Cahill as its candidate. It again has a new candidate on this occasion.

James Gaffney is based on North Circular Road in Limerick City. He is the director of an English language teaching company in Limerick, who also teaches at the English Language School in Dublin City University. He has a degree in Law and European Studies from University of Limerick. Campaigning for improved healthcare, public transport provision and proper, sustainable planning he has opposed the proposals to take large volumes of water from the Shannon at Parteen Weir and transfer it to the East Coast.

Anti-Austerity Alliance – People Before Profit:

Cian Prendiville has been a member of Limerick City and County Council for the Limerick City North electoral area since 2014. He polled 964 votes (9.6%) in that election and took the third of the six seats. He polled 721 votes (1.7%) when he stood as the United Left Alliance candidate in the 2011 Dáil election. He was active in politics in the University of Limerick in 2007, initially campaigning primarily for free fees but later for other local, national and international causes. He was a founding member of the local We Won't Pay anti-water charge campaign. During the 2011 election he was asked about how he combined politics and a 'twenty-something lifestyle'. He said that he didn't have the lifestyle.

Social Democrats:

Sarah Jane Hennelly is originally from Castlebar, County Mayo, and now lives in Castletroy. She was an unsuccessful independent candidate in the Limerick City East electoral area in the 2014 local elections when she polled 467 votes (3.9%) and was the last candidate eliminated. She has a Masters Degree in European Politics and Law from the University of Limerick where she is a population health researcher in the medical school, with a specific interest in understanding how environment and lifestyles impact physical and mental health and well-being. Standing as an independent candidate for Limerick City East in 2014 she polled 467 votes (3.9%). In 2015 she was a committee member for the inaugural year of the Limerick Spring Festival of Politics and Ideas and the Pay It Forward Festival of Kindness, two initiatives seeking to promote community and self-empowerment.

Limerick County

Outgoing Deputies:
Dan Neville (FG), Patrick O'Donovan (FG), Niall Collins (FF)

The Constituency:
This three-seater, formerly known as Limerick, and before that as Limerick West, now compromises that part of Limerick County not in the Limerick City constituency. In the redrawing of constituencies since 2011 the Kerry/Limerick county boundary has been reinstated and 18 electoral divisions, with a population of 13,352 have been returned to this constituency.

	% Vote 1997	% Vote 2002	% Vote 2007	% Vote 2011	Swing 2011	Quotas 2011
Fine Gael	37.19	41.65	39.95	48.68	8.73	1.9
Labour	4.22	–	5.63	17.56	11.93	0.7
Fianna Fáil	32.44	53.43	47.23	20.78	–26.45	0.8
Green Party	–	2.66	2.40	0.79	–1.61	0.03
Others	26.14	2.26	4.79	12.19	7.4	0.5

2016 Candidates will include:

Tom Neville (FG), Patrick O'Donovan (FG), Niall Collins (FF), Seamus Browne (SF), James Heffernan (SD), Mark Keogh (IDP), Emmett O'Brien (Ind), Richard O'Donoghue (Ind)

In Brief:

Dan Neville's retirement is the news story here. Fine Gael's other outgoing deputy, Patrick O'Donovan, is safe and Dan's son Tom Neville seems likely to hold the second seat for Fine Gael. Here too Fianna Fáil is running just one candidate and Niall Collins will also hold his seat. The independent Councillor Emmett O'Brien, who is based in the Adare–Rathkeale area, is also worth watching closely.

Fine Gael:

Tom Neville was co-opted to Limerick County Council for the Rathkeale area, replacing his father, when the dual mandate ban was introduced in 2003. In the 2004 local elections Tom topped the poll there with 2,599 votes (24.71%), and in 2014 his vote was 1,873 (15.19%). His father Dan Neville is retiring as a Dáil deputy on this occasion. Dan Neville was an unsuccessful candidate in the 1987 and 1992 Dáil elections and was first elected to Dáil Éireann in 1997, holding the seat very narrowly in 2002. He improved his total on his re-election in 2007 and with running mates Patrick O'Donovan and William O'Donnell managed to amass 48.7% of the first preference votes in 2011, taking the first seat, with O'Donovan taking the second. The Nevilles are based in Kiltannon.

Tom did a postgraduate course in business at the University of Limerick and then travelled before taking a job as an IT accounts manager in the Channel Islands and then coming back to Limerick, where he works in a recruitment consultancy. He plays piano and guitar and has a dance music show on FM102. He plays soccer with Shauntrade, surfs in Lahinch, Doonaha and Spanish Point, plays Gaelic football with Cappagh and 'loves a good hurling match.'

Patrick O'Donovan is a native of Newcastle West in Co. Limerick where he has a constituency office. In 2011 he was elected to the Dáil at his first attempt, polling 8,597 (19.1%). He had been a member of Limerick County Council for the Newcastle West electoral area since 2003 when he was co-opted to replace Michael Finucane TD. He was elected to the council in the 2004 local elections with 1,485 first preferences (13.26%) and in 2009 with 8,597 (19.09%). In 2007 he failed in a bid to be elected to the Seanad for the Labour panel. In Dáil Éireann he is a member of the Joint Committee on Transport & Communications. He is also the Chairperson of the Fine Gael internal committee on Public Expenditure and Reform. In December 2014 he was appointed to the Public Accounts Committee. In January 2014 he called for 'tougher controls on the use of open source internet browsers and payment systems' which he said allowed users to remain anonymous in the illegal trade of drugs, weapons and pornography. Before becoming a TD, he qualified and worked as an industrial chemist and later became a primary school teacher.

Labour Party:

The party's candidate in 2007 and 2011 was James Heffernan, who failed to be elected on both occasions, but was elected to the Seanad on the Agricultural Panel in 2011. In December 2012 Heffernan voted against the government on the Social Welfare Bill and lost the party whip. He is contesting for the Social Democrats in 2016. At the time of going to print the Labour Party had not announced anyone to replace him,

Fianna Fáil:

Fianna Fáil polled above 50% at every election from 1948 to 1992, while Fine Gael came in around the 30 or 40% mark. This gave the parties a 2:1 breakdown in seats that remained steady until Progressive Democrat John McCoy took one of Fianna Fáil's seats in 1987. Fianna Fáil took that seat back in 1989 and held it in the much more competitive 1992 general election. Party in-fighting cost Fianna Fáil the seat again in 1997, although between 1997 and 2002 it managed to re-integrate the dissident elements and regain the seat, with an increase in vote share of over 20%. 2007 saw a six-point drop in the Fianna Fáil vote, leaving it below 50% for only the third time in the constituency's history, but it managed to hold its two seats. One Fianna Fáil seat in the old Limerick West has been occupied by a member of the Collins family for the vast majority of the constituency's history and is now filled by Niall Collins. The other seat was occupied by Newcastle-based John Cregan, who stepped down in 2011 after a row with the party leadership. With only Collins holding his seat in 2011 he runs alone in 2016.

Niall Collins is based in Patrickswell and has been a member of Dáil Éireann since 2007. He is the party spokesperson on Justice and Equality. He topped the poll in that election with 10,396 first preferences (25.71%), a couple of hundred votes above the quota. In 2011 he polled 9,361 (20.8%) to take the third and final seat. In the current Dáil he was Fianna Fáil's spokesperson on Environment, Community and Local Government from April 2011 to July 2012.

Before his election to Dáil Éireann Niall Collins had been a member of Limerick County Council for the Bruff electoral area since 2004. He worked formerly as an accountant with Ernst & Young and as a lecturer at Limerick Institute of Technology. He previously served as deputy CEO of the Shannon Regional Fisheries Board. His uncle, Gerry Collins, was a minister in various departments, a member of Dáil Éireann from 1967 to 1997, and a member of the European Parliament from 1994 to 2004. Gerry Collins represented Limerick West from November 1967's by-election until 1997. Another of his uncles, Michael Collins, was a Dáil deputy from 1997 to 2002. Niall's grandfather, James J. Collins, was a member of Dáil Éireann from 1948 to 1967.

Sinn Féin:

Seamus Browne is a lawyer based in Abbeyfeale. He has been a member of Limerick City and County Council for the Newcastle West electoral area since 2014. In that year's local elections he polled 1,271 first preferences (9.7%) to take the fifth of six seats there. Sinn Féin is an emerging force in this constituency. In the 2014 local elections it won a seat in each of the six city and county electoral areas here. Browne is Sinn Féin's first Dáil candidate in County Limerick since 1992, when Coireall MacCurtain polled just 346 first preferences.

Green Party:

The party ran candidates here in 2002 and in 2007. In 2002 Marcus Briody polled 948 first preferences. James Nix contested in 2007 and polled 969. He was also unsuccessful in the Limerick North local electoral area in the 2009 local elections for the Green Party. The party have run candidates in Castleconnell, Newcastle and Rathkeale in recent local elections but have failed to make an impact. The candidate for the 2011 Dáil election was Stephen Wall who polled 354 votes (0.8%). At the time of going to print the party had not announced a candidate for this constituency.

Social Democrats:

James Heffernan is a native of Kilfinane. He has been a member of Seanad Éireann since 2011. He was the Labour party candidate in this constituency in the 2007 and 2011 Dáil elections. He polled 2,277 first preferences in 2007 and narrowly missed a seat in 2011 with 7,910 first preferences (17.6%). He was elected to Seanad Éireann in 2011 on the Agricultural panel. He lost the Labour Party whip in the Seanad in December 2012 after voting against the government on the Social Welfare Bill. In February 2015 he announced that he himself would form a new party but in September 2015 announced he would run in this election for the Social Democrats. There was a considerable amount of media interest in early 2015 when he was asked to leave the office he shared with Labour's John Gilroy on the Labour floor of Leinster house.

Heffernan was the youngest Labour candidate to run in the 2007 general election and was elected to Limerick County Council for the Kilmallock electoral area on the Labour ticket in 2009, topping the poll with 2,282 first preferences, almost two hundred over the quota. He is a politics graduate of the University of Limerick. His father, Pat Heffernan, who ran as an independent at the 2004 local elections for the Kilmallock local electoral area and won 917 first preference votes, was vice-Chairman of the Limerick County GAA Board.

The Irish Democratic Party:

Mark Keogh is based in Pallaskenry and studied robotics and fluid power systems at Limerick Institute Of Technology. An advocate of participatory democracy he has, like other members of the Irish Democratic Party been active in opposing home repossessions.

Independents:

Emmet O'Brien is based in Pallaskenry and has been an independent member of Limerick County council since 2014. He was a former member of the Fianna Fáil Ard Comhairle and resigned from the party having being unsuccessful in his attempt to be selected as a candidate for the 2014 local elections. There were furious scenes at a meeting of Fianna Fáil's cumann in December 2013 when members found that party head office had pre-selected three candidates for the 2014 local elections and they could only vote for the last place. Supporters of O'Brien formed a human chain to make sure that the ballots were counted in the room but their candidate lost. He later launched his independent local election campaign by marching through the streets of Limerick while supporters carried sticks topped with sods of burning turf, to symbolize that 'there is still life and hope in the community'. He topped the poll in the Adare–Rathkeale local electoral area with 2,270 votes (18.4%) of the first preferences almost 400 ahead of his nearest rival, Fine Gael's Tom Neville.

Launching his campaign for the 2016 Dáil election he said, 'Limerick needs a progressive, business-orientated and hardworking, independent TD who will represent the people of Limerick free from a party whip' adding that 'with the right policies and a strong voice', Limerick and the Mid West could become an economic counter-weight to Dublin.

Richard O'Donoghue is a Limerick City and County Councillor, He decided to run as an independent in Limerick County following the decision of Fianna Fáil to run only one candidate, outgoing TD Niall Collins, in Limerick County. The lifelong Fianna Fáil supporter – he became chairperson of the Dromin Cumann at the age of 18 – feels that the representations of the local grassroots that a second Limerick County candidate should be added have been ignored at national level. Councillor O'Donoghue is Cathaoirleach of the Adare Rathkeale municipal district, having been elected with 912 votes (7.4%) in the 2014 local election, which gave him the fifth of the six seats in this electoral area.

Married, with four children, he is a self employed contractor from Ballinagarry. His vintage Ferguson tractor can be seen at summer shows around the county and he has campaigned for vintage tractors to be exempted from the rigorous safety testing applied to more modern vehicles. He has been involved in the development of various heritage-based attractions around the county.

Longford–Westmeath

Outgoing Deputies:

Willie Penrose (Lab), James Bannon (FG), Gabrielle McFadden (FG), Robert Troy (FF)

Nicky McFadden (FG) was elected in 2011 but died in March 2014. Her sister Gabrielle McFadden (FG) won the seat in the resultant by-election in May 2014.

The Constituency:

This four seat constituency is composed of all of the county of Longford, together with most of the county of Westmeath, except for that more north eastern part, south and east of Castlepollard, which has been incorporated into the Meath West constituency. The boundaries of this constituency are unchanged since the 2007 election.

	% Vote 1997	% Vote 2002	% Vote 2007	% Vote 2011	Swing 2011	Quotas 2011
Fine Gael	25.88	27.20	30.95	38.05	7.10	1.9
Labour	24.51	26.05	17.65	26.71	9.06	1.3
Fianna Fáil	45.67	41.65	41.15	19.46	–21.69	1.0
Sinn Féin	–	3.44	3.89	7.54	3.65	0.4
Green Party	–	–	1.75	0.54	–1.21	-.03
Others	3.94	1.66	4.60	7.70	3.10	0.4

2016 Candidates will include:
James Bannon (FG), Peter Burke (FG), Gabrielle McFadden (FG), Willie Penrose (Lab), Connie Gerety-Quinn (FF), Robert Troy (FF), Paul Hogan (SF), Dom Parker (AAA–PBP), Frank Kilbride (Ind), Kevin 'Boxer' Moran (Ind), James Morgan (Ind), Barbara Smyth (Ind)

In Brief:
This is one of the most competitive constituencies in the country. Willie Penrose has been Labour's strongest candidate in the country in recent elections and he looks set to retain his seat, notwithstanding the fall in the party's vote nationally. Apart from him, however, none of the other deputies are secure. Fine Gael will win at least one seat but will have a fight on its hands to hold the second. There are a number of strong independents contesting in this constituency and three of them have joined the Independent Alliance. Kevin 'Boxer' Moran is a long-standing councillor in Athlone, originally from the Fianna Fáil gene pool. In the absence of a Fianna Fáil candidate from the Athlone end of Westmeath, Moran will do even better than he did in the 2014 by-election. James Morgan, who is running for the Independent Alliance in the Longford end of the constituency, performed surprisingly well in the 2014 by-election. If there is a good transfer between Morgan and Moran across the county boundary, one of them, probably Moran, will win a seat. The other candidate to watch is Sinn Féin's Paul Hogan, a councillor in Athlone who did very well both in 2011 and in the 2014 by-election. Fine Gael's Westmeath deputy Gabrielle McFadden, also based in Athlone, could get squeezed in such a scenario. If Morgan is the stronger of the independents then James Bannon could lose out. Fianna Fáil won a bare quota here in 2011 and there has been uproar within the party over its candidate strategy, especially in Longford. This means that Fianna Fáil's sitting deputy Robert Troy is far from safe and it could actually be Fianna Fáil that loses out to the Independents or Sinn Féin. So varied are the permutations that even an initial call would be foolhardy in this constituency.

Fine Gael:

In 2007 the team of James Bannon, Peter Burke and Nicky McFadden attracted over 30% of the vote for Fine Gael, although only James Bannon succeeded in capturing a seat. In 2011 the same team took 38.1% and both Bannon and Nicky McFadden took seats. The party is again running three candidates this time, two in Westmeath and one in Longford.

James Bannon is a native of Legan, in county Longford, where he worked as a farmer and auctioneer before entering politics. He was elected to Longford County Council for the Ballymahon electoral area in 1985, 1991 and 1999, taking the first seat on each occasion and was the youngest ever Chair of Longford County Council. In 2002 he was elected to Seanad Éireann on the Industrial and Commercial Panel. He was first elected to the Dáil in 2007, with a first preference vote of 7,652 (13.93%) and in 2011 he polled 7,652 first preferences. He was made Fine Gael's Deputy Spokesperson on the Environment with Special Responsibility for Local and Community Development in 2010. Bannon is often colourful in his public comments. In September 2015 when there were media suggestion that homeless people in Dublin might be given housing in county like Longford, Bannon suggested that 'instead of addressing the deprivation in my area, unnamed officials in the Department of the Environment are reported to be considering visiting further deprivation on my area by bringing possibly thousands more deprived people into the area.' His suggestion that this would lead to increased crime caused considerable anger.

Peter Burke is a Mullingar-based accountant and has been a member of Westmeath County Council since 2009. This is his third Dáil election. In 2007 he polled 3,988 votes and was eliminated on the fourth count. In the 2011 his 6,629 votes (11.5%) took him through to the final count without winning a seat. He was a campaign worker for former Longford–Westmeath Fine Gael TD Paul McGrath. Having unsuccessfully contested the 2004 local elections he was elected to Westmeath County Council for Mullingar East local electoral area in 2009, taking 13.31% of the poll with 866 votes, which gave him the third seat. He stood unsuccessfully for Seanad Éireann on the Industrial and Commercial Panel. In 2014 he was elected to Westmeath County Council for the Mullingar–Coole electoral area with 1,008 first preference votes (8.72%).

Burke is a graduate of NUI Galway from which he holds a Bachelor of Commerce degree and he is also qualified as a chartered accountant. A native of Clonmore, he grew up on a farm and is married with one child. He is an avid cyclist.

Gabrielle McFadden is a native of Athlone in county Westmeath and was elected to Dáil Éireann in the by-election caused by her sister Nicky McFadden's death in 2014. She won with 12,365 first preferences, which was just over 25% of the first preference vote. Gabrielle had been a member of Westmeath County Council for the Athlone area since 2009 with 892 votes (8.47%) in 2009 and she was Mayor of Athlone 2013/2014. In Dáil Éireann she is a member of the Public Accounts Committee and the Select Committee on Justice, Defence and Equality. Before becoming a full time county councillor she worked as a bank official and managed a family business. She is married, with two teenage children.

Fianna Fáil:

Connie Gerety-Quinn lives at Moydow in County Longford. She was selected unopposed as the only female candidate contesting the party convention for the Longford candidate held in October 2015. Twenty-four hours before the convention the Fianna Fáil national executive had issued a directive that only a female candidate could be selected, meaning that Cllrs Seamus Butler and Pat O'Rourke, who had been nominated in advance, could not contest. Some activists have threatened to resign from the party over the imposition of her candidature and some Longford party members went so far as to threaten a picket of party headquarters. In November 2015 the party Longford organisation passed a motion of no confidence in her candidacy.

Gerety-Quinn has been the Manager of County Longford Citizens Information Service for the last 16 years. Her husband is a dry stock farmer and off farm haulier and they have 3 young children.

Robert Troy is from Balynacargy near Mullingar. He was Fianna Fáil's only newly elected TD in 2011. He replaced the party's veteran Athlone-based deputy Mary O Rourke. Troy is currently the party spokesperson on Children and Youth Affairs. He was previously a member of Westmeath County Council representing the Mullingar West area. He was first elected to the council in 2004 on the 9th count, receiving 8.62% of the first preference votes, and was re-elected in 2009 with 21.36% of the first preferences. After leaving school, Troy spent 5 years working in Dublin before returning to the county to work as the Ballynacargy postmaster. His family have a long tradition of community activity and volunteer work – his parents were involved in local GAA and community games, while his uncle is a former Chairman of a Westmeath County Board.

Labour Party:

This is a very good constituency for the Labour Party, primarily because of the phenomenal electoral appeal of its sitting deputy, Willie Penrose. He polled 20% in his first election in 1992, increased that to 25% in 1997 and increased it again in 2002 to 26%. This was Labour's second best vote share in the country, bettered only in Wicklow, where the party had three candidates. He achieved only 17.65% in 2007 but still captured the most first preference votes. In 2011 the grafting of Mae Sexton's Longford base onto the Labour vote machine gave him 11,406 votes, a 19.8% share that was only 100 short of the quota.

Willie Penrose is based in Mulligar in County Westmeath and has been a member of Dáil Éireann since 1992. In March 2011 he was appointed Minister of State for Housing and Planning but in November of that year he resigned his post and the party whip in order to oppose the closure of Columb Barracks in Mullingar. In October 2013 he rejoined the party but in summer 2015 he suggested that he might not be a candidate in the 2016 election, making his decision conditional upon the reduction of the bankruptcy period to one year. Having received a commitment from the government to support his legislation on this point which was brought before the Dáil, he was selected as the sole candidate at the party's convention on December 15th 2016. Penrose was a member of Westmeath County Council from 1984 to 2002 for the Mullingar electoral area. He practices as a barrister on the midlands circuit.

Sinn Féin:

Paul Hogan is a member of Westmeath County Council for the Athlone electoral area. He was also the party candidate for the 2007 and 2011 Dáil elections. He was elected to Athlone Town council in 2004 at the age of 21. As the party candidate in the 2007 general election he polled 2,136 first preferences and was eliminated on the second count. He was Mayor of Athlone for the year 2007–2008. However, in 2009 he failed to be re-elected to the Town Council when his 836 votes (7.94%) did not attract sufficient transfers. In 2011 his Dáil election vote was 4,339 (7.54%). In the 2014 Longford–Westmeath by-election he almost doubled his first preference votes to 7,458 (7.54%). In 2014 he won a seat on Westmeath County Council with 1,423 votes (10.7%). He works for Sinn Féin.

Anti-Austerity Alliance – People Before Profit:

Dom Parker is the candidate of the new Athlone branch of the Anti-Austerity Alliance of which he is chair. The group says it has four key aims: the total abolition of Irish Water and related charges through non-payment, and the immediate reversal of all austerity taxes. Its goals also include retaining Costume Barracks and improving pay and resources for troops, as well as not forming a coalition with any right wing parties. Prior to becoming part of the Anti-Austerity Alliance, the Athlone grouping arranged marches, public meetings, and door to door leaflet drops about water charges.

Independents:

Three of the independents contesting the 2016 election in this constituency are doing so under the Independent Alliance banner:

Frank Kilbride is a hotelier from Edgeworthstown in County Longford and is a former member of Longford County Council. He is contesting this election as part of the Independent Alliance. He was originally a Fine Gael councillor. He was elected to the county council in 1999 and 2004, and on both occasions he topped the poll with 669 votes (16.58%) and 914 votes (20.47%) respectively. In 2007 he ran for the Senate on the Industrial and Commercial Panel but failed to take a seat. In 2009, while he held on to his seat in Granard, his vote fell to 669 (16.67%) for the third seat. He resigned from the party over the Protection of Life During Pregnancy Bill (2013) but subsequently rejoined. He failed to hold his county council seat in the 2014 local elections when his 499 votes (6.85%) saw him eliminated on the sixth count with three other Fine Gael candidates elected. A broadcaster, businessman and former showband star, he says he is running as an independent because there is a need for better representation of Longford, and particularly the Granard area, in the Dáil.

Kevin 'Boxer' Moran is from Athlone and he too is contesting under the Independent Alliance banner. He was a Fianna Fáil member of Westmeath County Council from 1999 to 2011 but announced his intention to contest that year's Dáil election as an independent when he failed to secure selection as a party candidate. He then polled 3,707 first preference votes (6.4%) in the 2011 Dáil election. He also contested the 2014 by-election as an independent and increased his vote to 5,629 votes (11.5%). In the 2009 local elections he topped the poll in the Athlone area with 1,771 first preference votes, and was the only candidate to achieve the quota on first preferences. In the 2014 local elections he further increased his local election vote dramatically to 2,897.

Moran lives in Cornamagh, Athlone and is married with two teenage children. He is a keen angler and works to promote Lough Ree and improve its shoreline amenities. His community involvement includes Athlone St. Patrick's Day Parade, TriAthlone and the European People's Festival. He supports Athlone Town Football Club, GAA and Rugby. He owns and operates a taxi company. He was prominent in local efforts in December to counter the risk to business and homes from the threatened flooding in the Shannon area.

James Morgan is a Longford-based accountant, financial consultant and business man. He is also contesting this election under the Independent Alliance banner. He ran as an independent candidate in the 2014 Dáil by-election and polled an impressive 5,959 votes (12.2%). A native of Longford he studied accounting and finance in Dublin City University before completing his professional training in Mullingar. He then moved to Tool Hire in Athlone and now lives in Longford with his wife and four children. He has run independent charitable events in support of relief efforts in Haiti, and sponsors his local school sports teams. He was involved in the development of Longford's N4 Axis Retail Centre.

Barbara Smyth is a former Sinn Féin candidate who this time is running as an independent. She ran unsuccessfully for Sinn Féin in the Longford electoral area in the 2014 local elections, polling 252 first preferences (4.41%). She and her husband and children own and run a small business providing a national service in sound system provision and repair from their home village of Newtownforbes. Both are originally from the Dublin area. She is involved with Longford Community Resources Ltd where she volunteers at the drop in centre two days a week and with many other community organisations. She studied social inclusion and community development at Maynooth. When she has time she plays golf.

Louth

Outgoing Deputies:
Séamus Kirk (FF), Gerry Adams (SF), Fergus O'Dowd (FG), Gerald Nash (Lab), Peter Fitzpatrick (FG)

In September 2015 Séamus Kirk (FF) announced that he would not contest this election.

The Constituency:
This is a five-seater encompassing the administrative county of Louth and the hinterland of Drogheda including Mornington, Bettystown, Laytown and the Meath coast.

2016 Candidates will include:
Peter Fitzpatrick (FG), Fergus O'Dowd (FG), Mary Moran (Lab), Gerald (Ged) Nash (Lab), Declan Breathnach (FF), Emma Coffey (FF), Gerry Adams (SF), Imelda Munster (SF), Mark Dearey (GP), Garrett Weldon (AAA–PBP), Michael O'Dowd (Renua), Anthony Connor (DDI), Pat Greene (DDI), Jeff Rudd (UP), Kevin Callan (Ind), Maeve Yore (Ind)

	% Vote 1997	% Vote 2002	% Vote 2007	% Vote 2011	Swing 2011	Quotas 2011
Fine Gael	27.90	20.23	29.38	31.48	2.10	1.6
Labour	10.50	6.69	4.98	19.13	14.15	1.0
Fianna Fáil	40.02	43.57	42.13	15.66	–26.47	0.8
Sinn Féin	8.11	14.95	15.04	21.74	6.70	1.1
Green Party	3.12	4.16	7.58	4.68	–2.90	0.2
Others	10.36	10.40	0.89	7.29	6.40	0.4

In Brief:

This constituency was effectively a four-seater in 2011 since Seamus Kirk (FF) was elected to the new Dáil automatically as the outgoing Ceann Comhairle. He is retiring on this occasion and Declan Bhreathnach (FF), who also ran here in 2011, is likely to win a seat on this occasion. The Fine Gael candidates are publicly fretting about whether the party can retain its two seats and Labour also knows that its seat is vulnerable. There are at least two seats for the government parties, however, and if Nash is not elected then Fine Gael will hold two seats. Gerry Adams will win a seat. If Nash does lose his seat then the second Sinn Féin candidate Imelda Munster is most likely to take it, although the Independent Alliance has two candidates in this constituency and one of them could take a seat. Interestingly two brothers will compete against each other for different parties. Outgoing Fine Gael deputy Fergus O'Dowd should hold his seat not withstanding the decision of his brother Michael to run for Renua Ireland here. Overall it looks like two Fine Gael, two Sinn Féin and one Fianna Fáil.

Fine Gael:

Peter Fitzpatrick is based in Dundalk and has been a member of Dáil Éireann since 2011. He was manager of the Louth GAA county football team when he stood in that election. He polled 7,845 first preferences (11.3%) and took the fourth of the contested seats. He is a native of Dundalk, and has lived there all his life. Married, with three adult children, he previously ran his own business, Fitzpatrick Electrical, having served in the army from 1987 until 1990. He was manager of the Louth GAA Senior Football team from 2009 to 2012, guiding them to the 2010 Leinster football final. He himself played GAA senior football for Louth from 1980 until 1996. In Dáil Éireann he has contributed to debates about issues relating to development in the north east and on public health issues such as alcohol abuse and road safety. He sits on the Oireachtas Committee on Health and Children. He is a loyal supporter of Dundalk Football Club and he played for the team in the late 1970's and early 1980s.

Fergus O'Dowd is based in Drogheda and has been a Dáil Deputy since 2002. Fergus O'Dowd was a Senator from 1997 to 2002 and replaced the retiring deputy Brendan McGahon as Fine Gael's only TD for Louth in the 2002 Dáil election. He increased his vote share by a further 3.69% in 2007. In 2011 he added another 5% and polled 13,980 (20.2%), six votes over the quota and took the second seat behind Gerry Adams. He was the party's spokesperson on Transport and the Marine from 2007 to 2011. On 10th March 2011, he was appointed Minister of State at the Departments of Environment and Communications with responsibility for the NewEra Project. He lost his position as Minister of State in the July 2014 reshuffle. He has been very critical of the manner in which Irish Water was established on several occasions in the Dáil since. He was a member of Louth County Council from 1979 to 2003 where he represented the Drogheda West local electoral area. O'Dowd served three terms as mayor of Drogheda He is a native of Kerry, but has lived in Drogheda since his schooldays, and is married, with three children, He worked previously as a teacher. He is a brother of Niall O'Dowd, owner of the Irish Voice newspaper in New York City and of the IrishCentral.com website for the Irish diaspora. Their brother Michael O'Dowd is the Renua Ireland candidate in this constituency.

Labour Party:

Gerald (Ged) Nash is based in Drogheda and has been a member of Dáil Éireann since 2011. He was elected to Dáil Éireann at his second attempt in 2011. On 11 July 2014, he was appointed Minister of State for Business and Employment with responsibility for small and medium business, collective bargaining and low pay commission at the Department of Jobs, Enterprise and Innovation. He was also made a 'Super Junior' Minister, which means he attends cabinet meetings but does not have a vote. He was the party candidate in the 2007 Dáil election when he was eliminated on the second count with 2,739 votes (5%). His vote improved dramatically to 8,718 first preferences in 2011 (12.6%), the best Labour performance in the constituency since 1992. Nash was a member of Louth County Council for the Drogheda West electoral area from 2004 to 2011. He was Mayor of Drogheda in the year 2004/2005.

Nash is a former Chairperson of the Labour Party branch in University College Dublin where he studied History and Politics. He is also a former National Secretary of Labour Youth. He has worked previously as a public relations consultant and as a teacher, and was also assistant to Nessa Childers when she was a Labour MEP.

Fianna Fáil:

The Fianna Fáil vote here in 2007 was down by nearly 1.5% on 2002, but the outgoing deputies, Dermot Ahern and Séamus Kirk, comfortably held their two seats, receiving over 18% of the vote share each. In 2011, with Kirk's seat as Ceann Comhairle guaranteed, the party fielded two candidates, Declan Breathnach and Senator James Carroll, neither of whom had run previously. In the event Carroll, at 8.2%, polled higher than Breathnach's 5,177 (7.5%) and even though 4,000 of Breathnach's votes transferred to Carroll the party did not win a seat.

Declan Breathnach is a native of Knockbridge and has been a member of Louth County Council since 1999, latterly for the Dundalk local electoral area. He was one of the party's two candidates for the 2011 Dáil election and polled 5,177 (8.2 %). Based in Knockbridge, he is the father of two adult children. He was formerly Principal of Walshestown National School, Grangebellew and taught before that in Dunleer NS. He has been chairperson of Louth County Council on two occasions and for 2014/2015 he was the first Chair of Dundalk Municipal District. He was re-elected to the county council in 2004, 2009 and 2014 with 12.95%, 11.87% and 12.87% (1,364 votes) of the first preference votes respectively.

Emma Coffey is a Drogheda-based solicitor living in Dundalk. There was considerable controversy locally when her candidacy was imposed by the party national executive headquarters since she has no previous electoral experience and had only recently joined the party. She is, however, the grand daughter of former Tánaiste Frank Aiken who was TD for this constituency from 1923 to 1977. Local activist John Temple, who had hoped to be the candidate himself, has agreed to act as her director of elections.

Sinn Féin:

In 2002 Arthur Morgan nearly doubled the Sinn Féin vote to take the second seat in this constituency. In that election as in subsequent elections Morgan proved more effective at attracting transfers than many of the party's candidates in other parts of the country. In 2007, Morgan again won a seat, this time on the sixth count, without reaching the quota. When Morgan retired in 2011 Sinn Féin President Gerry Adams resigned his seat in the House of Commons and announced his candidacy here.

Gerry Adams is based in Ravensdale and has been a member of Dáil Éireann since 2011. He has been President of Sinn Féin since 1983. In the 2011 election he topped the poll with 15,072 (21.7%) first preference votes, 116 over the quota. Adams was an abstentionist member of the Westminster Parliament for the West Belfast constituency from 1983–1987 and again from 1997 to 2010. In the 2010 Westminster election he polled 71% of the vote in the single seat West Belfast constituency. He was also a member of the Northern Ireland Assembly from June 1998 until December 2010. In 2014, he was arrested for questioning and held for four days by the Police Service of Northern Ireland in connection with the abduction and murder of Jean McConville in 1972. He was freed without charge. In May 2015, while on an official royal trip to Ireland, Prince Charles shook Adams' hand in what was described as a symbolic gesture of reconciliation.

Imelda Munster is originally from Drogheda's Ballsgrove area, She now lives in Mellifont Park. She has been has been a member of Louth County Council since 2009. She first ran in the Drogheda East electoral area in 2004 and got 736 votes (7.62%) but was not elected. In 2009 she increased her vote to 1,300 in the Drogheda electoral area and was elected. In the 2014 local elections she improved on that vote by more than another thousand and topped the poll with 2,317 first preferences to take the first seat. She chairs the Housing, Community, Planning and Emergency Services SPC on Louth County Council.

Munster is married with teenage daughters and describes herself as a committed trade unionist. She is former Chair of both Louth and Drogheda Sinn Féin, Secretary of the Cottage Hospital Action Group and a member of the Louth/Meath Education and Training Board.

Green Party:

The Green Party candidate in 2002 was Bernadette Martin from Port Togher. The party had previously polled just 3.12 % and Martin managed to push that up to 4.16 %.

Mark Dearey was the candidate in 2007. He was first elected to Dundalk Town Council in the 2004 local elections, where he polled 802 first preferences representing an 18.46 % vote share and took the second seat. In 2007 he got 4,172 first preference votes (7.58%) and was eliminated on the fifth count. In 2009 he was successful in the Louth County Council elections for the Dundalk South area with 1,448 votes (12.58%). He was appointed to the Seanad in February 2010 as a Taoiseach's nominee. In the 2011 Dáil election his vote fell to 3,244 first preference votes, a 3% fall in vote share. In the 2014 county council elections his 717 votes (7.31%) were just enough to prevent Sinn Féin acquiring a third seat in the Dundalk–Carlingford electoral area.

Dearey is based in Dundalk where he owns and manages the Spirit Store bar and music venue He previously worked as a secondary school teacher and then in organic horticulture. In 1994, he was one of the plaintiffs in a court action taken against British Nuclear Fuels Limited to seek an end to reprocessing at Sellafield. He is Director of Turas, a Dundalk-based addiction counselling service, a founding member of the Newry Dundalk Farmers Market, Chairman of the Dundalk St. Patrick's Day Committee, and a former board member of Friends of the Earth, Ireland.

Anti-Austerity Alliance – People Before Profit:
Garrett Weldon is a 44-year-old native of Dundalk, now living in Louth village. He has worked in the community sector for 20 years in the area of Youth and Community development. He sees his work as being about facilitating communities to realise their own strengths and abilities. He is married with two children.

Direct Democracy Ireland:
Anthony Connor is General Secretary of Direct Democracy Ireland. He lives in Collon but is originally from Drogheda and worked in retail management for 14 years before being made redundant. While unemployed he has volunteered in various sectors, including St Vincent de Paul, S.O.S.A.D. suicide prevention, coaching an under-14 football team and other youth work. He has also campaigned against water and property charges and home evictions In the 2014 Louth County Council elections he polled 383 votes (2.76%) in the Drogheda area.

Pat Greene is the Leader of Direct Democracy Ireland. He polled 124 votes (1.15%) in the 2014 Louth County Council elections in the Ardee area. Based in Monasterboice he describes himself as a 'reluctant candidate' for those elections. Married, with four children, he has a small gate supply business. He has organised regular advisory clinics with anti-repossession activist and former party leader Ben Gilroy.

Renua Ireland:
Michael O'Dowd was a Fine Gael member of Louth County Council from 1999 to 2014. He lost his seat in 2014. He is the brother of the Fine Gael TD for this constituency Fergus O'Dowd. In the 1999 local election he polled 560 votes (7.99%) in the Drogheda East local electoral area, in 2004 he retained that seat and added a seat on Drogheda Borough Council for the Laurence Gate ward, taking the first seat on both with 1,350 votes (13.98%) and 612 votes (18.81%) respectively. In 2007 he ran for the Seanad on the Administrative Panel but was unsuccessful. In the 2009 local elections he polled

1,366 votes (13.14%) and was reelected to the county council. In 2014 his vote collapsed to 433 (3.12%). He has twice been Mayor of Drogheda and has consistently opposed the moving of many of the former responsibilities of the Drogheda Borough Council to Dundalk. In June 2014 he left Fine Gael and is a founding member of Renua Ireland.

He is a qualified accountant with an MSc in Business Development and works in Enterprise Ireland. He is a founding member of the social enterprise 'Ablevision' which empowers people with an intellectual disability to speak up for themselves through the use of digital media and is involved with the social enterprise 'My Streets' which trains homeless people to become tour guides. He is a Council member of 'Gorta Self help Africa' and has in the past worked in Tanzania on development projects.

United Peoples Party:

Jeff Rudd in based in Mell and was the first national chairman of Direct Democracy Ireland but left the party complaining of issues about its internal democracy. He has now founded this new party, which he says will allow members to enjoy better participation. He is a former barman who has more recently returned to education. He qualified in a number of IT areas and has studied accountancy, taxation, business management and company law. He has also been an assistant in the ARCH Club of Drogheda, and campaigns against water fluoridisation.

Married with four children, Rudd says he was never involved in politics (apart from 'a year or two in Fianna Fáil as a teenager'), until in 2005, his daughter was born with severe scoliosis. With her appointments frequently cancelled at Crumlin hospital he joined a group of parents who protested to save services there in 2009, and subsequently 'went looking for something that would help to make things better for the country.'

Independents:

Two non-party candidates in this election are running under the Independent Alliance banner.

Kevin Callan has been a member of Louth County Council for the Drogheda local electoral area since 2009. He is contesting this election under the Independent Alliance banner. In 2009, as a Fine Gael candidate, he polled 855 (11.7%) votes in the Drogheda West ward and took a seat on the council. In 2014, again as a Fine Gael candidate, he retained his seat on the council polling 852 (6.14%) in the larger Drogheda electoral area. He was chosen as Mayor of the county in July 2014. However, in November 2014 he resigned from the party in protest at the government's handling of the introduction of water charges. He is a barrister and lists among his local activities as a volunteer his work with Drogheda Women's and Children's Refuge, Drogheda Youth Development, Drogheda Local Heroes Initiative, and SOSAD.

Maeve Yore has been a member of Louth County Council since 2014. She is contesting this election under the Independent Alliance banner In the 2014 local elections she polled 1,228 first preferences (11.58%) in the Dundalk South electoral area and won the third seat. She says her campaign on that occasion cost €476 of her own savings. Her general election website, maeveyore.ie, is the first Irish candidate website to be fully compatible with the international Web Accessibility Initiative. As a county councillor she opposed a chairman's allowance and proposed that all expenses should be vouched. She has been a fundraiser and volunteer for local schools, groups and committees for over 30 years and is a founder member of Special Needs Active Parents (SNAP) and a Board Member of Louth Volunteer Centre and Louth Meath Education & Training Board. Married, with four children, she worked in Dundalk Credit Union for 14 years and before that in Eircell/ Vodafone Call Centre for 13 years.

Mayo

Outgoing Deputies:

Enda Kenny (FG), Michael Ring (FG), Michelle Mulherin (FG), Dara Calleary (FF), John O'Mahony (FG)

John O'Mahony (FG) will contest in the Galway West constituency in 2016.

The Constituency:

This is now a four seat constituency. In the redraw of constituencies since 2011 nine electoral divisions in the Ballinrobe area in the south of the count have been transferred to the Galway West constituency. The area transferred includes Cong, Kilmaine, Neal and Shrule, as well as Garrymore in addition to Ballinrobe.

2016 Candidates will include:

Enda Kenny (FG), Michelle Mulherin (FG), Michael Ring (FG), Dara Calleary (FF), Lisa Chambers (FF), Rose Conway-Walsh (SF), Margaret Sheehan (GP), Tom Moran (AAA–PBP), Michael Farrington (Renua), Gerry O'Boyle (Ind), Michael Kilcoyne (Possible Ind)

	% Vote 1997	% Vote 2002	% Vote 2007	% Vote 2011	Swing 2011	Quotas 2011
Fine Gael	48.75	37.59	53.83	64.96	11.13	3.9
Labour	–	–	1.16	4.91	3.75	0.3
Fianna Fáil	42.95	39.98	24.46	16.07	–8.39	1.0
Sinn Féin	–	3.28	5.05	6.48	1.43	0.4
Green Party	1.52	1.05	0.81	0.36	–0.45	0.02
Others	6.77	18.09	14.68	7.22	–7.46	0.4

In Brief:

The reduction of this constituency from a five-seater to a four-seater means Fine Gael have definitely lost a seat. This reality and the fact that 8000 votes from his Ballinrobe base were transferred to Galway West prompted John O'Mahony (FG) to move constituencies. The question remains whether Fine Gael can hold the other three seats. Taoiseach Enda Kenny (FG) and Junior Tourism and Sports Minister Michael Ring are safe but backbencher Michelle Mulherin (FG) may be in some difficulty. Fianna Fáil's outgoing deputy Dara Calleary (FF) will be elected and his running mate Lisa Chambers (FF) will also poll well, but probably not well enough for the party to take two seats. The candidate to watch is Rose Conway-Walsh of Sinn Féin. That party ran two candidates in 2011 who between them polled almost 5,000 votes. This time running as the party's sole candidate Conway-Walsh will improve on that significantly, and probably enough to win a seat.

Fine Gael:
In 2007 the party again ran four candidates when sitting TDs Enda Kenny and Michael Ring were joined by Mayo football manager John O'Mahony and local councillor Michelle Mulherin. Kenny topped the poll with 14,717 first preferences for a 20.62% share. He was joined in Dáil Éireann by the re-elected Michael Ring, who polled 11,412, and by John O'Mahony, who received 6,869 first preferences. Michelle Mulherin finished seventh on the first count with 5,428 but did not win a seat. In total, the party received 53.83% of the first preference vote, making Mayo once again Fine Gael's best performance in the country. In 2011 Fine Gael nominated the same four candidates and in the then five seat constituency all four came home. Kenny again topped the poll, increasing his vote to 17,472 (23.6%), with Ring claiming 13,180 (17.8%), Mulherin 8,851 (11.9%) and O'Mahony 8,667 (11.7%). With the constituency reduced to four seats, and John O'Mahony following his electoral base into Galway West, the other three incumbents were selected unopposed by the constituency convention in October 2015.

Enda Kenny is based in Castlebar and has been a member of Dáil Éireann since 1975. He has been Taoiseach since March 2011. He won a by-election following the death of his father Henry Kenny who had been a TD from 1969 to 1975. At 24, Enda Kenny's election made him the youngest member of the 20th Dáil. He was

Minister of State at the Departments of Education and Labour with special responsibility for Youth Affairs from February 1986 to March 1987 and Minister for Tourism and Trade from 1994 to 1997. He was party chief whip from 1992 to 1994 and held a variety of frontbench spokesperson positions in opposition. Enda Kenny is the longest-serving TD in Dáil Éireann. He worked previously as a national school teacher.

Michelle Mulherin is based in Ballina and has been a member of Dáil Éireann since 2011. She was formerly a member of Mayo County Council. In the 2004 local elections she polled 1,202 first preferences in the Ballina electoral area. After her unsuccessful candidacy for the Dáil in Mayo in 2007 she was also unsuccessful in a run for the Seanad on the Administrative Panel. In the 2009 local elections she topped the poll in Ballina with 1,921 first preferences, almost 200 above the quota. She was also a member of Ballina Town Council from 1999 until 2011, being Mayor of Ballina in 2008/9. She practiced as a solicitor in Ballina.

Michael Ring is based in Westport and has been a member of Dáil Éireann since 1994. He has been Minister of State for Tourism and Sport since 2011. He was first elected to Dáil Éireann in the former Mayo West constituency in the 1994 by-election that followed Padraig Flynn's appointment to the European Commission. He has comfortably held his seat since, spectacularly topping the poll in two subsequent elections. He polled 10,310 (quota 10,310) in 1997 and in 2002 he polled 9,880 (quota 10,581). He increased his vote to 11,412 in 2007, but was knocked off the top of the poll by party leader Enda Kenny. He was the party spokesperson on Agriculture from 1997 to 2000 and deputy spokesperson on Health from 2000 to 2002. He was the party's frontbench spokesperson on Social and Family Affairs from June 2002 to October 2004. Following a frontbench reshuffle he declined the offer of the post of spokesperson on the Marine. He was the spokesperson on Community, Rural and Gaeltacht Affairs from 2007–10 and subsequently spokesperson on Social Protection. He was a member of Mayo County Council from 1994 to 2004 and took an unsuccessful High Court challenge to the constitutionality of the 'dual mandate' ban in 2004. He was formerly an auctioneer.

Labour Party:

At the time of going to print no Labour candidate has been announced for this constituency.

Fianna Fáil:

Dara Calleary is based in Ballina and has been a Dáil deputy since 2007. He is the party spokesperson on Jobs, Enterprise and Innovation. In 2007, as a first-time candidate, Dara Calleary finished comfortably ahead of his running mates John Carty TD and Councillor Frank Chambers on the first count with 7,225 votes, compared to 5,889 for Carty and 4,345 for Chambers. Calleary was elected on the eighth count with Beverley Flynn, who was running in that election as an Indepeendent and won 6,779 first preferences, taking the final seat.

From 2009 to 2011 Calleary was Minister of State at the Department of Enterprise, Trade and Employment with special responsibility for Labour Affairs and in March 2010, following a cabinet reshuffle, responsibility for Public Service Transformation was added to his role. In the 2011 Dáil election 2011 he polled 8,577 first preferences (11.6%) and took the fifth seat on the elimination of his running mate. Calleary was Fianna Fáil's spokesperson on Justice, Equality and Defence from April 2011 to July 2012 when he was appointed spokesperson on Jobs, Enterprise and Innovation. Dara Calleary studied Political Science and Business at Trinity College Dublin. Before his election he worked for Chambers Ireland, the national network of Chambers of Commerce, and as a bank official. He has previously been Chairman of the party's youth wing Ógra Fianna Fáil. Dara's father, Seán Calleary, was a TD for Mayo East from 1973 to 1992. His grandfather, Phelim Calleary, served as a TD for Mayo North from 1952 to 1969.

Lisa Chambers has been a member of Mayo County Council for the Castlebar electoral area since 2014. She was also a candidate in the 2011 Dáil election, when as Fianna Fáil's youngest candidate, and the youngest female candidate in the country, she polled 3,343 votes and was eliminated on the fifth count. She is a barrister. She hit national headlines in 2013 when, as party Vice-President, she called for former Taoiseach Bertie Ahern's resignation from the party in the wake of the publication of the Mahon tribunal report. In the 2014 local elections she took the second seat in the Castlebar area with 1,481 first preferences (9.6%). She is on the board of management of the Irish Women Lawyers Association and has worked with the National Women's Council of Ireland to try to get more young people and women involved in politics. Outside politics she is a member of the Reserve Defence Forces and enjoys competitive running.

Sinn Féin:

Rose Conway-Walsh lives in Belmullet and has been a member of Mayo County Council since 2009. She was also one of the party's candidates in the 2011 Dáil election when she polled 2,660 (3.6%) first preferences. Her running mate on that election was Thérèse Ruane who polled 2,142 (2.9%). Rose Conway Walsh first ran in Mayo County Council elections in Belmullet in 2004, failing to be elected with 924 first preferences. In the 2009 local election her 1,368 votes (15.11%) gave her the fourth seat. In the newly reconfigured West Mayo electoral area in 2014 she topped the poll with 2,075 votes (13.7%) and was comfortably re-elected. She is a community development worker and has a BA in Public Management and an MA in Local Government. She lives in Belmullet with her husband and children.

Green Party:

In 2011 the Green Party candidate was John Carey, from Kilmaine, who received 266 votes (0.4%). In 2007 the party ran Peter Enright, who polled 580. The candidate in 2002 and 1997 was Anne Crowley, who took 669 and 938 votes in those two elections. This time the party again has a new candidate.

Margaret Sheehan has lived in South Mayo for over twenty years. Returning to education as a mature student after rearing her family she has a first class BA in Sociology, Political Studies and History and an MA from NUI Galway in Gender, Globalisation and Rights. She is the Environmental Pillar Nominee and Vice-Chair of South West Mayo Development Company, and an active participant in Kilmaine Community Garden. As a member of Headford

Environment Group, she represents the environment college on County Galway Local Community Development Council.

Anti-Austerity Alliance – People Before Profit:
Tom Moran is a retired aviation engineer living in Westport. A long time socialist he has campaigned on environmental issues, such as opposition to the Corrib gas pipeline and working with the Federation of Irish Seat Trout and Salmon Anglers to protect Irish waters from fish farms and pollution. He has also supported the Occupy movement in both Dublin and Galway. Raised in Westport he learned his trade in Kevin Street technical college and then at North Dublin Polytechnic. He has worked in Africa and the Middle East and spent 30 years working in the control tower at Shannon Airport. He is standing in this election because during his working life he has seen inequality grow and the quality of life of working people eroded. He feels it is time to make a stand. He says 'We need to create a society where everyone has equality of esteem and a share in our natural resources, both in its lands and in its marine environment.'

Renua Ireland:
Michael Farrington is from Kiltimagh, in the Mayo East area of the constituency. He previously worked in a variety of positions in accountancy and financial control, and runs an import and distribution business into the hotel, catering, retail and allied trades. He is a director of Kiltimagh Community Centre. He says his priority is to build up infrastructure in areas such as tourism including Knock airport and the hotel and restaurant sector. He is married with three children and expressed the hope that his business experience would be of use to the people of Mayo.

Independents:
Gerry O'Boyle is a former auctioneer from Mayo who was a publican living in Castlerea when he ran in the 2014 Roscommon–South Leitrim by-election caused by the election of 'Ming' Flanagan to the European Parliament. On that occasion he polled 82 votes under the 'Land League West' banner. In March 2015 he was amongst a number of protesters who caused court proceed-

ings relating to home repossessions at the Registrar's Court to be disrupted on two occasions. He is a former student of Ballyhaunis Community School and also studied Real Estate, Auctioneering and Valuation at Galway Mayo Institute of Technology.

Meath East

Outgoing Deputies:

Dominic Hannigan (Lab), Regina Doherty (FG), Helen McEntee (FG)

Shane McEntee (FG) was re-elected in 2011. He died in December 2012. His daughter Helen McEntee (FG) won the seat in the resultant by-election in March 2013.

The Constituency:

This three seat constituency includes the urban areas of Ashbourne, Dunboyne, Dunshaughlin, Ratoath and Kells. It does not include the Meath coastal area of Stamullen, Julianstown, Laytown and Bettystown or the Drogheda environs which are included in the Louth constituency.

	% Vote 1997	% Vote 2002	% Vote 2007	% Vote 2011	Swing 2011	Quotas 2011
Fine Gael	36.92	27.23	25.88	40.87	14.99	1.6
Labour	7.93	4.26	11.94	21.04	9.10	0.8
Fianna Fáil	41.88	44.92	43.56	19.61	–23.95	0.8
Sinn Féin	3.53	9.34	3.94	8.88	4.94	0.4
Green Party	1.95	3.65	3.09	1.08	–2.01	–
Others	7.8	10.51	11.54	8.53	–3.01	0.3

2016 Candidates will include:

Regina Doherty (FG), Helen McEntee (FG), Dominic Hannigan (Lab), Thomas Byrne (FF), Darren O'Rourke (SF), Seán Ó Buachalla (GP), Aisling O'Neill (SD), Ben Gilroy (DDI), Seamus McDonagh (WP), Sharon Keogan (Ind)

In Brief:

This is one of handful of three-seaters where the government parties currently hold all the seats. Fine Gael's all female ticket of outgoing deputies is likely to hold onto its two seats but Labour is likely to lose its one seat. The question is whether former Fianna Fáil deputy Thomas Byrne or Sinn Féin's Darren O'Rourke will take it. Even on a very bad day in 2011 Fianna Fáil had twice as many votes as Sinn Féin, but Sinn Féin has a different candidate this time in Darren O'Rourke. On balance Thomas Byrne seems better placed to take the seat.

Fine Gael:

Regina Doherty is based in Ratoath and has been a member of Dáil Éireann since 2011. She had previously contested the 2007 Dáil election when she polled 4,363 and was eliminated on the seventh count. In 2011 she took the second seat with 8,677 first preferences (20.3%). She is a Member of the Joint Oireachtas Committee on Health and Children, the Joint Oireacthtas Committee on Finance, Public Expenditure and Reform and was also a member of the Constitutional Convention. Originally from Dublin she has lived in Ratoath with her husband and four children for many years. She was Deputy Director of Fine Gael's campaign for the Seanad Abolition referendum in 2013. She previously worked as a sales director for the Horizon Technology Group and subsequently operated her own ICT distribution company with her husband.

Helen McEntee has been a member of Dáil Éireann since March 2013. She worked as personal assistant to her father who was a TD when he died suddenly in December 2012 and she was subsequently elected in the by-election in March 2013 when she polled 9,356 first preference votes (38.5%). Her father had first been elected to Dáil Éireann in the 2005 by-election in the Meath constituency caused by the appointment of former Taoiseach John Bruton to the position of European Union Ambassador to Washington. Shane McEntee was re-elected for this Meath East three-seater in 2011, increasing his vote and share to 8,794 (20.6%) to take the third seat behind Labour's Dominic Hannigan and running mate Regina Doherty. Heather McEntee is a member of the

Oireachtas committee on Transport and Communications and of the Oireachtas Committee on Environment, Culture and the Gaeltacht. Now 29 years old, she is the second youngest member of Dáil Éireann. Before working for her father she gained a BA in Politics and Law and a Masters Degree in Media and Communications, both from Dublin City University. Between degrees she worked in banking.

Labour Party:

Although Labour's Dominic Hannigan topped the poll here in 2011 the party did disastrously in the 2013 by-election, coming in fourth with just 4.6 % of the vote. It also lost all of its four seats on Meath County Council in the 2014 local elections.

Dominic Hannigan is based in Dunshaughlin and has been a Dáil deputy since 2011. He was elected to Meath County Council in 2004 as an Independent, polling 908 votes in the Slane Local Electoral area. In 2005 he joined the Labour party and was the party's candidate in the 2005 by-election in Meath polling 5,567 votes. He ran again in the 2007 Dáil election and polled 5,136 seats. He was a member of Seanad Éireann from 2007 to 2011. He succeeded on his third attempt to win a Dáil seat when in 2011 he topped the poll with 8,994 votes (21%).

He has been Chair of the Joint Committee on the Implementation of the Good Friday Agreement, and Chair of the Joint Committee on European Union Affairs. Before his election he ran a home-based business consultancy that provided advice to the health, transport, communications and entertainment sectors. He holds a degree in engineering from University College Dublin, a Masters in Transport from City University London and a Master in Finance from the University of London. He worked in a private engineering consultancy in London for four years and also worked for Camden Council as a engineer in its policy and development team.

Fianna Fáil:

Fianna Fáil held three of the five seats in the old Meath constituency between 1987 and its abolition in 2007. In 2007 it won two seats in Meath East with Mary Wallace and Thomas Byrne. Wallace did not contest in 2011 and Byrne ran with Councillor Nick Killian. However, the Fianna Fáil vote more than halved and although the candidates got more than three quarters of a quota between them the party lost its seat.

Thomas Byrne lives in Colpe and has a constituency office in Donacarney. He has been a member of Seanad Éireann since 2011. He was a member of Dáil Éireann from 2007 to 2011. In 2007 he polled 7,834 first preferences for an 18.22% share. In 2009 he ran for the party in the East constituency of the European elections, coming sixth with a disappointing 31,112 votes. In the 2011 Dáil campaign, although he had 5,715 first preference votes (13.4%), he failed to hold the seat. In the 2013 by-election he polled 8,002 (32.9%) but came in second. He was again a candidate for the European Elections in 2014 when he polled 55,384 first preferences and lasted until the sixth count before he was eliminated.

A law graduate of Trinity College, Dublin, Byrne is a practising solicitor in Drogheda. He is married, with three children. His father, Tommy Byrne, represents Fianna Fáil on the Louth County Council for the Drogheda local electoral area, having previously been elected to Drogheda Borough Council as an independent in 1999 and 2004.

Sinn Féin:

Darren O'Rourke is based in Ashbourne and is a member of Meath County Council for the Ashbourne local electoral area. He was the party's candidate in the 2013 by-election, polling 3,165 (13%) of the vote. In the 2014 local elections he stood in the Ashbourne electoral area, polled 1,407 first preference votes (15.8%), which was 134 over the quota, and took the second of the six seats. He has a BSc in Biomedical Science from Dublin Institute of Technology, and an MSc in Molecular Pathology from Trinity College Dublin and an MSc in Leadership and Management Development from the Royal College of Surgeons. He worked as a Clinical Biochemist in Our Lady of Lourdes Hospital, Drogheda, before becoming Health Policy Advisor to Caoimhghín Ó Caoláin TD. He is also a competitive runner, who fundraises for local organisations, and an amateur boxer.

Green Party:

Seán Ó Buachalla ran for the Greens in Meath East in the 2007 Dáil election. He polled 1,330 first preferences. He also ran in the 2009 local elections in the Dunshaughlin electoral area but his 142 votes were disappointing. Even more disappointing were his 461 votes (1.1%) in the 2011 Dáil election. His support in the 2013 by-election was 1.7%, or 423 votes. In the 2014 local elections his 157 votes (1.44%) placed him bottom of the poll in the Ratoath electoral area. Ó Buachalla, who studied Modern Irish and History at NUI Maynooth, is a freelance Irish language translator and has worked as a youth club development officer for Ógras. He was active locally in the Save Tara campaign. He chairs the Green Party's Irish Language Policy Group.

Social Democrats:

Aisling O'Neill lives in Ashbourne. She is a registered general nurse and the mother of two children. She first stood as an Independent in the Ashbourne Electoral Area in the 2014 local elections campaigning on the need to save services in Navan Hospital, where she was working as an emergency nurse, and on water charges and property tax. On that occasion she received 249 first preference votes (2.8%) and survived into the sixth count on transfers before being eliminated.

Direct Democracy Ireland:

Ben Gilroy was one of the founder of Direct Democracy Ireland in November 2012. In December 2015 that organisation announced that it would be working together in this election with the National Citizens Movement. Gilroy was leader of DDI from its foundation in November 2012 until he stepped down as leader in February 2014 citing personal reasons. He has for some time been a leading figure in the campaign against home repossessions. He stood in the 2013 by-election in this constituency and polled 1,588 first preferences, which put him ahead of the Labour Party candidate. He was later a candidate in the Midlands–North West Constituency for the 2014 European elections when he polled 7,683 votes and was eliminated on the first count.

Workers Party:

Seamus McDonagh is a native of Wilkinstown and lives in Kells. He was the Workers Party candidate in Meath East in the 2013 by-election, when he polled 263 votes (1.1%). This will be his fourth attempt at election. He first ran in 1987 in the old five seat Meath constituency when his 790 votes gave him 1.43% of the poll, his highest figure so far. In 2011 he ran in Meath West, polling 189 votes (0.47%).

As a teenager he moved to England to find work on building sites and began working with the Irish community in Birmingham, providing employment advice to his fellow workers. Returning to Ireland in the late 1970s, he became active in campaigns supporting PAYE workers, for the public ownership of Ireland's natural resources and against discrimination. During the 1980s and 1990s, Seamus was active in campaigns against proposed water charges. He served as Chairman of the North Meath Campaign Against Household and Water Taxes (CAHWT). He has two daughters and three grandchildren, all of whom live in Meath.

Independents:

Sharon Keogan is an independent member of Meath County Council for the Laytown Bettystown electoral area. She was a member of the Fianna Fáil Ard Comhairle, but left the party when she was unsuccessful in her effort to replace Mary Wallace on the party's general election ticket for the 2011 election. She stood unsuccessfully as an independent in that year under the banner of 'New Vision.' She polled 1,168 first preference votes (2.7%).

In 2014 she contested as an independent in two separate local elections areas for Meath County Council. In the Laytown–Bettystown area she polled 1,150 first preferences (11.69%) and took the second seat. In the Ashbourne area she polled 452 first preference and survived until the last count but did not get a seat. She and her business partner Seamus O'Neill operate a pub and restaurant in Duleek. He was an independent member of Meath County Council from 2008 and he was re-elected to the county council for the Slane local electoral area in 2009 as an independent. He resigned in 2012 and her son Arian Keogan was co-opted in his place. Arian did not run in 2014.

Meath West

Outgoing Deputies:

Damien English (FG), Peadar Tóibín (SF), Ray Butler (FG)

The Constituency:

This three seat constituency includes that western portion of the administrative county of Meath not in the Meath East constituency, together with a north-eastern section of the county of Westmeath. It includes the towns of Kells, Trim, Oldcastle and Navan. The boundaries of the constituency are unchanged since 2011.

	% Vote 1997	% Vote 2002	% Vote 2007	% Vote 2011	Swing 2011	Quotas 2011
Fine Gael	36.92	27.23	29.03	45.92	16.89	1.8
Labour	7.93	4.26	4.04	13.52	9.48	0.5
Fianna Fáil	41.88	44.92	51.59	18.13	–33.46	0.7
Sinn Féin	3.53	9.43	11.29	17.40	6.11	0.7
Green Party	1.95	3.65	2.50	1.19	–1.31	0.05
Others	7.79	10.51	1.56	3.84	2.28	0.2

2016 Candidates will include:

Ray Butler (FG), Damien English (FG), Tracy McElhinney (Lab), Shane Cassells (FF), Peadar Tóibín (SF), Seamus McMenamin (GP), Alan Lawes (DDI)

In Brief:

The Sinn Féin seat seems safe. Fine Gael will win one seat and that will go to Minster of State Damien English. This is a key target constituency for Fianna Fáil who had almost three quarters of a quota even on a bad day in 2011. The second Fine Gael seat held by Ray Butler is in jeopardy and Fianna Fáil is likely to take it even though that means there will be three TDs from Navan.

Fine Gael:

The party secured one seat here in 2007 and two in 2011. The two outgoing deputies are again the only candidates in this election.

Ray Butler is originally from Kells and now lives in Trim. He has been a member of Dáil Éireann since 2011. He first stood for election for Trim Town Council in 2004, when he topped the poll and took the first seat with 406 votes (14.97% and 1.49 quotas). In the 2009 county council elections he again topped the poll this time in the Trim Electoral area where he obtained 0.99 of a quota with his 1,933 votes (19.73%). In the 2011 Dáil election his 5,262 first preference votes (13.1%) gave him the third seat in Meath West. In Dáil Éireann he is a member of the Joint Committee on Education and Social Protection. Before his election to Dáil Éireann in 2015 he had been self-employed for over 20 years. He lives in Trim with his wife Marie and four children.

Damien English is based in Navan and he has been a member of Dáil Éireann since 2002. He is Minister of State with responsibility for Skills, Research and Innovation, working across the Departments of Education and of Enterprise, Skills and Innovation. He entered local politics in the 1999 local election when he secured a seat on Meath county council in the Navan electoral area at just 21 years of age. He held that seat until the dual mandate ban was introduced in 2003.

In his first Dáil election outing in 2002 Dáil English polled an impressive 5,958 first preferences (9.3%). Importantly, he was 2,081 votes ahead of his running mate John Farrelly, and English went on to take the fourth seat without reaching the quota, becoming the youngest deputy in the 29th Dáil. In the 2007 Dáil election English was almost 4,000 votes ahead of his nearest running mate and saw off Sinn Féin's Joe Reilly to take the last seat. In 2011 he was again 4,000 votes ahead of running mate Ray Butler, with 9,290 first preferences (23.1%). English is married with four children. He has a diploma in Management Accounting. For relaxation he runs marathons.

Labour Party:

Tracy McElhinney is from Ballivora and is a former member of Meath County Council for the Trim electoral area. She was elected to Meath County Council in 2009, polling 1,225 votes (12.5%). In the 2014 local elections, however, she received only 434 votes (4.43%) and lost her seat. She is married with two sons. She comes from a family of Labour Party activists. She worked for NEC semi conductors for 12 years where she was a shop steward. After she was made redundant she set up the employment lobby group Next Era Calling with former employees and others from the local community. She chairs the parents' association at St Columbanus' National School.

Fianna Fáil:

Shane Cassells is based in Navan and has been a member of Meath County Council since 2004. He was first elected to Navan Town Council in 1999 at 21 years of age and has served two terms as Mayor of Navan. In 2004 he was elected to Meath County Council, polling 935 first preferences (6.77%) in the Navan electoral area. His vote share was almost exactly the same in the 2009 local elections when he polled 1,059 (6.76%). He got almost exactly the same vote in the 2014 local elections when he polled 1,051 first preferences. He was also the party candidate in the by-election in March 2005 in the Meath constituency. He polled 16,117 first preference votes (32.4%), which was a crucial 647 votes behind Shane McEntee (FG) who took the seat. Cassells was one of two candidates for the party, with outgoing deputy Johnny Brady in 2011. Cassells polled 3,496 first preferences while Brady polled 3,789, but both were ultimately eliminated. Cassells is the sole candidate for the party on this occasion.

Cassells holds a BA in Journalism and Media Communications. He is a Director of Navan Enterprise Board, Navan Civic Trust and Navan Leisure Centre.

Sinn Féin:

Peadar Tóibín is a first time deputy based in Navan. He first ran for Navan Town Council and for Meath County Council in the Navan electoral area in the 2004 local elections when he failed to be elected to either with 296 and 626 votes respectively. In November 2007 he was co-opted to the County Council but he was not re-elected in 2009.

In 2011 Tóibín was elected to Dáil Éireann with 6,989 first preference votes (17.4%). He holds a BA in Economics and Politics and a postgraduate qualification in Enterprise from University College Dublin. He was a self-employed management consultant. He was suspended from the Sinn Féin parliamentary party in 2013 when he voted against the Protection of Life During Pregnancy Bill 2013. After six months he was reinstated. He is the party's Dáil spokesperson on Trade, Jobs and Innovation and on the Irish language. Locally he chairs the Save Navan Hospital campaign and founded the campaign to develop a greenway along the Boyne from the source to the estuary.

Green Party:

Seamus McMenamin is a general practitioner from Navan and a first time candidate. A prominent member of the Irish Medical Organisation he has been active in GP protests around the negotiation of the new general practice contract. He is doctor to the Meath Senior Inter-county football team and is a member of the Navan Theatre group. He is married with two children. He lists among his priorities the retention of services at Navan hospital, a referendum to prevent the privatisation of Irish Water, free healthy school dinners and strengthened home care packages to support older people living at home.

Direct Democracy Ireland:

Alan Lawes is standing this time under the banner of Direct Democracy Ireland–National Citizens Movement. In the 2014 local elections he was a People Before Profit candidate in Navan, where he polled 333 votes (3.43%). He lives in Johnstown in Navan and is married with four children. He is one of the three founding members of the National Citizens Movement which is campaigning jointly with Direct Democracy Ireland. Employed in Cappagh Hospital for 30 years he volunteers as a SIPTU grassroots representative and safety representative there. He is Chair of the Johnstown Community Group. He has volunteered with the Garda Reserve and various local organisations.

Independents:
No independent candidates have confirmed in this constituency at the time of writing.

Offaly

Outgoing Deputies for Laois–Offaly:
Charles Flanagan (FG), Marcella Corcoran Kennedy (FG), Barry Cowen (FF), Brian Stanley (SF), Seán Fleming (FF)

Charles Flanagan (FG) and Seán Fleming (FF) will run in Laois in the 2016 election.

The Constituency:
This is a new three seat constituency. It comprises the county of Offaly together with twenty-four electoral divisions from the north west of Tipperary, 19 of these from the former Borrisokane Rural District and five divisions from the former Nenagh Rural District. The total population of the Tipperary area in this constituency was 10,953 at the time of the last census.

See Laois chapter for party results table for Laois–Offaly 1997 to 2011

2016 Candidates will include:
Marcella Corcoran-Kennedy (FG), Barry Cowen (FF), Eddie Fitzpatrick (FF), Carol Nolan (SF), John Leahy (Renua), Ken Smollen (IDP), John Foley (Ind), Joe Hannigan (Ind)

In Brief:
This new three seat constituency brings two sitting deputies with it out of the former Laois–Offaly five-seater. Both of them, Mar-

cella Corcoran-Kennedy (FG) and Barry Cowen (FF) are safe. The key question is what happens to the seat that has been added to the county. Sinn Féin have justifiable hopes of a Dáil breakthrough now that it has a councillor in each of the three local electoral areas. Its candidate Carol Nolan was the weaker of those three in the 2014 local elections but if she can garner the support for the party across the county she will win a seat. The other contender for the third seat is John Leahy, who was a poll topper as an independent candidate in the Birr area in the 2014 local elections. He has since joined Renua Ireland and represents that party's best prospect for a new TD. Fianna Fáil has also selected a strong second candidate in the form of councillor Eddie Fitzpatrick, but two out of three seats would be a dramatic achievement for the party. The Independent to watch is Edenderry area Councillor John Foley, a former Fianna Fáil Dáil candidate who polled well again as an independent Dáil candidate in the 2011 election. If he improves at all on his first preference this time out he could be well placed to gather any Fianna Fáil, Renua or other independent transfers which come available, particularly from the north of the county.

Fine Gael:

Marcella Corcoran-Kennedy is a first time deputy and is based in Birr. She is a former member of Offaly County Council for the Ferbane electoral area. She lost her council seat in the 2009 local elections. In 2011, however, she was elected to Dáil Éireann for the Laois–Offaly constituency with 5,817 first preference votes (7.8%). Among the campaigns she has been associated with was that for the provision of broadband to the four midland counties under the National County and Group Broadband Scheme. In Dáil Éireann she is a member of the Committee on the Environment, Culture and the Gaeltacht, the Select sub-Committee on Arts, Heritage and the Gaeltacht, the Committee on Jobs, Enterprise and Innovation and the Committee on Justice, Defence and Equality. She is also Deputy Chairperson of the Fine Gael LGBT group and was a prominent campaigner in the Marriage Equality referendum.

Based in Birr she says that the impact on family life for a rural TD can be quite considerable. She is fan of theatre and a big fan of the US political drama *The West Wing.*

Labour Party:

The party last held a seat in the Laois–Offaly constituency from 1992 to 1997, when Offaly based Pat Gallagher was the deputy. Gallagher gave up politics in 2000 to take up a position in local government administration. He went on to become County Manager in Offaly and then Galway. He is currently Chief Executive of Westmeath county council.

Many high profile Offaly members left the Labour party following the controversy over the selection of John Whelan as the party's Laois–Offaly candidate in 2011. At the time of writing the party has not yet announced a candidate in Offaly constituency.

Fianna Fáil:

The party is running two candidates in this new three seat constituency.

Barry Cowen is based in Tullamore and has been a deputy since 2011. He is the party spokesperson on Environment and Local Government. He is a brother of former party leader and Taoiseach Brian Cowen, Barry replaced his brother on the ticket for the 2011 election and took the third seat on that occasion with 8,257 first preferences (11.1%). Before his election to Dáil Éireann, Barry was a member of Offaly County Council for the Tullamore electoral area from 1991 to 2011. In the local elections he took the second seat in 1999 with 1,139 votes (11.96%), the fourth seat in 2004 with 1,169 (10.13%), and topped the poll in 2009 with 1,626 (13.86%). In Dáil Éireann he was Fianna Fáil's spokesperson on Social Protection from 2011 to July 2012 when he became spokesperson on Environment and Local Government. He was an auctioneer and valuer before his election.

Eddie Fitzpatrick is based in Portarlington and is a member of Offaly County Council for the North Offaly (Edenderry) electoral area. He was first elected to Offaly County Council as a Progressive Democrats candidate in 2004 when he won 503 votes (7.09%).

In the 2009 local elections he ran as an independent, holding his seat comfortably with 1,236 first preferences (12.93%). In the 2011 Dáil election he ran as independent again and was unsuccessful, but polled 2,544 votes (3.43%). In the 2014 County Council elections he polled exactly one quota with 1,250 votes (14.29%). He is a tillage and beef farmer and has worked on the county's economic planning and on the development of its education services. In his spare time he tries to fit in rugby, GAA and golf.

Sinn Féin:

In the 2014 local elections Sinn Féin had a councillor elected in each of the three local electoral areas in Offaly. Brendan Killeavy topped the poll in Tullamore with 2,778 first preferences, which was 1,255 votes above the quota. Martin O'Reilly topped the poll in Edenderry with 1,669 first preferences, 419 votes over the quota.

Carol Nolan received 1,166 (10.01%) first preferences in the Birr electoral area, two thirds of a quota, and she took the fourth of the six seats. She is from Cadamstown and is married, with two children. Nolan is a primary teacher and has served as the principal of a local Gaelscoil. She has an MA in Special and Inclusive Education and is studying for a PhD at NUI Galway. In 2015 she worked to ensure the survival of the traditional Banagher Horse Fair.

Green Party:

The party had selected no candidate at the time of going to press.

Renua Ireland:

John Leahy is based in Kilcormac and is a member of Offaly County Council for the Birr Local Electoral Area. He was first elected to Laois county council in June 2009, when he polled 1,144 first preferences. He contested the 2011 Dáil election in Laois–Offaly as an independent and polled 4,882 first preference votes (6.6%). In 2014 he again fought the local elections as an independent in Birr and polled 2,686 votes (23.05%) first preferences which gave him over a thousand votes to spare over the qouta. In January 2015 he joined Lucinda Creighton and Eddie Hobbs at the press conference which announced the establishment of a new party which was later named Renua Ireland. As well as being a public representative he is the Offaly GAA Coaching and Games Promotion Officer. In 2011 he funded his campaign from savings, without holding any benefit nights or other fundraising events.

Irish Democratic Party:

Ken Smollen is the chairperson and co-founder of the Irish Democratic Party. He is originally from Tullamore and is now based in Clara. Smollen is a retired member of An Garda Siochana and served 30 years in Tallaght, Dublin, Edenderry and Portlaoise. The Irish Democratic Party was founded in October 2013 and was officially launched in Tullamore in October 2014. It advocates participatory democracy and now has over 200 signed up members in Offaly and over 1,000 members nationwide. The group has focussed much of its attention on the ongoing home eviction crisis.

Independents:

John Foley is a member of Offaly County Council for the Edenderry Local Electoral Area who is contesting this Dáil election under the Independent Alliance banner.

He ran for Fianna Fáil in the 2007 Dáil election when he polled 5,899 (8.3%) and narrowly missed out to his Laois-based party running mate John Moloney. He also contested the 2011 Dáil election as an independent and won 4,465 first preferences (6%). He is a former Mayor of Edenderry. In the 2009 local election to Offaly County Council he polled 1,649 first preferences (quota 1,367) and took the first of the six seats in the Edenderry electoral area. In the 2014 local elections he polled 1,078 first preferences and took the third of the six seats in that area.

Announcing his 2016 candidacy for the Independent Alliance Foley said he would be to the fore 'in ensuring that Offaly was not left behind as the economy recovers'. He was a keen sponsor of local sporting clubs and children's activities until his business had to cease trading because of the impact of the recession.

Joe Hannigan is based in Nenagh and is a member of Tipperary County Council who is obviously hoping to attract support from the 9,500 North Tipperary voters included in this new Offaly constituency. He is from Kilbarron and has a grandmother in Ferbane. Asked whether he would join any of the new political groupings that have appeared in the last few years he has said 'The girls are only arriving into the hall. I will have a dance with all the girls in the hall, but if I'm going to take a girl home I will have to consult with my supporters to decide which one will have the best dowry for my area.' He topped the poll in the Nenagh district in the 2014 local election, his 2,028 votes (10.89%), being comfortably over the quota. He is current chairman of the Tipperary GAA County Football Board and widely seen as one of the forces behind the recent improvements in Tipperary football.

Teresa Ryan-Feehan is from Birr and sees herself as being well positioned to attract voters from that part of Tipperary included in the new Offaly constituency. Her decision to run comes from her belief that successive governments have neglected her area. She has worked in the BBC News and Current Affairs and World Service Television. She also worked in hospital administration in Saudi Arabia and managed a waste company with her late husband. She has received leadership training through Toastmasters International and has particular interests in the impact of wind energy on rural communities, the need for increased Garda resources and the need to defend Irish neutrality in the centenary year of the 1916 Rising.

Roscommon–Galway

Outgoing Deputies:
Michael Fitzmaurice (Ind), Frank Feighan (FG), Denis Naughten (Ind).

Denis Naughten (Ind) lost the Fine Gael party whip on 7th July 2011 and subsequently resigned from the party. He will contest the 2016 election as an independent,

Luke 'Ming' Flanagan (Ind) was elected to Dáil Éireann in 2011 but was elected to the European Parliament in 2014.

Michael Fitzmaurice (Ind) was elected in the resultant Dáil by-election in October 2014

Frank Feighan (FG) announced in July 2015 that he would not contest this election.

The Constituency:

This is a three-seater, consisting of the County of Roscommon augmented by the transfer of 33 electoral divisions from Galway East with a population of 20,521. Nine of the transferring electoral divisions were previously in a Roscommon constituency. They are in the Former Ballinasloe No. 1 Rural District, the Former Glennamaddy Rural District, the Former Mount Bellew Rural District and Dunmore North and Toberadosh in the Former Tuam Rural District. Meanwhile a large portion of South Leitrim which was combined with Roscommon to make up the Roscommon–South Leitrim constituency for the last election has now gone back to a reformed and redesigned Sligo–Leitrim constituency.

	% Vote 1997*	% Vote 2002*	% Vote 2007§	% Vote 2011§	Quotas 2011
Fine Gael	36.91	30.69	39.13	38.53	1.5
Labour	1.48	1.28	1.81	9.38	0.4
Fianna Fáil	47.02	40.76	38.84	14.95	0.6
Sinn Féin	–	3.37	8.41	9.76	0.4
Green Party	–	0.86	1.81	0.46	0.02
Others	14.59	13.63	23.05	26.92	1.1

* Counts Longford–Roscommon Figures

§ Counts Roscommon–South Leitrim Figures

2016 Candidates will include:

Maura Hopkins (FG), John Kelly (Lab), Eugene Murphy (FF), Shane Curran (FF), Claire Kerrane (SF), Miriam Hennessy (GP), Eddie Conroy (AAA–PBP), Anne Farrell (Renua), Michael Fitzmaurice (Ind)

In Brief:

Roscommon is one of two constituencies where siblings from two separate parties are competing against each other in this election. Senator John Kelly is again the Labour Party candidate and his sister Anne Farrell is running for Renua Ireland. Neither of them will get elected. All has changed utterly in Roscommon politics since 2011. Roscommon is no longer combined with South Leitrim, but is instead merged with some of east Galway to make this new three seat constituency. Meanwhile Roscommon County Hospital, which has been a potent political force for decades, has again given rise to dramatic political fallout since the last election. It has created such convulsions in Fine Gael that the party is without both of its outgoing deputies for this election. Frank Feighan is stepping down while Denis Naughten is contesting as an independent. Naughten is likely to retain his seat. In addition, the colourful independent Luke 'Ming' Flanagan, who was elected here in 2011, has since gone to the European Parliament and was replaced by the politically less volatile independent Michael Fitzmaurice in the 2014 by-election. Fitzmaurice too will retain his seat. The third seat will be a battle between Fine Gael, Fianna Fáil and Sinn Féin. The Fianna Fáil selection process from which new Dáil candidate Councillor Eugene Murphy emerged was particularly convoluted. Fine Gael's selection of its sole candidate, Maura Hopkins, was more straightforward and while it will be difficult for Fine Gael to win a seat alongside Naughten she is likely to do so. Notwithstanding all the drama since 2011 the allocation of seats between the parties and independents is likely to be the same as in the outgoing Dáil, one Fine Gael TD and two independents.

Fine Gael:

Denis Naughten and Frank Feigan have been the Fine Gael ticket in this county for two elections. Combined, the two of them took 39.2% of the first preferences in 2007 and 38.5% in 2011. Denis Naughten left the party shortly after the 2011 election. In 2014 Frank Feighan announced that he would not contest this election. Both of their decisions arose from the party's policy in government to reverse its stance on keeping the accident and emergency department of Roscommon County Hospital open. Naughten left the party over the failure to keep the original pledge and Feighan is not recontesting because of the backlash he received locally for the closure. Naughten is standing as an independent in 2016. The party has decided on a single candidate strategy for 2016.

Maura Hopkins is from Ballaghaderreen, and has been a member of Roscommon County Council since 2014. In the local elections she polled 840 votes (7.3%) in the Boyle electoral area and took the third of the six seats. She was also the party's candidate in the 2014 by-election and her 5,593 first preference votes (16.79%) put her in third place. She is an occupational therapist who works with stroke victims and lists her outside interests as Macra na Feirme and GAA. She says she stands for election because her generation has born the brunt of the economic collapse.

Labour Party:

John Kelly is based in Castlemore, Ballagaderreen and has been a member of Seanad Éireann since 2011. He first won a seat on Roscommon county council when he stood in the Ballagaderreen electoral area in the 2004 local elections. He polled 1,101 first preferences (22.83%). He performed equally impressively in the 2009 local elections when he stood in the Castlerea electoral area and polled 2,230 votes, which was almost a quarter of all votes cast. In the meantime he had stood as an independent in the 2007 Dáil election and polled 4,539 in what was then the Roscommon–Leitrim South constituency. In February 2010 Kelly joined the Labour party and when he stood for it in the 2011 Dáil election he got 4,455 votes. However, as the party's candidate in the 2014 by-election he polled only 2,037 (6.1%). He was elected to the Seanad in 2011 on the Administrative Panel, and is the Labour Party spokesperson on Arts, Heritage, Gaeltacht Affairs, Training and Skills in the Seanad.

Kelly was born in Ballintubber, County Roscommon but is now based in the Ballaghaderreen area. He worked as a Community Welfare Officer in the area for the HSE for 24 years. He is a brother of Anne Farrell who is the Renua Ireland candidate in this constituency.

Fianna Fáil:

Fianna Fáil ran two incumbents here in 2007 but had two new candidates in 2011, neither of whom won a seat. In the 2014 by-election Ivan Connaughton, an Athlone-based councillor, was the candidate. Although he topped the poll for the party with 22% he was 2,831 votes behind Michael Fitzmaurice for the seat on the last count. Fianna Fáil had some difficulty finalising its selection process in Roscommon for this election. In the summer of 2015 it was suggested that former Dublin South–West TD, Conor Lenihan, whose family have strong political roots in the Roscommon area, might either contest the convention or be imposed by party headquarters but there was a great deal of local resistance and he did not put himself forward for the final selection process. In October 2015 the party sought nominations for a selection convention for the constituency but did not fix a date for a convention. Cllr Ivan Connaughton was among those who put their names forward even though there had been earlier suggestion that he might leave the party. He subsequently withdrew his name from consideration for this election. By late December 2015 only two names remained on the list of ten possible candidates published in October, namely long-standing Strokestown-based councillor Eugene Murphy and Seán Óg Higgins from Ballintubber, the Chairperson of Roscommon Ógra Fianna Fáil. Ultimately on December 20th 2015 Eugene Murphy was selected to be the candidate but, in one final twist, the name of Shane Curran was added by national headquarters on January 10th 2016.

Eugene Murphy is based in Strokestown and has been a member of Roscommon County Council since 1985. Murphy was re-elected in 1991 and 1999. In November 2000 he failed by one vote to win the convention to be the party candidate for the 2002 election. He contested unsuccessfully for the Seanad election on the Agricultural Panel in 2007. He was re-elected comfortably to the county council in 2004, 2009 and 2014 polling 983, 964 and 1,149 (9.99%) first preferences respectively in the Boyle electoral area. Murphy works as a producer and presenter with a local radio station S.S.I.N.S.

Shane Curran is the former Connaught championship winning Roscommon county goalkeeper. Since retiring from inter-county football he has worked on developing his flood defence system business. He is involved in many community activities in the Castlerea area.

Sinn Féin:

Leitrim-based John McGirl once held a seat for Sinn Féin in this area. In 1957 he topped the poll in Sligo–Leitrim with 7,007 first preferences. He failed in subsequent election attempts in 1961, 1982 and 1987 but he remains the most successful candidate for Sinn Féin in this region. Martin Kenny was the candidate in 2011 and 2014, polling 4,637 in 2011 (9.8%) and 5,906 in 2014 (17.7%), although on that occasion Fine Gael's Maura Hopkins overtook him on transfers. The party has a new candidate in 2016.

Claire Kerrane from Castlerea is 23 years old and was previously secretary to the former independent deputy Luke 'Ming' Flanagan. A farmer's daughter and school teacher, she is now studying for an MA in Professional Education at NUI Galway.

Green Party:

The party ran candidates here in 2002, 2007 and 2011. Catherine Ansbro was the candidate in 2002, polling 426 votes. She later ran unsuccessfully for Boyle town council and that area of Roscommon County Council in 2004. Former south Leitrim spokesperson for the Labour Party, Garreth McDaid, was a Green Party candidate here in 2007 and 2011. He received 836 votes in 2007 and 105 when he unsuccessfully contested the Carrick-on-Shannon local election in 2009. In 2011 his vote fell to 220 (0.5%).

Miriam Hennessy made it to the final count in the Stillorgan area of Dún Laoghaire–Rathdown County Council in 2014 with 643 first preferences (6.51%). Originally from Roscommon she attended Ireland's first political campaign school EQUIP run by Women for Election in Athlone. The national organisation provides training and support to women from all backgrounds interested in a career in politics. She is a representative for the Environmental Pillar at the Board of the County Roscommon Integrated Local Development. She is also the Good Energy Alliance Ireland representative and very active in the anti-fracking campaign.

Anti-Austerity Alliance – People Before Profit:
Eddie Conroy is a community activist from Boyle who has been a leader in the local Right2Water campaign. He works at Trojan Computers in Boyle. He says it is hard to find a person aged between 18 and 27 in Boyle. 'Boyle has lost the fish factory, its hotel, two banks, its courthouse and the Garda station has had its hours much reduced. This is reflected in every community in Roscommon. We have been abandoned by the establishment parties.'

Renua Ireland:
Anne Farrell is from Oran, which is close to the Roscommon/Galway border. She initially joined the administrative and organisational staff of Renua because of her admiration for party leader Lucinda Creighton, although she has declined to back Creighton's position on abortion and describes herself as being both pro-life and pro-choice. She previously canvassed for President Michael D. Higgins and is the sister of Labour Senator John Kelly, who also runs in this constituency. She tried to persuade her brother to join her in Renua but says he was not interested. Before taking up a full time post with Renua she was a community welfare officer for twenty years and says that gave her particular concern about mental health services.

Independents:
Michael Fitzmaurice has been a member of Dáil Éireann since October 2014 and is contesting this election as part of the Independent Alliance. He was elected in the by-election caused by the election of Luke 'Ming' Flanagan (Ind) to the European Parliament in 2014. Fitzmaurice is a farmer and turf contractor and is head of the Turf Cutters and Contractors Association. He came second in the 2014 by-election on the first count with 6,220 first preferences (18.7%) but overtook Fianna Fáil's Ivan Connaughton with transfers. A close friend of Flanagan, he has described the importance of working with anyone in or out of government who will listen in order to bring services and opportunities to rural Ireland.

Denis Naughten is a native of Drum and is now based in Roscommon town. He has been a member of Dáil Éireann since 1997. He was elected to Seanad Éireann as a Fine Gael candidate in the Seanad by-election caused by the death of his father Liam the previous November. He was a Fine Gael member of Roscommon County Council from January 1997 to October 2003. He was first elected to Dáil Éireann in 1997, being re-elected in 2002 and 2007. He polled 6,652 in 1997, 6,660 in 2002 and 8,928 in 2007. In the 28th Dáil he was Fine Gael spokesperson on Youth Affairs, School Transport and Adult Education and on Enterprise, Trade and Employment. He later served as party spokesperson on Transport and on Agriculture from 2004–2007, and then as party spokesperson on Immigration and Integration between 2007 and 2010, when he lost his place on the front bench after supporting Richard Bruton's challenge to Enda Kenny's leadership. In October 2010, he was re-appointed to the front bench as party Deputy spokesperson on Health with special responsibility for Primary Care and Disability.

In the 2011 Dáil election Naughten polled 9,320 first preferences (19.6%) and took the third seat in the constituency. He was appointed Chairman of the Joint Oireachtas Committee on Health, Children and Youth Affairs in April 2011. In July of that year he voted against the government's decision to close the Roscommon County Hospital emergency department and lost the party whip. In September 2013 he and five of the Fine Gael parliamentarians who had voted against the Protection of Life During Pregnancy Bill 2013 formed the Reform Alliance. When some of them went on to form the new political party Renua Ireland in 2015 Naughten did not do so and confirmed he would contest this election as an independent. He is married, with four young children. He is a microbiologist with a science degree from University College Dublin and qualified as a researcher in biology from University College Cork.

SLIGO–LEITRIM

Outgoing Deputies:

John Perry (FG), Tony McLoughlin (FG), Michael Colreavy (SF)

In February 2015 Michael Colreavy (SF) announced that he would not be contesting this election.

The Constituency:

This is now a four-seater, consisting of the counties of Sligo and Leitrim with the addition of 36 electoral divisions from western Cavan with a population of 13,183. These are in the former Bawnboy Rural District, the former Cavan Rural District and the former Enniskillen No. 2 Rural District, and Loughdawan and Scrabby in the former Mullaghoran Rural District. The constituency also includes nine electoral divisions in South Donegal with a population of 8,779. These include the former Ballyshannon Rural District and the district of Ballintra, from the former Donegal Rural District.

	% Vote 1997	% Vote 2002	% Vote 2007	% Vote 2011	Swing 2011	Quotas 2011
Fine Gael	36.63	26.67	39.27	36.86	–2.41	1.5
Labour	10.86	4.96	3.89	10.25	6.36	0.4
Fianna Fáil	40.41	38.97	40.96	21.85	–19.11	0.9
Sinn Féin	7.10	10.21	11.73	13.30	1.57	0.5
Green Party	–	–	3.03	0.97	–2.06	0.04
Others	11.00	19.19	1.11	16.76	15.65	0.7

2016 Candidates will include:

Tony McLoughlin (FG), John Perry (FG), Gerry Reynolds (FG), Susan O'Keeffe (Lab), Marc McSharry (FF), Eamon Scanlon (FF), Martin Kenny (SF), Chris MacManus (SF), Leslie O'Hora (GP), Nigel Gallagher (AAA–PBPA), Finbarr Filan (Renua), Marie Casserly

(Ind), Declan Bree (Ind), Des Guckian (Ind), Bernard Sweeney (Ind), Gary Smylie (Ind)

In Brief:

All eyes will be on this constituency, not least to see if outgoing Fine Gael deputy John Perry, having gone to such lengths to get on the ticket, can retain his seat. Of the many constituency selection sagas in the lead in to this election this was the most dramatic, culminating as it did in a five day High Court hearing which raked over the coals of the Fine Gael selection convention held in Drumshambo on the 16th and into the early hours of the 17th of October 2015. The instruction to the convention to select one candidate from the Sligo end and one from the Leitrim end was always going to be contentious since the party already had two sitting TDs from Sligo. Tony McLouglin from Sligo and former Leitrim TD Gerry Reynolds were selected and the other Sligo deputy John Perry demanded to be added, citing what he said was a commitment to the parliamentary party from leader Enda Kenny that all sitting TDs would get the opportunity to contest the election. When irregularities in the convention process were exposed in evidence during Perry's subsequent High Court case the party, claiming a rise in support in recent months as rationale for running an additional candidate, added Perry to the ticket and settled the litigation. With either two or three candidates Fine Gael will struggle to win two seats in this newly configured constituency. Leitrim voters will be understandably tribal, since their county is once again united within one constituency and Gerry Reynolds will be the principle beneficiary of this. There is at most one Leitrim seat in this constituency and the county will rally to which ever of Reynolds or the Sinn Féin candidate Mark Kenny they perceive will most likely win the seat.

In Sligo the competition for the other two seats will be even more intense. Fianna Fáil's candidates are geographically close to each other, with Marc MacSharry in Sligo and former deputy Eamonn Scanlon in Ballymote. The two of them had 0.9 of quota in the Sligo–North Leitrim three-seater in 2011 and it would be a bad day for Fianna Fáil nationally if the necessary slight increase in vote share doesn't happen in this election. The party might have been in an even better place to win the seat if it had run just one Sligo candidate. Similarly, Fine Gael's chances of stopping Fianna Fáil would have been better if the party had only one Sligo candidate although the selection drama may engender a sympathy factor for Perry who had alienated some voters because of other controversies since 2011. Sinn Féin is without its outgoing deputy Michael Colreavy who has decided to retire after one term. However, it has a strong Leitrim candidate in Mark Kenny and has added Chris McManus. If he can gather sufficient votes and the party's typically strong internal transfer rate can be maintained across the county boundary the party will hang on to its seat. One Fine Gael seat is the only certainty here and the publication of any constituency polls during the campaign could have a decisive impact on the outcome, especially if they clarify who the strongest Leitrim candidate is.

Fine Gael:

When Sligo–Leitrim was last a constituency it was a four-seater; Fine Gael regularly split the seats two each with Fianna Fáil. However, Marian Harkin's election in 2002 meant that Fine Gael won just one seat. The outgoing frontbencher, Gerry Reynolds, who was based in Leitrim, lost his seat in that 2002 election. In 2007 the party ran a three-candidate strategy, with Michael Comiskey and Imelda Henry joining incumbent deputy John Perry on the ticket. Due to a belief that this strategy had not worked, Dublin Fine Gael HQ ordered that just two candidates be selected for the 2011 ticket, which caused some controversy at the convention. It had been widely assumed that three candidates would run and Michael Comiskey's failure to make the ticket meant that North Leitrim was unrepresented. Instead two Sligo candidates, Perry and Sligo Town based Tony McLoughlin, were selected and they each won a seat.

In October 2015 party headquarters issued a geographic directive to the convention, specifying that one candidate should be selected from Sligo–South Donegal and one from Leitrim–West Cavan. The convention selected one of the outgoing Sligo deputies Tony McLoughlin and the former Leitrim deputy Gerry Reynolds.

Tony McLoughlin is based in Barnasraghy, County Sligo and has been a member of Dáil Éireann since 2011. He was first elected to Sligo County Council in the mid-1970s and subsequently elected to Sligo Borough Council. He has served as mayor of Sligo on four occasions. His family has a long history in local politics. His uncle, Joe McLoughlin, represented Sligo–Leitrim in the Dáil from 1961 to 1979 and his late father, Pat, was a member of Sligo County Council and Sligo Borough Council and also served as Mayor of Sligo. McLoughlin ran unsuccessfully for a Dáil seat for the party in 1981. He took the first seat in each of the local elections he contested from 1991 to 2009, surpassing the quota on the first count on the last three occasions. He polled 2,054 in 2004 in Sligo Strandhill and 2,019 in 2009. In the 2011 Dáil election he took the second seat in Sligo–North Leitrim with 7,715 votes (17.37%). He is a member of the Joint Oireachtas Committee on the Environment, Culture and the Gaeltacht. Before his election to Dáil Éireann he worked in sales. He is married, with three grown up children, and is a keen GAA fan, having played for his local team in his youth. He worked formerly as a sales executive.

John Perry is a native of Ballymote in County Sligo. He has been a member of Dáil Éireann since 1997. In 1997 in Sligo–Leitrim he polled 5,786 first preferences and increased that to 6,897 in 2002 and to 7,910 in Sligo–North Leitrim in 2007. In 2007 he was the only Fine Gael candidate elected and took the second seat on the fifth count. In opposition he served as party spokesperson on Science, Technology, Small Business and Enterprise and the Border Counties and later as front bench spokesperson for the Marine. After the 2007 election he lost his position on the front bench but was appointed party spokesperson on Small Business in July 2010. In the 2011 Dáil elections he topped the poll with 8,663 votes (19.5%) and was appointed Minister of State for Small Business in the new Dáil. In July 2012 there was controversy over his claims for mileage expenses and in September 2013 he confirmed that he and his wife had reached an agreement with Danske Bank in relation to outstanding loans. In the July 2014 reshuffle he lost his post as Minister of State and in December of that year was reappointed to the Public Accounts Committee. In October 2015 he failed to be re-selected as a candidate in this constituency and then commenced a High Court challenge to the way in which the convention was conducted. On the 22nd December 2015 he was added to the Fine Gael ticket by the party's national executive. A native of Ballymote, he was educated at Corran College. He has been chair of a number of community groups, including Ballymote Community Enterprise. He is a former businessman.

Gerry Reynolds is a native of Ballinamore and now lives in Carrick on Shannon in county Leitrim. He was a member of Dáil Éireann from 1989 to 1992, and again from 1997 to 2002. He was a member of Seanad Éireann from 1987 to 1989 and from 1993 to 1997. He was first elected to Dáil Éireann for Sligo–Leitrim in 1989, polling 8,487 (19.8%) first preference votes. He lost the seat to Declan Bree in the 'Spring Tide' of 1992 with his vote falling to 6,348 (14.9%) but he regained his Dáil seat in 1997 with a very similar vote of 6,743 (14.9%). In 2002 he lost the Dáil seat to independent Marian Harkin, polling 6,192 (12.6%). He did not run in the Dáil elections of 2007 and 2011. In local elections he has been successful in the Ballinamore electoral area in 1999 and in Carrick-on-Shannon in 2004 and 2009. In 2014 he decided not to contest that seat citing personal reasons. In 2015 he decided to return to politics. He says that job creation in the region will be an important issue in this election campaign.

Labour Party:

Labour has suffered a steep decline here since Declan Bree won a seat for the party in 1992. In 1992 he took 17% of the vote to win, but in 1997 this fell to 10.86%, costing him his seat. In 2002 his vote fell a further 5%. By 2007, after Bree had left the party, candidate Jim McGarry polled just 3.89% of the first preferences. The party did not run a candidate in the old Sligo–Leitrim in 1987 or 1989, and recruited the one time Independent Socialist Bree, a regular Dáil candidate, to run in 1992. Bree's victory in 1992 was the first time that the party had made double figures in vote-share since 1965. Bree's election then was the only seat Labour has held in Sligo–Leitrim since the two counties first became an electoral constituency in 1948. In 2011 the party's new candidate was Susan O'Keeffe and she is again the candidate for the 2016 election.

Susan O'Keeffe is based in Sligo and she has been a member of Seanad Éireann since 2011. She is a member of the Oireachtas Banking Inquiry and was the party's candidate in the Ireland North West constituency in the 2009 European election. She finished eighth on the first count in that election, with 28,708 first preferences. In 2011, as the party's new candidate for the Dáil in the Sligo–North Leitrim constituency, she polled 4,553 first preferences, which grew with transfers to 6,646 votes before she was eliminated on the eighth count. She was subsequently elected to the Seanad on the Agriculture Panel. In 1995 as an investigative journalist it was her report on the World in Action programme on the Irish Beef Industry that led to the establishment of the Hamilton Tribunal of Inquiry.

Fianna Fáil:

Sligo–Leitrim has been a strong region for Fianna Fáil and it has held at least two seats here in each election from February 1973 until 2011. In 2007 Fianna Fáil employed a two candidate strategy here for the first time since 1977. John Ellis moved with his local area to Roscommon–South Leitrim, where he failed to get elected. leaving two of the 2002 candidates, Eamon Scanlon and Jimmy Devins, to contest in Sligo–North Leitrim where Devins took a seat. In 2007 Eamon Scanlon, surprised many by topping the poll ahead of sitting TD Jimmy Devins, who took the third seat. Devins did not contest the seat in 2011 and the party's two candidates were Eamon Scanlon and Marc MacSharry who polled 5,075 votes (11.4%) and 4,633 votes (10.4%) respectively although neither took a seat. The same two candidates are running on this occasion.

Marc MacSharry has been a Fianna Fáil member of Seanad Éireann since 2002 on the Industrial and Commercial panel. He is a member of the Oireachtas Banking Inquiry. He is the son of Ray MacSharry, former Fianna Fáil Minister and European Commissioner who was a TD for this constituency from 1969 to 1984. Marc has been Fianna Fáil's Seanad spokesperson on Communications, Marine and Natural Resources, then on Tourism and the Arts and more recently on Health. He has worked previously for the Irish Permanent Building Society, Celtic Foods and Sligo Chamber of Commerce. He currently has his own estate agency. This will be his second Dáil election after unsuccessfully contesting in 2011.

Eamon Scanlon was first elected to the Dáil for this constituency in 2007. He polled 9,258 for a 23.18% share in that election. In the 2002 election he polled 6,345 first preferences (almost 13% of the total vote) but failed to gain election. He was subsequently elected to the Seanad on the Agricultural panel. In 1991 and 1999 he was elected to Sligo County Council for the Ballymote electoral area. He is a butcher and an auctioneer and has been a member of the Governing Body of Letterkenny Institute of Technology and the Ballymote Community Enterprise Board. On 5th August 2009, he and fellow Sligo Fianna Fáil TD Jimmy Devins resigned the party whip over his opposition to cuts in breast cancer services at Sligo General Hospital. He rejoined the parliamentary party on 13th January 2011. He was re-elected to Sligo County Council in the 2014 local elections when he polled 1,106 (7.31%).

Sinn Féin:

The candidate in Sligo–North Leitrim in 2011 was Michael Colreavy, who polled 5,911 first preference votes (13.3%) to take the third of the three seats. In 2007 the party's candidate, Seán McManus, polled 4,684 for an 11.73% share of the vote. That share had been steadily rising in each of the previous three elections. In 1997 he polled 3,208 votes, which was just over 7% of the first preferences. In 2002 his support grew to over 10% as he polled 5,001 first preferences, which was just over half a quota. Colreavy is retiring at this election and this is the first time the party has run two candidates in this constituency.

Martin Kenny is from Aughavas and has been a member of Leitrim County Council for the Ballinamore electoral area since 2003. He was co-opted to replace Liam McGirl when he retired. Kenny topped the poll in the Ballinamore electoral area in the 2004 local elections with 860 votes (17.71%). He ran in the 2007 Dáil election in the Roscommon–South Leitrim constituency, polling 3,876 (8.41%) first preferences but not winning a seat. In the 2009 local elections he polled 661 votes (13.03%) and retained his seat. In 2011 he ran again in Roscommon–South Leitrim for the Dáil and increased his vote to 4,637 (9.76%). His vote share fell to 10.57% with 722 votes in the 2014 local elections, but that was because the party had added a third candidate to its team. In the October 2014 Roscommon–South Leitrim by-election caused by 'Ming' Flanagan's move to the European Parliament Kenny was third in the first preference poll with 5,906 votes (17.73%). He is a member of Sinn Féin's Ard Chomhairle and says he is determined to ensure that farmers can continue to cut turf on their own bogs. He is a member of his local GAA club and is interested in reading and history. He ascribes his membership of Sinn Féin to a long family background in the party as well as commitment to more recent issues. Married with four children, he did an engineering course with FÁS in Sligo and worked as coordinator for Lá Nua, a republican ex-prisoners group based in Leitrim – there were at one time over 80 ex-prisoners living in the area.

Chris MacManus is based in Sligo. He is the son of Seán MacManus, who was the party's candidate in Sligo in 1997, 2002 and 2007. He has served several years on Sinn Féin's national executive. In 1999 he was elected to Sligo Town Council with 525 votes (17.52%) and in 2004 he kept the seat with 462 votes (15.68%). He had a small part in the Ken Loach film *Jimmy's Hall*, which was released in 2014. Kenny was selected at the first party convention in March 2015 but Sinn Féin decided that it also needed a Sligo candidate and MacManus was selected at the Sligo convention in August. Supporters of Kenny have suggested that the move makes it less likely that any Sinn Féin candidate will be elected.

Green Party:

In 2007 the Green Party ran former Labour councillor for Sligo–Drumcliff Brian Scanlon in this constituency. Scanlon had left the Labour Party in 2006 and secured 1,209 first preferences in 2007. In 2011 the candidate was Johnny Gogan who managed only 432 votes (1.0%). It has a new candidate in 2016.

Leslie O'Hora is based in Carrick-on-Shannon. He is a founder member of the citizen science and education group Good Energies Alliance and has worked for a solar energy company for the last few years. Although he has been heavily involved in local anti-fracking campaigns he says his main issues are renewable energy, value added agri-food and tourism and digital hubs, and he wants to see rural communities using them to keep young people at home. He was involved in the set up of the Environmental Research Laboratory in Queens University Belfast.

Renua Ireland:
Finbarr Filan is a qualified Manufacturing Engineer who has worked in and managed in manufacturing, retail and construction. He is the brother of Shane Filan of Westlife, with whom he formed a property company to build 60 homes in Dromohair. The company went into receivership in 2012 owing €5.5 million and Shane Filan filed for bankruptcy in the United Kingdom. In 2010 Finbarr Filan bought the loss making Centra store in Castle Street and turned it into a success. In an interview in Hot Press magazine in August 2015 Finbarr talked extensively and emotionally about his younger brother Shane, going into business with the former Westlife singer and how their property development company went bust, forcing Shane to declare bankruptcy and move to England. He is Chair of the Sligo Business Improvement District, which works to offer a sustainable model for town and city centre management. He first took an interest in politics as a street ambassador when Sligo decided to work for the Purple Flag international nightlife tourism award.

Anti-Austerity Alliance – People Before Profit:
Nigel Gallagher is a 28-year-old graphic designer from Maugherow. He has recently been involved with the anti-water charges movement and the Yes Equality marriage referendum campaign. His platform will focus on emigration and Anti-Austerity issues. He works with the Hawks Well theatre.

Independents:
Declan Bree ran as an independent socialist candidate in 2011. He left the Labour party in 2007, citing differences with then-leader

Pat Rabbitte. He first ran for the Dáil as an independent representing the Sligo/Leitrim Independent Socialist Organisation, of which he was a founder, in 1977. In total he has run in ten Dáil elections in Sligo–Leitrim, winning election for the first and only time as a Labour Party candidate in 1992. He failed to defend his seat in 1997 and by 2002 his vote had fallen from 17.15%, when he won election, to 4.96%. He was first elected to Sligo Corporation and Sligo County Council in 1974 and has retained his seat on both authorities at each subsequent election, standing most recently in the Sligo local electoral area in 2014 and topping the poll with 1,848 first preferences. In the 2011 general election his vote was 2,284 (5.1%). He was Mayor of Sligo in 2004 and was Chairman of Sligo County Council in 1986. An active trade unionist, Bree is a former member of the western branch committee of the Federated Workers Union of Ireland and is currently a member of the Sligo branch of SIPTU. Bree is a former National Chairperson of the Connolly Youth Movement. He is also a member of the Executive of the Local Authority Members Association and was Cathaoirleach of the host branch of Comhaltas when Fleadh Cheoil na hÉireann was awarded to Sligo.

Marie Casserly is from Streedagh and has been an independent member of Sligo County Council since 2014. She is contesting the 2016 election as part of the Independent Alliance. She polled 1,195 first preferences (7.14%) in 2014 when she took the third seat in the Sligo electoral area. She has decided to refuse approaches from existing political parties and remain an independent. Her husband Mel unsuccessfully contested the 2011 Seanad Éireann on the Industrial and Commercial panel in 2011. Marie Cassidy is a school teacher and mother of five with a BA, an H Dip. Ed., and a postgraduate diploma in Guidance Counselling. Her community activities have included the provision of a playground in North Sligo, the founding of Grange Men's Shed, involvement in An Taisce National Spring Clean projects, coaching girls' gaelic games and helping to found a local Senior Athletics club.

Des Guckian has been an independent member of Sligo County Council since 2014. He unsuccessfully contested the 2009 local elections in the Carrick-on-Shannon electoral area and got just 281 votes (5.27%). In the 2014 local elections he ran again and polled 671 (12.49%) votes to take the fourth seat. In 2014 he also contested the Roscommon–South Leitrim by-election and he polled 902 first preference votes, a 2.7% share.

He proposes the creation of a Special Western Development Region, within Europe, with grants and incentives to support agriculture, tourism, 'employments such as meat processing, MBNA etc, integrated transport and a broad range of service employments to bring us into line with the far more developed East.' He campaigns against the repealing of the 8th Amendment and against fracking.

Gary Smylie is a Community Worker from Sligo town. Educated at Sligo IT who says he stands shoulder to shoulder with Right2Water.

Bernard Sweeney is a 40-year-old father of four from Market Yard, Sligo. He is a member of the Traveller community, and has a background as a community worker and in conflict resolution (including cross border reconciliation). He says 'Irish people are suffering and experiencing real austerity which I fully understand as the Travelling community have suffered this for decades. I see myself working very successfully with the parties of the left such as People Before Profit and the Anti-Austerity Alliance.' He is a computer technician contracted to several businesses in the Sligo region.

Tipperary

Outgoing Deputies Tipperary North:
Michael Lowry (Ind), Noel Coonan (FG), Alan Kelly (Lab)

Outgoing Deputies Tipperary South:
Tom Hayes (FG), Séamus Healy (WUAG), Mattie McGrath (Ind)

The Constituency:
This is a new five seat constituency consisting of the County of Tipperary with the exception of 19 electoral divisions in the former Borrisokane Rural District and 5 electoral divisions in the former Nenagh Rural District with a population of 10,953 which have been transferred to Offaly and the divisions of Kilmacomma and Kilronan in the former Clonmel No 2 Rural District with a population of 1,597 which have been transferred to Waterford.

Tipperary North

	% Vote 1997	% Vote 2002	% Vote 2007	% Vote 2011	Swing 2011	Quotas 2011
Fine Gael	11.32	14.91	15.89	23.67	7.78	0.9
Labour	10.33	13.52	10.27	19.80	9.53	0.7
Fianna Fáil	42.29	42.66	34.31	16.53	–17.78	0.8
Sinn Féin	–	–	3.76	6.28	2.53	0.3
Green Party	–	–	1.11	0.85	0.26	0.03
Others	36.07	25.39	34.66	32.87	–1.79	1.3

Tipperary South

	% Vote 1997	% Vote 2002	% Vote 2007	% Vote 2011	Swing 2011	Quotas 2011
Fine Gael	24.09	24.54	21.14	34.57	13.43	1.4
Labour	16.11	9.14	8.77	10.94	2.17	0.4
Fianna Fáil	37.28	38.51	46.42	13.10	–33.41	0.5
Sinn Féin	–	3.30	3.09	4.50	1.41	0.2
Green Party	–	–	1.51	0.89	–0.62	0.04
Others	22.51	24.50	19.05	36.00	16.95	1.4

2016 Candidates will include:

Noel Coonan (FG), Tom Hayes (FG), Marie Murphy (FG), Siobhán Ambrose (FF), Jackie Cahill (FF), Michael Smith (FF), Alan Kelly (Lab), Seamus Morris (SF), Seamus Healy (WUAG), Gearóid Fitzgibbon (GP), Caroline Hofman (Ind), Michael Lowry (Ind), Michael Dillon (Ind), Mattie McGrath (Ind)

In Brief:

The amalgamation of the two Tipperary constituencies into one five-seater follows on from the amalgamation of the North and South Riding County Councils into one council. The contest here will not lack for drama or colourful characters. Six outgoing deputies are contesting for the five seats, one Minister in the form of Labour Deputy Leader Alan Kelly, one junior minister in the form of Fine Gael's Tom Hayes, a government back bencher in the form of Fine Gael's Noel Coonan, the left wing TD Seamus Healy and two high profile and at times controversial independents in the form of Michael Lowry in the north and Mattie McGrath in the South.

Michael Lowry will hold his seat. Although his impressive political organisation is focused on North Tipperary he is strong enough there to get a quota or thereabouts.The two sitting Fine Gael TDs also look good to hold their seats. They are well positioned at either end of the county and have a strong sweeper in the form of Marie Murphy in Clonmel. The battle for the other two seats will be shaped by both geography and positioning on the political spectrum. Minister Alan Kelly's seat is in real jeopardy. In theory, and even on the 2011 figures, there should be enough space in the five-seater for Fianna Fáil, who once had four of the six seats in the county, to regain one seat. Michael Smith Jnr in the north looks the strongest of the Fianna Fáil candidates although Siobhan Ambrose in Clonmel could beat him, depending on the performance of other candidates in the south. The third Fianna Fáil candidate Jackie Cahill, the former Preident of the ICMSA, will have the advantage of name recognition countywide but has a weaker electoral record than the other two. The party's chances of winning a seat might be easier if they had one candidate less.

Another key factor which may shape the outcome is that in addition to Ambrose there are two sitting deputies at the Clonmel end of the county. Its difficult to see both Mattie McGrath and Seamus Healy getting elected out of Clonmel but whichever one of them is the stronger is likely to win a seat. In the last election Healy was the stronger and if Fianna Fáil recover that should harm McGrath.

The line up, the amalgamation, and the geographic considerations make this constituency difficult to predict but there should be two Fine Gael seats, a seat for Michael Lowry, a Clonmel seat for either Healy or McGrath and a Fianna Fáil seat for either Smith or Ambrose. Much will depend on whether Alan Kelly can appeal across the county and how Labour does generally in the campaign. If Kelly upsets things in the north that will impact both on which of the Fianna Fáil candidates are strongest and whether Healy wins a seat. At this stage Kelly's task looks insurmountable however.

Fine Gael:

Noel Coonan is based in Roscrea and has been a member of Dáil Éireann for Tipperary North since 2007. In 2002 he came very close to winning a Dáil seat. The Fine Gael resurgence of 2007 did not sweep through North Tipperary, the party's vote there increasing by just 1%, but that was enough to enable Coonan to finally win a seat. He polled 7,061 first preferences – about 1,000 more than his 2002 tally – and took the second seat on the sixth count. In 2011 he ran again as the sole candidate for the party, polled 11,425 first preferences (23.7%) and took the second seat behind Michael Lowry (Ind). Coonan was a member of Tipperary North County Council from 1991 to 2004 for the Templemore electoral area and was also a member of the town council. He was elected to the Seanad on the Cultural and Educational Panel in 2002 after an unsuccessful attempt at the Agricultural Panel in 1997. He is President of the Collins 22 Society, a Michael Collins remembrance group.

Tom Hayes is a farmer based in Golden and has been a member of Dáil Éireann for the Tipperary South Constituency since 2011. He has been Minister of State for Food, Horticulture and Food Safety since June 2013. He contested the two by-elections in 2000 and 2001, securing the vacant seat in the latter, after Theresa

Ahearn's death. Hayes held the seat as the only candidate in 2002 and 2007, topping the poll on both occasions. In the 2002 general election he was only 170 votes below the quota with 8,997 votes. In 2007 he held the seat again although his first count vote at 8,200 was nearly 1,500 votes below quota. In 2011 Clonmel-based councillor Michael Murphy joined Hayes on the ticket in a bid to add an extra seat in the context of the national anti-Fianna Fáil mood. However, former Fianna Fáil TD Mattie McGrath left the party and ran as an Independent and only Hayes came home for Fine Gael, topping the poll again with 8,896 votes (21.5%)

Hayes is a former member of Tipperary South Riding Council for the Cashel electoral area. He was a member of Seanad Éireann from 1997 to 2002 on the Agricultural Panel. He was chairman of the Fine Gael parliamentary party from September 2002 to March 2010. In October 2010 Hayes was appointed party Deputy spokesperson on Transport with special responsibility for Road Safety.

Marie Murphy is a native of Clogheen and has been a member of Tipperary County Council for the Clonmel-Cahir electoral area since 2009. In the 2014 local elections in the enlarged Clonmel electoral area she polled 1,060 (6.77%) first preferences to take the eighth of the nine seats. In the 2009 local elections she polled 980 (14.59%) first preferences in the smaller Cahir electoral area and took the fifth seat. She had unsuccessfully contested in the same area in 2004. As a county councillor she has been a member of both the Environment and Water Services and the Housing Policy and Social Development SPCs. She has a degree in accounting and has been a full time public representative since 2009.

Labour Party:

Labour's candidate in Tipperary North in the 2011 general election was Alan Kelly, who ran a strong campaign to take the third seat with 9,559 first preference votes (19.8%). Seamus Healy's Workers United Action Group assumed the mantle of the left in South Tipperary following the death of former Deputy Michael Ferris in 2000. Philomena Prendergast was Labour's candidate there in 2011 with 4,525 (10.9%). In this newly amalgamated constituency the party is wisely running just one candidate.

Alan Kelly is based in Nenagh and has been a member of Dáil Éireann since 2011. He has been Minister for Environment, Community and Local Government since July 2013. He is Deputy Leader of the Labour party. He first ran for national office when he contested on the Agricultural Panel for the 2007 Seanad Election and won a seat. He then ran as the party candidate in the Ireland South constituency in the 2009 European election. He polled 64,152 first preferences, which was a 12.88% vote share. He took the third and final seat, becoming the first Labour MEP elected here since the late Eileen Desmond in 1979. In 2011 he became the party's Dáil candidate in Tipperary North and at his first attempt polled 9,559 (19.8%) and took the third of the three seats. In his first week in Dáil Éireann he was was appointed Minister of State for Public and Commuter Transport. He was elected deputy leader of the party after the resignation of Eamon Gilmore as party leader. In July 2014 he became Minister for the Environment, Community and Local Government. Unusually for a senior politician he has never served in local government.

Kelly worked previously as an e-business manager with Fáilte Ireland. He was founder of the Jim Kemmy Branch of the Labour party in University College Cork in 1995 and was national Chair of Labour Youth in 2000. He is the author of *A Political History of County Tipperary 1916-1997*. He holds a BA in History and an MPhil in Politics from University College Cork and a MBS in eCommerce from University College Dublin.

Fianna Fáil:

The national party issued a directive to the convention in Tipperary in June 2015 to select just one candidate. Jackie Cahill, a new councillor in the Templemore area, was a surprise selection. The party since added two other councillors, Siobhán Ambrose in the south and Michael Smith, also in the Templemore area.

Siobhán Ambrose is based in Clonmel and has been a member of Tipperary South, and then Tipperary, county council since 2009. She is the only one of the three party candidates in this election who has previously contested a Dáil election. She ran for the party, with Mattie McGrath, in South Tipperary in 2007. On that occasion she polled 4,286 first preferences (11.1%) and her elimination gave McGrath the second seat. She comes from a political family – her father was mayor of Clonmel and she herself was Mayor of Clonmel 2010/2011 and says that she grew up 'putting leaflets into envelopes'. She was elected to Clonmel Borough Council in 2004 and In the 2009 local election she was elected to South Tipperary County Council polling 1,160 (10.82%) and taking the second seat in the Clonmel electoral area. In the 2014 local elections she polled 1,449 (9.25%) in the same enlarged electoral area. Ambrose has a Diploma in Marketing from Waterford Institute of Technology and a certificate with distinction in Community Waste Management. She is a member of South Tipperary General Hospital's 'Save Our Acute Hospital Services' Committee.

Jackie Cahill is based in Killinan, near Thurles, and has been a member of Tipperary County Council since 2014. He was just doing his Leaving Certificate and getting ready to head for university to study accountancy when his father asked him to take over the family farm instead. He says it was something of a shock but he stuck with the farm and instead of accountancy went into farming politics to complement the work on his 220 acre dairy and other livestock farm. Eventually he became President of the ICMSA, Chairman of the Irish Dairy Council, a member of Bord Bia and Director of Thurles Greyhound Stadium. When he finished his term leading the ICMSA he says it was perhaps inevitable that when he needed something to fill the time left over from farming he went into politics. He was elected to Tipperary County Council in the Templemore-Thurles electoral area on his first run in 2014, with 1,097 first preference votes (5.86%) and took the last of the nine seats. Fianna Fáil won four of the nine seats in that area in that election.

Michael Smith Jnr farms in Roscrea and has been a member of North Tipperary and then Tipperary County Council since 2004. He is another candidate who has grown up in politics, since his father, also Michael Smith, represented Tipperary North for almost 40 years, from 1969 to 2007, only failing to be elected in 1973 and the two elections of 1982. He was first elected as a County Councillor in 2004 in the Templemore electoral area with 1,206 votes

(14.64%). In 2009 he topped the poll there for the first time with 1,791 (20.36%). In 2014 he topped the poll in the Templemore-Thurles electoral area with 2,568 (13.72%) which was 1.37 quotas He is a former Vice Chairperson of North Tipperary County Council and in June 2014 was accused of 'backstabbing' his party colleagues when he was proposed by Sinn Féin and Independents, including Micheál Lowry Jnr to become district chairman and voted with them against his party's nominee.

Sinn Féin:

Seamus 'Séamie' Morris is based in Rathnaleen and was first elected to Nenagh Town Council in 2004 when he topped the poll and took the first seat with 396 votes. He was then the party's candidate in the 2007 Dáil election, their first since since Jimmy Nolan in 1992. In 2007 Morris polled just 1,672 first preferences, a 3.76% share. In the 2009 local elections he was elected to Tipperary North Riding County Council for the Nenagh electoral area, polling 933 first preferences (8.69%) and taking the sixth and final seat. In the 2011 Dáil election, again as the party candidate in Tipperary North, he improved his general election performance significantly to 3,034 votes, a 6.3% share. In 2014 he was again comfortably re-elected to the county council with 1,731 first preferences (9.29%). He comes from a very strong republican household, his father having been interned for six weeks in the late 1970s. He describes the impact on himself and his nine siblings as being traumatic. He worked previously as a postal worker.

Green Party:

In 2007 Paul McNally, an architect running a practise specialising in low-energy, ecological buildings, received 495 first preferences here for a 1.11% share of the vote in North Tipperary, while Bernard Lennon took 591 votes (1.5%) in South Tipperary. In 2011 McNally ran in South Tipperary where he got 367 votes (0.9%) while Olwyn O'Malley ran in North Tipperary polling 409 (0.8%). She runs in Offaly this time.

Gearóid Fitzgibbon is originally from a dairy farm in Effin Co. Limerick but is now a community development officer with North

Tipperary Leader partnership. He has worked on community energy schemes, community education and capacity buildup, and startup company support. He has also worked as a Human Rights Accompanier in occupied Palestinian territories and as a documentary film maker. He says he will campaign for energy transition in Tipperary and that if elected, he will give 35% of the TD's €87,358 salary to the Citizens Information Service.

Workers and Unemployed Action Group:

Seamus Healy is based in Clonmel and has been a member of Dáil Éireann from 2000 to 2007 and again since 2011. He runs under the banner of the local Clonmel Workers and Unemployed Action Group. He first contested a Dáil election in 1987 when his 1,457 votes represented 3.51% of the poll. After that he steadily increased his vote in the 1992 and 1997 general elections. He finally won a seat in a dramatic by-election victory in 2000. In the 2002 general election he retained it comfortably with 7,350 first preferences (20%). In 2007, however, there was a sharp reduction in his vote, to 14.72% and he lost the seat to Fianna Fáil's Martin Mansergh, albeit by just 59 votes.

In 2011 Healy and his Workers and Unemployed Action Group ran under the United Left Alliance banner. He topped the poll in the constituency with 8,818 votes (21.3%). In December 2011 he launched a national campaign against the household charge, which was subsequently abandoned in favour of the property tax. Healy is a former member of Clonmel Town Council and of Tipperary South Riding County Council for the Clonmel electoral area. When he last contested a local election in 2009 he received 2,336 first preferences in 2009. That total was 1,000 above quota, more than a thousand above his nearest rival and was a 21.78% share. 65-year-old Healy is a former hospital administrator. He is a brother of high-profile former Teacher's Union of Ireland (TUI) President and Seanad candidate Paddy Healy.

Independents:

Michael Dillon is a former Labour Party member who ran as in Independent in Nenagh for the Tipperary County Council in 2014, receiving 296 votes (1.59%). He has said that he will not be using posters and will not canvass. According to his FaceBook page 'Mickey Dillon is the only candidate seeking election that is on the dole. He is 24 and is from Portroe. He fights against Irish water and feels very strongly about mental health awareness and suicide awareness...believe me lads this man is a vault of knowledge and ideas'

Caroline Hofman is a 21-year-old based in Roscrea. She declared her candidacy in May 2015. She says that studying for a degree in government at University College Cork has allowed her to understand how the Irish political system works and that she can bring a fresh view and voice to Dáil Éireann. She says that rural Ireland is recovering more slowly than the east and that more energy needs to be put into jobs and infrastructure creation in Tipperary. Her parents have a business in the north of the county. She was a finalist in the Miss Cork competition. She works as an HR assistant in the legal firm McCann Fitzgerald.

Michael Lowry is based in Holycross and has been a member of Dáil Éireann since 1987. He has topped the poll in each of the four general elections in Tipperary North since he became an Independent before the 1997 general election. He was first elected to Dáil Éireann in 1987 as a Fine Gael deputy, He was appointed Minister for Transport, Energy and Communications in 1994 but resigned in controversial circumstances in November 1996. He resigned from the Fine Gael parliamentary party in 1997. In 2002 his vote was down from 11,638 first preferences in 1997 to 10,400 first preferences. This represented a 4% drop, which he reversed in the 2007 election. In 2007 he received 12,919 first preference votes (29.1%), and in 2011 14,104 (29.2%). He is a former chairman of the Tipperary county board of the Gaelic Athletic Association.

Lowry was a member of Tipperary North county council from 1979 to 1995. He was re-elected to the council in the 1999 local elections in the Thurles local electoral area, receiving more than two and a half quotas. He had to resign from the council because of the dual mandate ban in 2004. However, his 27-year-old son Micheál topped the poll in the Thurles electoral area with 1,671 first preferences. Micheál Lowry was re-elected in 2009, although with a reduced vote-tally. Micheál forms part of his father's electoral machine known as 'Team Lowry' which also includes several other members of North Tipperary County Council in Thurles and Templemore. In 2007 Michael Lowry Snr was one of four independent TDs who supported Bertie Ahern's re-election as Taoiseach. Despite threatening to withdraw his support on a number of occasions he continued to vote with that government and supported their 2011 Budget. Lowry is currently seeking a High Court judicial review to have proceedings brought against him by the Director of Public Prosecutions and the Revenue Commissioners in relation to the filing of tax returns struck out. Lowry disputes the charges and the matter has not yet come to trial.

Mattie McGrath is based in Clonmel and has been a member of Dáil Éireann since 2007. He was a Fianna Fáil member of Tipperary South Riding County Council for the Cahir electoral area from 1999 until his election to Dáil Éireann in 2007. He topped the poll in 2004's local elections in the area, with 1,902 first preferences, which was 600 votes over the quota, and was Chairperson of South Tipperary Co. Council in 2004/2005. In Dáil Éireann he was frequently at odds with the Fianna Fáil leadership and eventually lost the party whip in June of 2010 when he voted against legislation to restrict Stag Hunting. He continued to criticize Fianna Fáil government policy on many national and local issues such as Tipperary South General Hospital and finally left the party and ran as an Independent in 2011 when he took the third seat in Tipperary South with 6,074 votes (14.7%). Born in 1958, he has lived in Newcastle, Clonmel, ever since. He has a certificate in horticulture from Kildalton Agricultural College and a Diploma in communication skills from University College Cork. From 1977 to 1982 he was a Sales Representative servicing the agricultural industry in the local area and subsequently developed his own local plant hire business. He is married with eight children and is a former All Ireland set dancer.

WATERFORD

Outgoing Deputies:

John Deasy (FG), Paudie Coffey (FG), Ciara Conway (Lab), John Halligan (Ind)

The Constituency:

This four-seater encompasses the administrative city and county of Waterford. Kilmacomma and Kilronan in the Former Clonmel No2 Rural District with a population of 1,597 have been transferred from the former Tipperary South to this constituency since 2011.

	% Vote 1997	% Vote 2002	% Vote 2007	% Vote 2011	Swing 2011	Quotas 2011
Fine Gael	24.55	21.48	27.36	38.00	10.64	1.9
Labour	11.77	13.36	11.33	18.97	7.64	0.9
Fianna Fáil	35.79	46.34	46.49	13.99	–32.50	0.7
Sinn Féin	–	6.35	6.72	9.94	3.22	0.5
Green Party	1.81	2.92	2.12	0.86	–1.26	0.04
Others	16.85	9.56	6.00	18.23	12.23	0.9

2016 Candidates will include:

Paudie Coffey (FG), John Deasy (FG), Mary Butler (FF), Ciara Conway (Lab), David Cullinane (SF), Grace O'Sullivan (GP), Una Dunphy (AAA–PBP), Mailo Power (Ren), John Halligan (Ind)

In Brief:

The two Fine Gael seats are safe. The party got 1.9 quotas in 2011 and the two candidates are well placed in different areas. Coffey is seen locally as well in with the party leadership and his promotion to Minister of State has helped his position. Deasy, who cuts somewhat of an anti-establishment pose, attracts a strong personal and local vote. John Halligan, the outgoing independent deputy, also looks as if he will hold his seat. Halligan will benefit from the growth in support for independents generally since 2011, not least because he is one of the deputies behind the Independent Alliance initiative. The Labour seat is vulnerable. It had 0.9 quotas with two candidates in 2011. The poll trends suggest it will have considerably less than a quota on the first count in this election which is why it is running just one candidate, the sitting deputy Ciara Conway. The difficulties for her arising from the party's falling vote share are compounded by the fact that as a sole candidate she is not based in the city itself where most of the left wing vote is. Sinn Féin's David Cullinane was tipped for a Dáil seat here in 2011, but the Sinn Féin vote was only up marginally, in part because of the nationwide surge then for Labour. This time there is a more pronounced increase in the Sinn Féin vote and Cullinane is likely to take Conway's seat.

Fine Gael:

John Deasy is based in Dungarvan and has been a member of Dáil Éireann since 2002. He was elected to Dáil Éireann on its first attempt in 2002. He was then appointed the party's spokesperson on Justice, Equality and Law Reform by Enda Kenny, but was removed from that front bench position in April 2004 after a controversy about a breach of the smoking ban in the Dáil bar. In January 2007 he announced his intent to challenge Enda Kenny for leadership of Fine Gael if the party should fail to enter government, but in the event he did not carry out the threat. In the 2007 the party ran three candidates, Paudie Coffey, Jim D'Arcy and Deasy. Deasy was well ahead of the other two, and kept his seat comfortably. D'Arcy and Coffey were eliminated on the sixth and ninth counts respectively. In 2011 the party ran only two candidates, Deasy and Coffey. Deasy topped the poll with 10,718 first preferences (20.0%). He served as party Deputy Spokesperson on Foreign Affairs with special responsibility for Overseas Development Aid from 2007 to 2010. He was chair of the Joint Oireachtas Committee on European Affairs 2002 to 2007. He is currently a high profile and effective member of the Public Accounts Committee. A graduate of Mercyhurst College, he worked as a legislative assistant in the United State senate from 1990 to 1991 and in the United State House of Representatives from

1993 to 1995 before returning to Ireland to take a Bachelor of Law degree at UCC. He was a member of Waterford County Council for the Dungarvan electoral area from 1999 to 2004.

Paudie Coffey is based in Portlaw and has been a member of Dáil Éireann since 2011. He has been Minister of State with responsibility for Housing, Planning and Co-ordination of the Construction 2020 Strategy at the Department of the Environment, Community and Local Government. He was a member of Waterford County Council from 1999 to 2007. In the 2004 local elections he polled 834 first preferences in the Suir electoral area, where he took the last of the three seats. He polled 4,658 first preferences, almost half a quota, in his first Dáil contest in 2007. After his unsuccessful Dáil campaign in 2007 he was elected to the Seanad in July 2007 and in 2011 he took second place in the poll with 9,698 votes (18.1%). He was previously an engineering officer with the ESB. His brother. Brendan Coffey was co-opted to Waterford County Council when he was elected to the Seanad and Brendan was elected for the Comeragh LEA in 2009 on the first count with 1.21 quotas. In the 2014 however Brendan lost his council seat having polled just 577 first preferences.

Labour Party:

There was a delay in putting the Labour ticket in place in 2011 because of the late decision of sitting deputy Brian O'Shea to retire. O'Shea had been the party's deputy here since 1989 and their candidate since 1982. His strongest performance was in 1992 when he got more than 26%. In 2007 he polled 11.3%. With Labour's vote on the rise and Fianna Fáil shrinking the party would have been expected to hold its seat notwithstanding O'Shea's resignation. With a two candidate strategy the seat might have been vulnerable but in the event Ciara Conway and Seamus Ryan both polled well with a combined vote share of 18.9% for the third seat.

Ciara Conway is based in Dungarvan and has been a member of Dáil Éireann since 2011. In the 2011 as part of a two candidate ticket she polled 5,554 (10.3%). She is Vice-Chairperson of the Joint Oireachtas Committee on Health, Children and Youth Affairs and a member of the Oireachtas Committee on Finance, Public Expenditure and Reform. She was a strong supporter of steering the Protection of Life During Pregnancy Bill 2013 through the Dáil. Conway was formerly a Councillor on Dungarvan Town Council, to which she was elected in June 2009. She served as Anti-Discrimination Officer in NUI Galway Students Union between 1999 and 2000 while studying for a degree in Public and Social Policy. She has previously worked as a social worker and in family support services, and was a service and development facilitator for the Barnardos charity.

Fianna Fáil:

Fianna Fáil ran its outgoing deputy Brendan Kenneally in 2011. Kenneally was first elected to the Dáil in 1989 and retained his seat until losing it at the 2002 general election. He regained the seat in the 2007 general election at the expense of his party colleague Ollie Wilkinson. In 2011 Kenneally polled 7,515 (14%), but failed to get enough transfers to turn that into a seat. Fianna Fáil has a new candidate in 2016.

Mary Butler is a native of Comeragh and is based in Portlaw. She has been a member of Waterford County Council since 2014. She is the current chair of Portlaw Comogie club and Secretary of Portlaw Tidy Towns. Butler is keen to make it clear that she was not imposed to fulfill the gender quota, but was chosen by the Waterford Fianna Fáil convention over four male contenders for the candidacy. On her first electoral outing in 2014 she took the sixth seat in Comeragh with 639 votes (7.08%). She is a Board Member of Déise Link and of Waterford Theatre Royal.

Sinn Féin:

David Cullinane is based in Lisduggan in Waterford city and has been a member of Seanad Éireann since 2011. In the 2002 Dáil election he polled 2,955 first preferences and was eliminated on the seventh and last count. He was Sinn Féin's candidate in the Munster constituency in the 2004 European elections and received 6.74% of the first preference vote. On the same day in the 2004 local elections he was elected to Waterford City Council representing the No. 3 ward where he polled 1,109, well above the quota of

861. He was again the party candidate for the 2007 Dáil election, polling 3,327 first preferences (6.7%) and being eliminated on the 7th count. In the 2009 local elections he was re-elected to Waterford City Council representing the Waterford South ward. In 2011 he increased his vote to 5,342 (9.9%) but still failed to take a seat. He was subsequently elected to the Seanad on the Labour panel. He formerly worked in the motor trade. He is married to Kathleen Noctor who is again the Sinn Féin candidate for this election in the Carlow– Kilkenny constituency.

Green Party:

In 2011 the Green Party candidate was Jody Power who polled only 462 (0.9%). His vote was probably damaged not only by the previous Fianna Fáil coalition but by the presence on the ballot paper here of Ben Nutty, brother of Green Party official Stiofán Nutty, running on the platform of Green Party left wing breakaway party Fís Nua. Ben Nutty polled 257 votes (0.5%). The party has a new candidate for 2016.

Grace O'Sullivan is best-known for her high-profile activism during her 20-year career with Greenpeace. She is a former Irish surfing champion and has worked for the past number of years as an environmental education specialist and ecologist. She was Coxswain with the Tramore RNLI inshore lifeboat by the time she was 18 and left Tramore to join Greenpeace, crewing on the Rainbow Warrior, the boat that was bombed by the French secret service in Auckland, New Zealand. She later worked as assistant to the Campaign Director and as Human Resources Manager for Greenpeace International. Grace returned to Tramore in 2000 with her three children and undertook a distance learning course in Field Ecology at UCC as well as other courses at the Open University and the Waterford institute of technology. Following on from time spent working as Environmental Educationalist at the Smithsonian Environmental Research Center in Maryland, USA, Grace has worked as an eco guide with Oceanics Surf School and Marine Education Centre in Co. Waterford. She runs ongoing ecological tours and workshops with T-Bay Surf and Eco Centre in conjunction with the primary and secondary school curriculum and has been involved in the creative and strategic development of T-Bay from an exclusive surf base to the broadening of the business to cater for eco-tourism opportunities.

She ran as the Green MEP candidate for the Ireland South constituency in the 2014 European election polling 27,860 first preference votes (4.2%) and surviving to the eighth count.

Renua Ireland:

Mailo Power is a hotelier from Waterford who says she joined Renua because of the challenges facing small family run businesses. With a BA from Waterford IT and an MA from Gloucester University she has chaired the Winterval Hospitality Committee since 2012. As well as being on the committees of many leading hospitality industry organisations she previously served as Chairperson of the Inaugural OCS Irish Paralympic Awards.

Independent:

John Halligan is based in John's Hill in Waterford city and has been a member of Dáil Éireann since 2011. He was a candidate for the Workers' Party in the 2002 and 2007 Dáil elections. He achieved 2.7% in the 2002 general election and 3.4% in 2007 general election. In 2008 he left the Workers' party because he wanted to vote for local authority service charges, which the Workers' Party has long opposed as a form of double taxation. In 2009, he ran as an independent in the local elections, standing in the Waterford South electoral area for the city council. On that occasion he received 24.11% of the vote and took the sixth seat. He was Mayor of Waterford for the council year 2009/ 2010. In 2011 he contested the Dáil election as an independent and his vote increased dramatically to 5,546 votes (10.3%) and took the final seat in this four seat constituency. He joined the Technical Group in the Dáil in order to improve his speaking rights, which has allowed him to address issues such as the pension rights of former Waterford Crystal workers and the cutbacks at University Hospital Waterford. He also brought forward a bill on Restorative Justice, proposed a bill on assisted suicide and campaigned for the suspension of drivers charged with causing a fatal accident pending trial. Along with other independent deputies Shane Ross, Finian McGrath and Michael Fitzmaurice, Halligan has been one of the drivers behind the Independent Alliance.

Wexford

Outgoing Deputies:

Mick Wallace (Ind), Brendan Howlin (Lab), John Browne (FF), Liam Twomey (FG), Paul Kehoe (FG)

In July 2015 Liam Twomey announced that he would not be contesting this election.

In September 2015 John Browne announced that he would not be contesting the election.

The Constituency:

This five-seater coincides with the administrative county of Wexford. The four key towns are, from north to south, Gorey, Enniscorthy, Wexford and New Ross. The boundaries of this constituency are unchanged since 2007.

	% Vote 1997	% Vote 2002	% Vote 2007	% Vote 2011	Swing 2011	Quotas 2011
Fine Gael	38.58	25.74	31.56	34.46	2.90	2.1
Labour	19.69	13.23	13.77	20.47	6.70	1.2
Fianna Fáil	38.95	40.09	42.19	18.57	–23.62	1.1
Sinn Féin	–	8.22	7.39	5.76	–1.63	0.3
Green Party	1.68	–	1.17	0.52	–0.65	0.03
Others	1.11	12.72	3.93	20.22	16.29	1.2

2016 Candidates will include:

Michael D'Arcy (FG), Julie Hogan (FG) Paul Kehoe (FG), Brendan Howlin (Lab), James Browne (FF), Aoife Byrne (FF), Malcolm Byrne (FF), Johnny Mythen (SF), Ann Walsh (GP), Deirdre Wadding (AAA–PBP), Leonard Kelly (SD), David Lloyd (DD), Mick Wallace (Ind4Change), Ger Carthy (Ind), Caroline Foxe (Ind), Emmet Moloney (Ind)

In Brief:

There is definitely one safe Fine Gael seat for the Government: Chief Whip Paul Kehoe. Outgoing Independent deputy Mick Wallace is also safe. Although the Wallace family base is in Wellington Bridge in the south, his profile is such that he will get votes in every box in the county. There is also one safe Fianna Fáil seat and James Browne wears the strongest Fianna Fáil brand name in the county. He is likely to comfortably retain the seat that has long been held by his father John Browne, who is retiring. Unless there is a complete collapse for Labour in this election Brendan Howlin will hold his seat. He has a strong base in the Wexford area and recognition across the county for his work as a Minister. There is then a four-way scrap for the remaining seat. This is between two Gorey-based candidates, Fine Gael's Michael Darcy and Fianna Fáil's Malcolm Byrne, Sinn Féin's Johny Mythen, who is based in Enniscorthy, and independent councillor Ger Carthy, who is based in the Wexford area. Whether the Gorey end of the county, which currently does not have a TD, rallies behind one candidate or transfers strongly between the two will be a key factor. So too will be the transfer rate within the Fine Gael and Fianna Fáil tickets. Sinn Féin's candidate Johny Mythen has the advantage of being his party's only candidate. Although Sinn Féin did very well in the 2014 local elections and now has five members of Wexford County Council, it would take a dramatic increase in the party vote on 2011, when they only got a third of a quota, to win a seat here. Meanwhile if Carthy's base in the Wexford areas gets him high enough on the first preferences he would take transfers from all sides. It is impossible to call.

Fine Gael:

Fine Gael was traditionally a one-seat party in this constituency. It held that single seat in Wexford in every election from 1943 to 1981. In 1981 it became much more competitive, managing two seats at least up until 2002 when then independent Liam Twomey, who ran for Fine Gael in 2011, took a seat from Michael D'Arcy senior. The party's strong performance in the 1980s and 1990s corresponded to a jump in vote share to a consistent 30% or more. This established a pattern whereby Fianna Fáil would finish in the forties, Fine Gael in the thirties and Labour would fail to reach the twenties. Fine Gael did manage to exceed Fianna Fáil's seat tally in 1981 and November 1982, but did not beat its share of the vote in this constituency until 2011. In that year Fine Gael ran a three-candidate ticket and hoped to take three seats for the party with sitting deputies Kehoe and D'Arcy and former independent TD for the area Senator Liam Twomey. With the intervention of Independent Mick Wallace having changed the traditional patterns in the constituency and Liam Twomey deciding not to contest, the party is still adopting a three candidate strategy in 2016.

Paul Kehoe is based in Enniscorthy and was first elected to Dáil Éireann in 2002. He has been Government Chief Whip and Minister of State at the Department of Defence since 2011. He secured 7,048 first preferences then, which he increased to 8,459 on his re-election in 2007. His 2002 election tally was more than 2,500 ahead of the outgoing deputy Michael D'Arcy and more than 3,000 ahead of the MEP and former deputy Avril Doyle. In 2007 he similarly topped the party ticket, almost one thousand votes ahead of Michael D'Arcy junior and three thousand ahead of Liam Twomey. 2011 saw Twomey as the party's front-runner and Kehoe in second place with 8,386 votes (11.1%).

Kehoe was deputy spokesperson on Communications, Marine and Natural Resources from 2002 to 2004. He was Fine Gael whip in opposition before assuming the same role in government in 2011. A farmer, he is a former national chairman of Macra Na Feirme and a former youth officer with Wexford Gaelic Athletic Association.

Michael D'Arcy is based in Gorey and has been a member of Seanad Éireann since 2011. He was a member of Dáil Éireann from 2007 to 2011. He is a member of the Oireachtas Banking Inquiry. He was first elected to Wexford County Council for the Gorey electoral area in 2004, after having been co-opted to replace his father in 2003. He topped the poll in that election with 1,952 first preferences. In 2007's Dáil election he received 7,692 first preferences, an improvement of over three thousand votes on his father's showing in 2002, and he held onto the family seat. However, in 2011, although he polled fractionally ahead of Kehoe with 8,418 first preferences, Labour transfers favoured Kehoe and he did not get a seat. He was subsequently elected to the Seanad on the Administrative panel and he is Fine Gael spokesperson on Finance there. He is a farmer and, with a degree from the University of London, has been an apprentice solicitor and won an All-Ireland junior medal with Wexford. He is married with two children.

He is a former Director of Wexford County Enterprise Board, Wexford Organisation for Rural Development and Courtown Waterworld Ltd. His father Michael D'Arcy senior first ran for the party in the area in 1973. He was a member of Dáil Éireann from 1977 to 1987, from 1989 to 1992 and from 1997 to 2002 and was a member of Seanad Éireann from 1992 to 1997.

Julie Hogan is originally from Saltmills in the New Ross area in the south of county but has lived and worked in Wexford town for 25 years. This is her first election. She was added to the party's ticket in this constituency by the national executive in January 2016, thereby giving some gender balance to the ticket. She works as a manager with Eishtec, the outsource contact company which is a large employer in Wexford town. She has been a volunteer with Wexford Festival Opera and has taken part in various fund raisers for Ben5k and Run for Nepal. She says she 'contacted Fine Gael, having been supporter for a number of years, in September, to express my interest in representing Wexford town and south county'. She attended secondary school in Ramsgrange.

Labour Party:

Brendan Howlin is based in Wexford town and has been a Dáil deputy since 1987. He has been Minister for Public Expenditure and Reform since 2011. In the 1987 election he reclaimed the 'Corish' seat that Labour had long held in this constituency. He went on to top the poll in the 'Spring Tide' election of 1992, more than doubling his party's 1987 vote. The party saw only a slight decrease in 1997, but the vote share fell gradually from 1997 to 2011. In 2011 Labour ran a two-candidate ticket in Wexford for the first time in a generation, with clinical nurse Councillor Pat

Cody from Enniscorthy joining Howlin on the ticket. Cody polled 4,457 (5.9%) which transferred solidly to Howlin, who had himself polled 11,005. The party has sensibly decided to revert to a single candidate strategy for this election. From 1997 to 2002 Howlin was deputy leader of the Labour Party and he was an unsuccessful candidate for the leadership in 2002. He was Leas-Cheann Comhairle from 2007 to 2011, Minister for the Environment from 1994–7 and Minister for Health from 1993 to 1994. He was a Taoiseach's nominee to Seanad Éireann from 1982 to 1987. He is a former primary school teacher and a prominent trade unionist. His father, John, served on Wexford Corporation for 18 years and was a local trade union official. Brendan himself is named after former local TD Brendan Corish and served on Wexford Borough Council after 1981. His brother, Ted, has been a member of Wexford Town and Wexford County Council.

Fianna Fáil:

For 2016 the party will return to a three-candidate strategy. For the purpose of the constituency convention the national party directed that the county be divided (unusually) on an east-west basis with one candidate to be selected from the New Ross and Enniscorthy areas combined and another to be selected from the Gorey and Wexford areas combined. Malcolm Byrne was selected unopposed for the Wexford area and James Browne was selected for the New Ross/Enniscorthy area. Aoife Byrne was added to the ticket by party headquarters in December 2015 in order to ensure gender balance.

James Browne is based in Enniscorthy and has been a member of Wexford County Council since 2014. In that election he topped the poll and took the first seat with 1969 first preferences which was 1.33 quotas. He was elected to Enniscorthy Town Council in 2009 at the age of 25. He is the son of outgoing Fianna Fail TD John Brown who has been a member of Dáil Éireann since 1982. John Browne's last four first preference vote tallies were 8,646 in 1997, 9,150 in 2002, 12,768 in 2007 and a crash to 7,352 (9.7%) in 2011. James is a barrister and practises on the South Eastern Circuit. He studied at Waterford Institute of Technology, University College

Cork and Kings Inns. He played GAA for Marshalstown and Soccer for Moyne Rangers. Browne has been advised by his father to 'throw away all these Facebook and Twitter things' and get out on the road and meet the people.

Malcolm Byrne is from Gorey and has been a member of Wexford County Council since 2009. A former law student at UCD, he was Vice-President of the National Youth Council of Ireland, Education Officer of the Union of Students in Ireland and a member of the executive of the European Students Union. He is now Head of Communications with the Higher Education Authority. He was elected on the first count to Gorey Town council in 1999 and again in 2004, and to Wexford County Council in 2009. He was first elected to Wexford County Council in 2009 when he polled 1,927 votes (13.89%). In the 2014 local elections he topped the poll in the Gorey electoral area with 1,688 first preferences. He was the Chairman of Wexford County Council 2014/15. He does not come from a political background and in his spare time he runs marathons and is a member of his local musical society. He is a former Chief Executive of the National Community Games.

Aoife Byrne is originally from Fethard-on-Sea in the New Ross area, but has lived in Wexford town for the last 15 years. Her father Hugh Byrne was a member of Dáil Éireann for this constituency from 1981 to 1989 and from 1992 to 2002. She has been a member of Fianna Fáil throughout those years but was not always active. She says this was because she became disillusioned for a while. She has an MBA and then gained a job in AIB with the aid of JobBridge. Her addition to the ticket in early December 2015 caused significant controversy in the party organisation, particularly as her father had publicly supported New Ross Councillor Michael Sheehan for the selection convention on the 17th October.

Sinn Féin:

The party ran no candidate here in 1997 but in 2002 its new candidate, John Dwyer, put in an impressive performance, polling 4,674 first preferences. He saw his vote share slip in 2007, from 8.22% to 7.39%, but increased his vote tally to 5,068. Dwyer left the party in June of 2009 after failing to gain re-election to his Wexford

County Council seat. Citing what he said was the party's 'failure to win the hearts and minds' of the working class he was critical of what he said was a strategy of focusing particularly on high-profile candidates. He announced that he had decided to contest future elections as an independent left candidate, starting with general election 2011. Sinn Féin's 2011 general election candidate was Wexford Town Councillor Anthony Kelly who polled 4,353 first preferences and was eliminated on the fifth count. The party has a new Dáil candidate for this election.

Johnny Mythen is based in Enniscorthy and has been a member of Wexford County Council. He polled 1,812 (13.6%) first preferences in the Enniscorty electoral area in the 2014 local elections and was just behind James Browne (FF). His selection was something of a surprise since many had expected the party's new councillor in the New Ross area, Oisin O'Connell, to be the Dáil candidate as he would have been geographically well placed to maximise the chance of winning the seat. After being defeated at the convention, Councillor O'Connell pledged his 'complete support' to Councillor Mythen for the campaign.

Green Party:

The Green Party ran a candidate for the first time here in 1997. Marie Percival, who went on to contest unsuccessfully for local election in the Celbridge area in 1999 and 2004, polled 938 first preferences. Its candidate in 2007 was Ballymitty-based Tom Harpur who received 802 first preferences.

Ann Walsh is originally from New Ross but now lives in Castletown. She says the Green Party represents integrity and that in the present situation collaboration is more useful than conflict. With an MA in Forensic Psychology and Criminology and an H. Dip in Human Givens Psychotherapy she has particular personal and professional expertise in the areas of mental health and disability. She is married with two children. She is campaigning for a healthcare and mental healthcare system that is fit for purpose and focuses on prevention, and a political system with strong regulation that puts the responsibility for environmental action on government, rather than individuals.

Anti-Austerity Alliance – People Before Profit:

Deirdre Wadding is based in Gorey and has been a member of Wexford County Council since 2014. She is a recent arrival to political activism and says she was brought to the party by a wish to campaign effectively against home and water taxes. She ran in the 2014 local elections in the Wexford electoral area and took 599 first preference votes (3.76%) to take the final seat. She hopes to become the first pagan in the Dáil. A former teacher she worked with travellers in inner city Dublin and is a shamanic healer. Her election to Wexford County Council cost her her lone parent's allowance as the Councillor's wage of €16,500 a year plus allowances took her over the €425 a week qualifying level.

Social Democrats:

Leonard Kelly failed to take a seat in the 2014 county council elections when he ran as an independent. On that occasion he polled 499 first preferences (3.13%) and was the last candidate to be eliminated in the Wexford electoral area. The engineer and father of four young children has a long history of community involvement in the town. He is on the board of Wexford Educate Together primary school and Wexford County Childcare Committee and recently helped to set up the Friends of Its Good to Talk. He has degrees in Quality Management and in Counselling and Psychotherapy. He has worked in the medical devices, Pharmaceuticals and Manufacturing sectors. The party had initially selected sociologist and author Shay Dunphy to contest in this constituency but in October 2015 he pulled out of the election race in Wexford saying that he would not be able to devote the amount of time needed to his candidacy due to his work as a teacher at Waterford Institute of Technology.

Direct Democracy:

David Lloyd is a native of Wexford town where he has worked as an electrician for the last 15 years. He was a candidate for Direct Democracy Ireland in the Wexford LEA of Wexford County Council in 2014. His 114 votes saw him almost on the bottom of the poll. He trained in Waterford Institute of Technology and then

Cork Institute of Technology. Issues he highlights include household and water taxes, the withdrawal of heating and phone allowances, and the dangers of electromagnetic radiation from new electricity pylons.

Independents 4 Change:

Mick Wallace topped the poll in 2011 with 13,329 votes, 17.6% of the total poll and 739 over the quota. Interestingly that 739 vote surplus was shared around the other candidates of all political persuasions. Wallace's name has been in the news throughout the current Dáil. In 2011 the Commercial Court ordered him to repay more than €19 million to ACC Bank. In 2012 he made a seven figure settlement with the Revenue Commissioners for non-payment of VAT, having admitted to knowingly making false declarations and he has promised to pay over half of his Dáil salary as a gesture to pay down this revenue debt. As a TD he has used Dáil privilege to highlight information given to him by whistle blowers in An Garda Síochána, particularly about irregularities in the penalty point system, and whistle blowers about some contracts entered into by NAMA. In 2014 he and close political ally Clare Daly TD were arrested for trespassing airside at Shannon Airport and subsequently fined. Choosing not to pay their fines they were arrested, taken to prison and immediately released.

He was born and brought up in Wexford and lived there during his marriage but now lives in Dublin. His vote in the constituency in 2016 may be influenced by the fact that he is seen more as a national than a local politician. He is the founder and originally the principal funder of Wexford Youth, the League of Ireland soccer club based in Crossabeg.

Independents:

Breda Cahill, who was to have run, has had to pull out for health reasons but hopes to run in the future.

Caroline Foxe is the postmistress at Foulksmill in the southern part of the county. Her campaign will focus on the need to keep post offices alive because of the many community services they provide. As well as highlighting the importance of local businesses in keeping communities alive she has a special emphasis on the need to improve the health services.

Ger Carthy is based in Our Lady's Island and has been a member of Wexford County Council since 2014. He is the current Mayor of Wexford, and the first Mayor to come from the town's rural hinterland. He says he sees part of his role as Mayor being to promote job creation and help ameliorate the rates burden on small businesses. His father Leo was elected to Wexford County Council for the Wexford local electoral area in 1999 and 2004 but lost his seat in 2009. Ger topped the poll to retake the seat in the 2014 local elections with 1,932 votes, almost 500 over the quota. In his home parish of Lady's Island an emergency extra ballot box had to be shipped in when the original filled to capacity.

Ger Carthy qualified as a carpenter but joined the National Ambulance Service and has a diploma in Emergency and Medical Technology from University College Dublin. He now works as a Paramedic Supervisor. He has helped develop first responder schemes and anti-suicide initiatives, and chairs a community employment board that covers several rural parishes. Within the GAA he is development officer of the County Board. He is married, with two children.

Emmet Moloney is based in Selskar and his campaign is focusing on Wexford's crime problem. He previously canvassed for Colm O'Gorman in 2007. He worked as a manager for Dunnes Stores in various outlets before coming home to Wexford as a manager at the Eishtec contact centre. He says that while he is opposed to some of the austerity measures he is more centrist than parties such as People Before Profit. As well as highlighting issues such as Garda station closures and an excessively lenient judicial system he also wishes to emphasise the need to improve the county's mental health care.

WICKLOW

Outgoing Deputies:

Andrew Doyle (FG), Billy Timmins (Renua), Simon Harris (FG), Anne Ferris (Lab), Stephen Donnelly (SD).

In 2011 Billy Timmins (Renua) was elected as a Fine Gael candidate. He has since left the party and was one of the founders of Renua Ireland.

The Constituency:

This is a five-seat constituency. Its area incorporates the administrative county of Wicklow and a portion of county Carlow including Clonmore, Hacketstown, and Rathvilly. The boundaries of this constituency are unchanged since 2011.

	% Vote 1997	% Vote 2002	% Vote 2007	% Vote 2011	Swing 2011	Quotas 2011
Fine Gael	19.71	15.97	23.15	39.61	16.46	2.4
Labour	23.79	29.55	16.34	17.14	0.80	1.0
Fianna Fáil	29.87	31.27	38.06	10.59		0.6
Sinn Féin	–	2.80	4.98	10.06	5.08	0.6
Green Party	2.48	5.88	7.38	1.46	–5.92	0.1
Others	24.14	14.53	9.99	21.14	11.15	1.3

2016 Candidates will include:

Avril Cronin (FG), Andrew Doyle (FG), Simon Harris (FG), Anne Ferris (Lab), Pat Casey (FF), Jennifer Cuffe (FF), John Brady (SF), Steven Matthews (GP), Sharon Briggs (AAA–PBP), Anna Doyle (AAA–PBP), Billy Timmins (Renua), Stephen Donnelly (SD), Joe Behan (Ind), Robert (Bob) Kearns (Ind), Charlie Keddy (Ind)

In Brief:

Fine Gael pulled off quite a feat here in 2011, winning three of the five seats on just 2.4 quotas. Simon Harris took the third of those seats. The fast talking Minister of State will be one of the most high profile spokespersons in the national Fine Gael campaign for this election and he is likely to top the poll here in Wicklow. The poll topper in 2011 was Andrew Doyle who is based in Roundwood. He too should hold his seat on this occasion. The third Fine Gael seat was lost to them for the second half of this Dáil term because Billy Timmins was expelled for voting against the Protection of Life in Pregnancy Bill in 2013 and is now the Deputy Leader of Renua Ireland. Fine Gael will put in a determined effort to win it back off him in this election but geographic factors will assist Timmins in retaining it. Stephen Donnelly, who had no political base or experience before the 2011 election, still managed to take the last seat then. He has had a high national profile and built a strong local political operation even before he became joint leader of the new Social Democrats party and he too should hold his seat. Labour say that their new 2011 deputy Ann Ferris is one of their safest seats in the country. It difficult to see how this can be the case since she is a first term TD and this is a constituency which swings strongly with the national mood. In addition Fianna Fáil has a strong ticket here, seeking to regain a seat and the former Independent Fianna Fáil gene pool TD Joe Behan can also be expected to put in a determined effort to get back into Dáil Éireann. The strongest challenge to Ferris's seat may come from Sinn Féin's John Brady, who just missed out on a Dáil seat in 2011. One seat for Donnelly, one for Harris seems certain, one each for Doyle and Timmins seems probable, after that any of Ferris, Behan, either of the Fianna Fáil candidates or Sinn Féin's John Brady seems possible.

Fine Gael:

In 2011 the party ran three candidates: the two incumbents, Billy Timmins and Andrew Doyle, along with Simon Harris. They took the first three seats with 39.6% of the poll, but Billy Timmins has now left the party and runs for Renua in 2016. Fine Gael meanwhile is running the remaining two deputies and a new female candidate.

Avril Cronin is a native of Dunlavin and is a first time candidate. She has worked as a parliamentary assistant to formerly Fine

Gael and now Independent Dublin South TD Peter Mathews. She is 29 years of age and has an MA in Public Affairs and Political Communication. She is the secretary to the Dunlavin Fine Gael branch and before moving to the Dáil to work was an employee of Kildare County Council and Kildare–West Wicklow Community Addiction Services.

Andrew Doyle is Roundwood-based and has been a member of Dáil Éireann since 2007. In the 2007 elections he took the last seat on the ninth count. Doyle was a member of Wicklow County Council from 1999 to 2007, representing the east Wicklow electoral area. In the 2004 local elections he polled 2,008 first preferences, which was 168 above the quota in that electoral area. He was chairman of Wicklow County Council for the 2005–06 year. Having trained in agriculture in Rockwell College and New Zealand, where he also played rugby, he is the sixth generation running his family farm. In July 2010 he was made party spokesperson on Agriculture, Fisheries and Food, having served as deputy spokesperson on Agriculture with special responsibility for Food and Horticulture from 2007 to 2010. In 2011 he topped the poll and took the first seat in this constituency with 10,035 (14.2%). He is now chair of the Oireachtas Joint Committee on Agriculture, Food and the Marine. He is married, with four children.

Simon Harris is based in Greystones and has been a member of Dáil Éireann since 2011. He is Minister of State at the Department of Finance with special responsibility for the Office of Public Works, Public Procurement and International Banking. He was a member of Wicklow County Council and Greystones Town Council before being elected to Dáil Éireann, having been elected to the county council on his first attempt in 2009. He polled 3,119 in that election, which was almost a third of all votes cast in the Greystones electoral area and was the highest percentage vote of any county councillor in the country at 31.76%. He worked as political advisor to then Senator and now Justice Minister, Francis Fitzgerald, when she was a party front bench member and health spokesperson. In the 2011 Dáil election he polled 8,726 for the third seat in this constituency. He is the youngest member of the Dáil. He has been a member of the Public Accounts Committee and of the Joint Oireachtas Committee on Finance, Public Expenditure and Reform. As a member of the Oireachtas cross party group on Mental Health he introduced the Mental Health (Anti Discrimination) Bill 2013 in that year. In 2014 he was an unsuccessful Fine Gael candidate in the European Parliament election in the South constituency. He polled an impressive 51,483 first preference but was eliminated on the 12th count and his running mate Deirdre Clune won the only Fine Gael seat in the constituency. He has a BA in Journalism from the Dublin Institute of Technology. He is the founder of the Wicklow autism charity the Wicklow Triple A Alliance.

Labour Party:

In 2007 Labour ran two candidates here: the former Democratic Left deputy Liz McManus, who always had a strong base in the Bray and Greystones areas, and Arklow-based councillor Nicky Kelly. With neither McManus nor Kelly contesting the 2011 election the party ran three candidates, Anne Ferris, Tom Fortune and Conal Kavanagh, and transfers gave Ferris a very secure fourth seat despite an initial poll of only 5,436 (7.7%). The party's total vote share in 2011 was 17.2%. Ferris is the party's sole candidate in this election.

Anne Ferris is based in Bray and has been a member of Dáil Éireann since 2011. She was a close political associate of the Labour Party's Liz McManus, with whom she worked for two decades as personal assistant, whilst also managing the Labour Party constituency office in Bray. Ferris is a former Cathaoirleach of Wicklow County Council and of Bray Town Council. She was co-opted to the county council for the Bray area in 2003 and was elected there in the 2004 local elections. She did not contest the 2009 county council election. She holds a Diploma in Women's Studies from Maynooth University.

Fianna Fáil:

In 2011 Fianna Fáil's vote suffered particularly badly in this constituency with veteran TD Dick Roche and his running mate Cllr

Pat Fitzgerald achieving only 10.6% of the first preference vote between them. The party will run two new candidates in 2016.

Pat Casey is based in Glendalough and has been a member of Wicklow County Council since 2004. He stood as an independent candidate in the 2004 local elections and took the third seat in the Wicklow electoral area with 1,152 (11.2%). He joined Fianna Fáil in 2006. He contested the 2009 local elections as a Fianna Fáil candidate again in the Wicklow electoral area, receiving 1,595 first preferences, which was 0.8 of a quota. In the 2014 local elections he polled 1,152 and took the third of the six seats, again in the Wicklow electoral area. He announced almost immediately that he would seek the party nomination for the Dáil election, saying he believed the county was suffering because it had no Fianna Fáil TD. He is the proprietor of The Glendalough Hotel.

Jennifer Cuffe is based in the Greystones and Bray area. She was selected unopposed at the party convention because she was the only candidate from the north end of the constituency. The 29 year old family law barrister is a member of Dún Laoghaire–Rathdown county council for the Killiney–Shankhill electoral area which borders county Wicklow. In the 2014 local elections she polled 1,286 votes and took the third seat in Killiney–Shankhill. In April 2015 she sought unsuccessfully to be selected as the party candidate in the Dun Laoghaire constituency. In a YouTube video she says that it was her experiences with St Vincent de Paul, the Lions Club and Meals on Wheels that made here decide to get involved in politics.

Sinn Féin:

John Brady is based in Bray and has been a member of Bray Town Council since 2004, and of Wicklow County Council since 2009. He was previously the Sinn Féin Dáil candidate here in the 2007 and 2011 elections. In 2007 he received 3,324 votes, a 4.98% share of the poll, and was eliminated on the fourth count. In 2011 he improved that vote to 7,089 (10.1%), losing the fifth seat to Independent Stephen Donnelly by only 112 votes in the final count. In the 2004 Bray Town Council election his 492 votes (8.41%) gave him the fifth seat, in 2009 his 1,899 votes were over the quota and

the 2014 Wicklow County Council election he topped the poll and took the first seat in the Bray area with 2,142 votes (16.95%) which put him more than 800 votes over the quota.

Green Party:

The 2011 Green Party candidate, Niall Byrne, failed to gain election to Wicklow County Council in 2004 as an independent or as a Green Party candidate in 2009. In the 2011 general election his vote was 1,026 (1.5%). This time the party's candidate will be Steven Mathews.

Steven Mathews was a member of Bray Town Council from 2007–2009 after he was co-opted to replace Deirdre de Burca, but failed to hold the seat in 2009. He took the seventh seat in the Bray electoral area in 2014 with 752 votes (6.01%). A founder of Bray Cyclists Forum he holds a BSc in Planning and Environmental Management from DIT and is the Environment representative on Bray Town Council Planning and Infrastructure MPC and is Chairperson of the Wicklow Green Party. He has been an electrician at Irish Rail for 25 years.

Anti-Austerity Alliance – People Before Profit:

Sharon Briggs is based in Bray. In the 2014 local elections she polled 560 first preference votes (4.47%) in the Bray electoral area. She came within 20 votes of taking the eighth seat. She has been a prominent protester against water metering and has campaigned for the removal of head shops and the property tax, against the downgrading of the local A&E, and most recently as part of the Right2Water and Right2Housing movements.

Anna Doyle is based in Ashford. She ran in the Wicklow electoral area in the 2014 local elections and polled 165 votes (1.6%). She was a one of the founders of the Right2Water Wicklow movement and was also directly involved with the wider 'meter watch' community. She has participated in campaigns such as that against household and water tax and the Forest campaign. She is a member of the direct steering committee of People Before Profit, and she sits on the committee of Wicklow Pride as an LGBT activist. She is a member of the parent's council of CCM and a founding member of the Public and Private Tenants Union which is affiliated to Right2Housing.

Renua Ireland:

Billy Timmins is based in Baltinglass and has been a member of Dáil Éireann since 1997, He was comfortably re-elected in 2004. In 2007 he polled 8,072 first preference votes. From 2007 to 2010 Timmins was Fine Gael spokesperson on Foreign Affairs. He was appointed Deputy spokesperson on Social Protection in 2010. In the 2011 Dáil election he polled 9,165 first preference votes (13%), which gave him the second seat. In 2013 he was expelled from Fine Gael when he was one of those who voted against the Protection of Life During Pregnancy Bill (2013) and later that year he was one of those who formed the Reform Alliance. He is now deputy leader of Renua Ireland. From 1997 to 2004 he was a member of Wicklow County Council for the Baltinglass electoral area. He was educated at University College Galway, where he took a BA in Economics and Legal Science, and at the Military College at the Curragh. As an army officer he served in the Lebanon and Cyprus with the United Nations. His father, Godfrey Timmins, was TD for Wicklow from 1965–1997.

Social Democrats:

Stephen Donnelly is based in Greystones and has been a member of Dáil Éireann since 2011. He is joint leader of the Social Democrats. He was a management consultant with McKinsey & Company when he announced his intention to run as an independent candidate in January 2011. At that year's election he polled slightly behind Sinn Féin's John Brady on the first count with 6,530 (9.2%) but overtook him on transfers to take the final seat. In Dáil Éireann he is a member of the Joint Oireachtas Committee on Finance, Public Expenditure and Reform and has focused on education and economic issues. In Wicklow he has been active on issues such as the regeneration of Greystones Harbour, long term school planning, and business and community initiatives. He was one of the three TDs who founded the Social Democrats with Róisín Shorthall and Catherine Murphy. He lives in Greystones with his wife and three children. He has an MA from the Kennedy School of Government at Harvard University.

Independents:

Cllr Pat Kavanagh, who contested here in 2011 for Fís Nua, had hoped to run again here as an Independent candidate, but sadly she died on 16th December 2015.

Joe Behan is based in Bray and was a member of Dáil Éireann from 2007 to 2011. He was a Fianna Fáil member of Wicklow County Council for the Bray electoral area from 1992 to 2007. In his last local contest in the 2004 local election he polled 1,620 first preferences, which was 15.78% of the first preference vote. He was Cathaoirleach of Wicklow County Council in 2006–2007. He was elected as a Fianna Fáil TD in 2007 with 9,431 votes (14.5%). Behan resigned from Fianna Fáil in October 2008 in protest at the emergency Budget and particular at the proposals to withdraw the medical card from people over 70 and at the increase in school class sizes. He sat as an independent until 2011, occasionally supporting the government in various Dáil votes. In 2011 he came sixth in terms of first preference votes with 4,197 votes (6%). In 2014 he returned to Wicklow County Council as an independent, again in the Bray electoral area, coming second in the poll with 1,776 first preference votes (12.11%), 384 over the quota.

Robert (Bob) Kearns is a carpenter based in Wicklow. This will be his second Dáil election. He took only 406 votes in the 2002 general election and did not run in 2007 or 2011. He was an unsuccessful candidate for Wicklow County council in 1991 and 1999 and was elected to Wicklow Town Council in 1999, taking the third seat with 298 votes, which was almost a quota. He comes from an old Wicklow town family and was a Wicklow Town Councillor for 24 years. He says that the town and county are suffering as a result of many years of neglect.

Charlie Keddy is a plumber based in Kilcoole. He first ran on the Labour ticket in Greystones in the 1991 local elections, when he received his highest ever vote of 411. Since the 1995 Wicklow by-election he has always fought as an independent. He contested that election, the general elections of 1997, 2002 and 2011 in

Wicklow, the local elections of 1999, 2004 and 2009 in Greystones and the 2013 Meath East by-election, with his highest tally during that period being his 383 votes in the 2002 general election. He usually stands in several electoral areas. In the 2014 local elections he gained 50 votes in the Arklow area, 31 in Baltinglass, 49 in Bray, 178 in Greystones and 59 in Wicklow. He is currently highlighting water taxation. In 2015 he campaigned strongly against marriage equality.

Local Election Results Summary

	Seats	Seats 09/14	Vote	% Vote	% 09/14
Fianna Fáil	267	+49	430,040	25.3	0.3
Fine Gael	235	–105	408,289	24.0	–10.7
Sinn Féin	159	+105	258,650	15.2	7.4
Labour	51	–81	121,898	7.2	–7.0
People Before Profit	14	+9	29,051	1.7	0.9
Anti-Austerity Alliance	14	+10	21,097	1.2	0.3
Green Party	12	+9	27, 168	1.6	0.5
Workers' Party	1	–1	3,147	0.2	–0.1
United Left	1		2,879	0.2	New
South Kerry Ind.	1		2,139	0.1	–
Workers & Unemployed Action	1	–1	1,927	0.1	–0.1
Republican Sinn Féin	1		1,561	0.1	–
Direct Democracy	0		3,607	0.2	–
Éirígí	0		3,120	0.2	–
Independents for Equality	0		1,828	0.1	–
Fís Nua	0		930	0.0	–
Letterkenny Residents Party	0		428	0.0	–
Communist Party	0		215	0.0	–
Independents	193	+71	388,721	23.2	7.6
Totals	949	+66	1,706, 695	100	–

European Election Results 2014

	Votes	% Vote		Seats	Change
Fine Gael	369,120	22.3	+6.8	4	0
Sinn Féin	323,300	19.5	+8.3	3	+3
Fianna Fáil	369,545	22.3	–1.8	1	–2
Labour	88,229	5.3	–8.6	0	–3
Green Party	81,458	4.9	+3	0	0
Socialist Party	29,953	1.8	–0.9	0	–1
Direct Democracy Ireland	24,093	1.5	–	0	–
People Before Profit	23,875	1.5	–	0	–0.1
Catholic Democrats	13,569	0.8	–	0	–
Fís Nua	4,610	0.3	–	0	–
Independents	328,766	19.8	+8.3	3	+2
Totals	1,701,942	+66	1,706, 695	100	–

By-Election Results 2011–2016

Dublin West 27 October 2011

		%	1st	2nd	3rd	4th	5th
Patrick Nulty	Lab	24.3	8,665	8,885	10,186	13,027	**17,636**
David McGuinness	FF	21.7	7,742	7,935	8,720	9,873	11,590
Ruth Coppinger	SP	21.1	7,542	7,834	9,368	9,873	
Eithne Loftus	FG	14.7	5,263	5,410	5,942		
Paul Donnelly	SF	8.9	3,173	3,309			
Roderic O'Gorman	GP	5.0	1,787	1,925			
Barru Caesar Hunt	Ind	2.2	775				
John Frank Kidd	Ind	0.9	311				
Gary Bermingham	Ind	0.5	185				
Brendan Doris	Ind	0.3	95				
Jim Tallon	Ind	0.2	73				
Benny Cooney	Ind	0.1	51				
Peadar Ó Ceallaigh	Fis	0.1	40				

Turnout 36,391 (58.5%) Quota 17,852

Meath East 27 March 2013

		%	1st	2nd	3rd
Helen McEntee	FG	38.5	9,356	9,547	**11,473**
Thomas Byrne	FF	32.9	8,002	8,106	9,582
Darren O'Rourke	SF	13.0	3,165	3,370	
Ben Gilroy	DD	6.5	1,568	1,793	
Eoin Holmes	Lab	4.6	1,112	1,245	
Sean Ó Buachalla	GP	1.7	423		
Seamus McDonagh	WP	1.1	263		
Mick Martin	Ind	0.8	190		
Charlie Keddy	Ind	0.5	110		
Gerard O'Brien	Ind	0.3	73		
Jim Tallon	Ind	0.2	47		

Turnout 24,309 (38.3%) Quota 12,155

Dublin West 23 May 2014

		%	1st	2nd	3rd	4th	5th	6th	7th
Gabrielle McFadden	FG	25.2	12,365	12,459	13,414	14,390	15,841	17,564	**20,058**
Aengus O'Rourke	FF	18.2	8,910	8,966	9,289	9,763	10,811	12,431	14,581
Paul Hogan	SF	15.4	7,548	7,677	8,014	8,756	9,570	11,254	
Kevin Moran	Ind	11.5	5,629	5,849	6,085	6,833	7,797		
James Morgan	Ind	12.2	5,959	6,096	6,206	6,615			
Brian Fagan	Ind	8.6	4,195	4,378	4,985				
Denis Leonard	Lab	6.7	3,290	3,352					
John Mc-Namara	Ind	1.8	869						

Turnout 50,495 (57.4%) Quota 24,502

Dublin South West 10 October 2014

		%	1st	2nd	3rd	4th	5th	6th	7th	8th
Paul Murphy	AAA	27.2	6,540	6,579	6,622	6,890	7,079	7,436	7,726	**9,565**
Cathal King	SF	30.3	7,288	7,304	7,340	7,448	7,580	7,828	8,017	8,999
Ronan McMahon	Ind	8.9	2,142	2,167	2,227	2,265	2,464	3,049	3,416	
Cáit King	FG	8.8	2,110	2,117	2,194	2,203	2,267	2,575	3,857	
Pamela Kearns	Lab	8.5	2,043	2,053	2,155	2,170	2,239	2,492		
John Lahart	FF	8.6	2,077	2,085	2,138	2,152	2,200			
Declan Burke	Ind	2.8	681	711	746	818				
Nicky Coules	PBP	2.2	530	540	554					
Francis Noel Duffy	GP	1.9	447	453						
Tony Rochford	Ind	0.4	92							
Colm O'Keeffe	Ind	0.3	74							

Turnout 24,280 (34.5%) Quota 12,013

Longford Rossommon 10 October 2014

		%	1st	2nd	3rd	4th	5th	6th	7th
Michael Fitzmaurice	Ind	18.7	6,220	6,371	6,625	7,075	9.211	11,722	**14,881**
Ivan Con-naughton	FF	22.0	7,334	7,502	7,652	7,846	8,863	10,083	12,050
Maura Hop-kins	FG	16.8	5,593	5,742	5,864	6,075	7,312	8,476	
Martin Kenny	SF	17.7	5,906	6,184	6,283	6,447	7,022		
Johnn Mc-Dermott	Ind	8.8	2,944	3,018	3,187	3,468			
John Kelly	Lab	6.1	2,037	2,060	2,090	2,144			
Emmett Corcoran	Ind	3.8	1,262	1,305	1,483				
Tom Crosby	Ind	3.1	1,030	1,063					
Des Guckian	Ind	2.7	902						
Gerry O'Boyle	Ind	0.2	82						

Turnout 33,572 (51.8%) Quota 16, 656

Position of Parties in Dáil on 25 February 2011

Fine Gael*	76
Labour	37
Fianna Fáil	20
Sinn Féin	14
People Before Profit	2
Socialist Party	2
Indepdendents	15
Total	166

Position of Parties in Dáil on 14 January 2016

Fine Gael*	68
Labour	33
Fianna Fáil	21
Sinn Féin	14
People Before Profit	1
Socialist Party	3
Renua	4
Social Democrats	3
Indepdendents	19
Total	166

* includes Ceann Comhairle Sean Barrett TD

Turnout in Irish Elections 1967–2014

Year	Election	Turnout %
2014	Local (and European Elections)	52.4
2011	Dáil Election	70.0
2009	Local (and European Elections)	57.7
2007	General Election	67.0
2004	Local (and European Elections)	58.7
2002	Dáil Election	62.7
1999	Local (and European Elections/Ref)	50.3
1997	Dáil Election	65.2
1992	Dáil Election	67.4
1991	Local Elections	55.7
1989	Dáil Election	67.6
1987	Dáil Election	72.7
1985	Local Elections	63.0
1982/83*	Dáil Election	72.9–73.0
1979	Local (and European Elections/Ref)	66.0
1977	Dáil Election	75.6
1974	Local Elections	67.0
1973	Dáil Election	75.5
1969	Dáil Election	76.0
1967	Local Elections	69.0

*average of three elections held in 18 months

Seats Won Dáil Elections, 1923–2011

	Fianna Fáil	Fine Gael	Labour	Others	Total
2011	20	76	37	33	166
2007	78	51	20	17	166
2002	81	31	21	33	166
1997	77	54	17	18	166
1992	68	45	33	20	166
1989	77	55	15	19	166
1987	81	51	12	22	166
1982 (F)	81	63	15	7	166
1982 (N)	75	70	16	5	166
1981	78	65	15	8	166
1977	84	43	17	4	148
1973	69	54	19	2	144
1969	75	50	18	1	144
1965	72	47	22	3	144
1961	70	47	16	11	144
1957	78	40	12	17	147
1954	65	50	19	13	147
1951	69	40	16	22	147
1948	68	31	14	34	147
1944	76	30	8	24	138
1943	67	32	17	22	138
1938	77	45	9	7	138
1937	69	48	13	8	138
1933	77	48	8	20	153
1932	72	57	7	17	153
1927	44	47	22	40	153
1927	57	62	13	21	153
1923	44	63	14	32	153

% Vote Share Dáil Elections, 1923–2011

	Fianna Fáil	Fine Gael	Labour	Others
2011	17.5	36.1	19.5	26.9
2007	41.6	27.3	10.1	21.0
2002	41.5	22.5	10.8	25.2
1997	39.3	28.0	10.4	22.3
1992	39.1	24.5	19.3	17.1
1989	44.2	29.3	9.5	17.0
1987	44.1	27.1	6.4	22.3
1982 (F)	47.3	37.3	9.1	6.3
1982 (N)	45.2	39.2	9.4	6.2
1981	45.3	36.5	9.9	8.3
1977	50.6	30.5	11.6	7.3
1973	46.2	35.1	13.7	5.0
1969	45.7	34.1	17.0	3.2
1965	47.7	34.1	15.4	2.9
1961	43.8	32.0	11.6	12.6
1957	48.3	26.6	9.1	16.0
1954	43.4	32.0	12.0	12.6
1951	46.3	25.8	11.4	16.6
1948	41.9	19.8	7.5	30.8
1944	48.9	20.5	7.7	23.0
1943	41.9	23.1	15.7	19.3
1938	51.9	33.3	10.0	4.8
1937	45.2	34.8	10.3	9.7
1933	49.7	30.5	5.7	14.1
1932	44.5	35.3	7.7	12.5
1927	26.1	27.5	13.8	28.8
1927	35.2	38.7	9.5	16.6
1923	27.4	39.0	12.4	21.1